The Organization Man

William H. Whyte, Jr., was born in West Chester, Pennsylvania, and graduated from Princeton in 1939. He is now assistant managing editor of *Fortune*. He has contributed to *Harper's, Encounter,* and *The Saturday Review*. In 1952 he published *Is Anybody Listening?*, a collection of articles on communication which originally appeared in *Fortune*. In 1953 he won the Benjamin Franklin Award for the best magazine article on U.S. life.

THE ORGANIZATION MAN was first published in 1956 by Simon and Schuster.

WILLIAM H. WHYTE, JR.

The Organization Man

DOUBLEDAY ANCHOR BOOKS

DOUBLEDAY & COMPANY, INC.

GARDEN CITY, NEW YORK

ACKNOWLEDGMENTS

First of all I want to thank my colleagues on *Fortune*. So many of them were so helpful in so many ways that I could not name them without listing the whole masthead. But I do in particular want to thank Managing Editor Hedley Donovan, and not merely because I am a good organization man. For three years he gave me the time and the freedom to follow my own trails, and though some of the material in this book has appeared in *Fortune*, through his forbearance and understanding I was able to work on this as a book rather than a collection of articles. Where it lacks the cohesion I was aiming for the failing is mine and not the importunings of journalism.

I also want to thank those who were good enough to give a critical reading to my preliminary drafts: Alex Bavelas, Reinhard Bendix, Nelson Foote, Herbert Gans, Wilbert Moore, Thomas O'Dea, David Riesman, and Hugh Wilson.

W. H. W.

COVER BY GEORGE GIUSTI
TYPOGRAPHY BY EDWARD GOREY

CONTENTS

PART ONE

The Ideology of Organization Man

CHAPTER ONE

Introduction

THIS book is about the organization man. If the term is vague, it is because I can think of no other way to describe the people I am talking about. They are not the workers, nor are they the white-collar people in the usual, clerk sense of the word. These people only work for The Organization. The ones I am talking about *belong* to it as well. They are the ones of our middle class who have left home, spiritually as well as physically, to take the vows of organization life, and it is they who are the mind and soul of our great self-perpetuating institutions. Only a few are top managers or ever will be. In a system that makes such hazy terminology as "junior executive" psychologically necessary, they are of the staff as much as the line, and most are destined to live poised in a middle area that still awaits a satisfactory euphemism. But they are the dominant members of our society nonetheless. They have not joined together into a recognizable elite—our country does not stand still long enough for that—but it is from their ranks that are coming most of the first and second echelons of our leadership, and it is their values which will set the American temper.

The corporation man is the most conspicuous example, but he is only one, for the collectivization so visible in the corporation has affected almost every field of work. Blood brother to the business trainee off to join Du Pont is the seminary student who will end up in the church hierarchy, the doctor headed for the corporate clinic, the physics Ph.D. in a government laboratory, the intellectual on the foundation-sponsored team project, the engineering graduate in the huge drafting room at Lockheed, the young apprentice in a Wall Street law factory.

They are all, as they so often put it, in the same boat. Listen to them talk to each other over the front lawns of their suburbia and you cannot help but be struck by how well they grasp the common denominators which bind them. Whatever the differences in their organization ties, it is the common problems of collective work that dominate their attentions, and when the Du Pont man talks to the research chemist or the chemist to the army man, it is these problems that are uppermost. The word *collective* most of them can't bring themselves to use—except to describe foreign countries or organizations they don't work for—but they are keenly aware of how much more deeply beholden they are to organization than were their elders. They are wry about it, to be sure; they talk of the "treadmill," the "rat race," of the inability to control one's direction. But they have no great sense of plight; between themselves and organization they believe they see an ultimate harmony and, more than most elders recognize, they are building an ideology that will vouchsafe this trust.

It is the growth of this ideology, and its practical effects, that is the thread I wish to follow in this book. America has paid much attention to the economic and political consequences of big organization—the concentration of power in large corporations, for example, the political power of the civil-service bureaucracies, the possible emergence of a managerial hierarchy that might dominate the rest of us. These are proper concerns, but no less important is the personal impact that organization life has had on the individuals within it. A collision has been taking place—indeed, hundreds of thousands of them, and in the aggregate they have been producing what I believe is a major shift in American ideology.

Officially, we are a people who hold to the Protestant Ethic. Because of the denominational implications of the term many would deny its relevance to them, but let them eulogize the American Dream, however, and they virtually define the Protestant Ethic. Whatever the embroidery, there is almost always the thought that pursuit of individual salvation through hard work, thrift, and competitive struggle is the heart of the American achievement.

But the harsh facts of organization life simply do not jibe with these precepts. This conflict is certainly not a peculiarly American development. In their own countries such Europeans as Max Weber and Durkheim many years ago foretold the change, and though Europeans now like to see their troubles as an American export, the problems they speak of stem from a bureaucratization of society that has affected every Western country.

It is in America, however, that the contrast between the old ethic and current reality has been most apparent—and most poignant. Of all peoples it is we who have led in the public worship of individualism. One hundred years ago De Tocqueville was noting that though our special genius—and failing—lay in co-operative action, we talked more than others of personal independence and freedom. We kept on, and as late as the twenties, when big organization was long since a fact, affirmed the old faith as if nothing had really changed at all.

Today many still try, and it is the members of the kind of organization most responsible for the change, the corporation, who try the hardest. It is the corporation man whose institutional ads protest so much that Americans speak up in town meeting, that Americans are the best inventors because Americans don't care that other people scoff, that Americans are the best soldiers because they have so much initiative and native ingenuity, that the boy selling papers on the street corner is the prototype of our business society. Collectivism? He abhors it, and when he makes his ritualistic attack on Welfare Statism, it is in terms of a Protestant Ethic undefiled by change—the sacredness of property, the enervating effect of security, the virtues of thrift, of hard work and independence. Thanks be, he says, that there are some people left—e.g., businessmen—to defend the American Dream.

He is not being hypocritical, only compulsive. He honestly wants to believe he follows the tenets he extols, and if he extols them so frequently it is, perhaps, to shut out a nagging suspicion that he, too, the last defender of the faith, is no longer pure. Only by using the language of individualism to describe the collective can he stave off the thought that he himself is in a collective as pervading as any ever dreamed of by the reformers, the intellectuals, and the utopian visionaries he so regularly warns against.

The older generation may still convince themselves; the younger generation does not. When a young man says that to make a living these days you must do what somebody else wants you to do, he states it not only as a fact of life that must be accepted but as an inherently good proposition. If the American Dream deprecates this for him, it is the American Dream that is going to have to give, whatever its more elderly guardians may think. People grow restive with a mythology that is too distant from the way things actually are, and as more and more lives have been encompassed by the organization way of life, the pressures for an accompanying ideological shift have been mounting. The pressures of the group, the frustrations of individual creativity, the anonymity of achievement: are these defects to struggle against—or are they virtues in disguise? The organization man seeks a redefinition of his place on earth—a faith that will satisfy him that what he must endure has a deeper meaning than appears on the surface. He needs, in short, something that will do for him what the Protestant Ethic did once. And slowly, almost imperceptibly, a body of thought has been coalescing that does that.

I am going to call it a Social Ethic. With reason it could be called an organization ethic, or a bureaucratic ethic; more than anything else it rationalizes the organization's demands for fealty and gives those who offer it wholeheartedly a sense of dedication in doing so—*in extremis,* you might say, it converts what would seem in other times a bill of no rights into a restatement of individualism.

But there is a real moral imperative behind it, and whether one inclines to its beliefs or not he must acknowledge that this moral basis, not mere expediency, is the source of its power. Nor is it simply an opiate for those who must work in big organizations. The search for a secular faith that it represents can be found throughout our society—and among those who swear they would never set foot in a corporation or a government bureau. Though it has its greatest applicability to the organization man, its ideological underpinnings have been provided not by the organization man but by intellectuals he knows little of and toward whom, indeed, he tends to be rather suspicious.

Any groove of abstraction, Whitehead once remarked, is bound to be an inadequate way of describing reality, and so with the concept of the Social Ethic. It is an attempt to illustrate an underlying consistency in what in actuality is by no means an orderly system of thought. No one says, "I believe in the social ethic," and though many would subscribe wholeheartedly to the separate ideas that make it up, these ideas have yet to be put together in the final, harmonious synthesis. But the unity is there.

In looking at what might seem dissimilar aspects of organization society, it is this unity I wish to underscore. The "professionalization" of the manager, for example, and the drive for a more practical education are parts of the same phenomenon; just as the student now feels technique more vital than content, so the trainee believes managing an end in itself, an *expertise* relatively independent of the content of what is being managed. And the reasons are the same. So too in other sectors of our society; for all the differences in particulars, dominant is a growing accommodation to the needs of society—and a growing urge to justify it.

Let me now define my terms. By social ethic I mean that contemporary body of thought which makes morally legitimate the pressures of society against the individual. Its major propositions are three: a belief in the group as the source of creativity; a belief in "belongingness" as the ultimate need of the individual; and a belief in the application of science to achieve the belongingness.

In subsequent chapters I will explore these ideas more thoroughly, but for the moment I think the gist can be paraphrased thus: Man exists as a unit of society. Of himself, he is isolated, meaningless; only as he collaborates with others does he become worth while, for by sublimating himself in the group, he helps produce a whole that is greater than the sum of its parts. There should be, then, no conflict between man and society. What we think are conflicts are misunderstandings, breakdowns in communication. By applying the methods of science to human relations we can eliminate these obstacles to consensus and create an equilibrium in which society's needs and the needs of the individual are one and the same.

Essentially, it is a utopian faith. Superficially, it seems dedicated to the practical problems of organization life, and its proponents often use the word *hard* (versus *soft*) to describe their approach. But it is the long-range promise that animates its followers, for it relates techniques to the vision of a finite, achievable harmony. It is quite reminiscent of the beliefs of utopian communities of the 1840s. As in the Owen communities, there is the same idea that man's character is decided, almost irretrievably, by his environment. As in the Fourier communities, there is the same faith that there need be no conflict between the individual's aspirations and the community's wishes, because it is the natural order of things that the two be synonymous.

Like the utopian communities, it interprets society in a fairly narrow, immediate sense. One can believe man has a social obligation and that the individual must ultimately contribute to the community without believing that group harmony is the test of it. In the Social Ethic I am describing, however, man's obligation is in the here and now; his duty is not so much to the community in a broad sense but to the actual, physical one about him, and the idea that in isolation from it—or active rebellion against it—he might eventually discharge the greater service is little considered. In practice, those who most eagerly subscribe to the Social Ethic worry very little over the long-range problems of society. It is not that they don't care but rather that they tend to assume that the ends of organization and morality coincide, and on such matters as social welfare they give their proxy to the organization.

It is possible that I am attaching too much weight to what,

after all, is something of a mythology. Those more sanguine than I have argued that this faith is betrayed by reality in some key respects and that because it cannot long hide from organization man that life is still essentially competitive the faith must fall of its own weight. They also maintain that the Social Ethic is only one trend in a society which is a prolific breeder of counter-trends. The farther the pendulum swings, they believe, the more it must eventually swing back.

I am not persuaded. We are indeed a flexible people, but society is not a clock and to stake so much on counter-trends is to put a rather heavy burden on providence. Let me get ahead of my story a bit with two examples of trend vs. counter-trend. One is the long-term swing to the highly vocational business-administration courses. Each year for seven years I have collected all the speeches by businessmen, educators, and others on the subject, and invariably each year the gist of them is that this particular pendulum has swung much too far and that there will shortly be a reversal. Similarly sanguine, many academic people have been announcing that they discern the beginnings of a popular swing back to the humanities. Another index is the growth of personality testing. Regularly year after year many social scientists have assured me that this bowdlerization of psychology is a contemporary aberration soon to be laughed out of court.

Meanwhile, the organization world grinds on. Each year the number of business-administration majors has increased over the last year—until, in 1954, they together made up the largest single field of undergraduate instruction outside of the field of education itself. Personality testing? Again, each year the number of people subjected to it has grown, and the criticism has served mainly to make organizations more adept in sugar-coating their purpose. No one can say whether these trends will continue to outpace the counter-trends, but neither can we trust that an equilibrium-minded providence will see to it that excesses will cancel each other out. Counter-trends there are. There always have been, and in the sweep of ideas ineffectual many have proved to be.

It is also true that the Social Ethic is something of a mythology, and there is a great difference between mythology and practice. An individualism as stringent, as selfish as that often preached in the name of the Protestant Ethic would never have been tolerated, and in reality our predecessors co-operated with one another far more skillfully than nineteenth-century oratory would suggest. Something of the obverse is true of the Social Ethic; so complete a denial of individual will won't work either, and even the most willing believers in the group harbor some secret misgivings, some latent antagonism toward the pressures they seek to deify.

But the Social Ethic is no less powerful for that, and though it can never produce the peace of mind it seems to offer, it will help shape the nature of the quest in the years to come. The old dogma of individualism betrayed reality too, yet few would argue, I dare say, that it was not an immensely powerful influence in the time of its dominance. So I argue of the Social Ethic; call it mythology, if you will, but it is becoming the dominant one.

In the first part of this book I wish to go into some of the ideas that have helped produce the Social Ethic. I do not intend an intellectual history; my aim is the more limited one of suggesting how deep are its roots and that it is not a temporary phenomenon triggered by the New Deal or the war or our recent prosperity.

I will then pick up the organization man in college, follow him through his initial indoctrination in organization life, and explore the impact of the group way upon him. While I will speak of the corporation man more than any other, I wish to show the universality of the Social Ethic. I will turn, accordingly, to the research laboratory and academic life and argue that the inclination to the co-operative ideal has had just as important consequences in these areas also. To illustrate further the universality of the Social Ethic, I will take up its expression in popular fiction. This will bring me finally to what I consider the best place to get a preview of the direction the Social Ethic is likely to take in the future.

This is the new suburbia, the packaged villages that have become the dormitory of the new generation of organization men. They are not typical American communities, but because they provide such a cross section of young organization people we can see in bolder relief than elsewhere the kind of world organization man wants and may in time bring about. Here I will go into the tremendous effect transiency has had on the organization people and how their religious life, their politics and the way they take to their neighbors reveal the new kind of rootedness they are looking for. And, finally, the moral of it all as they explain it to their children—the next generation of organization people.

While the burden of this book is reportorial, I take a position and, in fairness to the reader, I would like to make plain the assumptions on which I base it. To that end, let me first say what I am *not* talking about.

This book is not a plea for nonconformity. Such pleas have an occasional therapeutic value, but as an abstraction, nonconformity is an empty goal, and rebellion against prevailing opinion merely because it is prevailing should no more be praised than acquiescence to it. Indeed, it is often a mask for cowardice, and few are more pathetic than those who flaunt outer differences to expiate their inner surrender.

I am not, accordingly, addressing myself to the surface uniformities of U.S. life. There will be no strictures in this book against "Mass Man"—a person the author has never met—nor will there be any strictures against ranch wagons, or television sets, or gray flannel suits. They are irrelevant to the main problem, and, furthermore, there's no harm in them. I would not wish to go to the other extreme and suggest that these uniformities per se are good, but the spectacle of people following current custom for lack of will or imagination to do anything else is hardly a new failing, and I am not convinced that there has been any significant change in this respect except in the nature of the things we conform to. Unless one believes poverty ennobling, it is difficult to see the three-button suit as more of a strait jacket than overalls, or the ranch-type house than old law tenements.

And how important, really, are these uniformities to the central issue of individualism? We must not let the outward forms deceive us. If individualism involves following one's destiny as one's own conscience directs, it must for most of us be a realizable destiny, and a sensible awareness of the rules of the game can be a condition of individualism as well as a constraint upon it. The man who drives a Buick Special and lives in a ranch-type house just like hundreds of other ranch-type houses can assert himself as effectively and courageously against his particular society as the bohemian against his particular society. He usually does not, it is true, but if he does, the surface uniformities can serve quite well as protective coloration. The organization people who are best able to control their environment rather than be controlled by it are well aware that they are not too easily distinguishable from the others in the outward obeisances paid to the good opinions of others. And that is one of the reasons they do control. They disarm society.

I do not equate the Social Ethic with conformity, nor do I believe those who urge it wish it to be, for most of them believe deeply that their work will help, rather than harm, the individual. I think their ideas are out of joint with the needs of the times they invoke, but it is their ideas, and not their good will, I wish to question. As for the lackeys of organization and the charlatans, they are not worth talking about.

Neither do I intend this book as a censure of the fact of organization society. We have quite enough problems today without muddying the issue with misplaced nostalgia, and in contrasting the old ideology with the new I mean no contrast of paradise with paradise lost, an idyllic eighteenth century with a dehumanized twentieth. Whether or not our own era is worse than former ones in the climate of freedom is a matter that can be left to later historians, but for the purposes of this book I write with the optimistic premise that individualism is as possible in our times as in others.

I speak of individualism *within* organization life. This is not the only kind, and someday it may be that the mystics and philosophers more distant from it may prove the crucial figures. But they are affected too by the center of society, and they can be of no help unless they grasp the nature of the main stream. Intellectual scoldings based on an impossibly lofty ideal may be of some service in upbraiding organization man with his failures, but they can give him no guidance. The organization man may agree that industrialism has destroyed the moral fabric of society and that we need to return to the agrarian virtues, or that business needs to be broken up into a series of smaller organizations, or that it's government that needs to be broken up, and so on. But he will go his way with his own dilemmas left untouched.

I am going to argue that he should fight the organization. But not self-destructively. He may tell the boss to go to hell, but he is going to have another boss, and, unlike the heroes of popular fiction, he cannot find surcease by leaving the arena to be a husbandman. If he chafes at the pressures of his particular organization, either he must succumb, resist them, try to change them, or move to yet another organization.

Every decision he faces on the problem of the individual versus authority is something of a dilemma. It is not a case of whether he should fight against black tyranny or blaze a new trail against patent stupidity. That would be easy—intellectually, at least. The real issue is far more subtle. For it is not the evils of organization life that puzzle him, *but its very beneficence*. He is imprisoned in brotherhood. Because his area of maneuver seems so small and because the trapping so mundane, his fight lacks the heroic cast, but it is for all this as tough a fight as ever his predecessors had to fight.

Thus to my thesis. I believe the emphasis of the Social Ethic is wrong for him. People do have to work with others, yes; the well-functioning team is a whole greater than the sum of its parts, yes—all this is indeed true. But is it the truth that now needs belaboring? Precisely because it *is* an age of organization, it is the other side of the coin that needs emphasis. We do need to know how to co-operate with The Organization but, more than ever, so do we need to know how to resist it. Out of context this would be an irresponsible statement. Time and place are critical, and history has taught us that a philosophical individualism can venerate conflict too much and co-operation too little. But what is the context today? The tide has swung far enough the other way, I submit, that we need not worry that a counteremphasis will stimulate people to an excess of individualism.

The energies Americans have devoted to the co-operative, to the social, are not to be demeaned; we would not, after all, have such a problem to discuss unless we had learned to adapt ourselves to an increasingly collective society as well as we have. An ideal of individualism which denies the obligations of man to others is manifestly impossible in a society such as ours, and it is a credit to our wisdom that while we preached it, we never fully practiced it.

But in searching for that elusive middle of the road, we have gone very far afield, and in our attention to making organization work we have come close to deifying it. We are describing its defects as virtues and denying that there is—or should be—a conflict between the individual and organization. This denial is bad for the organization. It is worse for the individual. What it does, in soothing him, is to rob him of the intellectual armor he so badly needs. For the more power organization has over him, the more he needs to recognize the area where he must assert himself against it. And this, almost because we have made organization life so equable, has become excruciatingly difficult.

To say that we must recognize the dilemmas of organization society is not to be inconsistent with the hopeful premise that organization society can be as compatible for the individual as any previous society. We are not hapless beings caught in the grip of forces we can do little about, and wholesale damnations of our society only lend a further mystique to organization. Organization has been made by man; it can be changed by man. It has not been the immutable course of history that has produced such constrictions on the individual as personality tests. It is organization man who has brought them to pass and it is he who can stop them.

The fault is not in organization, in short; it is in our worship of it. It is in our vain quest for a utopian equilibrium, which would be horrible if it ever did come to pass; it is in the soft-minded denial that there is a conflict between the individual and society. There must always be, and it is the price of being an individual that he must face these conflicts. He cannot evade them, and in seeking an ethic that offers a spurious peace of mind, thus does he tyrannize himself.

There are only a few times in organization life when he can wrench his destiny into his own hands—and if he does not fight then, he will make a surrender that will later mock him. But when is that time? Will he know the time when he sees it? By what standards is he to judge? He does feel an obligation to the group; he does sense moral constraints on his free will. If he goes against the group, is he being courageous—or just stubborn? Helpful—or selfish? Is he, as he so often wonders, right after all? It is in the resolution of a multitude of such dilemmas, I submit, that the real issue of individualism lies today.

CHAPTER TWO

The Decline of the Protestant Ethic

LET us go back a moment to the turn of the century. If we pick up the Protestant Ethic as it was then expressed we will find it apparently in full flower. We will also find, however, an ethic that already had been strained by reality. The country had changed. The ethic had not.

Here, in the words of banker Henry Clews as he gave some fatherly advice to Yale students in 1908, is the Protestant Ethic in purest form:

SURVIVAL OF FITTEST: *You may start in business, or the professions, with your feet on the bottom rung of the ladder; it rests with you to acquire the strength to climb to the top. You can do so if you have the will and the force to back you. There is always plenty of room at the top. . . . Success comes to the man who tries to compel success to yield to him. Cassius spoke well to Brutus when he said, "The Fault is not in our stars, dear Brutus, that we are underlings, but in our natures."*

THRIFT: *Form the habit as soon as you become a money-earner, or money-maker, of saving a part of your salary, or profits. Put away one dollar out of every ten you earn. The time will come in your lives when, if you have a little money, you can control circumstances; otherwise circumstances will control you. . . .*

Note the use of such active words as *climb, force, compel, control.* As stringently as ever before, the Protestant Ethic still counseled struggle against one's environment—the kind of practical, here and now struggle that paid off in material rewards. And spiritually too. The hard-boiled part of the Protestant Ethic was incomplete, of course, without the companion assurance that such success was moral as well as practical. To continue with Mr. Clews:

> *Under this free system of government, whereby individuals are free to get a living or to pursue wealth as each chooses, the usual result is competition. Obviously, then, competition really means industrial freedom. Thus, anyone may choose his own trade or profession, or, if he does not like it, he may change. He is free to work hard or not; he may make his own bargains and set his price upon his labor or his products. He is free to acquire property to any extent, or to part with it. By dint of greater effort or superior skill, or by intelligence, if he can make better wages, he is free to live better, just as his neighbor is free to follow his example and to learn to excel him in turn. If anyone has a genius for making and managing money, he is free to exercise his genius, just as another is free to handle his tools. . . . If an individual enjoys his money, gained by energy and successful effort, his neighbors are urged to work the harder, that they and their children may have the same enjoyment.*

It was an exuberantly optimistic ethic. If everyone could believe that seeking his self-interest automatically improves the lot of all, then the application of hard work should eventually produce a heaven on earth. Some, like the garrulous Mr. Clews, felt it already had.

> *America is the true field for the human race. It is the hope and the asylum for the oppressed and downtrodden of every clime. It is the inspiring example of America—peerless among the nations of the earth, the brightest star in the political firmament—that is leavening the hard lump of aristocracy and promoting a democratic spirit throughout the world. It is indeed the gem of the ocean to which the world may well offer homage. Here merit is the sole test. Birth is nothing. The fittest survive. Merit is the supreme and only qualification essential to success. Intelligence rules worlds and systems of worlds. It is the dread monarch of illimitable space, and in human society, especially in*

America, it shines as a diadem on the foreheads of those who stand in the foremost ranks of human enterprise. Here only a natural order of nobility is recognized, and its motto, without coat of arms or boast of heraldry, is "Intelligence and integrity."[1]

Without this ethic capitalism would have been impossible. Whether the Protestant Ethic preceded capitalism, as Max Weber argued, or whether it grew up as a consequence, in either event it provided a degree of unity between the way people wanted to behave and the way they thought they *ought* to behave, and without this ideology, society would have been hostile to the entrepreneur. Without the comfort of the Protestant Ethic, he couldn't have gotten away with his acquisitions—not merely because other people wouldn't have allowed him, but because his own conscience would not have. But now he was fortified by the assurance that he was pursuing his obligation to God, and before long, what for centuries had been looked on as the meanest greed, a rising middle class would interpret as the earthly manifestation of God's will.

But the very industrial revolution which this highly serviceable ethic begot in time began to confound it. The inconsistencies were a long while in making themselves apparent. The nineteenth-century inheritors of the ethic were creating an increasingly collective society but steadfastly they denied the implications of it. In current retrospect the turn of the century seems a golden age of individualism, yet by the 1880s the corporation had already shown the eventual bureaucratic direction it was going to take. As institutions grew in size and became more stratified, they made all too apparent inconsistencies which formerly could be ignored. One of the key assumptions of the Protestant Ethic had been that success was due neither to luck nor to the environment but only to one's natural qualities—if men grew rich it was because they deserved to. But the big organization became a standing taunt to this dream of individual success. Quite

[1] Henry Clews, *Fifty Years in Wall Street* (New York: Irving Publishing Company, 1908).

obviously to anyone who worked in a big organization, those who survived best were not necessarily the fittest but, in more cases than not, those who by birth and personal connections had the breaks.

As organizations continued to expand, the Protestant Ethic became more and more divergent from the reality The Organization was itself creating. The managers steadfastly denied the change, but they, as much as those they led, were affected by it. Today, some still deny the inconsistency or blame it on creeping socialism; for the younger generation of managers however, the inconsistencies have become importuning.

Thrift, for example. How can the organization man be thrifty? Other people are thrifty *for* him. He still buys most of his own life insurance, but for the bulk of his rainy-day saving, he gives his proxy to the financial and personnel departments of his organization. In his professional capacity also thrift is becoming a little un-American. The same man who will quote from Benjamin Franklin on thrift for the house organ would be horrified if consumers took these maxims to heart and started putting more money into savings and less into installment purchases. No longer can he afford the luxury of damning the profligacy of the public; not in public, at any rate. He not only has to persuade people to buy more but persuade them out of any guilt feelings they might have for following his advice. Few talents are more commercially sought today than the knack of describing departures from the Protestant Ethic as reaffirmations of it.[2]

In an advertisement that should go down in social history,

_____

[2] Helping in this task is what a good part of "motivation research" is all about. Motivation researcher Dr. Ernest Dichter, in a bulletin to business, says, "We are now confronted with the problem of permitting the average American to feel moral even when he is flirting, even when he is spending, even when he is not saving, even when he is taking two vacations a year and buying a second or third car. One of the basic problems of this prosperity, then, is to give people the sanction and justification to enjoy it and to demonstrate that the hedonistic approach to his life is a moral, not an immoral one."

the J. Walter Thompson agency has hit the problem of absolution head-on. It quotes Benjamin Franklin on the benefits of spending. "Is not the hope of being one day able to purchase and enjoy luxuries a great spur to labor and industry? . . . May not luxury therefore produce more than it consumes, if, without such a spur, people would be, as they are naturally enough inclined to be, lazy and indolent?" This thought, the ad says, in a meaningful aside, "appears to be a mature afterthought, qualifying his earlier and more familiar writings on the importance of thrift."

"Hard work?" What price capitalism, the question is now so frequently asked, unless we turn our productivity into more leisure, more of the good life? To the organization man this makes abundant sense, and he is as sensitive to the bogy of overwork and ulcers as his forebears were to the bogy of slothfulness. But he is split. He believes in leisure, but so does he believe in the Puritan insistence on hard, self-denying work—and there are, alas, only twenty-four hours a day. How, then, to be "broad gauge"? The "broad-gauge" model we hear so much about these days is the man who keeps his work separate from leisure and the rest of his life. Any organization man who managed to accomplish this feat wouldn't get very far. He still works hard, in short, but now he has to feel somewhat guilty about it.

Self-reliance? The corporation estates have been expanding so dynamically of late that until about now the management man could suppress the thought that he was a bureaucrat—bureaucrats, as every businessman knew, were those people down in Washington who preferred safety to adventure. Just when the recognition began to dawn, no one can say, but since the war the younger generation of management haven't been talking of self-reliance and adventure with quite the straight face of their elders.

That upward path toward the rainbow of achievement leads smack through the conference room. No matter what name the process is called—permissive management, multiple management, the art of administration—the committee way simply can't be equated with the "rugged" individualism that is supposed to be the business of business. Not for lack of ambition do the younger men dream so moderately; what they lack is the illusion that they will carry on in the great entrepreneurial spirit. Although they cannot bring themselves to use the word bureaucrat, the approved term—the "administrator"—is not signally different in its implications. The man of the future, as junior executives see him, is not the individualist but the man who works through others for others.

Let me pause for a moment to emphasize a necessary distinction. Within business there are still many who cling resolutely to the Protestant Ethic, and some with as much rapacity as drove any nineteenth-century buccaneer. But only rarely are they of The Organization. Save for a small, and spectacular, group of financial operators, most who adhere to the old creed are small businessmen, and to group them as part of the "business community," while convenient, implies a degree of ideological kinship with big business that does not exist.

Out of inertia, the small business is praised as the acorn from which a great oak may grow, the shadow of one man that may lengthen into a large enterprise. Examine businesses with fifty or less employees, however, and it becomes apparent the sentimentality obscures some profound differences. You will find some entrepreneurs in the classic sense—men who develop new products, new appetites, or new systems of distribution—and some of these enterprises may mature into self-perpetuating institutions. But very few.

The great majority of small business firms cannot be placed on any continuum with the corporation. For one thing, they are rarely engaged in primary industry; for the most part they are the laundries, the insurance agencies, the restaurants, the drugstores, the bottling plants, the lumber yards, the automobile dealers. They are vital, to be sure, but essentially they service an economy; they do not create new money within their area and they are dependent ultimately on the business and agriculture that does.

In this dependency they react more as antagonists than allies with the corporation. The corporation, it has become clear, is expansionist—a force for change that is forever a threat to the economics of the small businessman. By instinct he inclines to the monopolistic and the restrictive. When the druggists got the "Fair Trade" laws passed it was not only the manufacturers (and customers) they were rebelling against but the whole mass economy movement of the twentieth century.

The tail wagged the dog in this case and it still often does. That it can, in the face of the growing power of the corporation, illustrates again the dominance mythology can have over reality. Economically, many a small businessman is a counterrevolutionist and the revolution he is fighting is that of the corporation as much as the New or Fair Deal. But the corporation man still clings to the idea that the two are firm allies, and on some particulars, such as fair trade, he often makes policy on this basis when in fact it is against the corporation's interests to do so.

But the revolution is not to be stopped by sentiment. Many anachronisms do remain; in personal income, for example, the corporation man who runs a branch plant on which a whole town depends is lucky to make half the income of the local car dealer or the man with the Coca-Cola franchise. The economy has a way of attending to these discrepancies, however, and the local businessman can smell the future as well as anyone else. The bland young man The Organization sent to town to manage the plant is almost damnably inoffensive; he didn't rent the old place on the hill but a smaller house, he drives an Olds instead of a Caddy, and when he comes to the Thursday luncheons he listens more than he talks. But he's the future just the same.

I have been talking of the impact of organization on the Protestant Ethic; just as important, however, was the intellectual assault. In the great revolt against traditionalism that began around the turn of the century, William James, John Dewey, Charles Beard, Thorstein Veblen, the muckrakers and a host of reformers brought the anachronisms of the Protestant Ethic under relentless fire, and in so doing helped lay the groundwork for the Social Ethic. It would be a long time before organization men would grasp the relevance of these new ideas, and to this day many of the most thoroughgoing pragmatists in business would recoil at being grouped with the intellectuals. (And vice versa.) But the two movements were intimately related. To what degree the intellectuals were a cause of change, or a manifestation, no one can say for certain, but more presciently than those in organization they grasped the antithesis between the old concept of the rational, unbeholden individual and the world one had to live in. They were not rebels against society; what they fought was the denial of society's power, and they provided an intellectual framework that would complement, rather than inhibit, the further growth of big organization.

It is not in the province of this book to go into a diagnosis of the ideas of Dewey and James and the other pragmatists. But there is one point of history I think very much needs making at this time. Many people still look on the decline of the Protestant Ethic as our fall from grace, a detour from Americanism for which we can blame pragmatism, ethical relativism, Freudianism and other such developments. These movements have contributed much to the Social Ethic, and many of their presuppositions are as shaky as those they replaced. To criticize them on this score is in order; to criticize them as having subverted the American temper, however, is highly misleading.

Critics of pragmatism, and followers too, should remember the context of the times in which the pragmatists made their case. The pragmatists' emphasis on social utility may be redundant for today's needs, but when they made their case it was not a time when psychology or adjustment or social living were popular topics but at a time when the weight of conservative opinion denied that there was anything much that needed adjusting. Quite clearly, revolt was in order. The growth of the organization society did demand a recognition that man was not entirely a product of his free will; the country did need an educational plant more responsive to the need of the people. It did need a new breeze, and if there had been no James or no Dewey, some form of pragmatism would probably have been invented anyway. Nonphilosophical Americans sensed that changes were in order too; what the philosophers of pragmatism did was to give them guidance and tell them in intellectually responsible terms that they were right in feeling that way.

Pragmatism's emphasis on the social and the practical, furthermore, was thoroughly in the American tradition. From the beginning, Americans had always been impatient with doctrines and systems; like the Puritans, many came here because of a doctrine, but what they came to was a new environment that required some powerful adapting to, and whenever the doctrine got in the way of practicality, the doctrine lost out. Few people have had such a genius for bending ideals to the demands of the times, and the construction of fundamental theory, theological or scientific, has never excited Americans overmuch. Long before James, *Does it work?* was a respectable question to ask. If impatience at abstract thought was a defect, it was the defect of a virtue, and the virtue, call it what you will, has always been very close to pragmatism as Dewey and James defined it. By defining it they gave it coherence and power at a time when it needed assertion, but the inclination to the practical antedated the philosophy; it was not the product of it.

Reform was everywhere in the air. By the time of the First World War the Protestant Ethic had taken a shellacking from which it would not recover; rugged individualism and hard work had done wonders for the people to whom God in his infinite wisdom, as one put it, had given control of society. But it hadn't done so well for everyone else and now they, as well as the intellectuals, were all too aware of the fact.

The ground, in short, was ready, and though the conservative opinion that drew the fire of the rebels seemed entrenched, the basic temper of the country was so inclined in the other direction that emphasis on the social became the dominant current of U.S. thought. In a great outburst of curiosity, people became fascinated with the discovering of all the environmental pressures on the individual that previous philosophies had denied. As with Freud's discoveries, the findings of such inquiries were deeply disillusioning at first, but with characteristic exuberance Americans found a rainbow. Man might not be perfectible after all, but there was another dream and now at last it seemed practical: the perfectibility of *society*.

CHAPTER THREE

Scientism

JUST how these currents of reforms congealed into an orthodoxy is a problem in intellectual history I must duck. Trying to weigh whose ideas were most responsible is in any event somewhat fruitless, for it is what people want to believe that is important, and those whose ideas they so frequently misinterpret should not be whipped for the bowdlerization. Freud, for example, who once remarked that he was not a Freudian, never maintained that man was forever a hostage to childhood traumata; with resolution and intelligence, he believed, the individual could, by understanding these factors, perhaps surmount them. Nor did James or Dewey ever say that the convenience of society was the key test of morality, and they most certainly did not believe that man was totally the product of those around him.

The popular ideology I am describing is highly elastic but it has a remarkable unity nonetheless. Most believers in the many subbranches of American organization life are still unaware of the interlocking nature of their separate credos, and it is partly for this reason they so often feel themselves missionaries in the midst of the unbelieving. Change a word here and there, however, and what many an educator is prescribing is exactly what many a personnel man is prescribing, and many a research director, and so on through the roster of our institutions.

In these next three chapters I am going to outline three

principal denominators which bind them. While each is important in its own right, it is their interrelationship that I wish to illuminate. Until this unity is discerned, to attack the fallacies of technique in each separate field is as futile as hacking away at the hydra; it is the central, nourishing vision that we must address ourselves to.

The first denominator is scientism. This is the practical part of the Social Ethic, for it is the promise that with the same techniques that have worked in the physical sciences we can eventually create an exact science of man.[1] In one form or another, it has had a long and dismal record of achievement; even its proponents readily admit that the bugs are appalling. But this has not shaken the faith in scientism, for it is essentially a utopian rather than a technical idea.

The preamble of the believers is always the same. We are in a terrible fix and it is almost too late. We have applied science to things, and only now have we begun applying it to man himself. Already we have learned some useful social techniques; we can measure personality, can spot the obstacles to good group dynamics, and predict communication response. But these are merely the beginning; if only we provide the time and money, before long we can unwrap the whole enigma with a unified science of man.

---

[1] N.B.: This is a very rough definition, and most people who have used the term have a different way of analyzing its bases. Hayek describes it as based on three fallacies: objectivism, collectivism, and historicism. By this he means the attempt to dispense with subjective knowledge; to treat abstract wholes—such as "society"—as definite objectives, like biological organisms; the attempt to make history a science, and the only one, of social phenomena. (F. A. Hayek, *The Counter-Revolution of Science: Studies on the Abuse of Reason.* Glencoe, Illinois: The Free Press, 1952.) Another critic of cientism, Eric Voegelin, also divides scientism into three components: "(1) the assumption that the mathematized science of natural phenomena is a model science to which all other sciences ought to conform; (2) that all realms of being are accessible to the methods of the sciences of phenomena; and (3) that all reality which is not accessible to sciences of phenomena is either irrelevant or, in the more radical form of the dogma, illusionary." (*Social Research,* December 1948.)

Here, extracted from the proceedings of several conferences, is a fair composite of the message:

If we draw into our group increasing numbers of hard-headed students, some of whom are not afraid of mathematics, and if we have faith and daring, we can build a science of man. . . . The conditions which determine human happiness are discoverable scientific methods and are to a major extent capable of realization. . . . More than ever, the world's greatest need is a science of human relationships and an art of human engineering based upon the laws of such science. We should, to put it brutally, pay more attention, first to the scientific aspects of our problems rather than to the philosophical ones. . . . Although human relationship problems are extremely complicated, science is gradually reducing them to simple fundamentals through which these complexities are reduced to factors that respond to direct and simple treatment.

Inevitably, there is the atom-bomb analogy:

It is trite but true to say that if social science had been given early enough the four billion dollars that have been spent on the atomic bomb and on chemical and germ warfare—say, half for research and the other half for popular education—perhaps then the first release of atomic energy would have been for peaceful purposes.

And how very ancient it all is! Most of the people who hearken to the vision of a unified science of man believe theirs is a fresh new vision, but in reality it is a cliché that has been kicked around for centuries.[2] Ever since Newton, scores of natural scientists have stepped out of their area of competence to suggest the possibilities of a science of man, and Erasmus's *Praise of Folly* suggests that even before this some savants had much the same idea. It was an understandable dream for a natural scientist to have. Even Descartes himself was seized with the idea that the discipline of mathematics could be extended to the affairs of man. Even-

[2] For an excellent summary of early attempts at scientism, see "The Invention of the Ethical Calculus," by Louis I. Bredvold in *The Seventeenth Century: Studies in the History of English Thought and Literature from Bacon to Pope,* Richard F. Jones *et al.* (Stanford University Press, 1951.)

tually, he thought, a "Universal Mathematical Science" would solve the problem of society—if only there were sufficient funds and time for the job.

Later others tried the geometric tack: Thomas Hobbes worked out a complete set of algebraic equations to explain ethics. As Laurence Sterne remarked, his equations "plussed or minussed you to heaven or hell . . . so that none but the expert mathematician would ever be able to settle his accounts with Saint Peter." In 1725 one Francis Hutchison devised an even more elaborate mathematical calculation on morality, and without the advantages of modern technocracy, he was able to produce formulas fully as intricate as any being worked out today.

With the founding of the École Polytechnique in Paris at the end of the eighteenth century scientism was given another forward push; Saint-Simon and Auguste Comte energized a formidable school with the promise of positivism. If man would only apply the discipline of the natural sciences to the study of man, then only a sufficient expenditure of time, money, and thought would separate him from the good society.

If only . . . In a hundred variations, this promise has been phrased and rephrased. Yet one would gather from current exhortations that we are just about starting from scratch just the same. Current literature is full of dawn-of-discovery analogies—Balboa discovering the Pacific, Newton and the apple, etc. But it is precisely this figure of thought, this sense of being on the frontier that gives scientism so tremendous an appeal.

And for people in the commercial as well as the academic world. " 'SECOND INDUSTRIAL REVOLUTION' TO FORCE MAJOR CHANGES IN PRODUCTION, MERCHANDISING, AND SELLING" headlined *Advertising Age* (October 5, 1953). E. B. Weiss, perhaps the best-known consultant in the merchandising field, explained to readers that it isn't simply that such advances as electronic calculators and automatic factories are going to make for more efficiency. A whole new science, he says, is abuilding, and with the confusion between control of the physical and control of the mental which is characteristic of believers in scientism, he proclaims that

"The Second Industrial Revolution will substitute the machine for the common, and for some fairly uncommon functions of the human *mind*." It is not his contention, he says in qualification, "that the robot will replace *all* human endeavor." But almost all. After initial successes, such as cutting out the personal element in retail selling, making inventory-taking automatic, the machine will advance into hitherto sacrosanct areas, and with what seems unwonted relish, he cites a scientist's prophecy that in time the machine will replace man in the realm of reasoning and logical deduction. "NEXT WEEK: No. 2 in this series—How Cybernetic Principles Are Being and Will Be Applied in Factory, Office, and Warehouse."

The field of public relations is particularly susceptible. Here, for example, the *Public Relations Journal* editorializes on the subject:

> *Now, whether he knows it or not, every practicing public-relations man is an engineer too—a* social *engineer. He developes new relationships and operations in society, designs new organizations and institutions, sets up and lubricates the human machinery for getting things done. The challenge of social engineering in our time is like the challenge of technical engineering fifty years ago. If the first half of the twentieth century was the era of the technical engineers, the second half may well be the era of the social engineers.*

Dip into personnel journals, advertising trade journals, and you will find the same refrain. A lot of it is sheer malarkey, of course, but I think most of it is evidence of a genuine longing to be related to a faith.

We talk much about the alienation of the worker from the satisfaction of the whole job, but the same longing for a sense of continuity and purpose affects managerial people every bit as much. As our organizations have grown larger and more bureaucratic, they have created great layers of staff functions and the people in them often feel neither fish nor fowl—intellectuals, yet not of the intellectual world; managerial, yet without authority or prestige. Scientism, with its implications of the specialist as eventual savior, can give the frustrated a sense of purpose that cuts across organization and occupational lines. I do not believe I read into scientism a coherence that they themselves do not feel. No matter what branch of social engineering a man is engaged in—"mass" communication, "the engineering of consent," public relations, advertising, personnel counseling— he can feel himself part of a larger movement.

Their good will is overpowering. Thoreau once said if you see a man approach you with the obvious intent of doing you good, you should run for your life; it is hard to restrain the impulse in talking with social engineers. Theirs is not a mere limited desire to help out a bit with the scientific method; the vision that energizes them is total—and exclusive. Science is not merely a tool; it is the only path to salvation in a world where the laymen have gone mad. There is no justification, one angry social engineer writes, "in inflicting wounds on social scientists who might conceivably be blazing trails toward solutions of an otherwise hopeless crisis in civilization." If the techniques are faulty, and this they admit, that is a matter of unfinished detail and insufficient funds, not principles, and no one should criticize until he offers a counter-utopia himself.

One should not fall into the trap of equating social engineering with social science. Some social scientists do believe in social engineering but a great many do not, and the claims some make in the name of social science are a serious embarrassment to them. A pretty good case could be made that the field would be more productive were it now called social *studies*. The study of man and society is quite worthy enough an occupation without being saddled with the task of hammering out a finite, embracing science, and the ultimate test of a social scientist's particular way of looking at people cannot be absolute truth; only the arrogant—or the stupid—can so aspire.

Part of the trouble lies in our new-found ability to measure more precisely, and the idea that the successes of natural science were due in large measure to the objectiveness of the phenomena studied eludes social engineers. There are, of course, aspects of man's behavior that we can properly measure and we learn much by doing so. But how fascinating, alas, it all is! Here, it would seem, we can at last be rid of the bugbear of values. The median income level of a hundred selected families in an urban industrial universe correlates .76 with population density—not .78 or .61 but .76, and that's a fact. The next step beckons: having measured this far, it seems that there is nothing that can't be measured. We are purged of bias, and somehow by the sheer accumulation of such bias-free findings, we will have the basis of a theoretical formula that describes all. Just like physics.

In a pure example of scientism, psychologist James G. Miller has described how an institute could make this final integration.

In constructing theory, we can employ models from the physical sciences. All psychological phenomena are essentially naturalistic—that is, ultimately they can be translated into principles of physics. . . . By having individuals from different disciplines working closely together on both theory and research, communication between disciplines can be greatly improved. . . . If there are general principles running through them all, these are more likely to be discovered by groups from different fields working together, and in close communication, than by individuals working alone. . . . Another related possibility is the use throughout all theoretical work of what Bertalanffy has called "general system theory." This is the contention, developing from the unity of science movement, that every system—whether it be a strictly physical system like a dry cell, or an automobile; a biological system like a single nerve cell or organ; a total organism; or a society—has certain formal characteristics which make possible comparison of it with all others. Hence, generalizations about all systems are feasible. . . . Perhaps an over-all theory of behavior is too near the end of the rainbow to be reached; perhaps it is a will-o'-the-wisp. If so, our efforts may still be rewarded by the salvage of microtheories about limited areas."

Let us assume, for the moment, that a precise science of man is not a will-o'-the-wisp and that we are on our way to achieving it. We are left with a knotty problem. What do we do about good and evil, right and wrong? Believers in scientism confess that the question requires hard thinking. They are glad that ethical relativism has freed us from the narrow view that our own group's given values are the only correct ones. Obviously, then, a science of man could not freeze on one scheme of ethics. If we are to be governed by it, however, it would need some sort of ethics. How are we to determine just what they should be?

Social engineers have emboldened themselves to seek the final solution. Now, they say, we will *scientifically determine ethics*. This is to be done, in part, through the concept of "equilibrium." "How can we hope . . . to fix with assurity a particular class of behavior as right or good?" asks anthropologist Elliot Chapple. "From our point of view, this can be done by the use of the concept of equilibrium . . . hence good or bad, right or wrong, are comparable to the concept of health and medicine."

I have read definitions of many equilibrium concepts but I am still not sure just what they mean and I am not sure their creators do either; as far as can be determined, it is one of those mushy words so serviceable to obscuring contradictions. As Gunnar Myrdal, in explaining his own theoretical model in *An American Dilemma,* has pointed out, in borrowing the equilibrium notion from physics most social scientists have thought of only one kind of equilibrium, the *stable* equilibrium. This generally can lead to an acceptance of social harmony—either that of the status quo or some future one—and the companion terms such as disharmony, disequilibrium, maladjustment, disorganization, are by implication "bad" things.

This helps explain the bias against conflict that is so prevalent in most social-science literature. Where the by-products of harmony are the good things, the by-products of conflict—such as tension, frustration—are the bad things. Without taking the equally wrong position of saying that tension and frustration per se are good, one can point out that it takes a rather firm set of values to classify them as bad. Few social engineers would state categorically that they classify conflict as bad; nevertheless the practical gist of the ethics-of-equilibrium notion is that good values are values that allow groups to interact benevolently on one another and the individuals in them.

If we grant the concept of equilibrium we are still left with a formidable task in getting down to cases. How do we find what an organization's equilibrium is? If it isn't in it, how is it to be gotten there? If ethics is to be scientized, some specific people will have to do it, and some specific people are going to have to see to it the ethics are applied to society. Who, then, is to be in charge?

Being most of them democratically inclined, the new utopians take this question very seriously. If manipulating people is bad—and manipulation is one of the dirtiest words in the new lexicon—how can one justify the manipulation of people for good ends? At every convocation of believers the matter is dialectically treated, and the result of this soul-searching has been a new enrichment of the vocabulary. Though social engineers love to analyze semantic folly, no group has searched more arduously for the magic term which will combine manipulation with moral sanction. Thus we hear that the wielder of the new social techniques will be a "peace planner," a "group therapist," an "integrative leader," a "social diagnostician"—a person empowered to dominate society, but disciplined by a scientific code of ethics from using his knowledge in any but good ways.

In spelling this out social engineers characteristically shield themselves from the implication of their doctrine by describing how social engineering could be applied to a worthy cause. In a typical example, psychiatrist William Borberg explains how social engineering would be applied to the United Nations.

Now, the knowledge accumulated in the social sciences and the understanding of its possible value to the United Nations must of necessity be greater among the scientists themselves than among policy-making leaders and diplomats. I therefore wonder whether the social scientists might not consider the desirability of creating themselves an organ for the purpose of that relationship. . . . This would be one of the means by which we may gradually introduce into the thinking of policy-making leaders more and more scientific knowledge, scientific methods, and scientific mentality, and thus gradually substitute the present, essentially emotional basis for peace by a much better and much more reliable one, the scientific view of peace.[3]

[3] William Borberg, "On Methods of the Social Sciences in

As in other such suggested projects, the scientific elite is not supposed to give orders. Yet there runs through all of them a clear notion that questions of policy can be made somewhat nonpartisan by the application of science. There seems little recognition that the contributions of social science to policy-making can never go beyond staff work. Policy can never be scientific, and any social scientist who has risen to an administrative position has learned this quickly enough. Opinion, values, and debate are the heart of policy, and while fact can narrow down the realm of debate, it can do no more.

And what a terrible world it would be! Hell is no less hell for being antiseptic. In the 1984 of Big Brother one would at least know who the enemy was—a bunch of bad men who wanted power because they liked power. But in the other kind of 1984 one would be disarmed for not knowing who the enemy was, and when the day of reckoning came the people on the other side of the table wouldn't be Big Brother's bad henchmen; they would be a mild-looking group of therapists who, like the Grand Inquisitor, would be doing what they did to help you.

But such a specter is not the consequence of scientism that should preoccupy us. It's not merely that social engineers have no such vision in mind—they don't; the point is that they couldn't pull it off if they did. Curiously, many who have warned most urgently of the horrors of a scientific utopia are themselves awed by scientism; their fears are based on the premise that it can work. Science-fiction writers, perhaps our most vigorous moralists, often seem to say that what would be wrong would be *too much* scientism, and even those dead set against it appear impressed with the possibility of its dominance. Some European critics of America have gone them one better. They say it has already happened. If anybody wants to see man crushed by science and mechanization, it appears he has only to take a trip to the U.S. The latest such critic, Robert Jungk, draws a picture of white-coated men around UNIVAC, and docile robots listening to piped music. *Tomorrow*, he warns, *is already here*.

That kind of tomorrow isn't here and it probably never will be. The implied choice between science and humanity is a false one. The danger is not in science dominating man, and the fears of this rest on a false personalization of the inanimate, not to mention a romantic, if retrograde, longing for a past utopia. Nor need the specter of a scientific elite worry us. It need not worry us because a "science of man" cannot work in the way its believers think it can, and in subsequent chapters I hope to demonstrate how naïve some of the current techniques are.

But the gospel of scientism is no less important for that reason. To stretch a point, the trouble is not so much that these techniques work, but that they *do not* work. Schemes that don't work can have as much effect on society as schemes that do. Machiavellian rules ask one to compromise, in this case, on one's ethics. But at least they can work, and if we sell our souls we get some satisfying sin in recompense. Scientism asks that we make a compromise, but it can't deliver anything really in return. The scientific formulas for "mass communication," for example: using them we manage to debase our prose, assault our instincts, and insult our listeners—but never do we get that sure-fire communion promised for our surrender. A poor bargain.

What I am arguing is that the real impact of scientism is upon our values. The danger, to put it another way, is not man being dominated but man surrendering. At the present writing there is not one section of American life that has not drunk deeply of the promise of scientism. It appears in many forms—pedagogy, aptitude tests, that monstrous nonentity called "mass communication"—and there are few readers who have not had a personal collision with it.

CHAPTER FOUR

Belongingness

WHAT kind of society is to be engineered? Some critics of social engineering are sure that what is being cooked up for us is a socialistic paradise, a radically new, if not brave, world, alien to every tradition of man. This is wrong. Lump together the social engineers' prescriptions for the new society and you find they are anything but radical. Boiled down, what they ask for is an environment in which everyone is tightly knit into a belongingness with one another; one in which there is no restless wandering but rather the deep emotional security that comes from total integration with the group. Radical? It is like nothing so much as the Middle Ages.

And what, some have been asking, was so wrong with the Middle Ages anyway? They had excellent human relations. They didn't have the self-consciousness about their society to make them rationalize it or the scientific approach with which to do it. But belongingness they had. They knew where they stood—peasant and noble alike. They saw the fruit of their labor, and the tiny world about them protected as well as demanded. Psychologically, they had a home.

Not that we should go back to all this, mind you. The job, to paraphrase, is to *re-create* the belongingness of the Middle Ages. What with the Enlightenment, the Industrial Revolution, and other calamities, the job is immensely more difficult than it was in those simpler days. But with new scientific techniques we can solve the problem. What we must do is to learn consciously to achieve what once came naturally. We must form an elite of skilled leaders who will guide men back, benevolently, to group belongingness.

An unfair paraphrase? The young men who enthuse so unqualifiedly about human relations as the last best hope would be shocked to be accused of holding so reactionary a view. The people who have been the intellectual founders of the human-relations gospel, however, have not been so muddy-minded. They were not the cheery optimists their latter-day followers seem to be; they were rather pessimistic about the capacities of man, and the society they prescribed was by no means a utopia which would be all things to all men. A man would have to make sacrifices to enjoy it, and the prophets of belongingness stated this with admirable toughness of mind.

The father of the human-relations school is Elton Mayo. Mayo, professor of industrial research at the Harvard Business School, was concerned with the anomie, or rootlessness, of the industrial worker. Ever since he first started studying industry in Australia in 1903 he had been looking for a way to reconcile the worker's need for belongingness with the conflicting allegiances of the complex world he now finds himself in.

For Mayo, and his colleagues, the great turning point came as the result of what started to be a very modest experiment. In 1927 some of Mayo's colleagues began the now celebrated study at the Hawthorne, Illinois, plant of Western Electric.[1] The company had a challenging problem for them. For several years it had been trying to measure how much more telephone equipment the workers would produce as lighting was improved in the rooms they worked in. The researchers chose three rooms and progressively increased the illumination in each, at the same time

[1] For a full account of this experiment, see *Management and the Worker*, by F. S. Roethlisberger and William J. Dickson (Cambridge, Massachusetts: Harvard University Press, 1939). A good summary is to be found in Stuart Chase's *The Proper Study of Mankind* (New York: Harper & Brothers, 1948).

keeping a careful record of the work output. To their surprise, there seemed no clear relation between production and better illumination. They tried a more careful experiment: this time they would use only two rooms, one a "control" group where conditions would be left the same and the experimental room where the changes would be introduced. Again, mixed results: output went up in the experimental room—but so did it go up in the control room.

At this point the Harvard group entered the picture and collaborated with the company on a more elaborate experiment: in a "relay assembly" test room they isolated a group of women operators from others doing the same work and one by one introduced changes—not only lighting, but changes in rest periods, hours, and economic incentives. According to the commonly accepted "scientific management principles" earlier advanced by Frederick Taylor, these changes in physical conditions and, most particularly, incentives would make the test group more productive than the other. But they didn't. As experiment followed experiment (the research was to continue until 1932) it became abundantly clear that physical changes were not the key. As in the earlier experiments, output did shoot ahead where conditions were changed, but so did output shoot ahead where no changes had been made.

How come? The researchers came to the conclusion that output shot up in both groups because in both groups the workers' participation had been solicited and this involvement, clearly, was more important than physical perquisites. The workers were a social system; the system was informal but it was what really determined the worker's attitude toward his job. This social system could work against management, but if the managers troubled themselves to understand the system and its functions for the worker, the system could work for management.

In the literature of human relations the Hawthorne experiment is customarily regarded as a discovery. In large part it was; more than any other event, it dramatized the inadequacy of the purely economic view of man. The conclusions that flowed from the experiment, however, were a good bit more than a statement of objective fact, for Mayo and his group were evangelists as well as researchers. He had come to quite similar conclusions many years before, and for him the Hawthorne experiment did not reveal so much as confirm.

The two slim books Mayo published since Hawthorne have proved to be an immensely powerful manifesto. Mayo never pretended that he was free from values and he frankly presents an argument as well as a diagnosis. In *The Social Problems of an Industrial Civilization*, he opens his case by picturing man's happiness in more primitive times. "Historically and traditionally our fathers worked for social co-operation—and achieved it. This is true also of any primitive society. But we, for at least a century of the most amazing scientific and material progress, have abandoned the effort —by inadvertence, it is true—and we are now reaping the consequences."

In the Middle Ages people had been disciplined by social codes into working well together. The Industrial Revolution, as Mayo described the consequences, had split society into a whole host of conflicting groups. Part of a man belonged to one group, part to another, and he was bewildered; no longer was there *one* group in which he could sublimate himself. The liberal philosophers, who were quite happy to see an end to feudal belongingness, interpreted this release from the group as freedom. Mayo does not see it this way. To him, the dominant urge of mankind is to belong: "Man's desire to be continuously associated in work with his fellows," he states, "is a strong, if not the strongest, human characteristic."

Whether the urge to co-operate is in fact man's most dominant drive, it does not follow that the co-operation is necessarily good. What is he going to co-operate *about?* What ends is the group working toward? But these questions do not greatly interest Mayo, and he seems to feel that the sheer fact of "spontaneous" co-operation carries its own ethic. "For *all* of us," Mayo states, "the feeling of security and certainty derives *always* from assured membership of a group." (Italics mine.)

Suppose there is a conflict between the individual and the group? Mayo sees conflict primarily as a breakdown in communication. If a man is unhappy or dissatisfied in his work, it is not that there is a conflict to be resolved so much as a misunderstanding to be cleared up. The worker might not see it this way, and most certainly the unions do not, but we have already been told that the individual is a nonlogical animal incapable of rationally solving his own problems or, in fact, of recognizing what the problem is.

At this point the human relations doctrine comes perilously close to demanding that the individual sacrifice his own beliefs that he may belong. The only way to escape this trap would be through the notion that by the process of equilibrium, a clarification of which never seems to detain anyone very long, what's good for the group is good for the individual. In speaking of the primitive group Mayo writes, "The situation is not simply that the society exercises a forceful compulsion on the individual; on the contrary, the social code and the desire of the individual are, for all practical purposes, identical. Every member of the group participates in all social activities because it is his chief desire to do so."

How to get back to this idyllic state? Mayo does not recommend a return to the Middle Ages. Too much water —and damn muddy water too, if you ask Mayo—has flowed under the bridge for that. The goal must be "an *adaptive* society"—a society in which we can once again enjoy the belongingness of primitive times but without the disadvantages of them.

This won't come about naturally. What with the mischief caused by the philosophers of individualism, most contemporary leaders are untrained in the necessary social skill to bring the adaptive society to pass. What is needed is an administrative elite, people trained to recognize that what man really wants most is group solidarity even if he does not realize it himself. They won't push him around; they won't even argue with him—unfettered as they will be of "prejudice and emotion," they won't have any philosophy, other than co-operation, to argue about. They will adjust him. Through the scientific application of human relations, these neutralist technicians will guide him into satisfying solidarity with the group so skillfully and unobtrusively that he will scarcely realize how the benefaction has been accomplished.

When Mayo got down to cases he was entirely consistent with his philosophy. His advocacy of "nondirective counseling" is a good case in point. In the course of their interviewing at Hawthorne, Mayo and his colleagues became impressed with the therapeutic effects the interviews had on the workers and went on to make the interview a management tool. The idea was to have a group of counselors who would be paid by management but who would not report to management what the workers said to them when they spilled their troubles. Since the workers knew this they could feel free to talk out their problems.

Implicit in this technique is the assumption that the worker's problems can indeed be *talked out*. He is to adjust to the group rather than vice versa; and the alternative of actually changing reality is hardly considered. If a worker is sore at his foreman the chances are good that he is not really sore at the foreman because of some rational gripe but is merely venting on the foreman certain repressed feelings. By listening patiently, like a psychiatrist, the counselor helps such persons understand that what they are really sore about flows from inner, subjective conflict. Characteristically, Mayo cites a woman worker who "discovered for herself during an interview that her dislike of a certain supervisor was based upon a fancied resemblance to a detested stepfather."

In similar cases it is possible the worker might not be maladjusted at all. The foreman might have been dividing up the work load problem badly, and maybe he had a few syndromes himself. The nondirective counseling idea, however, pooh-poohs the possibility: if there is a conflict of values that can't be talked out the interview has no provision in it for action to be taken—the setup itself, in short, is a value judgment that adjustment, rather than change, is the desideratum.

For a number of reasons, one being the hostility of the unions to it, the nondirective counseling system as such has never taken hold of the American industry. But the basic idea has. As I hope to demonstrate in later chapters, many of the more popular techniques—such as psychological "personality" testing, conference techniques—are all manifestations of the same principle. The rock is the group and maladjustment is disharmony with it.

Ironically, the primary target of this adjustment has become the managers themselves. While Mayo intended human relations to apply to the workers and managers both, the managers first seized on it as an excellent tool for manipulating the workers into a chronic contentment that would turn them away from the unions. But manipulation is a two-edged weapon; having learned how illogical workers were, managerial pioneers of human relations soon began to ponder the fact that their colleagues weren't so logical either. They needed to belong too—and even more than the worker, for more of their life was involved in the organization. Looking at the neuroses about him, many a progressive young organization man resolved that here, not on the shop floor, was the place that needed human relations most.

The use of psychological tests, if I may get a bit ahead of my story, is symptomatic. Originally, they were introduced by the managers as a tool for weeding out unqualified workers. As time went on, and personality tests were added to aptitude tests, the managers began using them on other managers, present and prospective, and today most personality testing is directed not at the worker, but at the organization man. If he is being hoist, it is by his own philosophy.

Not so long after Mayo and his colleagues documented the importance of the group at Hawthorne, a former student of Mayo's, anthropologist Lloyd Warner, began coming to remarkably similar conclusions in a study of a New England town. This study, which has had a tremendous impact on social science, was an impressively large-scale undertaking in which some twenty researchers spent three years making a study of Newburyport, Massachusetts. Every conceivable fact about Newburyport was to be dug up, and through scientific evaluations, some objective conclusions were to be arrived at.

Several years before, Warner had studied a tribe of Australian aborigines and had been immensely impressed by the way in which the tribal customs and the unwritten laws kept the individual in harmony with the group. The rituals and sanctions seemed illogical at times, but they shielded man from the kind of individual decisions which a fast-changing industrial society could overwhelm him with.

When Warner began poking around Newburyport, he discovered strong parallels. It was a venerable old New England town rich in tradition and full of people with a strong attachment to the past.[2] There were Memorial Day celebrations instead of the Nurngin totem rites, but in many ways it seemed much the same, and Warner drew the same moral. Of the many conclusions that came out of the study, by all odds the most important finding was the function of social structure in fixing the individual in a satisfying relation to the society. Newburyport did not present altogether as happy a picture of stability as a medieval or primitive society would have. Even though it had been touched by the Industrial Revolution, however, it did provide excellent grist for Warner's argument that the happiness of man depended on the rootedness in a stable group. Like several other old communities, it had lost the economic basis of its early prosperity and thus was frozen somewhat in the mold of previous times.

Warner saw, and charted, seven class divisions in Newburyport, and from these generalized a concept of class and status for the country as a whole. The concept has long since been subjected to a thoroughgoing critical analysis by many social scientists; suffice it to say here that Warner's description carried with it a strong note of advocacy. Warner did believe that there should be some mobility between classes and he thought it healthy that a number of people could move up from, say, the upper-middle to the lower-upper. But not *too* many. The class structure would become meaningless in that case, and people would become

[2] It was also the home town of J. P. Marquand, a fact which was later to produce *Point of No Return* and some sharp passages about anthropologists studying a venerable old New England town.

bewildered for lack of a firm group to relate themselves to.

Conflict, change, fluidity—these are the evils from which man should be insulated. To Warner, the unconscious yearning for belongingness was all-important. During the time he and his associates were at Newburyport, the workers in the shoe factory there went on strike. Ostensibly, the strike was over economic matters; the workers thought they wanted more money. But Warner and his colleagues saw it another way. They saw so many other factors that they produced a book on the subject (called, somewhat flatly, *The Social System of the Modern Factory*). The real cause of the strike, the book implies, was not so much the economic plight of the workers as the social one. Back in the eighteen-hundreds they had enjoyed the status that comes from a firm hierarchy of skills and there had been the steadying hand of the paternal local capitalists. But now increased mechanization, while not rampant in the shoe industry, had downgraded the old high-status jobs; equally unfortunate, the absentee ownership of "Big City capitalism" had supplanted the local oligarchy. Whether they knew it or not, in short, the workers struck because the cohesive society of old had broken down.

Someday someone is going to create a stir by proposing a radical new tool for the study of people. It will be called the face-value technique. It will be based on the premise that people often do what they do for the reasons they think they do. The use of this technique would lead to many pitfalls, for it is undeniably true that people do not always act logically or say what they mean. But I wonder if it would produce findings any more unscientific than the opposite course.

That strike at Newburyport, for example. Warner did devote a couple of sentences to the logical, economic factors, but it's clear in reading the other three hundred pages that he feels that the real cause lay in the fact that there was no longer any "hierarchy of skills" that used to give workers a sense of satisfaction and status. Well, maybe so, but most of the workers who struck didn't happen to have been around to remember the idyllic days of old described by Warner, and it is somewhat debatable if they would have liked them quite as much as Warner seems to believe they would. As far as I can gather from a careful reading of Warner's account of it, the workers acted with eminent logic. They wanted more money; the employers didn't want to give it to them; the workers banded together in strike, and the employers gave in. Is it so very naïve, then, to explain this strike as very much of an economic matter? Any more naïve than to attribute it to a nostalgia for ancient paternalism? Who has the nostalgia?

In fairness to Warner, it should be pointed out that he has subsequently been coming to the view that there is more mobility than Newburyport would suggest. His followers, however, have not been so flexible, and the Warner thesis, for all the defections of its author, remains a very powerful force. Among educators in particular it is one of the principal ideological bases for the belief that only a segment of society should be schooled in the humanities. The majority, goes the idea, should be taught lesser skills; rather than tantalize themselves with aspirations, they should adjust to the fact of a fairly fixed social system.

Neither Warner nor Mayo had much enthusiasm for the union as a social group; in Mayo's case it split loyalties in the factory scheme of things; in Warner's case it split the loyalties of the stable, fixed, small community. It could be argued, however, that if workers needed an embracing group the union had as much right to be it as any other group. Which brings us to the third variation on belongingness—the proposition of Frank Tannenbaum. Unlike Mayo, he is the father of no school; he is an historian rather than a labor leader. But his views are well worth examining all the same; they may not be symptomatic of labor thought but they are symptomatic of the growing quest for belongingness.

In the opening pages of Tannenbaum's *A Philosophy of Labor* (New York: Knopf, 1951) there is the customary salute to the Middle Ages.

Membership in a guild, manorial estate, or village protected man throughout his life and gave him the peace and serenity from which could flow the medieval art and craft.

The life of man was a nearly unified whole. Being a member of an integrated society protected and raised the dignity of the individual and gave each person his own special role. Each man, each act, was part of a total life drama, the plot of which was known and in which the part allotted to each was prescribed. No one was isolated or abandoned. His individuality and his ambitions were fulfilled within the customary law that ruled the community to which he belonged.

Then came the Industrial Revolution and paradise lost.

The Industrial Revolution destroyed the solid moorings of an older way of life and cast the helpless workers adrift in a strange and difficult world. The peasant who had been reared in the intimacy of a small village . . . now found himself isolated and bewildered in a city crowded with strangers and indifferent to a common rule. The symbolic universe that had patterned the ways of men across the ages in village, manor, or guild had disappeared. This is the great moral tragedy of the industrial system.

To make matters worse, Tannenbaum continues, the philosophers of the enlightenment rationalized this breakdown of the old society in terms of individualism. "This doctrine gave the social disintegration then taking place a moral purpose. . . . In its extreme form the theory seemed to advance the idea that the best society was that in which organized human relations and responsibilities were least."

As Tannenbaum rightly points out, this doctrine of self-sufficiency was all very fine for the *bourgeoisie,* but for the workers, self-sufficiency was an illusion. In learning this, however, the workers were taking the first steps to re-creating a community. In making them recognize their individual helplessness, the employers made them recognize their common strength. "The trade-union," as Tannenbaum says, "was the visible evidence that man is not a commodity, and that he is not sufficient unto himself."

The kind of sufficiency Tannenbaum is most concerned with is social rather than economic, and thus to him the real promise of the unions lay in their potential as a social unit. But the workers, no less affected by the Protestant Ethic than their employers, had too pressing an agenda to be diverted from bread-and-butter economic matters. Thus, in fighting the unions, the employers were diverting the unions' energies from the ultimate goal. And the employers didn't do it just to save money; they resisted unionization "because a society tends to become an all-embracing way of life."

Now, however, Tannenbaum argues that the unions are at last in a position to become instruments of "governance" rather than instruments of war. "Only when the battle for recognition is finished can the institutional role come into its own. If the trade-union could not fulfill its larger responsibilities, it would have no reason for existence, would not be a true society, would have no moral role, and would disintegrate." The true end, then, is for a society in which the worker, like his ancestors in the Middle Ages, will be firmly rooted in a group with customs, laws, and guides. He will lose his mobility—not for him the upward—and individual—path to the managerial world; the "fluidity," both geographic and social, that we will see in suburbia is precisely the thing Tannenbaum wants to insulate man from. And the trend away from fluidity is not to be denied. "Institutionally the trade-union movement is an unconscious effort to harness the drift of our time and reorganize it around the cohesive identity that men working together always achieve. That is why the trade-union is a repudiation of the individualism of the French Revolution and the liberalism of English utilitarian philosophers."

Tannenbaum seems to be working the other side of the street from Mayo and Warner. But while they are truer to the medieval spirit in wanting the nobility rather than the serfs to be in charge, the outlook is the same. Any dispute is merely jurisdictional; they don't agree on *which* group should do the embracing but they are all of a piece on the idea the embracing should be done—although not by the state, for that would be totalitarian.

I do not mean to deprecate study of the function of groups. One can study something without deifying it, and a recognition that a society can be all embracing doesn't require belief that it should be. The most vigorous criticism of the human-relations doctrine has come from social scientists, and most of them have by no means been uninterested in the power of the group or its value. However one differs with the findings of particular studies, the point at issue should be the findings, not the fact of the studies. An obvious point perhaps, but there does seem too little middle ground between the near-evangelical acceptance of social-science research on the one hand, and the damnation of it as the improper study of mankind because its particulars are found wanting.

Nor do values mar it; the point is to recognize the values that we may judge them. Mayo made his quite explicit, and in fairness to him and the other pioneers of human relations, we must remember the prevailing climate of opinion at the time; as John Dewey was to authoritarian education, so they were to authoritarian industry. Mayo emphasized group cohesiveness and administrative social skill so much because he felt—with considerable justification—that Americans had been slighting these matters. At a time when the people in charge of big organizations clung to the mechanistic views of the efficiency experts, Mayo brought a badly needed shift in perspective; he helped sensitize a steady stream of influential management people to the importance of the whole vast informal network beneath them and the necessity of comprehending it. One does not have to go along with Mayo's philosophy of the adaptive society to recognize the benefits in better management that he helped bring about.

But what was once counter-cyclical is now orthodoxy. Already human relations is a standard part of the curriculum of the business schools and it will not be very long before it is standard in the high schools too. Human relations can mean a lot of things—as one critic defines it, it is any study called human relations to escape the discipline of established theory in the appropriate field. But, generally speaking, most human-relations doctrine is pointed toward the vision of Mayo, and this reinforces what many people are already very well prepared to believe.

Particularly, the organization man. Who is the hero in human relations? In the older ideology, it was the top leader who was venerated. In human relations it is the organization man, and thus the quasi-religious overtones with which he gratefully endows it. The older ideology provided an unsatisfactory view of the system for the large and growing bureaucratic slice of management. The human-relations doctrine, however, not only tells them that they are important, but that they are the key figures. As sociologist Reinhard Bendix has observed, in the new managerial ideology, it is not the leaders of industry that are idealized—if anything, they are scolded—but the lieutenants. The people that the workers are to co-operate with are not the top employers but enlightened bureaucrats.

At times it almost seems that human relations is a revolutionary tool the organization man is to use *against* the bosses. Listen to an unreconstructed boss give a speech castigating unreconstructed bosses for not being more enlightened about human relations, and you get the feeling the speech is a subtle form of revenge on the part of the harried underling who wrote it. For reasons of protocol, organization men publicly extol human relations for the beneficial effects it casts downward, but privately they spend most of their time talking about using it upward. Whenever there is responsible criticism of human relations, there is a hurt response from middle management staff people, and, invariably, the complaint boils down to something like this: Why, why hurt us? Many of the criticisms are true all right—some people have gone haywire on this—but we progressives have a tough enough fight converting the reactionaries on top, and any criticism at this time only gives aid and comfort to them.

It is not an easy complaint to answer—many older executives are indeed reactionary and many are against human relations for strange reasons. What makes the complaint particularly tough to answer, however, is the trusting way organization men assume that only techniques are subject for criticism and that surely the goals must be noncontroversial. They thought that battle was won long ago. So it was. If I do not dwell more in this book on the beneficial aspects of human relations, it is because they have been reiterated quite enough already.

In practice, of course, corporations have not changed their ways quite so much as their self-congratulations on human relations suggest, and many a highly publicized program is only a sugar-coating of the mixture as before. Because there remains a divergence between precept and practice, however, does not mean that precept is any the less important. While older men may appropriate the vocabulary of human relations without the underlying philosophy, the younger men believe. They have had an indoctrination their superiors did not, and though experience may disillusion them somewhat they view the day of their ascension with genuine missionary zeal.

The point I am trying to make is not that the corporation, or any other specific kind of organization, is going to be *the* citadel of belongingness. The union of Frank Tannenbaum, the community of Lloyd Warner, the corporation of Elton Mayo—each is in conflict as to which group is going to furnish the vital belongingness, and these three by no means exhaust the roster of groups proposed. Spokesmen in other areas have similarly bewailed the lack of an encompassing, integrated life, and in an excess of good will have asked that their group take over the whole messy job. Many a contemporary prescription for utopia can be summarized if you cross out the name of one group and substitute another in the following charge: Society has broken down; the family, the church, the community, the schools, business—each has failed to give the individual the belongingness he needs and thus it is now the task of —— group to do the job. It is fortunate there are so many groups; with such competition for the individual psyche it is difficult for any one of them to land the franchise.

But ideologically these pleas do not cancel each other out. For there is always the common thread that a man must belong and that he must be unhappy if he does not belong rather completely. The idea that conflicting allegiances safeguard him as well as abrade him is sloughed over, and for the people who must endure the tensions of independence there is no condolence; only the message that the tensions are sickness—either in themselves or in society. It does not make any difference whether the Good Society is to be represented by a union or by a corporation or by a church; it is to be a society unified and purged of conflict.

To turn about and preach that conflicting allegiances are absolute virtues is not justified either. But at this particular time the function they perform in the maintenance of individual freedom is worthy of more respect. Clark Kerr, Chancellor of the University of California, at Berkeley, has put it well:

> *The danger is not that loyalties are divided today but that they may be undivided tomorrow. . . . I would urge each individual to avoid total involvement in any organization; to seek to whatever extent lies within his power to limit each group to the minimum control necessary for performance of essential functions; to struggle against the effort to absorb; to lend his energies to many organizations and give himself completely to none; to teach children, in the home and in the school, "to be laws to themselves and to depend on themselves," as Walt Whitman urged us many years ago —for that is the well source of the independent spirit.*

CHAPTER FIVE

Togetherness

IT is the organization man, then, more than the worker whom he wishes to serve, who most urgently wants to belong. His quest takes many forms; in this chapter I would like to examine the most concrete one: his growing preoccupation with group work. The group that he is trying to immerse himself in is not merely the larger one—The Organization, or society itself—but the immediate, physical group as well: the people at the conference table, the workshop, the seminar, the skull session, the after-hours discussion group, the project team. It is not enough now that he belong; he wants to belong *together*.

One reason that he is so fascinated with group work, of course, is the simple fact that there is now so much more of it. Organization life being what it is, out of sheer necessity he must spend most of his working hours in one group or another, and out of self-defense, if not instinct, the committee arts must become reflex with him. But more than necessity is involved. Where the immersion of the individual used to be cause for grumbling and a feeling of independence lost, the organization man of today is now welcoming it. He is not attempting to reverse the trend and to cut down the deference paid to the group; he is working to increase it, and with the help of some branches of the social sciences he is erecting what is almost a secular religion.

There are two bases for this movement, one scientific, the

other moral. The scientific basis can be stated very simply. It is now coming to be widely believed that *science has proved the group is superior to the individual.* Science has not, but that is another matter. Mistaken or not, the popularized version of the science of the group is a social force in its own right, and it holds that experiments have shown that in human relations the whole is always greater than the sum of its parts and that through "interaction" we can produce ideas beyond our capabilities as individuals. The new dynamism, furthermore, is not to apply merely to the day-to-day work of getting things done; it is, presumably, going to envelop creative work too, and in areas until recently considered sacrosanct to the individual it is already having some effect. The scientific genius, for example. As I will take up in later chapters, there is a growing thought that he is an anachronism—a once valuable, but now unnecessary, prelude to the research team. And not an idle thought; in the name of science, administrators are taking some practical measures to insure that he will in fact be an anachronism.

As is so characteristic of scientism, there is an overriding faith that we are on the brink of superseding discovery. In previous eras people often worked in groups too, and sometimes, though one would not imagine so from current group literature, quite successfully. But they were merely being empirical. If people were successful before, some now exclaim, think what lies ahead! For there now exists, or shortly will, a scientific body of laws by which we can unleash hitherto untapped sources of creativity.

For their theoretical justification, group advocates lean heavily on the work being done in "group dynamics." This is a difficult field to define, all social science having a concern with the group, but generally it describes the work of those whose attention is focused on the face-to-face group. From its beginnings, it has attracted some of the most imaginative men in social science, and through a combination of attitude surveys of organizations and experiments with small groups, they have tackled a whole series of intriguing questions. If a group has high morale, will it produce more? What is the ideal size of the informal group? What is the effect of the group on the deviate?

Over-all, their intellectual ambition has been large. Not only have they aimed to discover the underlying principles of group activity, they have aimed to do it in a rather short time, and this promise has unduly excited lay followers in the organization world. There have been delays; originally the group-dynamics people had expected the basic program to be over in ten years, but now they feel more time may be needed. Such delays, however, have only made the eventual promise all the more tantalizing to organization people. Another ten years . . .

But the basis of the movement is primarily a moral one. To the organization man the search for better group techniques is something of a crusade—a crusade against authoritarianism, a crusade for more freedom, for more recognition of the man in the middle. The key word is "democratic"; with some justification the organization man argues that the old-style individualist was often far more of a bar to individualism in other people and that in the modern organization the desk-pounding type of leader drastically inhibits the flow of ideas, not to mention making life unpleasant for everybody. As organization men see it, through an extension of the group spirit, through educating people to sublimate their egos, organizations can rid themselves of their tyrants and create a *harmonious* atmosphere in which the group will bring out the best in everyone. This moral urge is not lightly to be dismissed, and though I wish later to suggest other reasons for the group quest, it is only fair to say that most group advocates would be sincerely disturbed at the thought that they are party to anything that would stifle the individual.

But they are. Much of what they say is correct: it is true that the health of organization life depends upon skillful group work; it is true that the group is tremendously effective in bringing out different points of view that would otherwise remain latent, that together members of a group can see more possible lines of action than if they were consulted individually; it is true that genius cannot function in a vacuum and that interaction with others in the field can be vastly stimulating and, indeed, often indispensable.

But other things are true too, and in this chapter I would like to dwell on a few of the aspects of group work that are currently being sloughed over. To anyone who has had to work in an organization, they will not be novel thoughts, but I believe they deserve far more reiteration than they are now getting. It is not so much the fallacies of specific techniques of group work that are critical as the continued imbalance of emphasis, for this emphasis is having a definite molding effect on the organization man.

The organization man is not yet so indoctrinated that he does not chafe at the pressures on his independence, and sometimes he even suspects that the group may be as much a tyrant as the despot it has replaced. It is the burden of the new group doctrine that such misgivings, if they are not maladjustment on the part of the individual, are simply a lack of knowledge, a lack of mastery of managerial techniques. The doctrine may be wrong, but the constant impress of it is helping to undercut the few personal defenses left the individual; more to the point, it is making an organization life increasingly hostile to the nonbeliever who hangs onto his defenses.

The central fallacy, I believe, lies in what can be called false collectivization. When are people in a group? Too often, we insist on treating a person—or ourselves—as a unit of a group when association with the particular group is not vital to the task in question, or may even be repressive. In some cases the group is a key entity—that is, the working together of individuals is necessary to perform the particular function, and in such cases the way each of the people affects the others is inextricably entwined with the total performance. The work of a combat squad is a good example of this. The soldier is conditioned to fight primarily by his group, and just as a contagion of fear drastically alters the individual, so can a unity of courage. In such cases, plainly, the group is primary and it produces something over and above the total of the individuals.

Can we generalize, however, that this is true of all collections of individuals? We are confusing an abstraction with a reality. Just because a collection of individuals can be called a group does not mean it functions as a group or that it should. In many situations the fact of groupness is only incidental. Take, for example, the men who sit together in a college classroom. At times, an *esprit de corps* is helpful in promoting lively discussion, but it is not vital, and the student's important relationship is not with other members of the group but to the content of the course and to the teacher as intermediary.

But this distinction between the functional grouping and the incidental grouping is easily blurred. To follow the example of the class, we find many teachers treating a course less as a worthy discipline in its own right than as a vehicle for stimulating interaction. In many institutions, as a consequence, the yardstick of a teacher's performance is the amount of interaction he develops in the group, and those who keep the students' focus on the discipline are apt to find themselves under censure.

One teacher who had been criticized on this score told me that he was glad in a way, for he had been forced to think through his own position. "If I didn't, I would stand accused as a reactionary. So I had to think out what I had always taken for granted. First, I made the point that in my course—during the first part of it, at any rate—the students were not qualified. I think it would be a mistake to encourage them to think that their opinions are as good as mine at this stage. They aren't, and I want to let them know that before they can question my interpretation, they must master the fundamentals. Sure, I want them to question and to come to their own conclusions, but they have to earn the right; they don't get fundamentals through glorified bull sessions but by hard work. The second point I made was on the value of the interaction that they talk about. What's so very important about it? Of all the groups that we are connected with in our lives, the classroom group is one of the least permanent and least vital ones. Try to remember who sat next to you in your classes at college. You'll have a hard time remembering."

Another example of false collectivization is the way many organizations treat their professional employees. Recently, to cite a typical case, one well-known corporation was worried over a morale problem among its engineers. Now it is convenient to talk of the engineers as a group—just as it is convenient to talk of hundreds of thousands of individuals as a "mass audience." A convenient method of description, however, is not necessarily a reality. The engineers appeared to be a group because physically many of them were housed in the same building, and in the organization charts and pay scales they were classified together for convenience' sake. But their real problem in this instance came from their vertical relationship—that is, their relationship to the particular task and the superiors above them—and their morale problem had very little to do with social harmony among themselves. The company insisted on treating them as a group, however, and in a vain effort to promote morale completely obscured the real nature of the problem. I am sure that many organization men can think of similar confusions.

The most misguided attempt at false collectivization is the current attempt to see the group as a creative vehicle. Can it be? People very rarely *think* in groups; they talk together, they exchange information, they adjudicate, they make compromises. But they do not think; they do not create.

Group advocates would agree that this has been so. But they do not see this as a natural limitation. To them it is a bug of human relations to be cured, and in the expectation that technique is the key, they are engaged in a wholesale effort to tame the arts of discovery—and those by nature suited for it. In part this effort is propelled by the natural distaste of the noncreative man for the creative, but again, there is the moral impulse. Among many there is a real belief that we can teach the individual to create in concert rather than as an individual and that his acceptance of the organization way will produce a combustion of ideas otherwise impossible.

Here would be the ultimate victory of the administrator. The creative individual he does not understand, nor does he understand the conditions of creativity. The messiness of intuition, the aimless thoughts, the unpractical questions—all these things that are so often the companion to discovery are anathema to the world of the administrator. Order, objective goals, agreement—these are his desiderata.

Vital they are to executing ideas, but not to creating them. Agreement? To concentrate on agreement is to intensify that which inhibits creativity. For any group of people to operate effectively some firm basis of agreement is necessary, and a meeting cannot be productive unless certain premises are so shared that they don't need to be discussed and the argument can be confined to areas of disagreement. But while this kind of consensus makes a group more effective in its legitimate functions, it does not make the group a creative vehicle.

Think for a moment of the way you behave in a committee meeting. In your capacity as group member you feel a strong impulse to seek common ground with the others. Not just out of timidity but out of respect for the sense of the meeting you tend to soft-pedal that which would go against the grain. And that, unfortunately, can include unorthodox ideas. A really new idea affronts current agreement—it wouldn't be a new idea if it didn't—and the group, impelled as it is to agreement, is instinctively hostile to that which is divisive. With wise leadership it can offset this bias, but the essental urge will still be to unity, to consensus. After an idea matures—after people learn to live with it—the group may approve it, but that is after the fact and it is an act of acquiescence rather than creation.

I have been citing the decision-making group, and it can be argued that these defects of order do not apply to information-exchanging groups. It is true that meeting with those of common interests can be tremendously stimulating and suggest to the individuals fresh ways of going about their own work. But stimulus is not discovery; it is not the act of creation. Those who recognize this limitation do not confuse the functions and, not expecting too much, profit from the meeting of minds.

Others, however, are not so wise, and fast becoming a fixture of organization life is the meeting self-consciously dedicated to creating ideas. It is a fraud. Much of such high-pressure creation—cooking with gas, creating out loud, spitballing, and so forth—is all very provocative, but if it is stimulating, it is stimulating much like alcohol. After the glow of such a session has worn off, the residue of ideas usually turns out to be a refreshed common denominator that everybody is relieved to agree upon—and if there is a new idea, you usually find that it came from a capital of ideas already thought out—by *individuals*—and perhaps held in escrow until someone sensed an opportune moment for its introduction.

I have been talking of the extension of the team to a field where it does not belong. Even in fields where the group is vital, however, the current emphasis on the team is having some equally inhibiting effects. Just as it has obscured the role of the individual in creation and discovery in such activities as research and communication, so in the regular work of running an organization it is obscuring the function of leadership.

Such emphasis is particularly unnecessary at this time because the whole tendency of modern organization life is to muffle the importance of individual leadership. In studying an organization, one of the most difficult things is to trace a program or innovation back to its origins, and this is just as true of organization successes as it is of failures. Who started what and when? This kind of question is the kind that makes organization people uncomfortable. To answer it would be an offense against the organization spirit, and even the man himself who first conceived the plan is apt to deny—except perhaps to his wife—that his contribution was really very important. A sense of the fitness of things requires that it be the team, everyone working together, a small part of the inexorable symmetry of the over-all plan. Repeated, time and again, it becomes official, and this is the face of organization—and the moral—that is presented to the apprentices.

But now to this inclination is added the force of ideology. On the surface it seems reasonable enough; the bogy is authoritarianism, and the aim is to free organization people from the pressures imposed on them by opinionated, unilateral people that all may express themselves more freely. But how do you define authoritarianism? In practice, current definitions of the authoritarian leader come perilously close to including anyone who has ideas of his own or who differs with others on basic policy.

Anti-authoritarianism is becoming anti-leadership. In group doctrine the strong personality is viewed with overwhelming suspicion. The co-operative are those who take a stance directly over the keel; the man with ideas—in translation, prejudices—leans to one side or, worse yet, heads for the rudder. Plainly, he is a threat. Skim through current group handbooks, conference leaders' tool kits, and the like, and you find what sounds very much like a call to arms by the mediocre against their enemies.

Let me cite a Bureau of Naval Personnel handbook on "Conference Sense." It is describing, with elephantine cheeriness, the different kinds of types one has to deal with in conferences. Among the bad people we meet is The Aggressor.

The conference leader's remedy: Place Donald Duck at your left (the blind spot). Fail to hear his objections, or if you do, misunderstand them. If possible, recognize a legitimate objection and side with him. Object is to get him to feel that he "belongs." If he still persists in running wild, let group do what they are probably by now quite hot to do, i.e., cut the lug down. They generally do it by asking Little Brother Terrible to clarify his position, then to clarify his clarification, then to clarify his clarification of his clarification, etc., until our lad is so hot and bothered that he has worked himself into role of conference comedian. Then soothe his bruised ego and restore him to human society by asking him questions that he can answer out of special experience.

The good people? One is The Compromiser. He "may offer compromise by admitting his error . . . by obviously disciplining himself to maintain group harmony, or by 'coming halfway' in moving along with the group. . . . This takes courage. Let him know he's appreciated. Give occasional cigar. A fifteen center. He deserves the best."

These defensive gambits against the leader are only a stopgap measure. What some group advocates have in mind is, quite literally, *to eliminate the leader altogether.*

For some time the National Training Laboratory in Group Development at Bethel, Maine, has been experimenting with the "leaderless group"—and with such zeal as to make some students of the group a bit uneasy. One of the most astute students of the group, sociologist William Foote Whyte, was moved to write some second thoughts on his experiences at Bethel. He recounts the well-meaning attempt that was made there to turn the group leader into a "resource person." The idea was that as the group jells, the leader would become less necessary and would retire into the background to be consulted, occasionally, for his special *expertise*. When this was tried out, a good bit of chaos resulted, but the group people hoped that the chaos—or "feeling-draining"—would be a valuable catharsis and a prelude to later agreement. But no agreement came. Unfortunately, the group could not agree on a topic to agree upon.

The causes of failure, as Whyte maintained, were not technical. Later he tried similar experiments on his own, and these led him to the conclusion that "if the group is to make progress in its discussions and avoid confusion and frustration, then there must be a well-defined leadership, at least in the sense of co-ordination of activity. . . . in some groups, and this was notably true at Bethel, such a high premium is placed upon fitting into the group and being sensitive to the group's wishes that the individual who shows some initiative on his own becomes suspect and is likely to be discouraged. We must remember that if every member simply wants to do what the group wants to do, then the group is not going to do anything. Somehow, individual initiative must enter into the group. Should we bring it in openly or should we try to bootleg it in an expression of group sentiment?"

The intellectual hypocrisy of the leaderless group has brought forth a new breed; into the very vacuum that they bespeak have moved the professional group expediters. The end they seek is compromise and harmony, but in their controlled way they can be just as militant as any desk-pounder of old, and a lot more self-righteous. Reuel Denney has written a wonderful account in *Commentary* of the puzzlement of an old-style convention-goer when he comes up against them. After attending a preconvention conference with a group of people interested in groups, it slowly dawns on him that "those fellows were deciding a lot of things. Not that they knew it. But they were, for instance, planning a strategy to prevent the bright and talkative men from intimidating the others at the convention; they were going to get participation even if they, in a nice way, had to slug somebody, and the role of slugger—not just a role-playing role, either—was assigned in advance."

The extent of this ferment was forcibly brought home to me several years ago when I encountered my first "buzz session." It was at a management convention. It had started conventionally enough with a panel discussion in which I and two other men spoke. Halfway through the proceedings, the program chairman called an intermission and, with the assistance of several helpers, began rearranging the seating so that the audience would be divided into groups of four, with the chairs turned around so that they faced each other, looking much like a huge bridge tournament with the bridge tables removed. When I asked him what was going on, he seemed surprised. Hadn't I ever heard of a "buzz session"? He was an old hand at it, having been one of the first graduates of the National Group Training Laboratory at Bethel. He explained that rather than have a "directed" discussion, we would stimulate ideas through interaction. By breaking the audience into a constellation of face-to-face groups, he said, we would create this interaction. The fact that the seating would be a random mixture of strangers would make no difference; the interaction itself would produce many provocative insights.

At last he banged down the gavel, and some two hundred grown men turned and faced each other for the discussion period. Minutes went by. There was no buzz. Something, obviously, was wrong, and it was only through the heroic efforts of two expediters that any questions from the floor were forthcoming. The chairman was not chastened. After the meeting he told me that the trouble was simply that the groups were too small. Four wasn't up to the ignition level. Next time they would do it with six to eight men.

While it would be wrong to dwell overlong on the more fatuous examples, they are not quite as unrelated to the main trend as many embarrassed organization men would like to believe. The Harwald Group-Thinkometer, for example. Most group-relations people would probably disown it as too stringent a tool, yet it seems a perfectly logical development. The Group-Thinkometer is an electric meter the dial of which is graduated in degrees of interest. Feeding into it are ten remote-control switches which can be distributed around, or under, the table, and by pressing the switch members of the group indicate approval or disapproval. Since the needle on the meter shows only the accumulated group reaction, one can veto a colleague's idea without his being the wiser, and, as the Harwald Company suggests, thus the personality factor is eliminated almost entirely. Extreme? The Harwald Company has only concretized, you might say, the underlying principles of the group philosophy.

Let me now take up the question of morale. Underpinning the current denigration of leadership are some very questionable assumptions about the relationship between morale and productivity. As usually expressed by organization people, these assumptions follow this general sequence. Once we used hard-driving leaders to get things done, but this was because we didn't know any better. As group-dynamics studies have proved, high group morale is the heart of production. This means that the ideal leader should not lead in the old sense—that is, focus his attention and that of the group on goals. He should instead concentrate almost wholly on the personality relationships within the group. If he attends to these and sees to it that the members get along, the goals will take care of themselves.

But the findings of the group-dynamics investigators themselves have been nowhere near as heart-warming as their lay followers would like to believe. Recently, Rensis Likert, Director of the Institute for Social Research at the University of Michigan—heartland of group dynamics—told a management audience of some second thoughts he had had.

"On the basis of a study I did in 1937 I believed that morale and production were positively related: that the higher the morale the higher the production. Substantial research findings since then have shown that this relationship is much too simple. In our different studies we have found a wide variety of relationships. Some units have low morale and low production; other units have fairly good morale and low production; still others have fairly good production but low morale; other units have both high morale and high production."

Likert saw many benefits in the increased attention paid morale. Among other things it had led people to expect more opportunities for expression, initiative, and participation. But he had grown suspicious, he said, of the laissez-faire approach in which the supervisor does not lead but tries to keep people happy. In companies in which human-relations training programs have been emphasized, he went on, "some supervisors interpret the training to mean that the company management wants them to keep employees happy, so they work hard to do so. The result is a nice country-club atmosphere in which the leadership function has been abandoned to all intents and purposes. Employees like it and absence and turnover are low, but since little production is felt to be expected, they produce relatively little."

Obviously, the study of group dynamics need not be antithetical to the individual, and here let me again make the distinction between analysis of a phenomenon and deification of it. One can study the group aspect of a man without deprecating his other aspects, and while many students of group dynamics have crossed the line, they don't have to. The more we find out about how a group actually behaves —and the scientific method is of immense help here—the more sophisticated we can become about its limitations, the more armed against its defects. But this won't be done unless there is a far more rigorous questioning of the value premises which underlie most current attacks on the problem. Consider the abstractions that are so taken for granted as good—such as consensus, co-operation, participation, and the like. Held up as a goal without any reference to ends, they are meaningless. Why participate, for example? Like similar abstractions, participation is an empty goal unless it is gauged in relation to the job to be done. It is a means, not an end, and when treated as an end, it can become more repressive than the unadorned authoritarianism it is supposed to replace.

And why should there be consensus? Must consensus per se be the overriding goal? It is the price of progress that there never can be complete consensus. All creative advances are essentially a departure from agreed-upon ways of looking at things, and to over-emphasize the agreed-upon is to further legitimatize the hostility to that creativity upon which we all ultimately depend.

Let me admit that I have been talking principally about the adverse aspects of the group. I would not wish to argue for a destructive recalcitrance, nor do I wish to undervalue the real progress we have made in co-operative effort. But to emphasize, in these times, the virtues of the group is to be supererogatory. Universal organization training, as I will take up in the following chapters, is now available for everybody, and it so effectively emphasizes the group spirit that there is little danger that inductees will be subverted into rebelliousness.

Over and above the overt praise for the pressures of the group, the very ease, the democratic atmosphere in which organization life is now conducted makes it all the harder for the individual to justify *to himself* a departure from its norm. It would be a mistake to confuse individualism with antagonism, but the burdens of free thought are already steep enough that we should not saddle ourselves with a guilty conscience as well. The hunch that wasn't followed up. The controversial point that didn't get debated. The idea that was suppressed. Were these acts of group co-operation or individual surrender? We are taking away from the individual the ability even to ask the question.

In further institutionalizing the great power of the majority, we are making the individual come to distrust himself. We are giving him a rationalization for the unconscious urging to find an authority that would resolve the burdens of free choice. We are tempting him to reinterpret the group pressures as a release, authority as freedom, and that this quest assumes a moral guise makes it only the more poignant. Of all the forms of wanton self-destruction, the Englishman A. A. Bowman once observed, there is none more pathetic than that in which the human individual demands that in the vital relationships of life he be treated not as an individual but as a member of some organization.

PART TWO

The Training of
Organization Man

CHAPTER SIX

A Generation of Bureaucrats

WHEN I was a college senior in 1939, we used to sing a plaintive song about going out into the "cold, cold world." It wasn't really so very cold then, but we did enjoy meditating on the fraughtness of it all. It was a big break we were facing, we told ourselves, and those of us who were going to try our luck in the commercial world could be patronizing toward those who were going on to graduate work or academic life. We were taking the leap.

Seniors still sing the song, but somehow the old note of portent is gone. There is no leap left to take. The union between the world of organization and the college has been so cemented that today's seniors can see a continuity between the college and the life thereafter that we never did. Come graduation, they do not go outside to a hostile world; they transfer.

For the senior who is headed for the corporation it is almost as if it were part of one master scheme. The locale shifts; the training continues, for at the same time that the colleges have been changing their curriculum to suit the corporation, the corporation has responded by setting up its own campuses and classrooms. By now the two have been so well molded that it's difficult to tell where one leaves off and the other begins.

The descent, every spring, of the corporations' recruiters has now become a built-in feature of campus life. If the col-

lege is large and its placement director efficient, the processing operation is visibly impressive. I have never been able to
erase from my mind the memory of an ordinary day at Purdue's placement center. It is probably the largest and most
effective placement operation in the country, yet, much as in
a well-run group clinic, there seemed hardly any activity.
In the main room some students were quietly studying company literature arranged on the tables for them; others were
checking the interview timetables to find what recruiter they
would see and to which cubicle he was assigned; at the central filing desk college employees were sorting the hundreds
of names of men who had registered for placement. Except
for a murmur from the row of cubicles there was little to
indicate that scores of young men were, every hour on the
half hour, making the decisions that would determine their
whole future life.

Someone from a less organized era might conclude that
the standardization of this machinery—and the standardized
future it portends—would repel students. It does not. For the
median senior this is the optimum future; it meshes so closely
with his own aspirations that it is almost as if the corporation was planned in response to an attitude poll.

Because they are the largest single group, the corporation-
bound seniors are the most visible manifestation of their
generation's values. But in essentials their contemporaries
headed for other occupations respond to the same urges.
The lawyers, the doctors, the scientists—their occupations
are also subject to the same centralization, the same trend
to group work and to bureaucratization. And so are the
young men who will enter them. Whatever their many differences, in one great respect they are all of a piece: more
than any generation in memory, theirs will be a generation
of bureaucrats.

They are, above all, conservative. Their inclination to accept the status quo does not necessarily mean that in the
historic sweep of ideas they are conservative—in the more
classical sense of conservatism, it could be argued that the
seniors will be, in effect if not by design, agents of revolution. But this is a matter we must leave to later historians.
For the immediate present, at any rate, what ideological fer-

ment college men exhibit is not in the direction of basic change.

This shows most clearly in their attitude toward politics. It used to be axiomatic that young men moved to the left end of the spectrum in revolt against their fathers and then, as the years went on, moved slowly to the right. A lot of people still believe this is true, and many businessmen fear that twenty years of the New Deal hopelessly corrupted our youth into radicalism. After the election of 1952 businessmen became somewhat more cheerful, but many are still apprehensive, and whenever a poll indicates that students don't realize that business makes only about 6 per cent profit, there is a flurry of demands for some new crusade to rescue our youth from socialistic tendencies.

If the seniors do any moving, however, it will be from dead center. Liberal groups have almost disappeared from the campus, and what few remain are anemic. There has been no noticeable activity at the other end of the spectrum either. When William Buckley, Jr., produced *God and Man at Yale,* some people thought this signaled the emergence of a strong right-wing movement among the young men. The militancy, however, has not proved particularly contagious; when the McCarthy issue roused and divided their elders, undergraduates seemed somewhat bored with it all.

Their conservatism is passive. No cause seizes them, and nothing so exuberant or willfully iconoclastic as the Veterans of Future Wars has reappeared. There are Democrats and Republicans, and at election time there is the usual flurry of rallies, but in comparison with the agitation of the thirties no one seems to care too much one way or the other. There has been personal unrest—the suspense over the prospect of military service assures this—but it rarely gets resolved into a thought-out protest. Come spring and students may start whacking each other over the head or roughing up the townees and thereby cause a rush of concern over the wild younger generation. But there is no real revolution in them, and the next day they likely as not will be found with their feet firmly on the ground in the recruiters' cubicles.

Some observers attribute the disinterest to fear. I heard one instructor tell his colleagues that in his politics classes he warned students to keep their noses clean. "I tell them," he said, "that they'd better realize that what they say might be held against them, especially when we get to the part about Marx and Engels. Someday in the future they might find their comments bounced back at them in an investigation."

The advice, as his colleagues retorted, was outrageously unnecessary. The last thing students can be accused of now is dangerous discussion; they are not interested in the kind of big questions that stimulate heresy and whatever the subject—the corporation, government, religion—students grow restive if the talk tarries on the philosophical. Most are interested in the philosophical only to the extent of finding out what the accepted view is in order that they may accept it and get on to the practical matters. This spares the bystander from the lofty bulling and the elaborate pose of unorthodoxy that my contemporaries often used to affect, but it does make for a rather stringent utilitarianism.

Even in theological seminaries, this impatience to be on with the job has been evident. Writes Norman Pittenger, professor at General Theological Seminary:

It is a kind of authoritarianism in reverse. Theological students today, in contrast to their fellows of twenty years ago, want "to be told." I have gone out of my way to ask friends who teach in seminaries of other denominations whether they have recognized the new tendency. Without exception they have told me that they find the present generation of students less inquiring of mind, more ready to accept an authority, and indeed most anxious to have it "laid on the line."

In the seminary this means that the lecturer or teacher must be unusually careful lest his opinion, or what "the Bible says" or "the church teaches," shall be taken as the last word. . . . What troubles many of us is that students today are not willing enough to think things through for themselves. If this is what the Bible says, then how does it say it and why, and how do we know that this is indeed the teaching of Scripture? If this is what the church teaches, why does it teach it, what evidence can be given for the teaching and what right has the church to teach at all? Or

*if a professor says that such-and-such a view is correct,
why does he say it and what real evidence can he produce that his statement is true? It would be better and
healthier if the new respect for authority were more frequently found in combination with a spirit of inquiry, a
ready willingness to think through what is authoritatively
declared, and a refusal ever to accept anything simply because some reputable expert makes the statement.*

In judging a college generation, one usually bases his
judgment on how much it varies from one's own, and presumably superior, class, and I must confess that I find myself tempted to do so. Yet I do not think my generation has
any license to damn the acquiescence of seniors as a weakening of intellectual fiber. It is easy for us to forget that if
earlier generations were less content with society, there was
a great deal less to be contented about. In the intervening
years the economy has changed enormously, and even in
retrospect the senior can hardly be expected to share former
discontents. Society is not out of joint for him, and if he
acquiesces it is not out of fear that he does so. He does
not want to rebel against the status quo because he really
likes it—and his elders, it might be added, are not suggesting
anything bold and new to rebel *for*.

Perhaps contemporaryism would be a better word than
conservatism to describe their posture. The present, more
than the past, is their model; while they share the characteristic American faith in the future also, they see it as more
of same. As they paraphrase what they are now reading
about America, they argue that at last we have got it. The
big questions are all settled; we know the direction, and
while many minor details remain to be cleared up, we can
be pretty sure of enjoying a wonderful upward rise.

While the degree of their optimism is peculiarly American, the spirit of acquiescence, it should be noted, is by no
means confined to the youth of this country. In an Oxford
magazine, called, aptly enough, *Couth,* one student writes
this of his generation:

*It is true that over the last thirty years it has been ele-
mentary good manners to be depressed. . . . But . . . we
are not, really, in the least worried by our impending, and*

other people's present, disasters. This is not the Age of Anxiety. What distinguishes the comfortable young men of today from the uncomfortable young men of the last hundred years . . . is that for once the younger generation is not in revolt against anything. . . . We don't want to rebel against our elders. They are much too nice to be rebellable-against. Old revolutionaries as they are, they get rather cross with us and tell us we are stuffy and prudish, but even this can't provoke us into hostility. . . . Our fathers . . . brought us up to see them not as the representatives of ancient authority and unalterable law but as rebels against our grandfathers. So naturally we have grown up to be on their side, even if we feel on occasion that they were a wee bit hard on their fathers, or even a little naïve.[1]

More than before, there is a tremendous interest in techniques. Having no quarrel with society, they prefer to table the subject of ends and concentrate instead on means. Not what or why but *how* interests them, and any evangelical strain they have they can sublimate; once they have equated the common weal with organization—a task the curriculum makes easy—they will let the organization worry about goals. "These men do not question the system," an economics professor says of them, approvingly. "They want to get in there and lubricate and make them run better. They will be technicians of the society, not innovators."

The attitude of men majoring in social science is particularly revealing on this score. Not so very long ago, the younger social scientist was apt to see his discipline as a vehicle for protest about society as well as the study of it. The seniors that set the fashion for him were frequently angry men, and many of the big studies of the twenties and thirties—Robert and Helen Lynd's *Middletown*, for example —did not conceal strong opinions about the inequities in the social structure. But this is now old hat: it is the "bleeding-heart" school to the younger men (and to some not so young, too), for they do not wish to protest; they wish

---

[1] Similar tendencies have been noticed among German youth. In *Der Junge Arbeiter von Heute*, Karl Bednarik, a former leader in the socialist youth movement, has commented on the "bourgeoisification" of younger workers as a response to the postwar situation.

to collaborate. Reflecting the growing reconciliation with middle-class values that has affected all types of intellectuals, they are turning more and more to an interest in methodology, particularly the techniques of measurement. Older social scientists who have done studies on broad social problems find that the younger men are comparatively uninterested in the problems themselves. When the discussion period comes, the questions the younger men ask are on the technical points; not the what, or why, but the how.

The urge to be a technician, a collaborator, shows most markedly in the kind of jobs seniors prefer. They want to work for somebody else. Paradoxically, the old dream of independence through a business of one's own is held almost exclusively by factory workers—the one group, as a number of sociologists have reported, least able to fulfill it. Even at the bull-session level college seniors do not affect it, and when recruiting time comes around they make the preference clear. Consistently, placement officers find that of the men who intend to go into business—roughly one half of the class—less than 5 per cent express any desire to be an entrepreneur. About 15 to 20 per cent plan to go into their fathers' business. Of the rest, most have one simple goal: the big corporation.

And not just as a stopgap either. When I was a senior many of us liked to rationalize that we were simply playing it smart; we were going with big companies merely to learn the ropes the better to strike out on our own later. Today, seniors do not bother with this sort of talk; once the tie has been established with the big company, they believe, they will not switch to a small one, or, for that matter, to another big one. The relationship is to be for keeps.[2]

[2] One reason why seniors prefer big business is that the big companies go after them and the small ones don't. Of the 450,000 incorporated firms in the U.S., only about 1,000 actually recruit on the campuses, and it is these active 1,000 firms—generally the biggest—that get the cream. Sometimes college placement directors do line up the small company position, but even then they find the students apathetic. "Frankly," says one placement director, echoing many another, "the only kind I can interest in the small company job is the dynamic sort—the one type that is least

It is not simply for security that they take the vows. Far more than their predecessors they understand bigness. My contemporaries, fearful of anonymity, used to talk of "being lost" in a big corporation. This did not prevent us from joining corporations, to be sure, but verbally, at least, it was fashionable to view the organization way with misgivings. Today this would show a want of sophistication. With many of the liberals who fifteen years ago helped stimulate the undergraduate distrust of bigness now busy writing tracts in praise of bigness, the ideological underpinnings for the debate have crumbled.

The fact that a majority of seniors headed for business shy from the idea of being entrepreneurs is only in part due to fear of economic risk. Seniors can put the choice in moral terms also, and the portrait of the entrepreneur as a young man detailed in postwar fiction preaches a sermon that seniors are predisposed to accept. What price bitch goddess Success? The entrepreneur, as many see him, is a selfish type motivated by greed, and he is, furthermore, unhappy. The big-time operator as sketched in fiction eventually so loses stomach for enterprise that he finds happiness only when he stops being an entrepreneur, forsakes "21," El Morocco, and the boss's wife and heads for the country. Citing such fiction, the student can moralize on his aversion to entrepreneurship. His heel quotient, he explains, is simply not big enough.

Not that he is afraid of risk, the senior can argue. Far from being afraid of taking chances, he is simply looking for the *best* place to take them in.[3] Small business is small because of nepotism and the roll-top desk outlook, the argument goes; big business, by contrast, has borrowed the tools of science and made them pay off. It has its great laboratories, its market-research departments, and the time and

likely to get lost in a big company. I would sooner interest the other kind; I point out to the shy, diffident fellows that in a small outfit they'd be something of a jack-of-all-trades, that they'd get a better chance to express themselves, to grow out of their shell. They still don't want it."

[3] A Youth Institute Survey of 4,660 young men indicated that only 20 per cent felt they could not achieve all their economic desires by working for someone else.

patience to use them. The odds, then, favor the man who joins big business. "We wouldn't hesitate to risk adopting new industrial techniques and products," explains a proponent of this calculated-risk theory, "but we would do it only after we had subjected it to tests of engineers, pre-testing in the market and that kind of thing." With big business, in short, risk-taking would be a cinch.

In turning their back on the Protestant Ethic they are consistent; if they do not cherish venture, neither do they cherish what in our lore was its historic reward. They are without avarice. Reflecting on the difference between the postwar classes and his own class of 1928, an erstwhile Yale history professor confessed that the former were so unmercenary he was almost a little homesick for his own. "We were a terrible class. It was the days of the roasted lark, Hell's entries, of the white-shoe boys. Everyone was playing the stock market—they even had a ticker down at the Hotel Taft—and I wound up for a while in a bucket shop down in Wall Street. But today you don't hear that kind of talk. They don't want a million. They are much more serious, much more worth while." He shook his head nostalgically.

Others have been similarly impressed. One recruiter went through three hundred interviews without one senior's mentioning salary, and the experience is not unusual. Indeed, sometimes seniors react as if a large income and security were antithetical. As some small companies have found to their amazement, the offer of a sales job netting $15,000 at the end of two years is often turned down in favor of an equivalent one with a large company netting $8,000. Along with the $8,000 job, the senior says in justification, goes a pension plan and other benefits. He could, of course, buy himself some rather handsome annuities with the extra $7,000 the small company offers, but this alternative does not suggest itself readily.

When seniors are put to speculating how much money they would like to make twenty or thirty years hence, they cite what they feel are modest figures. Back in forty-nine it was $10,000. Since then the rising cost of living has taken it up higher, but the median doesn't usually surpass $15,000.[4] For the most part seniors do not like to talk of the future in terms of the dollar—on several occasions I have been politely lectured by someone for so much as bringing the point up.

In popular fiction, as I will take up later, heroes aren't any less materialistic than they used to be, but they are decidedly more sanctimonious about it. So with seniors. While they talk little about money, they talk a great deal about the good life. This life is, first of all, calm and ordered. Many a senior confesses that he's thought of a career in teaching, but as he talks it appears that it is not so much that he likes teaching itself as the sort of life he associates with it—there is a touch of elms and quiet streets in the picture. For the good life is equable; it is a nice place out in the suburbs, a wife and three children, one, maybe two cars (you know, a little knock-about for the wife to run down to the station in), and a summer place up at the lake or out on the Cape, and, later, a good college education for the children. It is not, seniors explain, the money that counts.

They have been getting more and more relaxed on the matter each year. In the immediate postwar years they were somewhat nervous about the chances for the good life. They seemed almost psychotic on the subject of a depression, and when they explained a preference for the big corporation, they did so largely on the grounds of security. When I talked to students in 1949, on almost every campus I heard one recurring theme: adventure was all very well, but it was smarter to make a compromise in order to get a depression-proof sanctuary. "I don't think A T & T is very exciting," one senior put it, "but that's the company I'd like to join. If a depression comes there will always be an A T & T." (Another favorite was the food industry: people always have to eat.) Corporation recruiters were unsettled to find that sen-

[4] The figures depend a great deal on the college. In the study done by the Youth Research Institute on a cross section of college seniors the median figure is about $8,000. At Princeton and Williams, by contrast, the figure is almost double.

iors seemed primarily interested in such things as pension benefits and retirement programs.

Seven years of continuing prosperity have made a great difference. Students are still interested in security but they no longer see it as a matter of security *versus* opportunity. Now, when they explain their choice, it is that the corporation is security *and* opportunity both. If the questionnaires that I have been giving groups of college seniors over the past six years are any indication, students aiming for the big corporation expect to make just as much money as those who say they want to start their own business or join a small one.[5]

Who is to blame them for being contented? If you were a senior glancing at these ad headlines in the *Journal of College Placement,* how much foreboding would you feel?

A WORLD OF EXPANDING OPPORTUNITY

OPPORTUNITY UNLIMITED

CAREERS UNLIMITED

THE HORIZONS ARE UNLIMITED FOR COLLEGE GRADU-
    ATES AT UNION CARBIDE

A GATEWAY TO LIFETIME SECURITY

A WISE CHOICE TODAY PUTS YOU AHEAD OF YOUR FUTURE

WHY THEY'RE SURE THEY'RE IN THE RIGHT JOB AT
    HARNSCHFEGER

TO THE YOUNG MAN BENT ON CONQUERING THE UN-
    KNOWN

A SECOND EDUCATION

GROWTH COMPANY IN A GROWTH INDUSTRY

"BRAIN BOX" NEEDS BRAINS

SO YOU WANT TO GO INTO BUSINESS

WHY COLLEGE GRADUATES SHOULD CONSIDER UNION
    CARBIDE

[5] This faith in the beneficence of the corporate salary is fairly universal. In the Youth Research Institute study previously mentioned this question was put to 4,660 high-school seniors, college seniors, recent graduates and veterans: "Do you feel that you will be able to achieve all of your economic desires by working for someone else?" 61.1 per cent said yes; 20.4 per cent said no; and 18.5 per cent couldn't make up their minds. There were no significant differences in optimism among any of the four groups.

A MAN CAN GROW AND KEEP ON GROWING WITH
    OWENS-ILLINOIS GLASS CO.
A BRIGHT FUTURE WITH RCA
DOW OFFERS THE GRADUATE A BRIGHT FUTURE
MORE AND BETTER JOBS
EXCEPTIONAL OPPORTUNITIES FOR COLLEGE MAN IN
    TEXTILE SALES
AN EQUITABLE LIFE INSURANCE MAN IS "A MAN ON
    HIS WAY UP"
GROUND-FLOOR OPPORTUNITIES IN TRANSISTORS
VITRO OFFERS YOUR GRADUATES THE ENGINEERS OF TO-
    MORROW!
YOUR OPPORTUNITY FOR A LIFETIME CAREER
OPPORTUNITY FOR YOUR COLLEGE GRADUATES
OPPORTUNITIES FOR MATH MAJORS
AN UNUSUAL OPPORTUNITY FOR OUTSTANDING MATH
    MAJORS
THE SKY IS OUR WORLD
THE SKY IS THE LIMIT!

It would be enough to make a man cynical. But the students are not a cynical lot. When they talk about security
they like to make the point that it is the psychic kind of
security that interests them most. They want to be of service. Occasionally, their description of service borders on the
mawkish, as though the goal was simply to defend the little
people, but underneath there is real concern. Seniors want
to do something *worth while*.

This worth-whileness needs some qualification. To listen
to seniors talk, one would assume that there has been an
upsurge of seniors heading toward such service careers as
the ministry. There is no evidence of such a rush. The public variety of service doesn't attract either. Seniors scarcely
mention politics as a career and even for the more aseptic
forms of public service they show little enthusiasm; the number aiming for the foreign services or the civil services has
been declining, and this decline was well under way before
the Washington investigations.

If they are going to be worth while, seniors want to be
worth while with other people. Their ideal of service is a
gregarious one—the kind of service you do others right in
the midst of them and not once removed. A student at a

round-table discussion on the pursuit of happiness put it this way: "People who are just selfish and wrapped up in themselves have the most trouble. And people who are interested in other people . . . are the type of person that is not too much concerned with security. Somehow the security is provided in the things they do, and they are able to reach out beyond themselves."

The kind of work that students want to do within the corporation illumines the character of this concept of worthwhileness. What the preferences show is a strong inclination toward the staff rather than the line. In a check I made of two hundred corporation-bound students of the classes of '55 and '56, only 12 per cent said they were aiming for production work, while roughly a third indicated a staff job.

Of these, the personnel slot is the glamour one. When seniors first expressed this yen for personnel work right after the war, many people thought it was simply a temporary phenomenon. The veterans of the postwar classes labored under the idea that because they had "handled people" in the services they were ideally suited for personnel work, and the advice given them by Veterans Administration counselors further confirmed them in the belief. But the years have gone by, and the quest has persisted. Wearily, placement directors explain that the work is semiprofessional, that there are few openings in it, and that in any event they are rarely open to recruits. It still doesn't seem to make much difference. With a phrase that has become a standing joke in placement circles, the senior explains that it is the job for him just the same—he *likes people*.

His vision of the job is a mirage. The actual work is connected more with time study, aptitude testing, and stop watches than adjusting people, but to the senior it seems to promise the agreeable role of a combination YMCA worker, office Solomon, and father confessor to the men at the lathes. It promises also to be somewhat out of the main stream. Much like life in the services, it seems to offer a certain freedom from competition; it is a technician's job, the job of one who services others. For a class intent on the happy mean, it is the all-round package: not only does it promise economic security, it promises spiritual security as well.

Because the quest has been so long unrequited, seniors have been turning to public relations. In some colleges it has already outdistanced personnel work as a choice. But it is really the same job they are thinking about. The senior does not see himself worrying about seating lists for banquets, ghostwriting speeches, or the like; in his vision he sees the universal man of the future, testing the pulse of the workers to see that they are happy, counseling with educators and clergymen for better inter-group communication, spellbinding the mossbacks with advocacy of the common man. As in personnel work, he will be nice to everybody on company time.

When seniors check such ostensibly line occupations as sales, they still exhibit the staff bias. For they don't actually want to sell. What they mean by sales is the kind of work in which they will be technical specialists helping the customer, or, better yet, master-minding the work of those who do the helping. They want to be sales engineers, distribution specialists, merchandising experts—the men who back up the men in the field.

If they must sell in the old, vulgar sense of the word, they want to do it as a member of a group and not as a lone individual. And most definitely, they do not want to sell on commission. This has been made quite clear in the reception given life insurance recruiters. Except when they have home office jobs to offer, insurance recruiters have always had fairly rough going in the colleges, but it's now so difficult that sometimes they sit in the interview room a whole day without a senior once coming near them. Mainly out of commiseration for the recruiters, one placement director uses a stratagem to force students into signing up for insurance interviews. "I tell them it's good for the practice," he explains. "I also tell them that if they don't turn up for these interviews I won't let them have a crack later at those nice big corporations."

Those who mark down finance as a choice are also staff-minded. Few ever mention speculating or investing in stocks and bonds. Their interest in finance is administrative rather than accumulative; they are primarily interested in credit, mortgage loan work, trust and estate work, and financial analysis.

A distinction is in order. While the fundamental bias is for staff work, it is not necessarily for a staff job. If the choice is offered them, a considerable number of students will vote for "general managerial" work, and many who choose personnel or public relations do so with the idea that it is the best pathway to the top line jobs. Seniors see no antithesis; in their view the line and staff have become so synonomous that the comfortable pigeonhole and the ladder, to mix some favorite metaphors, are one and the same. Their concept of the manager subsumes the two. As older executives are so fond of telling them, the "professionalization" of the executive is making a new kind of man, and more literally than the older men know, the younger ones believe every word of it. In fact, of course, as well as in the senior's fancy, the manager's work has been shifted more to the administrative. But not half so much as seniors would like to see it. In this respect, as so many business-school people hopefully say, seniors are way ahead of everybody else.

But not so very much. The bureaucrat as hero is new to America, and older, conventional dreams of glory do linger on—the lawyer brilliantly turning the tables in cross-examination, the young scientist discovering the secret in the microscope late at night. Even in corporations' institutional advertising there is some cultural lag—many an ad still shows us the young man dreaming by himself of new frontiers as he looks up at a star or a rainbow or a beautiful hunk of alto-cumulus clouds. But slowly the young man at the microscope is being joined by other young men at microscopes; instead of one lone man dreaming, there are three or four young men. Year by year, our folklore is catching up with the needs of organization man.

In *Executive Suite* we catch a glimpse of the hero in midpassage. In clean-cut Don Walling, the hitherto junior executive, what senior could not feel that there, with the grace of God, would go he? In Walling have been resolved all the conflicts of organization life; he puts everything he has into his work and plays baseball with his boy; he cares little about money and his ranch house is beautiful; he is a loyal subordinate and gets to be president. He is not fully the new model—he is too pushy, he plays too rough in the clinches for that—but he could almost be the class valedictorian as he electrifies his elders with his ringing, if somewhat hazy, statement of belief. Management man does not work to make money for himself and the company. Business is *people,* and when you help people to rise to their fullest you make them fulfill themselves, you create more and better goods for more people, you make happiness.

While the trust in organization is very strong among the majority group of college seniors headed for a business career, it is less so with a smaller group who say, at least, that they prefer a small firm. In the course of sessions during the past few years I have had with different undergraduate groups, to get the discussion rolling I have asked the students to answer several hypothetical questions on the "ideal" relationship between an individual and the demands of organization. I attach no great statistical significance to the actual figures, but I have kept the terms the same with each group, and I have noticed that consistently there is a difference between the answers of those headed for big organization and those not. As is brought out more forcefully by the kind of questions that the students themselves later asked, the big-corporation men are more inclined to the group way than the others.

Here is how a total of 127 men answered the two chief questions: on the question of whether research scientists should be predominantly the team player type, 56 per cent of the men headed for a big corporation said yes, versus 46 per cent of the small-business men. On the question of whether the key executive should be basically an "administrator" or a "bold leader," 54 per cent of the big-corporation men voted for the administrator, versus only 45 per cent of the small-business men. Needless to say, the weightings varied from college to college, and often the influence of a particular teacher was manifest—in one class the students complained that they probably seemed so chary of big business because they had been "brain-washed" by a liberal instructor. Whatever the absolute figures, however, there was generally the same relative difference between the big-business and the small-business men.

These differences raise an interesting question. It is possible that the majority group might be less significant than the minority—that is to say, the more venturesome may become the dominant members of our society by virtue of their very disinclination to the group way. As a frankly rapacious young salesman put it to me, the more contented his run-of-the-mill contemporaries, the freer the field for the likes of him.

While this can only be a matter of opinion at this date, I doubt that our society, as it is now evolving, will suffer such a double standard. The corporation-bound man may be an exaggeration of his generation's tendencies but only in degree, not in character. Other occupations call for different emphases, but on the central problem of collective versus individual work, young men going into other fields, such as teaching or law or journalism, show the same basic outlook.

Seniors do not deny that the lone researcher or the entrepreneur can also serve others. But neither do they think much about it. Their impulses, their training, the whole climate of the times, incline them to work that is tangibly social. Whether as a member of a corporation, a group medicine clinic, or a law factory, they see the collective as the best vehicle for service.

To a degree, of course, this is a self-ennobling apologia for seeking the comfortable life—and were they thoroughly consistent they would more actively recognize that public service is social too. But it is not mere rationalization; the senior is quite genuine in believing that while all collective effort may be worth while, some kinds are more so. The organization-bound senior can argue that he is going to the main tent, the place where each foot pound of his energy will go the farthest in helping people. Like the young man of the Middle Ages who went off to join holy orders, he is off for the center of society.

CHAPTER SEVEN

The Practical Curriculum

How did he get that way? His elders taught him to be that way. In this chapter I am going to take up the content of his education and argue that a large part of the U.S. educational system is preparing people badly for the organization society—*precisely because it is trying so very hard to do it.* My charge rests on the premise that what the organization man needs most from education is the intellectual armor of the fundamental disciplines. It is indeed an age of group action, of specialization, but this is all the more reason the organization man does not need the emphases of a training "geared for modern man." The pressures of organization life will teach him that. But they will not teach him what the schools and colleges can—some kind of foundation, some sense of where we came from, so that he can judge where he is, and where he is going and why.

But what he has been getting is more and more a training in the minutiae of the organization skills, and while it is hardly news that the U.S. inclines to the vocational, the magnitude of the swing has been much greater than is generally recognized. Only three out of every ten college graduates are now majoring in anything that could be called a fundamental discipline—in the liberal arts *or* in the sciences. Figures also indicate that this trend has been gathering force for a long time and that it is not to be explained away as a freak of current supply and demand or a hang-over from the disruptions of World War II.

There are signs of a countermovement. Spokesmen for the liberal arts have been making a strong case to the interested public. The foundations have been stimulating studies designed to reinvigorate the humanities. Friends of the liberal arts have been organizing more conferences to get the message across. Even businessmen seem to have become alarmed; executives of many of our best-known corporations have been arguing in print and speech that for the corporation's own good, the value of fundamental education needs to be restressed. Looking at all these signs, some people hopefully conclude that at last we are now on the verge of a great resurgence in the humanities.

I do not believe any such thing is going to happen. All these agitations for fundamental education are welcome and necessary, but they are minute, I submit, to the forces working in the other direction. Each June since the war, commencement speakers have been announcing that at last the humanities are coming back, and each fall more and more students enroll in something else. This increase in vocationalism, furthermore, carries with it the seeds of a further multiplication. The leaders of today's organizations graduated while the straight A.B. was still the fashion, and many have at least a sentimental attachment to the humanities.[1] But they will be replaced, and each year more and more of those who will replace them will be vocational graduates. If the climate for the humanities is poor now, what will it be when the current, vocationally trained majority comes of age? The present situation is only a harbinger of what is yet to come.

Let me first face up to two comforting hypotheses. One is the rose-by-any-other-name theory that much of the seem-

---

[1] Out of curiosity, Edward E. Booher, executive vice president of McGraw-Hill Book Co., Inc., checked the educational background of the top executives of *Fortune*'s list of the 500 biggest corporations. Of 365 men who indicated their educational background, 115 were not college graduates, 119 had liberal arts degrees, and 131 had degrees in the practical or applied fields, such as engineering. (*Antioch Notes,* March 1956.)

ing specialization is only a refreshening of the old disciplines—that Business English, for example, can convey just as many fundamentals as English, and that a change in labels need not worry us. The other hypothesis is to the effect that the decline of the humanities is only a statistical illusion. The number of degrees for vocational study, according to this view, is not a subtraction from fundamental education but an addition to it. It is simply that more people are going to college now, and thus the relative decline of the humanities is a necessary price to pay for the democratization of our culture. And not a very steep one, these people hold; just as the sale of comic books has not stifled the sale of first-rate paperbacks, so in education the increase in vocational training has accommodated those who previously would not have gone to college, and done it without denaturing the education of those who would have.

But this is not what has happened. Because of the way statistics have been gathered, precise comparisons with former years are not possible, but it is obvious that there has been a long and steady decline in the proportion of students majoring in the humanities, and the rate of decline has been so steep that it has not been offset by the increase in the numbers of people going to college. In actual numbers as well as proportion, only a small minority of students is now majoring in a basic subject.

In 1954-55, 183,602 men were graduated. Let's take *all* of the men majoring in mathematics, *all* of the men majoring in the physical sciences, *all* of the men majoring in the biological sciences, *all* of the men majoring in the liberal arts, *all* of the men majoring in the basic social sciences. Together they come to 48,999—26.6 per cent of the total.

The rest? Most were studying to be technicians: 22,527 were in engineering (12.3 per cent); 7,052 (3.8 per cent) were in agriculture; 14,871 (8.1 per cent) were in education. The largest single group of all: the 35,564 (19.4 per cent) in business and commerce—*more than all of the men* in the basic sciences and the liberal arts put together. (And more than all the men in law and medicine and religion: 26,412.)

These figures bring out a very important point. The conflict is not, as some embattled humanists believe, between the sciences and the liberal arts. The conflict is between the fundamental and the applied. Quite clearly, the increase in vocational students is not just an overlayer—it is a subtraction, and one that has affected the liberal arts and the sciences in the same degree.

The changing fashions in Ph.D. degrees also shows how closely united are the fortunes of the basic sciences and the humanities. Both have declined at about the same rate of speed. In the years between 1939 and 1946 the physical sciences accounted for 25 per cent of the doctorates; by 1955 the figure was down to 20 per cent. During the same period the humanities also dropped 5 percentage points, going from 12 per cent to 7 per cent.

What went up? As in the Bachelors, so in the Ph.D.s, the increase was in the number of men majoring in agriculture, engineering, and education. All three had proportionately the same rate of increase: in 1939-46 they together furnished 15 per cent of the total; by 1955 they were 29 per cent.

The social sciences seem to be the pivot point. Straddling, as they have, both camps, they lost in some subjects, gained in others, and, on the whole, advanced only 1.3 per cent— going from 17.7 per cent in 1939-46 to 19 per cent in 1954-55. An analysis of just where the gains and losses were registered indicates how fruitless is the usual quibbling over what should be included in the humanities and what in the social sciences. It can properly be argued that history and economics should be included under the heading of the humanities rather than the social sciences, but even if this were done it would not affect the rate of decline. While the other social sciences, notably psychology, were gaining, history and economics were losing—in almost exactly the same proportion as English, philosophy, and languages. The conflict, to repeat, is between the fundamental and the applied.[2]

[2] In charting the trends I have followed the classifications set by the Office of Education's statistical reports. In the physical sciences, accordingly, I have included: astronomy, chemistry, geology, metallurgy, meteorology, and physics. In the social sciences: anthropology, sociology, history, economics , international relations, plus psychology (listed separately by the Office

TREND IN PH.D. DEGREES

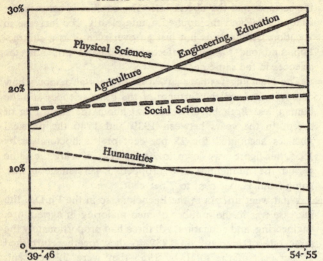

Let me now turn to the rose-by-any-other-name argument. Ironically enough, it is the schools of education that illustrate most clearly how real is the schism between fundamentals and the new dominant fields. Theoretically, a degree in education and a basic education are not antithetical; people go to teachers college not necessarily because they are seeking a vocational training for teaching—in many states it is one of the principal vehicles for a higher education.

But it doesn't make too much difference whether the student seeks the degree for a general education or for teacher preparation; in either event, the curriculum he will take is just about as far removed from fundamental education as it is possible to get. Nor is it likely to change for the better in the foreseeable future. There has been much

of Education). In the humanities I have included English, all of the foreign languages, and philosophy. Incidentally, the proportion in history and economics was 9.6 per cent in 1939-46, 6.3 per cent in 1954-55. Psychology, meanwhile, went up from 3.7 per cent to 7.5 per cent.

criticism recently of the fact that teachers colleges are far more interested in technique of pedagogy, personality adjustment, audio-visual *expertise,* and the like than the content of what is supposed to be taught, but the criticism has had little tangible effect. Teachers-college people are baffled and hurt by it, but a fairly exhaustive reading of current literature in the field fails to reveal any disposition to constructive self-criticism on this score. Quite the contrary, some leaders in teacher education have been saying that there still is *too much* content. Looking at the scene, Professor Percival M. Symonds, teacher of education at Teachers College, Columbia University, recently announced that there should be a change of emphasis in teacher education. The change? ". . . from purely intellectual courses to experiences for the better personal adjustment of teachers." (*The New York Times,* Sunday, June 26, 1955.)

There are no grounds for optimism discernible in this matter. If the level of the curriculum is low so is the level of the students, and the interaction of these two facts bodes no reform from within. No one likes to make invidious remarks about people who have entered a field that calls for so much work for so little pay, but the facts are too critical for euphemism. It is now well evident that a large proportion of the younger people who will one day be in charge of our secondary-school system are precisely those *with the least aptitude for education of all Americans attending college.*

In connection with its draft deferment program, the Army has had the Educational Testing Service administer a series of nationwide scholastic aptitude tests to undergraduates, and the by-product of this has been the brutally objective index of the caliber of students in different fields and in different institutions. Of students majoring in a particular field, students majoring in education have been scoring at the very bottom of the heap—no more than about 27 per cent have been able to make a passing grade. Another study furnishes corroboration. In checking I.Q. scores of a wide cross section of students, the Commission on Human Resources and Advanced Training found that in the field of graduate work, here also students majoring in education score the lowest.[3]

Close on the heels of education majors for the cellar was another group, and in numbers it takes precedence as the principal diversionary movement. Which brings us to the schools of business administration. In the last thirty years the number of men majoring in business has swelled almost in direct ratio as those in the humanities majors have declined, and since 1940 the rate of increase has been growing

[3] Here are the percentages of the 339,000 students tested in 1951 who got a passing score of 70 or more: in first place were students majoring in engineering (68 per cent passed); next, those in the physical sciences and mathematics (64 per cent); biological sciences (59 per cent); social sciences (57 per cent); humanities (52 per cent); general arts (48 per cent); business and commerce (42 per cent); agriculture (37 per cent); education (27 per cent). Relative rankings have not materially changed since 1951. The high scores of men majoring in the sciences would seem to indicate that while fewer people are interested in basic science these days, those that are come from the top layer. The mediocre scores of the humanities men—just under the average of 53 per cent for all students—is open to a number of interpretations, but it does seem clear that whatever the causes, the humanities are not attracting a large share of our most gifted people.

When the humanities are broken down into specific subjects, the prospect is a little more cheerful. In the study of I.Q. scores for a wide cross section of undergraduates and graduate students, the Commission on Human Resources and Advanced Training found that among students earning Bachelor degrees, men in English and foreign languages did quite well. Going up to the graduate level, humanities majors rank just below those in the natural sciences, just above those in the social sciences. Graduate students of education score abysmally: of the people in the bottom fifth of graduate students in all fields, students working for advanced degrees in education account for *46 per cent*. For results of the Army test program see Henry Chauncey, "The Use of the Selective Service College Qualification Test in the Deferment of College Students," *Science,* Volume CXVI, No. 3004, July 25, 1952, pages 73-79. Also, Chapter 7, *Proceedings of the Conference on the Utilization of Scientific and Professional Manpower,* Columbia University Press, 1954. For a résumé of the I.Q. study done by the Commission on Human Resources and Advanced Training see Dael Wolfle and Toby Oxtoby, "Distribution of Ability of Students Specializing in Different Fields," *Science,* September 26, 1952, pages 311-314.

steeper. Between 1940 and 1950 the number of business students doubled. By 1955, they had become the largest single undergraduate group—more than the majors in mathematics, all the natural sciences, all the physical sciences, all the biological sciences, and English put together.

Something has had to give and it has been fundamental education. The great increase in business education has not been channeled into graduate schools of business administration which, like those of Harvard and the University of Chicago, require a basic education as a prerequisite. The increase has been in the undergraduate "schools of commerce," and the students who are enrolling in them include many who ten years ago would very likely have majored in economics or politics or history.

Not only have the business schools been diverting more and more men away from basic studies, they have been subtly changing the climate of the whole campus. It is often the business school of the college that sets the dominant tone, and those students who major in the humanities are on the defensive, not to mention their professors. In a remarkably frank appraisal of the situation at the University of Pennsylvania, *The Daily Pennsylvanian* (January 14, 1955) had this to say about the effect of the business school on the rest of the campus.

The first and most important destructive influence at Pennsylvania of the atmosphere important for the nourishment of the humane arts is the Wharton School of Finance and Commerce. Justly famed for the excellent business training which it offers, and for which it grants an academic degree, the Wharton School by the sheer force of its reputation and undergraduate appeal has given to undergraduate social and extracurricular life an atmosphere which, while it is seldom anti-intellectual, is usually nonintellectual, and which tends to discourage the popularity of those interests which ordinarily occupy the time of the students of other universities where the school of liberal arts is the main impetus for student activity.

An undergraduate body where half the members have definite educational interests of a material, nonacademic nature is bound to create an atmosphere that reflects something less than enthusiasm for the theoretical sciences and the liberal arts. This is especially so when those members are frequently people of particular intelligence who are adept at pointing out to their fellow students the apparent flaws of an education seemingly for "nothing at all," and whose idea of what they are in the philistine habit of calling "culture" is an elementary course in fine arts or history, judiciously chosen for its adaptability to the not inconsiderable demands of a thorough business school.

Theoretically, a man could major in business and still learn a lot about the humanities. But it would take some doing. To be accredited by the American Association of Collegiate Schools of Business, a college must make the student take 40 per cent of his work in nonbusiness courses, and as a consequence there is a smattering of liberal arts courses, but as soon as these are dispensed with—and the wording of college catalogues these days suggests that "dispensed with" is the appropriate phrase—there remains only a vestigial trace of anything connected with the humanities. The University of Denver's College of Business Administration, to cite one of the more flagrant examples, suggests a variety of specialized curriculum for the student who "does not wish to specialize." Translated, this means that in his junior year he will take one nonbusiness course. It is called "Literature and the Other Arts." In his senior year he will take "The Philosophy of Life."

This might well be a rich offering compared to what will be served in the future. All signs point to a further specialization within the business schools, and in the name of "Professionalization" one school after another is beginning to spawn sub-schools. The momentum is irresistible; let a single course in one technical aspect of business become popular and before long a whole program of studies is built around it—instead of a single course offering in, say, air-line stewardess training, we now have, as at the University of Georgia, a whole program built on this rock.

Once a specialty is made into a program, the next step is to go on and design a degree around it, or, as is sometimes the case, a whole new school complete with buildings and separate new faculty. Not so many years ago, for example, the subject of public relations was generally considered a by-product of regular courses in personnel and publicity; today the subject is being constructed into programs, and in one institution, Boston University, a school has been set up that awards a Master's degree in the subject. Just how quick this cycle from course to program to school can be is illustrated by New York University. In the fall of 1953 it announced that the following year it would offer its first public-relations course. The ink still wet on the release, it went on to add that as soon as other courses were added it would offer a major in public relations.

Advertising is coming up fast, too. "The clamor is growing for advertising schools with college degrees available for the students," *Printer's Ink* announced in 1953. "Last month a resolution on the subject was passed at the Advertising Association of the West's convention in San Francisco. Now the American Newspaper Guild is urging 'all liberal arts colleges and universities to enlarge schools of advertising and establish a degree in advertising for those who complete the curriculum.' Only a slight progress has been made in this direction so far. Three liberal arts colleges give degrees in advertising (Denver University, Whitworth College in Spokane, and San José State College). And the University of Oregon has recently expanded its school of advertising and expects to cap it with a degree in advertising by next year. It is significant that in the East, center of the ad business, there are no degrees in advertising given by any college."

But the stumbling block is only temporary. In a cruel irony, the advertising professors have recognized that business was under the impression they were too much up in the clouds. Heatedly, the professors have been replying that this just isn't so, and they certainly are right to say so. In a more recent *Printer's Ink* article (May 27, 1955), titled "Advertising Education Has Come of Age—but Advertising Men Don't Know It," Philip Burton, chairman of the advertising department in the business school at Syracuse University, gives business a run-down. "Right on the campus students work in fully equipped radio and television studios or learn typography in a production lab with the latest equipment. For advertising photography there are cameras, developing equipment, and skilled men to teach all the tricks." There is a picture of students at the University of Texas doing "lab" work in the writing and production of radio commercials in an elaborate studio constructed for the purpose. This practical kind of training, Burton argues, is "cutting out guesswork for employers. An advertising student who has had some facts beaten into him in school is going to be a better employee risk for the employer. He has been pre-conditioned."

What debate there is in the business schools on the subject of specialization has now reached the level where the issue is how much you should specialize within a specialty. "Students might tend to specialize too much," an official of Miami University says, "but our school of business doesn't permit overspecialization. Here, all business-school graduates must have one or more courses in all of the basic business fields, including management, finance, marketing, business law, business statistics, economics, accounting, and business English." Many other business schools hold the redoubt against overspecialization in the same fashion.

They say this specialization is practical. In one sense it is; when a school enshrines a particular vocational specialty in its curriculum, it provokes grants and support from the grateful toilers in the commercial field thus legitimatized. The practicality for the student, however, is another matter. Even if he followed the specialty he studied at the business school, employers can find him lacking; he didn't learn what business can't teach him because he was too busy learning what business could teach him, and teach him better. In the majority of cases, furthermore, the business school graduate doesn't even get what benefits specialization does provide, for he is likely to end up in a different field. Professor William T. Kelley, of the Wharton School of Finance at the University of Pennsylvania, questioned alumni of the Wharton School as to the majors they took in school and the work they did in business afterward. Between the two he found a low correlation.

There are some first-rate men to be found on business school faculties, but there are not too many of them, and their chances of withstanding the pressures to further vocationalization are poor. It is not entirely facetious to suggest that the only way any reform could be effected would be through a subversive movement by the humanists. In what would be poetic justice to the vocationalists, humanists in disguise could appropriate their terminology and smuggle education into the curriculum by pretending to specialize it further. Who would dare cavil at the humanities were they presented as "Mercantile Influence in the Renaissance," "Market Patterns in Pre-Industrial England," or "Communication Techniques in Elizabethan Drama"?

When we turn to the influence of engineering, we come upon what seems an anomaly. On the face of it, one would gather that engineering was being put to rout by the victorious forces of medievalism. With great concern, spokesmen for engineers point to a decline in engineering graduates since 1950 as evidence that the country has turned its back on the technical and is being led hell bent back to the Middle Ages by the academicians. With little debate from the other side, engineers have gotten across the case that enrollment at engineering schools must soar if a balance is to be achieved. Indeed, they go on to add, it must soar if we are to survive; with Russia turning out fifty thousand engineers a year in contrast to our twenty-five to thirty thousand, not only good sense but patriotism demands a reversal of the tide.

It is not my intention to dispute that we need more engineers. When engineering enrollment swelled so greatly after the war, the government mistakenly warned that there would soon be more engineers than jobs, and in time this warning kept many—too many—people from enrolling in engineering schools. What I am disputing is the way people have accepted as established fact the idea that the shortage of engineers is our most pressing shortage and that an over-renaissance of the humanities is the cause. This is wrong. There has indeed been a shortage of engineers—but so has there been a shortage of almost every other kind of trained person too. It happened that in the Depression years of the early thirties people didn't raise as many mouths to feed, and those that were raised are coming of age at the very time when there are more jobs of every kind to be filled. When the great baby crop of the forties comes of age, supply and demand may come into better balance, but, even then, there will be shortages of trained people—shortages of doctors, of lawyers, of psychologists, of certified public accountants, of market researchers, and of chemists—and then as today each group will cry at the folly of the country for not honoring it more.

Engineers are right in assuming that if there are to be more engineers, something has to give somewhere, but it is curious that they should demand that the humanities be the place. As we have seen, the most cursory check of enrollment figures would reveal that it is to the business schools, not the ivory towers, that the extra young men are going— i.e., if there are less engineers, one strong reason is that more young men want to grow up to be people who boss engineers—and given the way business uses its technical people, to get ahead of our story, the impulse isn't entirely misguided.

That engineers should seize on the humanities as the villain of their piece reveals something more deep-seated than current exigency. While it is another subdivision of technocratic education that is currently the actual rival, engineers are right in sensing that the humanities are the core of the opposing tradition. The conflict has always been there, but so long as shortages of men weren't pressing, few people felt impelled to say anything mean about the humanities. But the live and let live era is over, and some seem to sense that the climate is now propitious for coming right out and naming the humanities as enemy. Let me cite Mr. George Tichenor, writing in M.I.T.'s *The Technology Review* (March 1955). He calls his essay "Interrupting the Great Conversation," and he says with such admirable ferocity what many others believe privately that he is worth quoting at some length.

After saying that he had a liberal arts education himself, Tichenor charges that they are useless, and though the pungency of his style belies the assertion, he goes on to venture that they may be even worse than useless. "A liberal arts education . . . is a relatively harmless adornment to a solid education if one has the time and the money for it in normal times. But these are not normal times." Warming to the needs-of-modern-man theme, he pictures a mass return to medievalism led by such as Nathan Pusey, Harvard ("probably the best example of this Renaissance warmed over"), and, inevitably, Robert Hutchins, who, as is usual in such strictures, is viewed as unquestioned commander of a monolithic army of academicians. "He is worth a full division in the onslaught on technical education. He is witty, he has a flair for making the news . . . and worst of all, he is eminently fair-minded and liberal, so that the weight of his authority can be disastrous when he plunges into areas where his blind spots are total."

It is not the humanists' own groves that concern Tichenor, vulnerable to the criticism though they may be. What he fears is that the humanists will successfully infiltrate the engineering schools and insinuate their message in these last fortresses of practicality. "In these trying times," he complains, "the humanists among our educators seem to intensify their efforts to crowd their elegancies into technical schools, at the expense, probably, of professional subjects crowded out of the curriculum, so that engineers are graduated with watered-down training." He flatly recommends that technical schools make any courses in the humanities optional. There is no proof, he irrelevantly adds, that the humanities ever made men more democratic. ("I am quite sure that Davy Crockett was every whit as patriotic as Thomas Jefferson—and a better shot.")

In the battle for men's minds, we are told, Russia has us hands down. No silly humanities crowd their engineering curriculums; the state, furthermore, sees to it that there is no shortage. "In Russia, very serious efforts are made to find technological talent; engineering students are exempt from military service, since in Russia engineering *is* military service, and the nation offers cash subsidies to students of technology." The moral for us? "Our government might put engineering and scientific training on the same footing as West Point and Annapolis; selected students would be enrolled in any of the fine technical schools we have and given cash allowances, with the proviso that upon graduation they will serve an allotted time in government service. The method of awarding scholarships in our colleges should be revised as far as possible. Less emphasis should be on brilliance, more on financial need."

Just why anyone should be so alarmed at the dangers of the curriculum's being liberalized is hard to understand. There has, it is true, been much talk lately about how engineering schools are recognizing the dangers of overspecialization and are liberalizing their curriculums, but the facts indicate that the reform remains more or less talk. With the exception of a few places like Case, Cal. Tech, Carnegie Tech and M.I.T., there has been practically no change in this respect in the last fifty years. Let me document. Back in 1903 the average time devoted to straight technical courses in the engineering schools was 84.1 per cent of the total curriculum hours. By 1944, four decades later, it was about the same. After a study of the situation, the Society for the Promotion of Engineering Education recommended that more time be given the "humanistic-social" division of the curriculum: "we believe that it can be achieved only through a *designed sequence* of courses extending throughout the four undergraduate years and requiring a minimum of approximately 20 per cent of the student's educational time." What has happened since? In 1953, the time for straight technical courses was 82 per cent. Even the slight increase in nontechnical hours is more in name than in fact. In its study of engineering curriculums, the Office of Education has pointed out that some of the presumably liberal courses are highly specialized courses much closer to engineering than to English or similar fundamentals. "The oft-expressed ideal of better balance . . . ," it reported, with hard-won restraint, "has been only imperfectly realized."

It is again relevant to pose the distinction between the fundamental and the applied. Those who cry the loudest against the humanities to justify the need for more engineers make their point in the name of *science*. But they have no more right to this association than those in the humanities—and, as a matter of fact, a good bit less. It may be correct

to say that we need more engineers; it is not correct, however, to say that we need them because we need more
scientists.

The training of the two is anything but synonymous, and
there is no evidence that engineering schools have produced
any appreciable number of fundamental scientists. In their
study, *Origins of American Scientists* (Chicago, 1952), R.
H. Knapp and H. B. Goodrich found "production of
scientists is inversely related to size and to vocationalism of
curricular emphasis. We found the most productive class of
institutions to be small liberal arts colleges with a strong
commitment to general education, whereas universities,
even after the most charitable adjustments had been made,
were seen to be less productive. Engineering institutions
were conspicuously unproductive. . . . The inferiority of
engineering institutions to both universities and liberal arts
colleges is perhaps not surprising, considering that such institutions are primarily dedicated to limited vocational
training."

Let's turn to the small number of students who do major in
the humanities. The number is dismal enough as it is, but
the actual decline is more than the figures alone would indicate. For when we look at the supposedly fundamental
courses, we find on closer look that many of them have
been made almost as narrow as the frankly vocational disciplines.

Let's take the subject of psychology as an illustration. In
some universities, psychology is taught as one of the humanities, but in more of them it is a catch-all phrase applied to a
weird assortment of utilitarian courses. The sheer number
of the courses tells the story; instead of demanding the
discipline of a hard core of basic courses, psychology departments tempt the student with as many as forty to eighty
separate offerings which, like a conglomeration of ever-
decreasing circles, pull the student further and further into
particulars.

It is as if high-school driver-training courses were split
into courses in Chrysler Driving or Ford Driving. A course
in personnel counseling, for example, could be considered

already pretty far down the line of specialization. But this is not enough for some departments; going a step further, they break the subject down into personnel counseling in specific kinds of situations—at Ohio State we have *University* Personnel Psychology, in other institutions we have *Corporation* Personnel Psychology or Civil Service Psychology.

But there is a denominator to such courses and it is a highly appealing one; dangled before the student is the secret of happiness, for the courses explicitly instruct one in the skills of manipulating other people or the skills of adjusting oneself. The student can hardly be blamed if he passes up an opportunity of poring through William James. Why read books by dead people when you can take:

36-250	PERSONALITY DEVELOPMENT. *Factors contributing to personality development. Mental hygiene principles will be introduced. Offered at College of Business Administration. Prerequisite: 36-10 and Upper Division status.*
36-251	MENTAL HYGIENE. *The purpose of this course is to provide the student with sufficient information and understanding of the factors contributing to good mental health to enable him to make a more satisfying type of adjustment with himself, with others and his environment.*
36-261.1, .2	PSYCHOLOGY APPLIED TO LIFE AND WORK. *The application of psychological principles to practical problems in business, industry and professional fields. Some application to personal problems will be included along with a consideration of such topics as work and rest, monotony, accidents and incentives. Prerequisite: Upper Division status and course in introductory or general psychology.*

And look what's happened to English. Now it is becoming "Communication Skills," and in what is called an interdisciplinary effort everybody from the engineers to applied psychologists are muscling in. In some places, Michigan State, for example, they not only have whole departments of communication but have made it the center of required under-class courses. In others, it has been made the heart of a vocational training in advertising and journalistic research.

As a way of looking at society, communication can be a very absorbing subject—but one of the reasons it can be very absorbing is because nobody is quite sure yet just what communication amounts to, or, for that matter, whether it is really a separate discipline at all. Until a good bit more is known, it has no business whatsoever as a basic undergraduate discipline. As anyone who has ever tried to teach composition knows, the student who has yet to master it would give anything to be done with the chore. Of all times this is not the one to fascinate him with mass media content analyses and experiments in audience behavior; they not only divert him from first things, they delude him into thinking that he has long since outgrown them and is poised on the very frontier of discovery.

And who are the technicians who are his mentors in this? Read their output in the learned journals. Many of these people don't even *like* the language. They torture it with charts, they twist it with equations, and they have so little respect for the devices they recommend as the avenue to the masses that they never demean themselves with their use. Rarely has brevity been advocated so interminably.

People concerned about overspecialization have been very much encouraged by the growth of the "general-education" movement. This, first given currency in the Harvard report of 1945, *General Education in a Free Society,* was not forwarded to denigrate specialization but rather to argue for a sounder underlying base. The free-elective system, pioneered by Harvard's Eliot, had liberalized the curriculum, but in time it had led to a fragmentation in which the electives moved further and further away from a unifying center. In most cases the courses that the student took outside of his major were not designed for him but for men who would go on to specialize in the particular subject, and even were he not bored by it, the student would fail to grasp the relevance of this subject to other subjects, and thus the relevance to him. A unifying goal, the report argued, was sorely needed; the schools and colleges, it urged, should now set to work welding the different disciplines into a program by which the general student could be instructed in the parts in such a way that he would grasp a meaningful whole.

So far, so good, and many colleges have undertaken a program that does just that. But "General Education," alas, was too good a thing not to be for, and with tremendous flexibility educators committed to utilitarianism very quickly appropriated the term to clothe programs that achieved the opposite of what the Harvard report was talking about. For them, the term rationalized their dislike of "subject matter" —i.e., knowledge—and what they proceeded to construct were superficial "survey" and "core" courses which were, if anything, a step backward from the electives they supplanted. In the latter the student was at least prodded to master something, and while the subject itself might not have compelled his attention it did provide a standard of accomplishment—and one not unlike the standards enforced in what is called real life. In the "survey" courses, by contrast, he merely samples, and, worse yet, he is persuaded that this sampling is itself a discipline.

A "survey" course can show the relationship between different areas of learning and thereby illuminate the whole. But it cannot do this at the expense of the parts; before he can see any relevance between two things—between, say, the Reformation and England's industrial revolution—the student must learn what the two things were. But can he do this in the compass of courses that in a handful of semester hours touch on just about everything that has happened to man since the Deluge? This is precisely what many "survey" and "general-education" courses attempt to do. They do not combine the parts; they eliminate the parts.

They eliminate the parts because the whole that the college often has in mind is quite frankly not intellectual development at all. It is, rather, the same old "personal-social development," and again the familiar needs-of-modern-man theme is wrung in to refreshen it. I quote from a recent conference of educators on general-education programs. "We may devise a new cosmotron," exclaimed a co-ordinator from Florida State, "some new design in curriculum structure, which would fit the atomic-age collegian with whom we work. And I would say that this planning is no less exciting than is the planning of 'accelerator-development groups' of our friends, the nuclear physicists." Queries directed at a cross section of colleges, it was reported, revealed that much had already been accomplished along these lines. "The centralizing course in basic education here," one college had declared, "is the course in Personal-Social Adjustment." "This institution," another said for the record, "believes that extracurricular counseling and assistance in real-life situations is as important and perhaps more important than a course using the method of didactic teaching."

Has vocationalism reached a saturation point? Those who like to think so would do well to ponder the history of U.S. education. Emphasis on utility is not a new development in our history. Many people speak of the education of a hundred years ago as an education tailored for an aristocracy, but American education was even then more utilitarian than the European model, and it was, in its way, a vocational training for the professions. When the great land-grant college movement began in the sixties, the country was so ready for a more "universal" education that in a remarkably few years a whole new slice of the population was enfranchised by scores of technical and agricultural schools. During this time the curriculum of the traditional liberal arts colleges was undergoing great changes too, and when Eliot introduced the elective system, college after college veered away from the old fixed regimen of studies. In similar fashion, the professional-school movement started by Johns Hopkins University was altering the institution of the college itself; by the turn of the century the liberal arts college was no longer the center of education but was becoming one more unit in a whole series of technical and professional schools. The changes that took place after 1900 in the great expansion of the high schools were also in character. In retrospect they seem revolutionary, but they were an extension, not a reversal.

Whether exaggerated or not, the inclination to the practical, the contemporary, has been thoroughly in the American tradition. Education can never go back in the sense that so many fear, because what it is supposed to go back to never really existed in this country. This fear of medievalism resurgent is a bogy; American education will always lean toward the practical, toward the larger number than the smaller, and no reformation can ever succeed that runs counter to this tradition.

Parents would not have it otherwise. They are not unwitting dupes of a cabal of educators; talk as they will of "fundamentals," when they have to get down to cases they reveal themselves far more interested in the immediately practical. In 1949 Elmo Roper surveyed for *Fortune* a wide cross section of Americans on their attitude toward education. One of the questions asked was how much time they would like their children to devote to the liberal arts while in college. Of those who answered, college graduates were the most tolerant. They divided up this way: 7 per cent wanted the student to spend all his time on the liberal arts; 7 per cent wanted him to spend three quarters of his time. By contrast, 30 per cent wanted him to spend only one half his time; 28 per cent, a quarter of his time, and 10 per cent wanted him to spend all the time on technical or professional study. Today, the bias against the liberal arts is stronger yet. In the chapters on suburbia we will see how the new generation of parents wish their children to be educated, and suffice it to say here that they demonstrate themselves even more vocational in their leanings than their opposite numbers of a decade previous.

The seeming opposition between traditionalism and modernism, as the Harvard report said, is a tragedy for Western thought. A more universal education does not have to be antithetical with the humanities. Granted that our national character inclines us excessively to the practical; granted that our youth must be prepared for an organizational world and not an entrepreneurial one—with all these qualifications an invigoration of the humanities can still make sense. It would not be a "return"; we cannot divide the U.S. into a vocationally trained majority with a small group of mandarins leading them—our society is much too national, much too transient for this. If the humanities are to flourish, their relevance to everyone must be demonstrated.

Only the boldest kind of leadership can accomplish this. There is a real battle to be fought. It cannot be adjudicated, for there are deep philosophical differences over ends. The people who have been working for the social-adjustment curriculum are dedicated. You may feel, as this writer does, that they are profoundly wrong in their emphasis, but you must also acknowledge that they *care*. In preparing students for the organization life, they feel very strongly that what they are doing is for the common good, and this has given them an ideological sustenance that has united and invigorated them. They have earned their dominance; it is they who have harnessed contemporary social forces, and for many years it is they who will reap the rewards.

In this struggle the stewards of the liberal arts have little reason for the smug self-satisfaction so many display. It was the liberal arts colleges which at the turn of the century abdicated to the normal schools their historic function of training teachers. Eventually, this abdication came home to roost, in the poorly prepared students the normal-school graduates were sending to the colleges. The colleges have been complaining loudly over the low level of high-school teaching, but only a handful have lifted a finger to do anything constructive about it. Rather than help educate secondary-school teachers, the majority have reacted in a negative sense; they have set up courses to make up for the freshmen's deficiencies in fundamentals, but the nub of the problem they have left alone.

The private schools have an even more dismal record. Potentially, they have a value far beyond their numbers as models and pace setters, but while most still give a good education they do it in camera. They are content simply to be. With very few exceptions—five would be too generous a number—they display no energy in showing their relevance to the rest of society, and the only issue which has roused them from their shameful torpor is the possibility of being taxed. The thought that the best way to insure that they won't be is to display some of their usefulness to the rest of secondary education is rarely voiced, and the great debate in education continues without them. When the layman reads anything about the private schools, it is apt to be in reminiscences of a well-spent life, pious tributes to the whole man, and the like, and this is not enough. Read the *Independent School Bulletin* and then read the journals of the National Education Association, and you have a good clue as to why the life-adjustment educators are dominant. The NEA articles are often appalling but they throb with excitement. The voice of the private school is the still, small voice —and so content, so very content, that it is small and still.

The stewards of the liberal arts are to blame for its low estate in another respect. If people swing away from them on the grounds that they are not useful enough, this cannot be explained entirely as a worship of false gods. There is nothing wrong with usefulness as a criterion; from the beginning, after all, the liberal arts were intended as a highly functional training. That they no longer seem so to the majority of people is rather strong evidence that something more is at fault than people's judgment.

Let's go back to the subject of English a moment. Of all subjects none is potentially more useful—as Peter Drucker has remarked, the most vocational course a future businessman can take is one in the writing of poetry or short stories. That English is being slighted by business and students alike does not speak well of business. But neither does it speak well for English departments. They are right to recoil from justifying English on the narrow grounds of immediate utility, as better report writing and the like. But one can recoil too far. In so resisting the vocationalizing of English, they have contributed to it. If technicians of "business writing" and the psychologists have been able to denature English into a "communication" science, it is because the greater relevance of English has been left undrawn.

And this, in the long run, means a less useful English. Who has the most to teach us about any subject? The geniuses—or the also-rans? It is to such as Lamb and Swift and Shakespeare that we should look and not to the prose engineers. The great models of thought and expression can seem far removed from our own immediate problems, but almost for this detachment they are the truest guide of all.

It is the universals, not the particulars, that are important; only through them can we learn that simplicity is the product of thought, rather than the mechanics of chopping the number of sentences per hundred words. It is a long and tough discipline, yet in the long run what is more down-right practical? It is sad that the prose engineers do not realize this. It is sadder still when the teachers of English do not.

There are some good omens. The Ivy League universities and some of the smaller liberal arts colleges have shown great energy and, if the word can be pardoned, pragmatism, in revitalizing the humanities, and their graduates remain in great demand. They are in demand, let it be conceded, largely for reasons other than the nature of the curriculum, but companies have found that the graduates weren't permanently hurt by it. In time there could be more than this negative tribute; in running counter to the rest of U.S. education, such colleges are carving out a function that may be more important than any they have performed before.

There are a few other good omens. As we have noted, several of the technical schools have been revamping their curriculums to give students some notion of what went on in the outside world the last 3,000 years; M.I.T., the California Institute of Technology, and the Carnegie Institute of Technology, among others, now require students to devote at least a fifth of their hours to the humanities, which, though hardly overpowering, is to be welcomed. Meanwhile, the number of commissions, programs, and conventions devoted to the humanities problem has been increasing. A series of studies has been exploding the myth of the thirteen-year-old I.Q. We do not lack for native talent, they have been demonstrating; the problem, indeed, is that most of our high-I.Q. people are not sufficiently challenged, and half of them never go on to college.

But the trend may be more powerful than the counter-trend. By default, the anti-intellectual sector of education has been allowed to usurp the word "democratic" to justify the denaturing of the curriculum, and while liberal arts people may win arguments on this score, the others won the war long ago. Once the uneducated could have the humility of ignorance. Now they are given degrees and put in charge, and this delusion of learning will produce consequences more critical than the absence of it.

I return to my pessimistic forecast. Look ahead to 1985. Those who will control a good part of the educational plant will be products themselves of the most stringently anti-intellectual training in the country. Nor will the laymen be out of tune with the vocationalists; to judge by the new suburbia the bulk of middle-class parents of 1985 will know no other standards to evaluate education of their children than those of the social-adjustment type of schooling. And who will be picking the schools to endow and sitting on the boards of trustees? More and more it will be the man of The Organization, the graduate of the business school—the "modern man," in sum, that his education was so effectively designed to bring about.

CHAPTER EIGHT

Business Influence on Education

IN this chapter I would like to bring into sharper focus the part business is playing in these educational changes. Business has been only one of many influences, but it is going to become a great deal more important in the years ahead. Simply by virtue of the changing economics of university financing, the organization man is going to be much more than an alumnus. As overseer of the corporation's fund giving, he is becoming a sort of extra trustee of education. What he thinks about education, whether we agree with it or not, is a matter of some moment.

This brings us to an interesting anomaly. Lately, leaders of U.S. business have been complaining that there are nowhere near enough "generalists." The average management man, they have been declaring, has been far too narrowly educated. One company, the Bell Telephone Company of Pennsylvania, feels so strongly on this it has been detaching some of its most promising middle-management men to the University of Pennsylvania for a year of special study in the humanities. But this, executives concede, is a stopgap measure: it is the kind of education a trainee should have gotten in the first place. Give us the well-rounded man, business leaders are saying to the colleges, the man steeped in fundamentals; we will give him the specialized knowledge he needs.

Convention after convention they make this plea—and

their own recruiters go right on doing what they've been doing: demanding more specialists. This does not spring from bad faith. The top man may be perfectly sincere in asking for the man with a broad view—he might even be a liberal arts man himself. Somewhere along the line, however, this gets translated and retranslated by the organization people, so that by the time the company gets down to cases the specifications for its officer candidates are something quite different.

Nobody knows this better than college placement directors. Every year the order sheet that corporation recruiters bring to the campus has been increasingly loaded against the liberal arts major. Five years ago we checked placement directors of eighty colleges to make up a cumulative listing of the different majors that recruiters were asking for. Out of every hundred jobs offered, it turned out, all but a handful were for men with vocational degrees. "What recruiters want," as one placement director explained, "goes in this order: (first) specialists, (second) specialists with some liberal education on the side, (third) any college graduate, (fourth) liberal arts graduates." Most of all, corporations have wanted engineers; they have wanted them so badly that recruiters, normally a friendly lot with one another, have competed for the available supply with every trick in the book.

Year by year the bias against the liberal arts has deepened. In 1950, to cite one of the most preferred of liberal arts colleges, some sixty-six manufacturing companies reserved interviewing space at Yale. Twenty-eight per cent of these companies at least mentioned that they might have a position for a liberal arts student. The next year, ninety-one manufacturing companies reserved interviewing space, but this time only 16 per cent even mentioned an interest in seeing liberal arts students. In 1952, out of 117 manufacturing companies only 14 per cent indicated interest. In other colleges the same trend was manifest. When we re-queried placement directors in 1953, one half reported that companies were demanding more specialists than before; of the few that reported less demand, several explained that it was only because recruiters were resigned to accepting some liberal arts men as a stopgap. Between 1953 and 1956, the number of business speeches bewailing overspecialization increased. So did the demand for specialists.

Out of sheer lack of enough candidates for the maw, the recruiters do get around to the liberal arts man these days, but it is only a stopgap measure. Relatively speaking, the liberal arts man remains in the cellar. About the only kind of a job he is seriously considered for at the outset is sales work, and others regard this as a dog job offered people unqualified for anything else. If he still doesn't get the point, the salary differential should drive it home; with very few exceptions he is offered less money than his classmates who majored in business administration or engineering. (In 1956 the average going rate for engineers has been $394; for students in general, $366.)

As soon as the mounting enrollment in vocational schools catches up with the demand, it would appear, a good many liberal arts men will be lucky if they can get to see the recruiters at all. For the bias against them seems to be a matter of policy more than current exigency. Frank Endicott, Director of Placement, Northwestern University, asked companies this question: "If a college man really has management potential, will it make any difference in the long run whether he is technically trained or broadly trained in the liberal arts?" 189 companies replied. Only twelve were willing to vote for a liberal arts background. Sixty-six favored technical training and 111 said it wouldn't make any difference.[1]

Won't it make any difference? My colleagues and I at *Fortune* had an unusual opportunity to put this professed tolerance to an acid test. A young man walked into our office looking for a job. He was blatantly well-rounded: he had an excellent liberal arts background (he was about

[1] "Employment Trends in 1955," "Employment Trends in 1956," Frank S. Endicott, Director of Placement, Northwestern University, *Journal of College Placement,* March 1955 and 1956, respectively. These surveys also indicate that after five years with business the outstanding liberal arts men overtake the specialists in earning capacity. Students, unfortunately, don't think much about this possibility.

to get a Master's degree in history), a good record of extracurricular work, and he did not lack self-confidence and gregariousness. It was quite obvious that his real interest lay in business rather than in journalism, and he explained to us that the interview was merely a warm-up for the lengthy series he was about to go through with corporations. An idea occurred to us: if he would write down verbatim what happened to him in each interview, we would pay his expenses for two weeks. He jumped at the idea, and together we made up a list of the leading companies in the area, making sure to include the ones whose leaders had been most articulate about the need for liberal arts men.

He got short shrift. If only, personnel people explained, he had had some technical training. Being a self-assured young man he didn't let them off without some thorough argument, and this unsettled some interviewers into passing him on up to the next echelon. Here he got a better hearing. Several executives, he found, thought the liberal arts training wouldn't hurt him, and two actually offered him a job. In the other twelve cases, however, the response was standard—they just didn't have any opening for a man with such an unusual educational background.

Unfortunately, this bias against the humanities is self-proving. Let's go back for a moment to the "shortage" of engineers. Companies have been downright frenetic in their search for engineers; look at the business pages of the newspapers, and the ads promise everything but the sun to the engineering graduate. But what do they do when they get him? Many companies don't use the graduates as engineers but as draftsmen. Other companies demand them for every opening in their trainee cadre, and since it wants the best to be executives, it puts them to work studying the non-engineering view of things they didn't get because the company wanted them to be engineers. Given this kind of attention, they respond, and the company finds its judgment of the rightness of using engineers confirmed.

Conceivably, the lack of enough engineers to satiate business could help the liberal arts men. Even in quasi-engineering jobs, some companies have rediscovered, liberal arts men weren't so bad after all. Several years ago one firm hired thirty-two liberal arts graduates for selling work usually done by engineers; after giving them a cram course in engineering, it found they did as well as regular engineers. The lesson, apparently, has not excited U.S. industry. The liberal arts men who got in under the wire are safe, but engineering-school enrollments are once again swelling and as soon as the new classes come of age, the liberal arts man will be in even less demand than before.

It is among undergraduates that the business bias against the liberal arts sets up the most far-reaching chain of consequences. When the upperclassman finds at first hand that the recruiters prefer men with the technical specialties, the word gets around the campus very quickly indeed. To the freshmen and sophomores who are pondering a choice of major, this is the real world talking. Why, then, the liberal arts? Sales work, they hear, is about the only slot they would qualify for if they took English or history or politics or such, and they have the strong feeling, not entirely erroneous, that the offer is made only because the recruiters can't interest the preferred ones in sales. So they listen politely when an occasional alumnus or speaker at a career-counseling meeting speaks glowingly of the liberal arts and the full man, the need for culture, and so on. Then they go sign up for something practical.

Already this drift has had a considerable effect on the composition of the student body enrolled in the liberal arts. In many cases, the liberal arts group seems divided between a small number of people who wish to teach and write and another group with no clear idea of anything particular they want to do. While roughly 53 per cent of all seniors plan to go into business, only about 29 per cent of the liberal arts men do. At the rate things are going, it would seem, liberal arts is well on its way toward being made into a specialty—a preprofessional training considered useful only for those who intend to lead the gentle life.

As the college catalogues make obvious, most administrators have been following the if-you-can't-beat-'em-join-'em line, and in meeting the demand they have lagged but slightly in setting up new courses. In some cases the business demand has also influenced them in the type of man they favor in the selection of students and the awarding of scholarships. One Dean of Freshmen told me that in screening applicants from secondary schools he felt it was only common sense to take into account not only what the college wanted but what, four years later, corporations' recruiters would want. "They like a pretty gregarious, active type," he said. "So we find that the best man is the one who's had an 80 or 85 average in school and plenty of extracurricular activity. We see little use for the 'brilliant' introvert who might spend the rest of life turning out essays on obscure portions of D. H. Lawrence's letters."

The influence of business is going to increase, in character as well as degree. Up until recently, business was one of many supporters of education, and its support was diverse—it was an accumulation of gifts by businessmen as individuals. But, business giving is rapidly becoming more institutionalized, more collective. Somebody is going to have to foot the bill for the increased costs of education and, unless the state is to take over, the corporation must assume a much greater share of the burden. Not just as an alumnus, but, ex officio, the organization man is becoming a trustee of education.

There is nothing inherently wrong with this kind of support—the growing interest in higher education among corporation leaders does not spring from a desire to dominate education but rather from a genuine sense of social obligation. Yet the pitfalls are considerable nonetheless. As long as the businessman was only one of many supporters, it was understandable that he would channel so much of his support to the vocational. Now that he is the agent of a dominant institution rather than an independent donor, he no longer has this justification. Some recognize this; elder statesmen of business like Frank Abrams have repeatedly made the point that what management needs from education is what our whole society needs. Whether the business-school graduates who will one day succeed them will make the same point remains to be seen.

Yet the crux of the situation may not be so much the

pressures of business as the acquiescence of the colleges. The burden is on the educators. They may complain with some justice of Babbitt's influence, but they help create the stereotype by catering to it. As many people who have sat in on business-academic meetings recognize, it is often the businessmen who seem the philosophers. In contrast, many of the same academics who privately throw up their hands at the horror of our materialistic culture act like so many self-abasing hucksters when it comes to pleasing grant-givers. If they have been so supine in catering to the vocational while there are still some liberal-educated business-men left around, one can only wonder what their posture will be in the future.

One solution that everyone seems to be getting enthusiastic about is the formalizing of more "channels of communication" between industry and the colleges. Businessmen have been showing much initiative in this; their organizations have been staging an increasing number of industry-college conferences, and some corporations have been host to groups of professors at special summer seminars. Much of this has been worth while. Where the businessmen have acted in their capacity as laymen they have been discharging an obligation rather than asserting a power, and they have learned much about academic problems thereby. The academic people, similarly, have learned much about business, and this has helped undercut the stereotyped and anachronistic kind of criticism of business so long characteristic of academia.

Nonetheless I would like to enter a caveat. Of all our problems, the businessman's complaints about the ivory tower's lack of esteem for business is one of our least pressing ones. No one should bespeak ignorance of the great changes that have taken place in corporate life, but it is questionable if even uninformed criticism is any more dangerous than a posture of reverence would be. The academic man should never discover himself beholden to business. Between the academic and the business world there must be some conflict of interests, and a running fire of criticism is a cross that business can well afford to put up with. As a dominant force in American society, and prime guardian of orthodox thought, business must stir unease from others, and we would have an unhealthy imbalance of power if it had not, and did not still. Many historians and novelists have been unfair to business, it is true, but it is hard, looking at the way business has managed to thrive, to feel that there was not some logic to the impulse. Would businessmen be better if *Babbitt* had been less a caricature? Humility may come from within, but an assist from others can help a lot.

The trouble with many industry-college conferences is that so little gets said. The very nature of such occasions, with their emphases on "communication" and agreement, leads the participants to devote themselves largely to the common denominators that everyone agrees on. This makes for good feeling, but the net effect is to suppress the real issues. The businessman and the educator may both agree that, say, general education is a good thing and yet have totally differing concepts of what they want. Such debate is in bad odor; the differences are not aired and everyone goes his way with the problem untouched.

Occasionally people speak out with candor, and then the interchange becomes valuable. Kenneth Brasted, Education Director of the National Association of Manufacturers, performed such a service not so long ago when he addressed the College English Association at Corning, New York. Instead of concealing the NAM's disapproval of certain aspects of education, he came out frankly with the charge that education is not vocational enough for the needs of his constituents. "Paramount in my mind," he said, "is the need for higher education to stop purposeful avoidance of any and all vocational or practical training. . . . You in liberal arts education should urge and encourage your students to pick up some employee skill or tool—e.g., statistics, accounting, mathematics generally; for girls—typing." One does not have to agree with the point to see how the making of it helps clarify the issues.

Because the conferences are so often held on business's home grounds, the academic people are under wraps. No one likes to bite the hand of his host, especially at the time of eating, and thus businessmen are robbed of the kind of

comment that could serve them well. It would be instructive
for them to hear frank appraisal of the caliber of the textbooks they subsidize for their training courses, or of their
version of economic history. They don't. Occasionally, some
academics do revolt; during a conference staged for academics by a large corporation one of the most noted wind-
bags in U.S. business started talking nonsense to his academic guests, at which juncture several pointedly got up and
left. Usually, however, academics suffer in silence.[2]

In the conflict of power the academic person has more
advantages than laymen suspect. The businessman is awed
by him. Considering the somewhat contemptuous way businessmen often describe academia, this sounds farfetched,
but you'll note that the contempt is expressed at a safe distance. In actual practice, the businessman is the biggest
sucker in the world for the trappings of scholasticism; and
while his own hired intellectuals may lose esteem through
continued familiarity, he will take an almost childish delight
in introducing as *professor* a simon-pure visitor from the
campus. Even the rawest Ph.D. can command a deference
in the business world never accorded him on the campus.
In the latter he is just another "mister"; in the business world
he becomes a "doctor," and the executive is in a quandary
as to what simulated rank he should be given. "We may
not make much money," one Ph.D. confessed to me, "but,
by God, they can't *place* us." There is another, and more
important, weapon. The businessman wants more than
power; he wants it rationalized, and so long as the academic
withholds the final blessing, he keeps a weapon of consider-

[2] In one exception Frederick Allis, of Andover School, wrote
for *Fortune* an account of his experiences at an elaborate convention the automotive industry had staged for secondary-school
teachers. He didn't think much of it. The teachers, he said, would
really like to know more about business, but they heard only the
commonplace (he would never be able to think of trucks any
more, he said, except as "the workhorses of industry") and
similarly low-level fare. Outrage greeted the article—it was
rotten of Allis to have said such things, many wrote. It did, however, stir some second thoughts by the automotive people, and
in the end was possibly more salutary than the bushels of easily
won praise solicited.

able power. Let him look to it zealously. To repeat the point of these paragraphs: the crux of the problem is not the pressure from business, but the posture of the academics.

There are issues, and vigorous debate of them is more vital than immediate "co-operation." Communication, yes, but the active kind too—the kind, for example, in which educators do *not* accept grants for further vocationalism. For the burden of leadership is theirs; instead of looking forward to the upsurge of the humanities so regularly proclaimed every year, educators can serve all of us, businessmen especially, by boldly reasserting the integrity of their own institutions. Those who do will inspire hostility from some businessmen, but business is not monolithic in distrust of the humanities. Not yet.

CHAPTER NINE

The Pipe Line

BEFORE we follow the senior into the corporation's post-graduate training schools, we must pause a moment longer on the campus. For it is here, in one important respect, that these new schools are being shaped. They are a projection of what the senior wants, and more than corporations care to admit, what the senior wants these days has a lot to do with what he gets. Corporation people talk much about the intensive screening by which they have sifted out of the common ruck such a superlative group of recruits for their particular organization. The blunt fact, however, is that these days it is the college senior who does most of the screening. With more job vacancies than there are graduates, the attractive senior will usually have some eight or nine offers to choose from. He does not throw the advantage away.

What he wants, above all, is the guarantee of a training program. Almost every recruiter implies to him that he will find security, happiness, and perpetual advancement if he chooses Ajax, but he is apt to remain visibly unimpressed unless the recruiter can back up the promise with a training program—and a formal, highly organized one too. Seniors don't leave it at that either. Having narrowed the choice to companies whose brochures promise training ("individual development program tailored to your particular needs" . . . "no dead-end jobs" . . . "no ceiling"), the senior starts applying other yardsticks. How long is the training program? Is it a real training program or just afterhours indoctrination about the company? Will he be exposed to many different operations of the company or will he be pigeonholed in a specialty? How will he be rated? Is the program geared to a fixed salary increase schedule?

What he wants is a continuation. He is used to formal training and he is wary of stepping out into the arena without a good deal more. This is one of the reasons he does not incline to the smaller firm; it may offer opportunity, but it offers it too soon. By contrast, big business's reassuringly institutionalized schools—sometimes complete with classrooms, dormitories, and graduating classes—is an ideal next step. It will defer opportunity until he is ready for it. For the same reason, it offers him far more security; the more the company spends on him, goes a popular line of thought, the less likely is it to let its investment in him lapse. The training program, in short, promises to obviate the necessity of premature decision, and to those concerned because they don't yet know what kind of subspecialty they want to follow, enrollment in the formal program is a sedative. "We tell them, in effect, 'You don't have to make up your mind,'" says one executive. "'Come with us and you will find out while you're in training.'"

The companies which deliver best on this promise, as a consequence, are the ones that get the most applicants. Students are not easily fooled; by spring they are connoisseurs of placement interviewing, and their information network is quick to pass along the word about specific company situations. If the placement director is energetic he will have checked up with recent alumni as to how well the companies have done by them. If the company welched by taking on more trainees than it would promote, or otherwise exploited them, the placement director then warns his men away from it—though, as we will see later, there are exceptions to the rule.

The placement director is in a sellers' market, and half the fun of the game for him is to get a most-favored-college position with the companies that do best by trainees. He schools his men in the way to deport themselves with particular recruiters, the weighting of the personality profile each is looking for, the right answers to the curved-ball questions. In some colleges, regular courses have been set up for the task, and seniors can't enter the placement competition until they've taken them. The Carnation Company's Wallace Jamie, one of the leaders in the field of corporate recruiting, tells of an experience at Indiana University: "I began to notice that every applicant wore a dark-blue suit and a conservative tie and had ready and right answers for most of my questions." As he had suspected, it turned out that the students had trained for the interview in a special class. Like other recruiters, who have similar experiences, he rather admires their sophistication. The eager beaver of today, he points out, knows the value of not being too eager, and only the company with the first-rate training program can command his attention.[1]

But corporations have not been setting up training schools simply because seniors want them to. Corporations started experimenting with such programs many years ago, and while the predilections of the young men have been a powerful prod, in time many corporations would have made the shift anyway. For the training schools are not simply a sugar-coating, a more attractively packaged indoctrination; they are a manifestation of a deep change in the organization's own view of what *kind* of man it wishes to achieve.

There are two divergent conceptions, and the question of which is to become dominant is still at issue. On the surface the trainee programs of most big corporations would seem

[1] In their own way, English undergraduates are becoming connoisseurs too. The London *Sunday Times* (March 18, 1956) writes of the way business executives are haunting the provincial universities in search of bright young men. There is now such a shortage, the *Sunday Times* writer reports, that "one young physicist I know has spent every weekend since he came down from the university voyaging up and down the country in first-class compartments to interviews, lodging at four-star hotels, dining with directors, and drinking more than is good for him. He has no intention of taking any of the posts he is offered, since he is very well placed already, thank you. But these weekly outings have become a hobby with him."

very much alike. Beneath such new standardized trappings as testing, automatic rating, rotation, and the like, however, is a fundamental difference in policy.

One type of program sticks to what has been more or less the historic approach. The young man is hired to do a specific job; his orientation is usually brief in duration, and for many years what subsequent after hours training he will get will be directed at his particular job. If he proves himself executive material he may be enrolled in a management development course, but this is not likely to happen until he is in his mid-thirties.

The newer type of program is more than an intensification of the old. The company hires the young man as a potential manager and from the start he is given to thinking of himself as such. He and the other candidates are put together in a central pool, and they are not farmed out to regular jobs until they have been exposed, through a series of dry-run tasks, to the managerial view. The schooling may last as long as two years and occasionally as long as four or five.

At the risk of oversimplification, the difference can be described as that between the Protestant Ethic and the Social Ethic. In one type of program we will see that the primary emphasis is on work and on competition; in the other, on managing *others'* work and on co-operation. Needless to say, there are few pure examples of either approach; whichever way they incline, the majority of training programs have elements of both approaches, and some companies try to straddle directly over the fence. But an inclination there is, and the new training program may prove the best of introductions to the "professional manager" of the future.

To sharpen the fundamental differences, I am going to contrast two outstanding trainee programs. For an example of the first type, I am going to take the training program of the Vick Chemical Company as it was in the late thirties. There are several reasons for the choice. First, it has been one of the best-known programs in the whole personnel field. Second, though it has often been cited as a pioneer example of modern practice, it was in its fundamentals the essence of the Protestant Ethic and so undefiled by change that there was nothing in it which Henry Clews would take exception to. Third, I happen to have gone through it myself. If I grow unduly garrulous in these next pages, I bespeak the reader's indulgence; I have often pondered this odd experience, and since it furnishes so apt an illustration of certain principles of indoctrination, I would like to dwell on it at some length.

It was a school—the Vick School of Applied Merchandising, they called it. The idea, as it was presented to job-hunting seniors at the time, was that those who were chosen were not going off to a job, but to a postgraduate training institution set up by a farsighted management. In September, some thirty graduates would gather from different colleges to start a year's study in modern merchandising. There would be a spell of classroom work in New York, a continuing course in advertising, and, most important, eleven months of field study under the supervision of veteran students of merchandising and distribution. Theoretically, we should be charged a tuition, for though we understood we would do some work in connection with our studies, the company explained that its expenses far outweighed what incidental services we would perform. This notwithstanding, it was going to give us a salary of $75 a month and all traveling expenses. It would also, for reasons I was later to learn were substantial, give us an extra $25 a month to be held in escrow until the end of the course.

Let me now point out the first distinction between the Vick program and the more current type. It was not executive training or even junior-executive training. Vick's did argue that the program would help produce the leaders of tomorrow, and prominent on the walls of the office was a framed picture of a captain at the wheel, with a statement by the president that the greatest duty of management was to bring along younger men. This notwithstanding, the question of whether or not any of us would one day be executives was considered a matter that could very easily be deferred. The training was directed almost entirely to the immediate job. The only exception was an International Correspondence Schools course in advertising, one of the main virtues of which, I always felt, was to keep us so occupied during the week ends that we wouldn't have time to think about our situation.

The formal schooling we got was of the briefest character. During our four weeks in New York, we learned of Richardson's discovery of VapoRub, spent a day watching the VapoRub being mixed, and went through a battery of tests the company was fooling around with to find the Vick's type. Most of the time we spent in memorizing list prices, sales spiels, counters to objections, and the prices and techniques of Plough, Inc., whose Penetro line was one of Vick's most troublesome competitors. There was no talk about the social responsibilities of business or the broad view that I can remember, and I'm quite sure the phrase *human relations* never came up at all.

What management philosophy we did get was brief and to the point. Shortly before we were to set out from New York, the president, Mr. H. S. Richardson, took us up to the Cloud Club atop the Chrysler Building. The symbolism did not escape us. As we looked from this executive eyrie down on the skyscraper spires below, Golconda stretched out before us. One day, we gathered, some of us would be coming back up again—and not as temporary guests either. Some would not. The race would be to the swiftest.

Over coffee Mr. Richardson drove home to us the kind of philosophy that would get us back up. He posed a hypothetical problem. Suppose, he said, that you are a manufacturer and for years a small firm has been making paper cartons for your product. He has specialized so much to service you, as a matter of fact, that that's all he does make. He is utterly dependent on your business. For years the relationship has continued to be eminently satisfactory to both parties. But then one day another man walks in and says he will make the boxes for you cheaper. What do you do?

He bade each one of us in turn to answer.

But *how much* cheaper? we asked. How much time could we give the old supplier to match the new bid? Mr. Richardson became impatient. There was only one decision. Either you were a businessman or you were not a businessman. The new man, obviously, should get the contract. Mr. Richardson, who had strong views on the necessity of holding to the old American virtues, advised us emphatically against letting sentimentality obscure fundamentals. Business was survival of the fittest, he indicated, and we would soon learn the fact.

He was as good as his word. The Vick curriculum was just that—survival of the fittest. In the newer type of programs, companies will indeed fire incompetents, but a man joins with the idea that the company intends to keep him, and this is the company's wish also. The Vick School, however, was frankly based on the principle of elimination. It wouldn't make any difference how wonderful all of us might turn out to be; of the thirty-eight who sat there in the Cloud Club, the rules of the game dictated that only six or seven of us would be asked to stay with Vick. The rest would graduate to make way for the next batch of students.

Another difference between Vick's approach and that now more characteristic became very evident as soon as we arrived in the field. While the work, as the company said, was educational, it was in no sense make-work. Within a few days of our session at the Cloud Club, we were dispatched to the hinterland—in my case, the hill country of eastern Kentucky. Each of us was given a panel delivery truck, a full supply of signs, a ladder, a stock of samples, and an order pad. After several days under the eye of a senior salesman, we were each assigned a string of counties and left to shift for ourselves.

The merchandising was nothing if not applied. To take a typical day of any one of us, we would rise at 6:00 or 6:30 in some bleak boarding house or run-down hotel and after a greasy breakfast set off to squeeze in some advertising practice before the first call. This consisted of bostitching a quota of large fiber signs on barns and clamping smaller metal ones to telephone poles and trees by hog rings. By eight, we would have arrived at a general store for our exercise in merchandising. Our assignment was to persuade the dealer to take a year's supply all at once, or, preferably, more than a year's supply, so that he would have no money or shelf space left for other brands. After the sale, or no-sale, we would turn to market research and note down the amount sold him by "chiseling" competitors (i.e., competitors; there was no acknowledgment on our report blanks of any other kind).

Next we did some sampling work: "Tilt your head back, Mr. Jones," we would suddenly say to the dealer. For a brief second he would obey and we would quickly shoot a whopping dropperful of Vatronol up his nose. His eyes smarting from the sting, the dealer would smile with simple pleasure. Turning to the loungers by the stove, he would tell them to let the drummer fella give them some of that stuff. After the messy job was done, we plastered the place with cardboard signs, and left. Then, some more signposting in barnyards, and ten or twelve miles of mud road to the next call. So, on through the day, the routine was repeated until at length, long after dark, we would get back to our lodgings in time for dinner—and two hours' work on our report forms.

The acquisition of a proper frame of mind toward all this was a slow process. The faded yellow second sheets of our daily report book tell the story. At first, utter demoralization. Day after day, the number of calls would be a skimpy eight or nine, and the number of sales sometimes zero. But it was never our fault. In the large space left for explanations, we would affect a cheerful humor—the gay adventurer in the provinces—but this pathetic bravado could not mask a recurrent note of despair.[2]

To all these bids for sympathy, the home office was adamantine. The weekly letter written to each trainee would start with some perfunctory remarks that it was too bad

---

[2] I quote some entries from my own daily report forms: "They use 'dry' creek beds for roads in this country. 'Dry!' Ha! Ha! . . . Sorry about making only four calls today, but I had to go over to Ervine to pick up a drop shipment of ¾ tins and my clutch broke down. . . . Everybody's on WPA in this county. Met only one dealer who sold more than a couple dozen VR a year. Ah, well, it's all in the game! . . . Bostitched my left thumb to a barn this morning and couldn't pick up my first call until after lunch. . . . The local brick plant here is shut down and nobody's buying anything. . . . Five, count 'em, *five* absent dealers in a row. . . . Sorry about the $20.85 but the clutch broke down again. . . ."

about the clutch breaking down, the cut knee, and so on. But this spurious sympathy did not conceal a strong preoccupation with results, and lest we miss the point we were told of comrades who would no longer be with us. We too are sorry about those absent dealers, the office would say. Perhaps if you got up earlier in the morning?

As the office sensed quite correctly from my daily reports, I was growing sorry for myself. I used to read timetables at night, and often in the evening I would somehow find myself by the C & O tracks when the George Washington swept by, its steamy windows a reminder of civilization left behind. I was also sorry for many of the storekeepers, most of whom existed on a precarious credit relationship with wholesalers, and as a consequence I sold them very little of anything.

The company sent its head training supervisor to see if anything could be salvaged. After several days with me, this old veteran of the road told me he knew what was the matter. It wasn't so much my routine, wretched as this was. It was my state of mind. "Fella," he told me, "you will never sell anybody anything until you learn one simple thing. The man on the other side of the counter is the *enemy*."

It was a gladiators' school we were in. Selling may be no less competitive now, but in the Vick program, strife was honored far more openly than today's climate would permit. Combat was the ideal—combat with the dealer, combat with the "chiseling competitors," and combat with each other. There was some talk about "the team," but it was highly abstract. Our success depended entirely on beating our fellow students, and while we got along when we met for occasional sales meetings the camaraderie was quite extracurricular.

Slowly, as our sales-to-calls ratios crept up, we gained in rapacity. Somewhere along the line, by accident or skill, each of us finally manipulated a person into doing what we wanted him to do. Innocence was lost, and by the end of six months, with the pack down to about twenty-three men, we were fairly ravening for the home stretch back to the Cloud Club. At this point, the company took us off general store and grocery work and turned us loose in the rich drugstore territory.

The advice of the old salesman now became invaluable. While he had a distaste for any kind of dealer, with druggists he was implacably combative. He was one of the most decent and kindly men I have ever met, but when he gave us pep talks about this enemy ahead of us, he spoke with great intensity. Some druggists were good enough fellows, he told us (i.e., successful ones who bought big deals), but the tough ones were a mean, servile crew; they would insult you, keep you waiting while they pretended to fill prescriptions, lie to you about their inventory, whine at anything less than a 300 per cent markup, and switch their customers to chiseling competitors.

The old salesman would bring us together in batches for several days of demonstration. It was a tremendous experience for us, for though he seemed outwardly a phlegmatic man, we knew him for the artist he was. Outside the store he was jumpy and sometimes perspired, but once inside, he was composed to the point of apparent boredom. He rarely smiled, almost never opened with a joke. His demeanor seemed to say, I am a busy man and you are damned lucky I have stopped by your miserable store. Sometimes, if the druggist was unusually insolent, he would blow cigar smoke at his face. "Can't sell it if you don't have it," he would say contemptuously, and then, rather pleased with himself, glance back at us, loitering in the wings, to see if we had marked that.

Only old pros like himself could get away with that, he told us in the post-mortem sessions, but there were lots of little tricks we could pick up. As we gathered around him, like Fagin's brood, he would demonstrate how to watch for the victim's shoulders to relax before throwing the clincher; how to pick up the one-size jar of a competitive line that had an especially thick glass bottom and chuckle knowingly; how to feign suppressed worry that maybe the deal was too big for "the smaller druggist like yourself" to take; how to disarm the nervous druggist by fumbling and dropping a pencil. No mercy, he would tell us; give the devils no mercy.

We couldn't either. As the acid test of our gall the company now challenged us to see how many drugstores we could desecrate with "flange" signs. By all the standards of the trade this signposting should have been an impossible task. Almost every "chiseling competitor" would give the druggist at least five dollars to let him put up a sign; we could not offer the druggist a nickel. Our signs, furthermore, were not the usual cardboard kind the druggist could throw away after we had left. They were of metal, they were hideous, and they were to be screwed to the druggists' cherished oak cabinets.

The trick was in the timing. When we were in peak form the procedure went like this: Just after the druggist had signed the order, his shoulders would subside, and this would signal a fleeting period of mutual bonhomie. "New fella, aren't you?" the druggist was likely to say, relaxing. This was his mistake. As soon as we judged the good will to be at full flood, we would ask him if he had a ladder. (There was a ladder out in the car, but the fuss of fetching it would have broken the mood.) The druggist's train of thought would not at that moment connect the request with what was to follow, and he would good-naturedly dispatch someone to bring out a ladder. After another moment of chatter, we would make way for the waiting customer who would engage the druggist's attention. Then, forthrightly, we would slap the ladder up against a spot we had previously reconnoitered. "Just going to get this sign up for you," we would say, as if doing him the greatest favor in the world. He would nod absent-mindedly. Then up the ladder we would go; a few quick turns of the awl, place the bracket in position, and then, the automatic screw driver. Bang! bang! Down went the sign. (If the druggist had been unusually mean, we could break the thread of the screw for good measure.) Then down with the ladder, shift it over to the second spot, and up again.

About this time the druggist would start looking up a little unhappily, but the good will, while ebbing, was still enough to inhibit him from action. *He* felt sorry for us. Imagine that young man thinking those signs are good looking! Just as he would be about to mumble something about one sign being enough, we would hold up the second one. It had a picture on it of a woman squirting nose drops up her nostrils. We would leer fatuously at it. "Just going to lay this blonde on the top of the cabinet for you, Mr. Jones," we would say, winking. We were giants in those days.

I suppose I should be ashamed, but I must confess I'm really not, and to this day when I enter a drugstore I sometimes fancy the sound of the awl biting irretrievably into the druggist's limed oak. I think the reader will understand, of course, that I am not holding up the Vick School of Applied Merchandising as an ideal model, yet I must add, in all fairness to Vick, that most of us were grateful for the experience. When we get together periodically (we have an informal alumni association), we wallow in talk about how they really separated the men from the boys then, etc. It was truly an experience, and if we shudder to recall the things we did, we must admit that as a cram course in reality it was extraordinarily efficient.

The General Electric program to which I now turn was in full force in the thirties and is actually an older one than the Vick's program. Where the latter was a late flowering of a philosophy already in the descendant, however, GE's was a harbinger of things to come. Even today, it is still somewhat ahead of its time; at this moment there are not many corporation training programs which come near General Electric's, either in the size or elaborateness of facilities or, more importantly, in consistency of principles. Yet I believe that as we take up these principal features of the General Electric program, we will be seeing what in a decade or so hence may be the middle of the road.[3]

The most immediately apparent thing about the General

[3] Even Vick has moved considerably in this direction. The heroic years are over; now it is "The Vick Executive Development Program," and though there has been no basic shift in underlying philosophy (Mr. Richardson is still at the helm), Vick now offers many of the material features of the GE program. Security is reasonably guaranteed; no longer are trainees "graduated"—of the roughly one hundred seniors taken in each year, all but a handful can remain as permanent employees. They are exposed to many more aspects of management and they don't have to do things like putting up flange signs.

Electric program is the fact that it *is* a school. While the plants serve as part of the campus, the company maintains a full-time staff of 250 instructors and an educational plant complete to such details as company-published textbooks, examinations, classrooms, and alumni publications. In direct operating costs alone the company spends over five million dollars annually—a budget larger than many a medium-sized college.

The program is highly centralized. To keep this plant running, GE's corps of recruiters each year delivers between 1,000 and 1,500 college graduates, mostly engineers, to the company's Schenectady headquarters. There the trainees enter what is for them a continuation of college life. Like fraternity brothers, they live together in boarding houses and attend classes in groups. For afterhours recreation, they have the privileges of the Edison Club where, along with other GE employees with college degrees, they can meet after classes to play golf, bridge, and enjoy a planned series of parties and dances. (GE employees who haven't gone to college are eligible to join if they have achieved a supervisory rating.)

The curriculum is arranged in much the same manner as a university's. The trainee enters under one of several courses, such as engineering and accounting. All these courses will have much in common, however, for the trainee's first eighteen months are regarded as the basic part of his training. At the end of this time he will then go on to a "major." If he has been in the manufacturing training course, for example, he can elect as a major factory operations, manufacturing engineering, production and purchasing, or plant engineering.

The work the trainee does during this training is not, like Vick's applied merchandising, considered an end in itself. From time to time the trainee will work at specific jobs, but these jobs, while not mere make-work, are outside the regular cost-accounted operations of the company. The company considers them vehicles for training, and it rotates students from one to another on a regular schedule.

The most noteworthy feature of the General Electric approach is the emphasis on the "professional" manager. As in all training programs, the bulk of the instruction is on specifics. Unlike most, however, there is considerable study in subjects that cut across every kind of job. Trainees study personnel philosophy, labor relations, law, and, most important, the managerial viewpoint.[4]

Only a minority of the trainees will ever become managers; in ten years 1,500 to 2,000 executive slots will open up, and this means that most of the thousands of young men trained during this time will never get further than middle management. Nevertheless, it is those future executive slots that the company is thinking of, and it makes its concern plain to the trainee. On the report card form for trainees, there is a space for an evaluation as to whether the trainee is suited "for individual contribution" or whether, instead, he is suited "to manage the work of others." The company tells the trainees that it is perfectly all right for them to aim at "individual contribution," which is to say, a specialty. It would be a dull trainee, however, who did not pause before consigning himself to such a role. In one of GE's textbooks there is a picture of a man looking at two ladders. One leads up to a specialty, the other to general managing. The question before the young man, the textbook states, is: "Will I specialize in a particular field?"—or "Will I become broad-gauge, capable of effort in many fields?"

Who wants to be narrow-gauge? Trainees do not have to read too strenuously between the lines to see that one should aim to manage; as a matter of fact, they are predisposed to read a good bit more between the lines than many of their elders would like them to. Which brings us to an important point. In gauging the impact of the curriculum on the young man, his predispositions are as important as the

[4] Among other things, the trainees take HOBSO. This is the course in How Our Business System Operates, originally developed by Du Pont to inoculate blue-collar employees against creeping socialism. Though GE has no reason to fear its trainees are ideologically unsound, it explains that the course will help them "detect any bad guidance they receive from union and political leaders, and even from educational and spiritual leaders."

weighting of the courses. Elders at General Electric can demonstrate that the actual amount of time devoted to the abstract arts of management is far less than the time devoted to specific skills. But the managerial part is what the trainees want to hear—and they want to hear it so much that one hour's exposure to the managerial view can be as four or five hours of something else in proportion to its effect on impressionable minds. Trainees are interested, to be sure, in how turbines are made, in the techniques of the accounting department and such, but they do not want to be *too* interested. It would make them unbalanced.

They regard specific work very much as many educators view "subject matter" courses: narrowing. As trainees play back the lesson, they see a distinction, sometimes a downright antithesis, between the qualities of the broad-gauge executive and the qualities that one must have to do a superlative piece of concrete work. Not work itself but the managing of other people's work is the skill that they aspire to. As they describe it, the manager is a man in charge of people getting along together, and his *expertise* is relatively independent of who or what is being managed. Or why.

Not surprisingly, the part of the curriculum for which they have the greatest affinity is the human-relations instruction. They are particularly enthusiastic about the "Effective Presentation" course worked up by the sales-training department. They can hardly be blamed. "YOU CAN ALWAYS GET ANYBODY TO DO WHAT YOU WISH," the textbook proclaims. To this end the students spend four months eagerly studying a battery of communication techniques and psychological principles which General Electric tells them will help them to be good managers. (Sample principle: "Never say anything controversial.")

There is nothing novel about teaching people how to manipulate other people, and GE's scientific psychological techniques bear a strong resemblance to the how-to-be-a-success precepts standard in the U.S. for decades. What is different about them is their justification. They are not presented on the grounds that they will help make people do what you want them to do so that you can make more money. GE trainees see it in much more eleemosynary terms. They do like the part about selling yourself to others so you can get ahead, for they think a lot about this. But they don't abide the thought of enemies on the other side of the counter; they see the manipulative skills as something that in the long run will make other people *happy*. When in years to come the trainees are charged with the destiny of subordinates—a possibility most take remarkably much for granted—they will be able to achieve a stable, well-adjusted work group. They won't drive subordinates, they explain. They will motivate them.

Trainees are also predisposed to emphasis on co-operation rather than competition, and this they get too. The emphasis is built into the structure of the school. For one thing, the student is given a high measure of security from the beginning, and while there may be promotion of the fittest there can be survival for all. There are exceptions, but one must be a very odd ball to be one. For the first two years the trainee is part of a system in which his salary raises will be automatic, and while later on he will be more on his own there will be no planned elimination as there was at Vick, nor an up-or-out policy such as the Navy's.

To get ahead, of course, one must compete—but not too much, and certainly not too obviously. While overt ambition is a bad posture for the ambitious anywhere, the GE system has especial sanctions for the rate-buster. The trainee is, first of all, a member of a group, and the group is entrusted to a surprising degree with the resolution of his future. How well, the company wants to know, does he fit in? His fellow trainees provide the answer, and in the "case study" group discussions the eager beaver or the deviant is quickly exposed. And brought to heel. Trainees speak frequently of the way close fraternity life atmosphere is valuable in ironing out some trainees' aberrant tendencies. It may be tough on him, they concede, but better now than later. In a few years the trainee will be released from this close association and the social character that he has perfected will be a fundamental necessity; he will be moving from one company branch to another, and he must be able to fit into the same kind of integrated social system.

The company officially recognizes the disciplining of the

group. In its periodic rating of the man, the company frequently calls on his comrades to participate in the rating. If a man is liked especially well not only by his superiors but by his peers, he may be given the job of guiding about eight or ten of his fellow trainees. He is now a "sign-up," and if he keeps on maturing he may become a "head-of-tests," the seven "sign-ups" reporting to him. Since the opinions of one's peers are so integral to advancement, this system virtually insures that the overzealous or the "knocker" type of man will not get ahead—or, at the very least, that he will successfully remold himself to the managerial image.

The fact that the trainee must spend so much time thinking of what other people think of him does not oppress him. Quite the opposite, the constant surveillance is one of the things the average trainee talks about most enthusiastically. The rating system is highly standardized, he explains; it is the product of *many* people rather than one, and this denominator of judgments frees him from the harshness or caprice that might result from the traditional boss-employee relationship. He is also freed from being ignored; the system insures that other people must be thinking about him quite as much as he is thinking about them, and for this reason he won't get pigeonholed. At General Electric, as one trainee remarked, not only can't you get lost, you can't even hide.

Needless to say, ambition still pulses, and I am not trying to suggest that the General Electric man is any less set on the main chance than my Vick comrades. It is quite obvious, nevertheless, that he must pursue the main chance in a much more delicate fashion. To get ahead, he must co-operate with the others—but co-operate *better* than they do.

The rules of the game do permit a few lapses, but these lapses, characteristically, are the display of personality. Somewhere along the line the trainees must get themselves hired into a regular job, and to do this they must attract the attention of superiors. There is a tacit understanding among trainees that it is perfectly all right to make a bald play to get on a first name-basis with superiors that might do one some good. "As soon as you know your way around a new department you start telephoning," one trainee explains, tapping the intercommunication telephone directory.

"Believe me, this little green book here is a man's best friend." The company encourages superiors to encourage this kind of contact. "I or anybody else," another trainee says, "can walk into a manager's office just as easily as we can each other's. By ten o'clock of the day I hit the New York office I was calling everybody by his first name."

In contrasting the General Electric type program with the old Vick's program, I have been contrasting extremes. The dividing line they illustrate, however, is one that more and more companies are having to recognize. For a long time businessmen have been rather carelessly talking about the coming of the "professional manager" as if this development was merely a further refinement of the mixture as before. When executives began expanding trainee programs right after the war, management literature on the subject gave no evidence that there were any policy issues involved, and the matters discussed were mainly those of the length of time men should be trained, the frequency of their rotation, and the like.

As time has gone on, however, executives have found that the trainee programs are forcing them to think a lot more than they wanted to about questions more fundamental. Was not the trainee program itself producing a rather definable type? Was this what the company wanted? And what was the company "character," anyway? For a long time executives have sensed that organizations tend to select and fashion a certain type, and while they cannot actually put their finger on it they know that, say, a Union Carbide man is somehow different from a W. R. Grace man. But they would like to leave it at that—in the realm of mystique. Now they have to analyze it.

Eventually, they would have to ponder the compatibility of the "professional manager" with the company spirit whether they put in a centralized training program or not. Times are moving fast, and from the great proselyting centers of the business schools the new man will be going forth to leave his mark on every kind of organization, traditional or otherwise. In the centralized training program, however, he does it ahead of time. It is the ideal culture for him, and though it is a case of evolution rather than revolution, the suddenness of his growth has been rather unsettling to many executives. Here, all at once, is an advance view of the man of the future, and for many a management it has proved too advanced to assimilate.

What the programs have done is accentuate the difference between generations. Ordinarily, this shift in outlook is so gradual as to be imperceptible, except in retrospect, and the company ideology can be revised without pain, or, for that matter, without anyone's knowing it's been revised at all. But not now. More consciously than other age groups before them, today's trainees see themselves as a new breed, and when you talk to them you cannot help but feel a certain premature condescension on their part for the present managers. One of the points younger men frequently make in praising their advanced training is its value to *older* men. "It brings them out of their shells," one twenty-three-year-old engineer explains. "It teaches them that there is an outside world and that there are good ideas and procedures around that the company has not come up with yet." The trainees make the same point about human-relations teaching; even if they don't need to be converted, they explain, the teaching does percolate up to the older, less progressive levels of management. "It's sad," one trainee said, "that you have to teach people how to be human in business. But the brass do need it."

Thanks to a misadventure of the Ford Motor Company, there exists a case study of what happens when this advanced view is introduced without a comparable change in the company spirit. For many reasons, including, perhaps, a certain sensitivity to charges that it was old-fashioned, shortly after the war Ford introduced an ambitious "field training program" for college graduates. Somewhat like the General Electric program, it was a centralized observation-orientation program through which incoming recruits were taken on a grand tour of the company which lasted some two years.

Ford executives now grimace at the memory of it. While no one planned it that way, the program created a cadre of "crown princes" that did not jibe at all well with the organization. As older hands were quick to remark, the trainees had gotten such a broad view of things that they had become quite confused as to what, specifically, they wanted to do in the way of actual work. Eventually they were placed in regular jobs, but to do it personnel people had to peddle them around and use a good bit of persuasion. Today the recruit gets a physical examination, a one-day orientation, and then is put to work. He is not encouraged to call the brass by their first names, and his advancement depends on what his line superior happens to think of his work.

The basic collision has been a philosophical one. Quite perceptibly, the schooling in the broad view produced a definite attitude toward work, and in Ford's case, an attitude 180 degrees away from what the company was used to. In companies like Ford—and this would include General Motors and Du Pont—the emphasis on a specific task as an end in itself shows quite readily in the way people talk about their jobs. Talk to a non-program Ford man or a Du Pont or a GM man and he will rarely dwell on abstractions that cut across the organization, but instead will talk on the concrete work he's connected with, like designing transmissions or opening new markets for paint. He may accuse himself of being too narrow, but he really doesn't worry about it— at that time, anyway—and even the highly ambitious will tend to leave to the president and the executive committee the chore of pondering the big picture. Where at General Electric a young man is likely to talk about managing, in short, at Ford he will talk about cars.

This identification with work was long regarded as the natural order of things, and it has been with some surprise that executives have found it necessary to make the reasons for it explicit. Looking back on the training program, one Ford executive summed up his complaint this way: "I always felt that human relations and getting along with people was all very important. But these trainees made me do a lot of thinking. At Ford we judge a man by results. I mean, what he gets accomplished. And I think this is the way it should be. Sure, human relations is important, but it should be subsidiary to results. Look at it this way: if the girls in a steno pool run away when a man comes around to give dictation on account of his manners, or other people hold out information on him, his results will be bad. I think that the colleges that send these men to us ought to put more emphasis on *doing things*. A lot of the young fellows I talk to think that most engineering problems are all solved and that it's just a question of human engineering. That's just not right."

Interestingly, it is management people in the thirty-five to forty-five age range who are most sensitive to the difference of viewpoint stimulated by centralized programs. Not only do they see more of the trainees than the older executives do, they expect less difference between their generation and the younger one and are surprised to find how much difference there is. Common to almost all of their criticisms is the charge that the younger men are much more sanguine than they had ever been and that the great expectations should be chastened rather than stimulated. Robert C. Landon, Industrial Relations Manager of Rohm & Haas, puts it this way: "Since the time they entered kindergarten they have spent sixteen years during which the world has been presented to them in study courses to be absorbed in an atmosphere of security. To extend this kind of thing when they reach the corporation—except for a well-founded research program—is a dangerous concept." Executives of this persuasion feel that present-day organizations are benevolent enough already. "We should let the wheel of fortune turn," one says. "It's all right for a young man to develop himself, but he shouldn't *be* developed."

I do not wish to overdraw the present distinctions. The first-rate General Electric trainee would not find it insuperable adjusting to the climate at Ford, and a first-rate Ford trainee could adapt to General Electric. Neither do I wish to suggest that a gulf is yawning between two kinds of companies. There has always been more diversity within the business creed than the nonbusinessman suspects and there always will be. But there is a problem of weighting common to all organizations, and this is my reason for dwelling on the "social character" developed by the training programs; exaggerated somewhat, here is the most likely alternative to the past. In these terms no one would choose, certainly not businessmen. The choice will be made through a multitude of day-to-day decisions which at the time will seem squarely poised over the middle way. But a shift there will be for all that.

CHAPTER TEN

The "Well-Rounded" Man

Let's examine first the model as younger men see him. They are in remarkable agreement on the matter. There are dissenters, precious few that they may be, and no generalization can do justice to all the different shadings in the majority's view. On the fundamental premise of the new model executive, however, the young men who hope to be that vary little, and from company to company, region to region, you hear a litany increasingly standard. It goes something like this:

Be loyal to the company and the company will be loyal to you. After all, if you do a good job for the organization, it is only good sense for the organization to be good to you, because that will be best for everybody. There are a bunch of real people around here. Tell them what you think and they will respect you for it. They don't want a man to fret and stew about his work. It won't happen to me. A man who gets ulcers probably shouldn't be in business anyway.

This is more than the wishful thinking normal of youth. Wishful it may be, but it is founded on a well-articulated premise—and one that not so many years ago would have been regarded by the then young men with considerable skepticism. The premise is, simply, that the goals of the individual and the goals of the organization will work out to be one and the same. The young men have no cynicism about the "system," and very little skepticism—they don't see it as something to be bucked, but as something to be co-operated with.

This view is more optimistic than fatalistic. If you were to draft an organization chart based on some junior-executive bull sessions, the chart wouldn't look too much like the usual hierarchical structure. Instead of converging toward a narrow apex, the lines on the chart would rise parallel, eventually disappearing into a sort of mist before they reached any embarrassing turning points.

The prosperity of recent years has had a lot to do with the rosiness of the view. Corporations have been expanding at a great rate, and the effect has been a large-scale deferral of dead ends and pigeonholes for thousands of organization men. With so many new departments, divisions, and plants being opened up, many a young man of average ability has been propelled upward so early—and so pleasantly—that he can hardly be blamed if he thinks the momentum is a constant.

The unity they see between themselves and The Organization has deeper roots, however, than current expediency. Let's take the matter of ambition as further illustration. They do not lack ambition. They seem to, but that is only because the nature of it has changed. It has become a *passive* ambition. Not so many years ago it was permissible for the ambitious young man to talk of setting his cap for a specific goal—like becoming president of a corporation, building a bridge, or making a million dollars. Today it is a very rare young man who will allow himself to talk in such a way, let alone think that way. He can argue, with good grounds, that if it was unrealistic in the past it is even more so today. The life that he looks ahead to will be a life in which he is only one of hundreds of similarly able people and in which they will all be moved hither and yon and subject to so many forces outside their control—not to mention the Bomb—that only a fool would expect to hew to a set course.

But they see nothing wrong with this fluidity. They have an implicit faith that The Organization will be as interested in making use of their best qualities as they are themselves, and thus, with equanimity, they can entrust the resolution of their destiny to The Organization. No specific goal, then, is necessary to give them a sense of continuity. For the short term, perhaps—it would be nice to be head of the electronics branch. But after that, who knows? The young executive does not wish to get stuck in a particular field. The more he is shifted, the more broad-gauge will he become, and the more broad-gauge, the more successful.

But not *too* successful. Somewhat inconsistently, trainees hope to rise high and hope just as much not to suffer the personal load of doing so. Frequently they talk of finding a sort of plateau—a position well enough up to be interesting but not so far up as to have one's neck outstretched for others to chop at. It figures, the young man can explain. Why knock yourself out when the extra salary won't bring home much more actual pay? You can make a very good living in the middle levels—well, not exactly middle, a little higher than that—and the work, furthermore, can be just as fulfilling. If The Organization is good and big, to put it another way, there will be success without tears.

For the executive of the future, trainees say, the problem of company loyalty shouldn't be a problem at all. Almost every older executive you talk to has some private qualifications about his fealty to the company; in contrast, the average young man cherishes the idea that his relationship with The Organization is to be for keeps. Sometimes he doesn't even concede that the point need ever come to test.

Their attitude toward another aspect of organization shows the same bias. What of the "group life," the loss of individualism? Once upon a time it was conventional for young men to view the group life of the big corporation as one of its principal disadvantages. Today, they see it as a positive boon. Working with others, they believe, will *reduce* the frustrations of work, and they often endow the accompanying suppression of ego with strong spiritual overtones. They will concede that there is often a good bit of wasted time in the committee way of life and that the handling of human relations involves much suffering of fools gladly. But this sort of thing, they say, is the heart of the organization man's job, not merely the disadvantages of it. "Any man who feels frustrated by these things," one young trainee with face unlined said to me, "can never be an executive."

On the matter of overwork they are particularly stern. They want to work hard, but not too hard; the good, equable life is paramount and they see no conflict between enjoying it and getting ahead. The usual top executive, they believe, works much too hard, and there are few subjects upon which they will discourse more emphatically than the folly of elders who have a single-minded devotion to work. Is it, they ask, really necessary any more? Or, for that matter, moral?

Tom Rath, hero of *The Man in the Gray Flannel Suit*, puts the thought well. He has just been offered a very stimulating, challenging, and perhaps too-demanding job by his dynamic boss. As the dust jacket says, Rath is a true product of his times. He turns the job down. "I don't want to give up the time," he tells the boss. "I'm trying to be honest about this. I want the money. Nobody likes money better than I do. But I'm just not the kind of guy who can work evenings and week ends and all the rest of it forever. I guess there's even more to it than that. I'm not the kind of person who can get all wrapped up in a job—I can't get myself convinced that my work is the most important thing in the world. I've been through one war. Maybe another one's coming. If one is, I want to be able to look back and figure I spent the time between the wars with my family, the way it should have been spent."

The boss should be damn well ashamed of himself. As Rath implies so strongly, when the younger men say they don't want to work too hard, they feel that they are making a positive moral contribution as well. In this self-ennobling hedonism, furthermore, they don't see why they shouldn't have the good life and good money both. There doesn't have to be any choice between the two.[1]

---

[1] Tom Rath, incidentally, found he wasn't making any sacrifice at all. After his speech he asked the boss if he still wanted him to work for him. "Of course," the boss says. "There are plenty of good positions where it's not necessary for a man to put in an unusual amount of work. Now it's just a matter of finding the right spot for you."

Which brings us to the best part of all. Younger men don't believe there has to be a choice because they believe organizations have been coming around to their own way of thinking. It's just plain good sense for The Organization, they argue, not to have people getting too involved in their jobs. Overwork may have been necessary once, they say, and perhaps you still need a few, very few, dynamic types, but business now sees that the full man is the model. What it needs is not the hard driver but the man who is so rested, so at peace with his environment, so broadened by suburban life, that he is able to handle human relations with poise and understanding.

So they believe, and because they believe this they see the organization life of the future as one in which tensions will be lessening. Again, it figures. The people who will be moving into the key slots then will be people like themselves, and as the last, unreconstructed drivers disappear there will be less trouble for everyone. Out of necessity, then, as well as natural desire, the wise young man is going to enjoy himself—plenty of time with the kids, some good hobbies, and later on he'll certainly go in for more reading and music and stuff like that. He will, in sum, be the apotheosis of the well-rounded man: obtrusive in no particular, excessive in no zeal. He will be the man in the middle.

A young man's idle dream? It is a playback only mildly exaggerated of a vision of the future that is becoming stronger and stronger among personnel executives and the business-school people who intellectualize for business. And their influence should not be underrated. The personnel men are of the staff, rather than the line, but it is they who choose the trainees and administer the schools that affect trainees in their formative years with the corporations.[2]

What personnel men have in mind as the manager of the

[2] The number of personnel people, compared to other employees, has been rising at a rapid rate. A study made by Dale Yoder and Mona L. Walz of the University of Minnesota's Industrial Relations Center indicates that by 1955 there were 8 personnel people per 1,000 employees—a jump of 15 per cent over the 7 per 1,000 in 1954.

future is more of a departure than is generally recognized. Personnel executives don't care to insult the company's brass and, except in the privacy of the conferences and workshops endemic to the field, they manage to muffle the criticism of the top executives their new model implies. For another thing, most definitions of executive traits are so encompassing that no matter how radical or conservative one's views of the future executive, there will be comfort in almost any of the usual all-purpose definitions. The executive, everyone agrees, must be forceful, patient, able to get along with other people, foresighted, imaginative, decisive, and of sound views.

But what, among these contradictions, is to be emphasized? To draw personnel people and executives out on the matter I tried an experiment. Out of the usual inventory of executive qualities I drew out two antithetical definitions. One description of the ideal executive hewed fairly close to the Protestant Ethic; the other to the Social Ethic. I then wrote to 150 personnel directors and asked them to say which one they inclined toward. At the same time, I sent an identical letter to 150 corporation presidents.

If they *had* to choose, I asked them, which of the following schools of thought would they favor:

a. *"Because the rough-and-tumble days of corporation growth are over, what the corporation needs most is the* adaptable *administrator, schooled in managerial skills and concerned primarily with human relations and the techniques of making the corporation a smooth-working team."*

b. *"Because the challenge of change demands new ideas to keep the corporation from rigidifying, what the corporation needs most is the man with strong personal convictions who is not shy about making unorthodox decisions that will unsettle tested procedures—and his colleagues."*

The response was spirited. Many of the hundred who answered jumped on me for asking such a question, but most of them did choose one way or the other and, more importantly, they went into their reasons at length.[3] The vote: presidents voted 50 per cent in favor of the administrator, 50 per cent in favor of the other type; personnel men: 70 per cent for the administrator.

In the wording of their letters the personnel men showed an inclination to the administrator even stronger than the vote indicated. Presidents who favored the administrator generally noted that the individualist had his place too; personnel men quite often not only failed to make such a qualification but went on to infer that the individualist should be carefully segregated out of harm's way if he should be tolerated at all. They were, furthermore, strikingly unanimous in their explanations: among the 70 per cent voting for the administrators the explanations offered so complemented one another as to produce a quite cohesive philosophy. Here, in paraphrase, is the gist of it:

The rough-and-tumble days are over. Since the job is to keep things going, more than pioneering, the leader must be the professional manager, "the man who knows how to elicit participative consultation, how to motivate groups and individuals, how to enhance job satisfactions . . . how to conduct problem-solving meetings." He will be a generalist who will not think in terms of specific work but in the science of making other people work.

In the old sense of work, he does not work; he encourages others to work. He does not create; he moderates and adjusts those who do create. "Primarily he is the balance wheel on the tendency of the professional-type individual to wander into new, unexplored, and perhaps dangerous territory."

Unorthodoxy can be dangerous to The Organization. The pro-administrators sometimes conceded that the administrator could have unconventional ideas himself at times. But, they were in haste to add, he ought to be rather sober about

[3] We had expected that the type of industry the executive was in and the size of the company would have a great deal to do with the way he answered. This did not turn out to be the case. No matter how we tried to correlate the answers, by type of company, age, etc., no pattern manifested itself; the choice, evidently, was primarily a reflection of the executive's own personal outlook.

it, and it was on the dangers rather than on the advantages of such unorthodox thinking that they dwelled.[4]

Unorthodoxy is dangerous to The Organization. Some personnel men didn't simply omit mention of inner qualities such as "drive" and "imagination"; they went out of their way to warn against them. "Any progressive employer," said one personnel director, "would look askance at the individualist and would be reluctant to instill such thinking in the minds of trainees." Another personnel man put it in more direct terms: "Men of strong personal convictions, willing to make unorthodox decisions, are more frequently given to the characteristics of 'drive' *rather than* 'leadership.' " (Italics mine.) This invidious pairing of qualities once thought congenial with each other was not restricted entirely to personnel men. "We used to look primarily for brilliance," said one president. "Now that much-abused word 'character' has become very important. We don't care if you're a Phi Beta Kappa or a Tau Beta Phi. We want a well-rounded person who can handle well-rounded people."

Ideas come from the group, not from the individual. The well-rounded man is one who does not think up ideas himself but mediates other people's ideas, and so democratically that he never lets his own judgment override the decisions of the group. "The decisions should be made by the group," says a personnel director, "and agreement reached after discussion and consultation prior to action." "The leader must be attentive and receptive to the ideas of his followers," says another personnel man, "and he must adjust his ideas accordingly."

If the corporation concentrates on getting people who will process other people's ideas, where will it get the other people—that is, the people with ideas? Some of the pro-administrators did concede that a question was left begging.

[4] When we checked the words which recurred most often in letters, we found that among presidents the most frequent were "imagination," "vigor," "judgment," "dynamic," and "aggressive." Except for those personnel men who voted for the individualist (and in fairness it should be noted that some were as strong as presidents on this score), personnel men tended to use words like "harmonious," "co-operative," etc.

Where would the spark come from? How could a corporation ever change to new ways if the top man was so concerned with equilibrium? They submitted a solution:

Creative leadership is a staff function. Organizations need new ideas from time to time. But the leader is not the man for this; he hires staff people to think up the ideas. While the captive screwball thinks about the major problems of the corporation, the leader—a sort of nonpartisan mediator —will be able to attend to the techniques of solving the problem rather than the problem itself. "He will be able to accomplish change without upsetting relationships," explains one, "because he has been trained to think about *how* the change should be accomplished quite as much as to think about what the change should be." His job is not to look ahead himself but to check the excesses of the kind of people who do look ahead. He does not unbalance himself by enthusiasm for a particular plan by getting involved with the basic engine. He is the governor.

In part, this vision of the new management can be explained away as rationalization. For the trainee it masks the conflicts ahead; for the personnel man it affords a function and status for what is still a highly ambiguous field of work. "From where we sit in the company," says one of the best personnel men in the country, "we have to look at only the aspects of work that cut across all sorts of jobs—administration and human relations. Now these are aspects of work, abstractions, but it's easy for personnel people to get so hipped on their importance that they look on the specific tasks of making things and selling them as secondary. It's heresy, but I swear I am not so sure human relations are really any better than they were twenty years ago. We just talk about them more, and the muddy-headed way so many of us do gives young men a very bum steer."

But even if the "well-rounded" ideal were no more than rationalization, the concept would still be powerful. It is self-proving. As an example of one very practical consequence we have only to note that in many large corporations the junior executives help out on the interviewing and selecting necessary to restock the cadres. As the trainees go back to the campus to search for their own image, they go back strengthened more than ever in their anti-intellectualism, and in a great Mendelian selection process well-rounded men who were chosen by well-rounded men in turn chose more well-rounded men.

It is possible that a genius, supposing he wanted to join the company in the first place, could so feign the role of the well-adjusted extrovert as to hoodwink a trainee into giving him a job. But he'd have to be skillful about it. A group of GE trainees were asked what they would do if a brilliant person like Steinmetz were to apply to them for a job. After some thought, a few trainees said they thought maybe he could work out; because of the fraternity-like life of the training program, they "could iron out his rough spots." Others disagreed; the man would be too hopelessly antisocial to remold. "I don't think we would put up with a fellow like that now," one said. (Fortunately for GE's research division, as we will see later, it does not use trainees as recruiters.)

From company to company, trainees express the same impatience. All the great ideas, they explain, have already been discovered and not only in physics and chemistry but in practical fields like engineering. The basic creative work is done, so the man you need—for every kind of job—is a practical, team-player fellow who will do a good shirt-sleeves job. "I would sacrifice brilliance," one trainee said, "for human understanding every time."

And they do, too.

PART THREE

The Neuroses of
Organization Man

CHAPTER ELEVEN

The Executive: Non-Well-Rounded Man

LISTENING too long to trainees and personnel men describe the future is likely to unnerve one into assuming that the complete bureaucrat is just about ready to take over. Now whether or not these people are riding the waves of the future or wallowing in some kind of trough is a matter of pure prophecy, and later I will take a crack at it. Before we can do it, however, it is necessary to have a look at another kind of corporation man—the man who is running the corporation.

If the criteria set up by many personnel men were to be applied across the board, the majority of U.S. corporation executives would be out of a job tomorrow. As a matter of fact, one gets the feeling that some corporation men don't think it would be an entirely bad idea. ("Because of their philosophy that the way of handling a corporation is based on the past," one personnel man wrote me, "they should not be in a position to influence the younger men being trained today.")

Top executives, of course, can seem just as balanced as the next man, and by the example they set—from the modulation of their voice in the conference room to the ease with which they handle afterhours affairs—they can sometimes appear almost as given to the Social Ethic as the newcomers. Certainly they are more given to it than the executives, say, of thirty years ago—it is, after all, these men who have been in great part responsible for the changes in corporations during the last decade.

Fundamentally, however, they are motivated by the Protestant Ethic. In the sense that younger men conceive the quality, they are not well rounded for the simple reason that if they had been well rounded, they wouldn't have gotten to be executives in the first place. Officially, the organizations they run deify co-operation; in actuality, they remain places where success still comes to those motivated essentially by the old individualistic, competitive drives. This may alter, as the personnel men and the trainees hope; certainly the vigor with which they seek the goal of well-roundedness cannot help but influence the climate of the organization as the new generation replaces the old.

But there is a flaw in their dream which all the wishing in the world will not eliminate. In this chapter, by looking at the older executive's attitude toward his work, I am going to submit that the goal of well-roundedness is an illusion—and in many ways, a cruel illusion. As long as our organizations remain dynamic—which is, of course, only a hopeful premise—The Organization will still be a place in which there is a conflict between the individual as he is and wishes to be, and the role he is called upon to play. This is a perennial conflict, and the sheer effort to exorcise it through adjustment may well intensify it. The new executives will probably mold themselves much closer to the bureaucratic type and thus seem to mitigate the difference, but they will not find the surcease they are looking for. Unfortunately, the drives that produce the executive neurosis so feared are entwined with the drives that make him productive. In denying this harsh reality the well-rounded ideal makes morally illegitimate the tensions now accepted as part of the game, and if the old flexing of the ego was a mixed blessing, so would be the new suppression of it.

There is a widespread assumption that executives don't work as hard as they used to, for which apparent fact many people voice thanks. We are hearing more and more now about the trend to more hobbies and outside interests, a more rational appreciation of the therapy of leisure, the desirability of being fully involved in community life, and it has now become virtually a cliché that today's effective executive is not the single-minded hard driver of old, but the man who is so well organized himself as to strike a sane balance between work and the rest of his life.

My colleagues and I, half persuaded that executives were in fact working more moderately, tried to test the proposition. We checked such things as country club attendance, commuter peak hours and travel schedules, and, more to the point, talked at length to several hundred organization men.[1] We came to the conclusion that: (1) executives are working as hard as they ever did—possibly even harder; (2) grumbling notwithstanding, high income taxes have had little effect on executive drive; (3) executives are prey to more tension and conflict than ever before, for while the swing to committee management has eliminated many old work pressures it has substituted new ones just as frustrating.

By "executive" I do not mean management men in general; in many respects the two are rather different. I am arbitrarily defining "executive" as corporation men who are presidents or vice-presidents plus those men in middle management who have so demonstrably gone ahead of their contemporaries as to indicate that they are likely to keep on going.

Common to these men is an average work week that runs between fifty and sixty hours. Typically, it would break down something like this: each weekday the executive will put in about 9½ hours in the office. Four out of five week-

---

[1] While it is difficult to classify or distinguish the executive from the nonexecutive, we had to make an effort so that we could distinguish between denominators which applied to all organization men—which to executives, which to the older, which to the younger, which to large companies, which to small, etc. For the "executive" category we interviewed: (1) fifty-two company presidents (average age, fifty-five); (2) twenty-three vice-presidents (average age, fifty-three); (3) fifty-three middle-management men who have marked themselves or been marked by the company as comers (average age, thirty-seven). In the "nonexecutive" category were studied: (4) thirty-three men working their way up from lower to middle management (average age, thirty); (5) sixty college graduates in their first two years as corporation trainees.

days he will work nights. One night he will be booked for business entertaining, another night he will probably spend at the office or in a protracted conference somewhere else.

On two of the other nights he goes home. But it's no sanctuary he retreats to; it's a branch office. While only a few go so far as to have a room equipped with dictating machines, calculators, and other appurtenances of their real life, most executives make a regular practice of doing the bulk of their business reading at home and some find it the best time to do their most serious business phone work. ("I do a lot of spot-checking by phone from home," one executive explained. "I have more time then, and besides most people have their guard down when you phone them at home.")

While corporations warn against such a work load as debilitating, in practice most of them seem to do everything they can to encourage the load. Executives we talked to were unanimous that their superiors approved highly of their putting in a fifty-hour week and liked the sixty- and sixty-five-hour week even better. In one company, the top executives have set up a pool of dictaphones to service executives who want to take them home, the better to do more night and week-end work.

In almost all companies the five-day week is pure fiction. Executives are quick to learn that if they drop around the office on Saturday to tidy things up a bit it won't be held against them in the slightest. Similarly, while the organization encourages executives to do extensive reading of business periodicals and trade journals—often by free subscriptions—few executives would dream of being caught reading them in the office. Such solitary contemplation during the office day, for some reason, is regarded by even the executive himself as a form of hooky.

Executives admit that they in turn impose exactly the same kind of pressure on their own subordinates. Some lean toward praising men pointedly for extra work, others prefer to set impossible goals or to use the eager beaver as a "rate-busting" example to others. "What it boils down to is this," one executive puts it, "you promote the guy who takes his problem home with him."

Why do they work so hard? No voice has been louder than the businessman's in damning the income tax as encouraging slothfulness, and they have repeatedly complained that its worst effect has been to rob management of the incentive to hard work. With this plaint in mind, we asked each of the executives we interviewed this question: "Would you, personally, be working harder now if your taxes were less?" Well, said the executives, now don't get them wrong, they don't take back anything about taxes, but as far as their own particular case went—no, they wouldn't be working harder now.

Unhappy as executives are about high taxes, to them the key aspect of salary is not its absolute but its relative size. And the relative size does depend on the income *before* taxes. The part of the pay stub that shows gross salary may be cause for hollow laughter, but it is still the part that is critical, and the man who gets $30,000 a year finds very little comfort in pondering the thought that his $37,000-a-year rival takes home only half of the extra $7000. Even those with independent incomes are just as concerned in this relative figure as anybody else. With one exception, those executives we talked to who were independently wealthy worked just as hard as the others, and sometimes, under the baleful gaze of the steely-eyed old gentleman in the picture on the wall, a good bit harder.

When the executive talks of himself and why he works—a subject of quite compelling interest to him—he speaks about many things. He speaks often of service to others. It is a genuine feeling on his part, for he does not himself belabor the point. Convention rhetoric notwithstanding, he has so little self-doubt on the matter that he is rather bored with the kind of soul-searching questions ("Is management a profession?" "Is public relations at the crossroads?") that worry the staff. He takes it for granted that management work is one of the most vital functions in the United States —sometimes he talks as if it were the only one.

Labor leaders talk like any other executive. Here, in excerpt, is a vice-president of a big CIO union on the subject of work load:

I'm working harder than I ever have in my life, and I once was a cushion builder. The incentive isn't monetary gain. There is much more than that. There is never a dull moment in the labor movement. I feel I'm part of a crusade, making the world a better place in which to live. I like everything about my job.

My usual work week is seventy to eighty hours, I would say. I get to the office at 8:30 A.M. and usually am at my desk until 6:00 P.M. There's usually a luncheon conference daily, and three nights a week I take home a brief case with reading material and reports. I spend about two hours those nights on the reports.

Two nights a week is about the average for attending local union meetings that require my attention. Every Saturday and Sunday there is a membership conference, an executives' conference, a convention, or a union picnic.

Forty per cent of the time I'm on the road in top-level negotiations, trouble-shooting, speaking or attending a CIO board meeting. Here is an example of out-of-town work: Last week end a workshop conference was ending at Purdue University. I left Detroit at 3:05 P.M., flying to Indianapolis and taking a car from there to Lafayette, Indiana. I spoke at 7:30 P.M., finished at 9:30, and then was in a conference until 11:15 P.M. I drove back to Indianapolis, left at 1:10 by plane and got home at 3 A.M.

Do I work too hard? My doctor and my wife think so, but I don't. If I am, it's my own fault because I don't delegate enough work.

Service is not the basic motivation. In talking about why he works, the executive does not speak first of service, or of pressures from the organization; very rarely does he mention his family as a reason. He speaks of himself—and the demon within him. He works because his ego demands it. "People are like springs," explains one company president. "The energy you have within you has to come out one way or another. I would really get in bad shape if I didn't work." "It's like baseball," another president puts it. "A good player doesn't think of the contract when he is up to bat. He drives for the fences." Whatever the analogy—two presidents compare themselves to concert pianists—the theme is self-expression.

Work, then, is dominant. Everything else is subordinate and the executive is unable to compartmentalize his life. Whatever the segment of it—leisure, home, friends—he instinctively measures it in terms of how well it meshes with his work. Is it *over*work? The executive's ability to describe a crushing work load and in the next breath deny that it's overwork is prodigious. Here, for example, is the way a utility company president answered the overwork question:

In the old days, I used to work eighteen and twenty hours a day, but when it was all finished, I didn't give a damn until work rolled around again the next day. Now, hell, I go home thinking about decisions I have to make. I just don't like to sit and think, so I pick up a detective story—something light—and sit there wondering what I'll tell Mike Quill when he says such-and-such or what I'll say at the next fare-increasing hearing.

In the middle of a rate or a wage fight, I lie awake nights wondering what the hell I'll say next. Sometimes I get up from one wage-bargaining session, go home, lie awake thinking until it gets light, and then go back to the bargaining table with maybe only an hour's sleep. I've got an ulcer that acts up on me in times like that. It goes to sleep again when the bargaining is all over and I can start eating decent meals again. I turn in at the hospital every once in a long while just to get some time off to think quietly. Is it overwork? Well . . . I grew up in this business. I like it. There's always something happening. I like it for itself and the fact that I've got some share in helping millions of people get where they want to go. That gives me some feeling of accomplishment.

Most executives are not as sheepish. For some reason the question of whether they overwork touches a very sensitive nerve; equally as they discuss other aspects of their life, on this one they fairly jump. Ninety per cent of the executives we queried said they didn't work too hard, and when they said it they answered with "Absolutely not!" "Of course not!" and similar expostulation. (The few executives who did say they worked too hard were described by colleagues as lazy.)

Why do they protest so much? Executives' reactions to a follow-up question give a clue. Did other people—their wives, their doctors, their friends—think they worked too hard? A little sadly the executive would answer, Yes, others did think that he worked too hard. *They just didn't understand.*

To the executive there is between work and the rest of his life a unity he can never fully explain, and least of all to his wife. One of the few secrets many an executive manages to keep from his wife is how much more deeply he is involved in his job than in anything else under the sun. Thus he can never really explain to his wife that what he is doing is not overwork, for the explanation would be tactless. "Overwork as I see it," says one company president, "is simply work that you don't like. But I dearly love this work. You love only one time and you might as well do something you like." He was not talking about his wife.

Unlike the Catholic Church, the corporation cannot require celibacy, and because its members are subject to the diversions of family ties, the corporation does fall short of complete effectiveness. But not so very far short, and if it officially praises the hearth and family, it is because it can afford the mild hypocrisy. It is true that wives often try to have their men violate their contract, and it is also true that many men have a much stronger attachment to afterhours with their families than to their work, but such cases are the minority; the men on whom The Organization depends most are generally the ones able to resolve successfully any dual allegiance.

Executives try to be dutiful husbands and parents, and they are well aware that their absorption in work means less time with their family even when they are physically with them. Younger executives in particular accuse themselves. They are not, they say, the fathers they should be and they often mention some long-term project they plan to do with their boy, like building a boat with him in the garage. But, they add ruefully, they probably never will. "I sort of look forward to the day my kids are grown up," one sales manager said. "Then I won't have to have such a guilty conscience about neglecting them."

What of leisure? When they talk about it, executives betray a curiously split feeling. They envy the worker his forty-hour week and they deplore the impulse that bedevils them into thinking about work after hours. Yet . . . "Instead of relaxing at night with a mystery story," one executive said of himself, "I keep at it until eleven o'clock and finally I say to myself, The devil with it, I'm going to have a highball or two and go to bed. But I sit there stewing until 12:30 or 1:00. As a result, I am very uncompanionable at breakfast. My wife says I just sit there and dream and maybe she's right. But I do get a kick out of being well informed in business."

Even those who make a great point of not taking a brief case home with them confess that they cannot shut off the business stream of consciousness. "I don't carry a thing home with me," a leading automobile executive said. "When I leave the office, except for the two or three nights when I attend meetings, I keep myself free for my wife and my family. After dinner, though, I take my dog for a walk. I guess you'd call them 'meditation walks.'" The president of a New England firm confessed that it had gotten so bad with him he had to swear off working at home evenings. "I can't read the shortest report," he explained, "without my mind going into action to plan what to do next. I found this stimulated me so much I just couldn't get to sleep at a reasonable hour." He is still on the wagon but he's not happy about it at all; what he really wishes, he says, is that there were more hours in the business day.

Civic work? Executives don't particularly like it. Rightly or wrongly, most of them consider it a diffusion of energy, and only those who see a clear relationship between civic work and their careers perform it with any enthusiasm. Many businessmen plunge into civic work with gusto; but these are not organization men—usually they are the bankers and merchants and others for whom civic work is part of their regular job.

The organization man does some civic work, but it is largely out of a sense of obligation rather than from any personal impulse. Characteristically, he is involved in civic work at that state of his career when, as a branch manager to the national organization, he is ex officio a leader in the local community. Many years later when he has reached the elder-statesman state he is once again involved. But this involvement, as many privately concede, is more a case of entrapment than free choice. "I had looked forward to taking it easy," says one sixty-five-year-old executive. "But the trouble is that just about the time you've trained the people under you to take over and you look forward to taking it easy the word gets around that you are available and then they put the finger on you."

Culture? Executives do tend to have broader tastes in music, reading, and the like than their less successful contemporaries. But that, as executives themselves concede, isn't saying very much. Most of those questioned were conscious that they didn't read enough good books about something besides business, and some executives went out of their way to berate themselves on that score.

But where, the executive asks, can he find time? Much as he might like to read more history or take in more plays, he looks on this as too marginal, too little relevant to his career to warrant making the time. His judgment is debatable on this point, but that is another story. The fact is that he doesn't see much relationship, and thus, as with the long-deferred project to build a boat with the boys, he will keep on planning that reading he hopes to get around to. One of these days.

Hobbies? Even here, the executive applies the yardstick of business relevance. While some executives are genuinely absorbed in a hobby for the sheer creative bang of it, for a larger number the pursuit carries strong therapeutic overtones. For them the hobby is not a joy in itself but simply a means of restoring themselves between rounds. To this end some executives go through an almost compulsive ritual—like watering the flowers at a regular week-end time whether or not it has just rained. To borrow an old phrase, they are never less at leisure than when they are at leisure.

We have, in sum, a man who is so completely involved in his work that he cannot distinguish between work and the rest of his life—and is happy that he cannot. Surrounded as he is by a society ever more preoccupied with leisure, he remains an anomaly. Not only does he work harder, his life is in a few respects more ascetic than the businessman of half a century ago. His existence is hardly uncomfortable, yet, save for the Cadillac, the better address, the quarter acre more of lawn, his style of living is not signally different from that of the men in middle management. And the fact doesn't concern him overmuch; the aspects of luxury that he talks about most frequently concern things that are organic to his work—good steak dinners, comfortable hotels, good planes, and the like. No dreams of Gothic castles or liveried footmen seize his imagination. His house will never be a monument, an end in itself. It is purely functional, a place to salve the wounds and store up energy for what's ahead. And that, he knows full well, is battle.

CHAPTER TWELVE

The Executive Ego

IN this absorption in work, many people believe, lies the seat of the executive neurosis. From Dodsworth on, the figure of the businessman self-alienated from the wider life has been held up to Americans as a somewhat tragic figure. Why, when the purpose of our vast productive apparatus is the release of man from toil, do the people in charge of it so willfully deny themselves the fruits of it? Even the executive, as he curses the demon within him, tends to feel a little guilty about it.

But this is not the nub of his problem. His long absorption in work to the exclusion of everything else may hit him very hard when he retires and finds himself illiterate in the other kinds of life. But if work is a tyranny, it is a self-imposed tyranny. He sees the disparity between work and leisure only as a minor conflict. It is something he feels he *should* worry about. And he hasn't the time.

The real conflict, I am going to argue in these chapters, is the conflict *within* work. Of all the organization men the true executive is the one who remains most suspicious of The Organization. If there is one thing that characterizes him, it is a fierce desire to control his own destiny and, deep down, he resents yielding that control to The Organization, no matter how velvety its grip. He does not want to be done right by; he wants to dominate, not be dominated.

But he can't act that way. He must not only accept control, he must accept it as if he liked it. He must smile when he is transferred to a place or a job that isn't the job or place he happens to want. He must appear to enjoy listening sympathetically to points of view not his own. He must be less "goal-centered," more "employee-centered." It is not enough now that he work hard; he must be a damn good fellow to boot.

And that is the rub. Executives have always had to play a role, but the difference between role and reality is becoming increasingly difficult to resolve. Even executives who would hate to be accused of philosophical thought sense that they are poised midway in a rather perplexing shift of values. They applaud better human relations, permissive management, and the like, yet for them personally these same advances ask them to act out something of a denial of the kind of people they really are. The organization ideology can help people endure the pressures, and the mere playing of the role of the well-adjusted team player can help quiet the inner worries. As Pascal pointed out, if one acts long enough as if one believes, the grace of faith will eventually be given.

But not to the executive. Many people from the great reaches of middle management can become true believers in The Organization—and, in this sense, I think laments over the plight of the white-collar man can miss a very important point. Of all the people in organization life, they are best able to reconcile their own modest aspirations with the demands of organization. But the most able are not vouchsafed this solace.

Here lies the executive neurosis. Some of the executive's tensions and frustrations are due to psychoses—his own and others'—and these are amenable to individual treatment. To a very large degree, however, the tensions of organization life are not personal aberrations to be eliminated by adjustment; they are the inevitable consequence of the collision between the old ethic and the new.

How does the executive really feel about the organization? On almost every question that illumines the relationship between the individual and the system you will find a definite difference in attitude as you go up the scale from trainee to middle management to top management. Let us take first the matter of the group way. As I have mentioned before, younger executives see it as a positive boon, the grist of the professional manager's job. Older executives are partly responsible for the younger men's outlook, for when they make a progressive-type speech, or deliver one written by their public-relations man, they often sound as if the thing they love most is deferring to colleagues, delegating authority to subordinates, and in general submerging themselves in the team.

They most certainly do not. "You're always selling," as one executive complains. "Even in my position, everything I do is subject to review by all sorts of people, so I have to spend as much time getting allies as I do on the project. You have to keep peace with people on all levels. Sometimes I get home worn to a frazzle over all this." The complaint is characteristic. In one variation or another executives make the point that when one's job is inextricably involved with others, the sense of individual creativity and the satisfaction of being able to deliver a tied-up package of achievement is hard to come by.

One of the most mouthed shibboleths in business is that a good executive is a man who can so organize his job that he enjoys this satisfaction and can leave at 5:30 with no worries left dangling over. The efficient executive can make a good show of this—the clean desk top, the brisk memo, the impressive charts—but a lot of this appearance of control is sheer self-defense. How, they complain, can you really control a job when it's others who are doing it?

When the executive was a younger man on the way up he felt differently about the group. For a young man on the make there is no better vehicle than the conference way. Where fifty years before he might have had to labor unseen by all but his immediate superior, now via the conference he can expose himself to all sorts of superiors across the line of command. Given minimum committeemanship skills, by an adroit question here and a modest suggestion there, he can call attention to himself and still play the game.

But as he succeeds in the struggle he comes into contact more and more with the frustrating nature of the process. He is, let it be noted, very, very good at team playing—he wouldn't have risen if he wasn't.[1] But more and more he begins to see the other side of the coin of "multiple management." He still presents the equable façade—he listens as if he really liked to and suggests rather than orders—and he half persuades himself that he is just suggesting. But down underneath, that ego is hardening.

The executive is very gregarious when he sees some practical utility to the gregariousness. But if he doesn't see that utility, good fellowship bores him to death. One of the most recurring notes in executives' complaints about their work loads is the uselessness of so much of the socializing they have to put up with—whether it is entertaining after hours or human relations during hours. One rather studious executive, who at the time was bucking for a vice-presidency, put it this way: "It is when you get where I am that you see the difference between the 'contributory' and the 'noncontributory' aspects of the job. You've got to endure a tremendous amount of noncontributory labor—this talking back and forth, and meetings, and so on. The emptiness and the frustration of it can be appalling. But you've got to put up with it, there's no mistake about that, and you just hope that you can keep your eye on the contributory phases which put you on the glory road."

[1] Let me add a personal testimonial on this score. Comparatively speaking, of all the kinds of people I have come in contact with, corporation men have seemed to me the least given to backbiting and personal animadversions. Most of the popular novels, movies, and plays on the subject give a quite contrary impression, but I think this is due to failure to distinguish between the entrepreneur and the organization man. The businessmen who draw popular attention are apt to be entrepreneurs who, like Robert Young, exist on strife and are never so happy as when they are publicly reviling their enemies. The corporation man is a different breed; he has obeyed the precept to team play so long it has become part of his personality. One result is often a rather automatic, and icy, bonhomie, but another is a remarkable capacity to disagree with colleagues professionally without having to dislike them personally. By contrast, the academic and literary worlds often seem like a jungle.

A majority of executives say about the same thing: the constant interruptions, the necessity to be fraternal, are the impedimenta of their lives—but impedimenta they cannot shed. "There's only about 10 per cent of your job you can control," one complains, "the rest is up to the others, so you've got to try to move people. Any program you're pushing, you've got to lay the groundwork. It's a drain on your time, but if the top people haven't been educated the program will get axed. Worrying about this is the part of the job that gives you butterflies in the stomach." "There's too much of this group stuff, but you don't want to be left out," another puts it. "This sort of thing has a sort of velocity."

Executives have much the same feeling about entertaining. When they are in the junior-executive bracket, the high life afforded by the expense account is very welcome, but this soon loses its savor. If the executive sees something pertinent to his work, the steak tastes very good indeed, but entertaining for entertaining's sake makes him fret. And more than anything else, he detests *being* entertained. To put it another way, if the entertaining is useful for work, it's play—but if it is just play, then it is just work. "Actually, it's hard to tell where the workday ends and the 'pleasure' begins," one executive says. "If you count all the time required for cocktails, dinners, conferences, and conventions, there is no end to work. I think any responsible executive these days works practically all the hours he is awake. That's the part that kills you off. You can stand the office hours, but you can't stand the rest."

This involvement with others, as young men see it, is the heart of the manager's job; not specific work itself, but the managing of *other* people's work is to be the goal. These matters are indeed central to the executive job, and when he has reached the elder-statesman phase he will talk a great deal about such managerial satisfactions as having inspired others, brought out the best in the group, and so on. For all this, however, the executive is much more concerned with the concrete nature of his work than current literature suggests. He does not talk like a neutralist lubricator of other human beings, but rather as a person who identifies himself with quite a specific challenge. Ask him to describe what he does and he will not dwell long on abstract principles of management; he will talk about the terrific job they're doing on nylon, the uphill fight the company has been having with the competition, the chaotic distribution of the industry, and what he's doing to set it right. It is when the executive talks of these things that he generates a sense of excitement. Sometimes, when he dwells overlong on the romance of the industry—how this is increasing more jobs for more people, how it's separating the men from the boys —he can also generate a good bit of hot air. But the excitement is there.

Another index of the difference between executive and trainee lies in the matter of conformity. In an inverse way, how much a man thinks himself a conformist tells a lot about how much spiritual fealty he feels for The Organization, and as subjective as this attitude may be, there is a discernible difference between older and younger men. The younger men are sanguine. They are well aware that organization work demands a measure of conformity—as a matter of fact, half their energies are devoted to finding out the right pattern to conform to. But the younger executive likes to explain that conforming is a kind of phase, a purgatory that he must suffer before he emerges into the area where he can do as he damn well pleases. "You take this business of entertaining," an ambitious assistant plant manager told me. "You have to go through all that stuff for ten years or so, but then you can chuck it. It's like running for the President of the United States; during the campaign you have to do a lot of things you might not like, but when you get to be President that's all over with."

Older executives learned better long ago. At a reunion dinner for business-school graduates a vice-president of a large steel company brought up the matter of conformity and, eying his table companions, asked if they felt as he did: he was, he said, becoming more of a conformist. There was almost an explosion of table thumping and head noddings. In the mass confessional that followed, everyone present tried to top the others in describing the extent of his conformity.

"A help-wanted ad we ran recently," one executive said, "asked for engineers who would 'conform to our work patterns.' Someone slipped up on that one. He actually came out and said what's really wanted in our organization." And it gets worse rather than better, others agreed, as one goes up the ladder. "The further up you go," as one executive put it, "the less you can afford to stick out in any one place." More and more, the executive must act according to the role that he is cast for—the calm eye that never strays from the other's gaze, the easy, controlled laughter, the whole demeanor that tells onlookers that here certainly is a man without neurosis and inner rumblings. Yet again the drive, the fierce desire to control one's own destiny, cannot help but produce the inner conflicts that the demeanor would deny. "The ideal," one company president recently advised a group of young men, "is to be an individualist privately and a conformist publicly."

Presidents appear considerably less disturbed by the pressure to conformity than those just beneath them. Yet the latter entertain few illusions that, even if there were not one rung higher—a board chairman, perhaps a not-too-friendly board of directors—things will ever get much easier. For now they must conform *downward*, just as much as upward. Less than before can they afford the luxury of an inadvertent frown, for their position now means that it will be transmitted all down the line, and eventually come back and smite them. An executive cannot have it said about him that he is an authoritarian; he must, above all, be permissive. Or, as is more customary, make a good show of it. Democracy, as many executives learn, is a lot more fun when you're going up than when you get there.

Some could interpret this attitude on conformity as proof that top executives are conformists. I interpret it otherwise. To be aware of one's conformity is to be aware that there is some antithesis between oneself and the demands of the system. This does not itself stimulate independence, but it is a necessary condition of it; and contrasted with the wishful vision of total harmony now being touted, it demonstrates a pretty tough-minded grasp of reality.

CHAPTER THIRTEEN

Checkers

Now, finally, the matter of ambition—for here is where we see most clearly the collision between the Social Ethic and the needs of the organization man. So far I have been arguing that the older executive is far more suspicious of organization than the professional manager who is the model of the next generation of management. I have further argued that this is not simply a difference in age but a portent of a long-range shift to the professional manager of men. I would now like to buttress my charge that the harmony it promises is a delusion.

The young men speak of "the plateau." If they were to find this haven they would prove that the Social Ethic is personally fulfilling. For the goal of the plateau is in complete consonance with it; one's ambition is not a personal thing that craves achievement for achievement's sake or an ego that demands self-expression. It is an ambition directed outward, to the satisfactions of making others happy. Competitive struggle loses its meaning; in the harmonious organization one has most of the material rewards necessary for the good life, and none of the gnawing pains of the old kind of striving.

As rationalization for the man who isn't going anywhere and doesn't much care, this goal has some utility. For others, however, the plateau has a fatal flaw. During the initial years the vision is proof against the facts of organization life.

When he is on the lower rungs of The Organization the young man feels himself wafted upward so pleasantly that he does not think high-pressure competition really necessary, and even the comparatively ambitious tend to cherish the idea of settling in some comfortable little Eden somewhere short of the summit. As the potential executive starts going ahead of his contemporaries, however, the possibility of a top position becomes increasingly provocative. After all, he got this far by being a little quicker on the uptake. Perhaps . . . maybe . . . *and why not?* The apple has fallen into the garden.

He will never be the same. No longer can he console himself with the thought that hard work never hurt anybody and that neuroses don't come from anything but worry. He knows that he has committed himself to a long and perhaps bitter battle. Psychologically he can never go back or stand still, and he senses well that the climb from here on is going to involve him in increasing tensions.

Just when a man becomes an executive is impossible to determine, and some men never know just when the moment of self-realization comes. But there seems to be a time in a man's life—sometimes 30, sometimes as late as 45— when he feels that he has made the irrevocable self-commitment. At this point he is going to feel a loneliness he never felt before. If he has had the toughness of mind to get this far he knows very well that there are going to be constant clashes between himself and his environment, and he knows that he must often face these clashes alone. His home life will be shorter and his wife less and less interested in the struggle. In the midst of the crowd at the office he will be isolated—no longer intimate with the people he has passed but not yet accepted by the elders he has joined.

In talking to men who have been selected by their companies to attend advanced management courses at graduate business schools, I have been struck by how mixed are the feelings of many a man so honored. Up until the moment the sword touched his shoulders his life has been fairly equable. He had done well in the company but not so obviously as to leave his contemporaries behind. If he had been on the special bonus list it was still too early for the implications to do much unfolding, and when he gathered with the rest of the gang around the barbecue pit on Saturday night it was with the easy camaraderie of equals.

But it will never be the same again. Sometimes the man cherishes the idea he's going to have it both ways, but if he does he is in for some poignant experiences. Let him pick up where he left off as if nothing at all had happened (they had to send somebody; just a fluke it was me), and he will soon be reminded by others that he and his wife are now different. He begins to notice the little edge in the joking remarks of his friends (What did that crack mean about the car? So it's a ranch wagon. So what?). For his wife, unless she is exceptionally shrewd, the disillusionment is even more cutting. More than her husband she has bucked the idea that getting ahead in the company will mean any sacrifice of the modulated life and, unlike her husband, she must suffer the ambiguities of her new status unshielded by the rules of the game and the trappings of rank that set up a buffer zone in the office.

Repeatedly, I keep running into management wives who bitterly resent (one to the extent of physically shaking me) a study I did on the subject four years ago. What they seem to resent most is the point made about the social demands of success. They actually believe in the plateau—or, rather, they desperately want to. Indignantly, they deny that becoming a boss's wife will mean any shedding of old associations. In other companies maybe, but not in this one. And why should we ever want to leave Crestmere Heights? Not the snappiest section of town perhaps, but they're real people here and none of us cares a hang about that rank stuff. Furthermore, that crowd out in the Brinton Hills is not our dish of tea. You were exaggerating terribly. Weren't you, really?[1]

[1] I would be more shaken by these protestations were it not for our mailing list change-of-address records. To interpolate from *Fortune*'s circulation records, promotion for the man and change of address for his family correlate rather highly—and rather quickly. In the case of the wives I interviewed for the articles I have gone back from time to time in connection with follow-up studies and have found that some of those most insistent about staying put and happy have been the first to move out to Brinton Hills or its equivalents. Crestmere Heights, it now

Husbands who have come to the fork in the road may also ponder the idea of finding the plateau, but unlike their wives they don't really believe it. The few who still try to convince themselves that the earlier dream is possible will now find scant comfort from their colleagues, who while not cynical have become too sophisticated to keep a straight face on the matter. "The trouble with you men," I heard one young executive exclaim to two friends, "is that you're still small-town Baptists at heart."

The figures of speech younger executives use to describe the situation they now find themselves in are illuminating. The kind of words they use are "treadmill," "merry-go-round," "rat race"—words that convey an absence of tangible goals but plenty of activity to get there. The absence of fixed goals, as we remarked before, may make them seem less ambitious, less competitive than their forebears, but in the more seemingly co-operative climate of today lies a prod just as effective. They are competing; all but the fools know this—but for what, and against whom? They don't know, and there is the trap. To keep even, they must push ahead, and though they might like to do it only slightly, who is to say what slightly is. Their contemporaries are in precisely the same doubt, and thus they all end up competing against one another as rapaciously as if their hearts were set on the presidency itself.

This co-operative competition can be observed rather clearly in the postgraduate business schools. At one school an up-and-coming plant manager told me that he was puzzled at the apparent lack of ambition in the others. Since they represented a good chunk of the cream of their age group in U.S. corporation life, he couldn't understand why so few of them had no specific goal in mind. (He wanted to be president of his corporation's major subsidiary.) "But the funny thing is," he told me, "that they work just as hard as I do. Frankly, I'm knocking myself out to get top grades because that will mean a lot to the people back in New York. The only thing the others here are working for is just to get an okay grade. But the grades here depend on

---

appears, was just a phase. And not the last one either, by a long shot.

how everybody else does, so how can you tell what a good grade is? They can't take any chances so they do just as much night work, give up just as many week ends as I do."

Back at the office the job of steering the right middle course requires more and more skill. The increasingly "democratic" atmosphere of management has opened up opportunities for the executive, but it has also made more difficult the task of sizing up the relative rankings around the place and judging the timing of one's pushes. The overt differences in status and office amenities are much less than before, but the smaller the differences the more crucial they can become to the individual. It is easy to joke about whether or not one has a thermoflask on his desk or whether the floor is rubber tiled or carpeted, but the joking is a bit nervous and a number of breakdowns have been triggered by what would seem a piddling matter to the observer. Where does one stand in this shifting society in which standing depends so largely on what other people think? Even a thermoflask is important if it can serve as a guidepost— another visible fix of where one is and where others are.

"You get into a certain position," one forty-year-old executive explains, "and you start getting scared that somebody else might want the job you have. You can't tell who he might be, so you take on the protective coloring so you won't look as if you are ambitious and have the others move in on you." The best defense against being surpassed, executives well know, is to surpass somebody else, but since every other executive knows this also and knows that the others know it too, no one can ever feel really secure. Check vacation records, and you will find that the higher up the man is, the more likely is the vacation to be broken up into a week here and a week there and, furthermore, to be rescheduled and postponed to suit the company rather than the family. "I like to take my vacation in two or three stretches instead of three or four weeks," one executive confesses. "I don't do it for my health. If you go away for three weeks, when you come back you find that they have rearranged your entire job. Someone has to carry on while you are gone and they are in your files, and when you get back the people will ask you questions about your job on account of what others did while you were away. I don't blame them, mind you; I would do exactly the same thing." (In *Blandings' Way*, Eric Hodgins has sketched a commuter's reverie that has occurred to many a management man. Today, the executive thinks miserably to himself, is the day they *find me out*.)

Can he "belong?" Let us turn now to the question of company loyalty. It is at the heart of the clash between the Protestant Ethic and the Social Ethic, for, ideologically, all the new emphases call for a closer spiritual union between the individual and The Organization. As the prophets of belongingness have maintained, greater fealty to The Organization can be viewed as a psychological necessity for the individual. In a world changing so fast, in a world in which he must forever be on the move, the individual desperately needs roots, and The Organization is a logical place to develop them.

There are some highly practical forces at work to compel more loyalty. With the great increase in fringe benefits, the development of pension and annuity plans, the individual's self-interest is bound up more tightly than before in continued service in one organization. Why, then, should a man leave a company? If a man breaks the ties at such expense to himself, some now maintain, it can only be because of a serious maladjustment—either in the individual or in the company.

As in other aspects of organization life, the younger generation of managers-to-be show themselves markedly more in favor of loyalty than their elders. When I asked a group of executives whether they thought that in the years ahead they should make a point of keeping their eyes open for opportunities elsewhere, two thirds stated, emphatically, that they should. I asked the same question of several groups of younger men. Only one third thought the executive should keep his eyes open; the consensus was to the effect that such behavior was characteristic of the What-Makes-Sammy-Run type, and the companies would be better off without such people.

With The Organization growing ever more benevolent, it would seem logical to assume that there are fewer defections these days, and many people (including the author) have done so. But the assumption may be false, and let me now introduce some contrary evidence. One available measure of company loyalty is the change in the number of people moving from one company to another. When you look into this you find indications that since the war there has been somewhat more movement, rather than less.

According to a study by the management-consultant firm Booz, Allen & Hamilton, there are now twenty-nine more personnel changes per hundred management jobs than before the war, and a great part of the increase is caused by switches from one company to another. An analysis of the alumni records of several colleges reveals the same trend. Of the men who were graduated in the late thirties, the number who have worked for only one corporation are in a minority (between 20 and 35 per cent). A hefty majority have changed jobs two or three times; among men fifteen years and more out of college the men who have worked for four or more corporations is likely to outnumber those who have worked for only one. Similarly, a great many men are shifting out of their original fields entirely. In twenty-five years four out of every ten Harvard '26ers have switched fields; in only ten years three out of ten '39ers have switched.

Are job changers the unsuccessful, the "floaters"? Some of them are, of course, but many of the job changers are among the most obviously successful of their age group. A study we made at *Fortune* of nine hundred top executives reveals that only a third of America's leading corporation executives are in the same firm they started with; 26 per cent had been with another company, and 40.5 per cent had been with two or more. Of the chief executives of companies, forty-three had been hired directly into their present positions from another company—and for many of these men this was only one of a long series of moves.

As the growing number of business-school graduates goes up the ranks, furthermore, top management may become even more fluid. A study made by the Harvard Business School of alumni of selected classes since 1911 is an indication. Making allowances for the different time lapse for each class and the disruption of the war, the record of job changes indicates that the professional manager is shifting companies—and fields—with increasing facility. The class of 1936 is typical of the developing pattern: only 22 per cent have stuck with one company since graduation, 26 per cent have worked for two, 24 per cent for three, and 28 per cent for four or more. Later classes haven't had as much chance to move, but they seem to anticipate that they will: of the 137 members of the class of 1951, only 28 per cent said that they expected to stay with their present companies.[2]

The corporations' pension and benefit programs do lead to a certain entrapment, but there are counter-forces. For the simple reason that most large organizations have remarkably similar programs, this adhesive factor tends to wash out. It is true, of course, that the longer a man stays, the more equity in the form of company-paid annuities and deferred profit sharing he builds up, and he cannot take all this with him. If a man finds a good slot in another corporation the latter will more than make up the difference in the annuity payments and deferred profit sharing the man left behind in the other company. The same prosperity which has helped corporations to be so munificent in benefits has also created expanding opportunities, so the executive does not have to be overly preoccupied with the security that a fixed position affords.

And how important to him, really, is this kind of security? Booz, Allen & Hamilton analyzed the attitudes of some 422 executives, who have made the jump. The findings appear to come together on one vital point: in the majority of cases the primary reason for switching was not money, increased

[2] Let me note that there are other ways of interpreting the figures I have given. While I believe they indicate a slight increase in the amount of job switching, other observers have held the opposite. With much the same source material, David R. Roberts of the Graduate School of Business Administration, Carnegie Institute of Technology, has argued that there is less job switching ("The Determinants and Effects of Executive Compensation"). I think he's wrong, but this area of activity is so difficult to measure with any statistical surety that conclusions can only be tentative.

security, or location. The executives switched most often because advancement was blocked. With executives who checked only one reason for switching, the order was: (1) bigger job, more responsibility; (2) don't like present management policies; (3) advancement in company uncertain; (4) change of activity desired. In seventh place: increased income. It is clear between the lines that the great motivating factor was the sense of a ceiling, psychological or actual, in one job and the need for more self-expression through another. Security was rarely mentioned.

The executive's own dissatisfactions are not the only factors stimulating switching. Though the executive may not know it, if he has been doing a notably good job his name is probably in the card files of one or more of the management-consultant firms. And the files are active; if an executive is getting restless the intelligence has a way of reaching the consultants, and even if he isn't restless they might approach him anyway. To a degree not commonly recognized, a great proportion of consultants' work consists of matching such men with clients dissatisfied with some of their own people—and the secret talent hunt that has resulted is not abating. "More than they used to," one consultant says, "corporations seem to feel that around the corner is the dream boy."

The fact is not unnoticed within companies. Since so many corporations do look elsewhere for their top executives, many men shy at committing their psyche wholly to the company because they know that when the time comes for their crack at a particular spot the company is as likely as not to go out and hire a banker or a lawyer or some other outsider to fill it. The result is a good bit of almost premature restlessness. "I have to battle with my clients to keep them from changing jobs too much," says a veteran of a big placement agency. "My boys see this going on all around them and they get restless. There is one top man who has made five different connections in eight years, each time being lured away by another of the consultants at a bigger salary."

Ironically, it is the corporation itself that taught the executives how to fly. Because transfer policy has exposed its young men to a succession of environments and new contacts, cutting old roots has not the terrors for them that it does for those who have never moved. Yet for the corporation as well as the individual, the individual's ability to move is profoundly necessary.

The fact that ties are increasingly easy to sever acts as a counter-force against the tendency for an organization to inbreed itself into a static, encompassing bureaucracy. As long as corporations have any life in them, they will always be productive of conflicts and tensions, and thus mobility, or the prospect of it, is a necessary safety valve. Complete allegiance is a snare; for all the injunctions to "get along" with people, it is important for the organization that the executive know that there are times when he very well ought *not* to get along. And to be able to dissent, to champion the unpopular view, he must be able to move. He may not move —but the knowledge that he can, that he is psychologically capable of it, is the guarantee that he can maintain his independence.

He knows that he can never fully "belong." The continuity that he seeks in his life is work that satisfies *his* drives, and thus he remains always a potential rebel. In a letter to the author, Richard Tynan describes the situation well: "For the sake of his career the executive must appear to believe in the values of his company, while at the same time he must be able to ignore them when it serves his purpose. What is good for the company is good for the executive— with exceptions. *Perceiving these exceptions is the true executive quality.*"

Above all, he must be able to perceive the possibility of leaving the organization, for if he does not he will never pressure his way to the top of it. He has high capacity for loyalty; he too wants to identify himself with the company. But he must also take frequent readings of the loyalty coming from the other direction and tacitly remind the company that he is desirable to other organizations too. (This, he explains ingeniously, is really the highest form of company loyalty since it makes the company more alert to make the best use of him, and so he doesn't have to leave at all.) While he can grow as misty-eyed as the next man at the banquet honoring the Grand Old Man and the Unique Spirit of the company, the mist will clear away rapidly if the Spirit overlooks the opportunities that he feels are his due. Once again, it is he against the system.

In citing the amount of moving around as evidence that many executives are resisting the organization, I recognize that I thereby have somewhat undercut my argument about the long-range trend. I can only say (1) I am happy that the facts show the resistance; (2) I hope that they continue to. But it is hard to be persuaded that trends will automatically keep on balancing each other out. The vision of the younger men and the growing philosophy of the encompassing organization are not lightly to be dismissed because they have not yet created that which is sought.

It can be argued that nothing will change; that the difference between the older executives and the professional managers seniors want to be is only one more variant of the customary difference between myth and reality; that it is a new way of making supportable to organization people the harsh fact that they have always been without independence. Or, possibly, that the difference is due to lack of experience and that the young men talk the way they do because they don't know any better and the personnel managers talk that way because they never will.

But I do not think so. The Social Ethic is no mere opiate of the white collar. This would suppose a cynicism The Organization could not abide; furthermore, there would be no feasible way of telling promising young men in advance that it's not meant for them but for those who can't get ahead. Nor is it simply the wishful dream of the young. The growing volume of books, speeches, and training courses for the new outlook is symptomatic of a deep and long-range shift. It is an orthodoxy for all a-building, and wishful thinking that it may be, it will have a deep effect on all organization people.

I am not trying to prophesy that these beliefs will create a unified, contented drone. Rather than tranquilize the individual, these human-relations aspects of organization life that are to assuage insecurity are just as likely to provoke another kind of insecurity. This is not to say that the fluidity of organization life is an absolute boon, nor is it to demean the more democratic climate of the modern organization. But these advances carry a price. Benefits too, yes, but we can resolve the conflicts in organization life only if we openly recognize their existence, rather than if we deny them.

It is not so much that The Organization is going to push the individual around more than it used to. It is that it is becoming increasingly hard for the individual to figure out when he is being pushed around. The older and more authoritarian systems may have confined a man's area of maneuver, but, like the military, they did provide a clear set of rules. A man knew where he had to bend to the system and he knew where he could assert himself against it—where he could put the telescope to the wrong eye.

But not now. As always, the way to success in an organization life depends upon being aware that most of the decisions that affect one's destiny are made by others, and that only rarely will one have the opportunity to wrest control into his own hands. And it is this vital point that the Social Ethic blurs, for it denies that there is any antithesis. What are the standards by which one should judge whether he is co-operating or surrendering? One wrong turn can destroy all that has gone before, but how do you know when it has come? What are the terms of the struggle?

"One of the hazards of the kind of life we lead," says a man now poised at the threshold of the top management of one of our largest corporations, "is the loss of well-defined objectives. What is the purpose? What is the end? I was deeply a part of my job in the chemical division. My wife and I were deeply a part of the community; I was contributing and was effective. Then they asked me to come to New York—the V.P. in charge told me that by coming here I'd have a box seat in the 'Big Time.' If his guess has been bad, it's a terrible waste. I hope the company isn't playing checkers with me. I feel a lack. I don't know what I'm being groomed for. I don't know what contacts to keep alive. A sales manager knows he should keep his customer contacts, but in the broad management philosophy you can't do this. You have to guess. I felt I had trained for twenty years for a tremendous job that had plenty of challenge, and I was in it for only nine months. Somehow I feel this move is out of my pattern—whatever that is. I'd hate to lose all that's behind me because somebody is playing checkers with me."

These apprehensions are not maladjustments. No one likes to be played checkers with, and the man The Organization needs most is precisely the man who is most sensitive on this point. To control one's destiny and not be controlled by it; to know which way the path will fork and to make the turning oneself; to have some index of achievement that no one can dispute—concrete and tangible for all to see, not dependent on the attitudes of others. It is an independence he will never have in full measure but he must forever seek it.

PART FOUR

The Testing of
Organization Man

CHAPTER FOURTEEN

How Good an Organization Man Are You?

IN the foregoing chapters, I have argued that the dominant ideological drift in organization life is toward (1) idolatry of the system and (2) the misuse of science to achieve this. I would now like to go into some detail on one manifestation of this drift: the mass testing of "personality." These curious inquisitions into the psyche are becoming a regular feature of organization life, and, before long, of U.S. life in general. And these tests are no playthings; scoff as the unbeliever may, if he has ambitions of getting ahead he would do well to develop, or simulate, the master personality matrix the tests best fit.

I hope these chapters will be instructive in this respect, and in examining the curious ways tests are scored, I will give some quite practical advice on how to beat them. But it is the underlying principles of testing that will be my main consideration. Ordinarily, The Organization's demands for conformity are so clouded in mystique that their real purport is somewhat obscured. In personality tests, however, they are abundantly evident. Here is the Social Ethic carried to the ultimate; more than any other current development, these tests dovetail the twin strands of scientism and the total integration of the individual. The testers can protest that this is not so, that really the tests are for the individual, that they encourage difference, not conformity. But the tests speak otherwise. They are not, I hope to demonstrate, objective. They do not respect individual difference. They are not science; only the illusion of it.

Personnel testing of one kind or another has been going on for a long time, but the testing of personality has been a fairly recent development. Spiritually, it is not descended so much from the scientific-management movement of the twenties but rather from the later, and presumably more liberal, human-relations movement. The scientific-management people, such as Taylor, were primarily interested in getting *things* done, and their concern with the employee was with those aspects that contributed to this—such as his ability to distinguish distance, or the dexterity of his hands. The development of testing during this period was almost wholly concerned with aptitudes, and some fair success was accomplished along these lines; by having job applicants try their hand at putting wiggly blocks together and such, management was much better able to tell what kind of work a man was best suited for.

Concurrently, organizations were finding vocabulary and intelligence tests similarly useful. During World War I, psychologists had developed, in the "Alpha" tests, a very serviceable vocabulary and intelligence test, and civilian organizations were quick to see its usefulness. While these were not precise, enough people were being tested to produce rough norms that would enable an organization to tell whether a person's mental capacities were sufficient for the particular work at hand. While schools and colleges have been the primary users of such tests, industry found that with the growing complexity of certain kinds of jobs, I.Q. tests were just as valuable as physical-aptitude tests in gauging employees. By the time of World War II, the use of aptitude and intelligence tests had become so widespread that it was almost impossible for any white-collar American to come of age without having taken a battery at one time or another.

But something was eluding The Organization. With aptitude tests The Organization could only hope to measure the specific, isolated skills a man had, and as far as his subsequent performance was concerned, it could predict the future only if the man was magnificently endowed or abysmally deficient in a particular skill. Aptitude tests, in short, revealed only a small part of a man, and as more and more group-relations advocates have been saying, it is the whole man The Organization wants and not just a part of him. Is the man well adjusted? Will he remain well adjusted? A test of potential merit could not tell this; needed was a test of potential *loyalty*.

For a long time applied psychologists had been experimenting with inmates of mental institutions and prisons to plumb the deeper recesses of maladjustment, and in the course of this work they had developed some ingenious pen and pencil tests. While most of these were originally designed to measure abnormality, they could not do this unless they were applied to normal people to get some sort of standard. Before long, the psychologists, spurred by the lively interest of professional educators, began applying these to ordinary groups of people. At first there were only crude indexes—chiefly of the degree people were extroverted or introverted. But the psychologists were nothing if not ingenious, and they designed tests which presumably can measure almost any aspect of a man's personality. Now in regular use are tests which tell in decimal figures a man's degree of radicalism versus conservatism, his practical judgment, his social judgment, the amount of perseverance he has, his stability, his contentment index, his hostility to society, his personal sexual behavior—and now some psychologists are tinkering with a test of a sense of humor. More elaborate yet are the projective techniques. With such devices as the Rorschach Inkblot test and the Thematic Apperception test, the subject is forced to apply his imagination to a stimulus, thereby X-raying himself for latent feelings and psychoses. Asking a normal adult to reveal himself is not the same thing as asking an inmate of a mental institution, of course, and some adults have balked at the self-revelation asked. But this recalcitrance, psychologists have advised organizations, is no great stumbling block. Testers have learned ways to attach great significance to the manner in which people respond to the fact of the tests, and if a man refuses to answer several questions, he does not escape analysis. Given such a man, many psychologists believe that they can deduce his suppressed anxieties almost as well as if he had co-operated fully.

Here, in short, was just what The Organization wanted. Not all organizations, to be sure, but since the war there has been a steady increase in the numbers which have taken up this tool. In 1952, one third of U.S. corporations used personality tests; since then the proportion has been climbing—of the 63 corporations I checked in 1954, some 60 per cent were already using the tests, and these include such bellwether firms as Sears, General Electric, and Westinghouse. Today, there remain some companies opposed to personality testing, but most of the large ones have joined and a fair number of smaller ones too.

The most widespread use of tests has been for the fairly mundane job of screening applicants. Even in companies which aren't yet fully sold on personality tests, it is part of standard operating procedure to add several personality tests to the battery of checks on the job applicant. If business declines, the tests may also be used to help cut down the work force. "For trimming inefficiency in the company operation," Industry Psychology Inc. advises clients, "there is no better place to direct the ax than in the worker category." And there is no better way to do this, it adds, than to run the work force through tests.

But the most intriguing development in personality testing lies in another direction. In about 25 per cent of the country's corporations the tests are used not merely to help screen applicants for The Organization but to check up on people already in it. And these people, significantly, are not the workers; as in so many other aspects of human relations it is the managers who are being hoist. Some companies don't bother to give personality tests to workers at all. Aside from the fact that testing can be very expensive, they feel that the limited number of psychologists available should concentrate on the more crucial questions.

Should Jones be promoted or put on the shelf? Just about the time an executive reaches fifty and begins to get butterflies in his stomach wondering what it has all added up to and whether the long-sought prize is to be his after all, the company is wondering too. Once a man's superiors would have had to thresh this out among themselves; now they can check with the psychologists to find out what the tests say. At Sears, for example, for the last ten years no one has been promoted in the upper brackets until the board chairman has consulted the tests. At Sears, as elsewhere, the formal decision is based on other factors too, but the weight now being given test reports makes it clear that for those who aspire to be an executive the most critical day they may spend in their lives will be the one they spend taking tests.

Giving them has become something of an industry itself. In the last five years the number of blank test forms sold has risen 300 per cent. The growth of psychological consulting firms had paralleled the rise. In addition to such established firms as the Psychological Corporation, literally hundreds of consultants are setting up shop. Science Research Associates of Chicago, a leading test supplier, reports that in one year seven hundred new consultants asked to be put on its approved list of customers. Colleges are also getting into the business; through research centers like Rensselaer Polytechnic's Personnel Testing Laboratory, professors in mufti have been tailoring tests for companies on a consultant basis—a kind of competition, incidentally, which annoys a good many of the frankly commercial firms.

Types of service offered vary greatly. Some firms will do the entire operation by mail—the Klein Institute for Aptitude Testing, Inc., of New York, for example, within forty-eight hours of getting the completed test back will have an analysis on its way to the company. Usually, however, the job is done on the premises. Sometimes the consultant group, like the Activity Vector Analysts, will process the entire management group at one crack. More usually the analysts will come in and study the organization in order to find the personality "profiles" best suited for particular jobs. They will then work up a battery of tests and master profiles. (Somehow, most batteries always seem to be made up of the same tests, but they are presumably just the right mix for the particular client.) The analysts may help out with the day-in, day-out machinery of testing, but the company's personnel department generally handles the rest of the job.

A dynamic would appear to be at work. The more people who are tested, the more test results there are to correlate, and the more correlations, the surer are many testers of predicting success or failure, and thus the more reason there is for more organizations to test more and more people. Some companies have already coded their executives onto IBM cards containing vital statistics, and adding test scores would seem an inevitable next step. What with the schools already doing much the same thing, with electronics making mass testing increasingly easy, there seems no barrier to the building of such personnel inventories for every organization. Since so many of the tests are standard, in time almost everyone can be followed from childhood on, as, echelon by echelon, he makes his way up the ladder of our organization society.

Fanciful? There's no limit to what some people would like to see done. Several years ago, I wrote a little piece for *Fortune* satirizing current integration trends. Under the nom de plume of Otis Binet Stanford, I presented a plan for a Universal Card. The idea was to do away with the duplication of effort in which each company goes about testing independently. Instead of each company tackling the job on its own, there would be one central organization. Eventually everyone would be processed by it—from school on. One's passport to organization life would be his card. On it would be coded all pertinent information: political leanings, marital relations, credit rating, personality test scores, and, if the states co-operated, the card would also be one's operator's license and car registration. (We had a very realistic card gotten up, complete with laminated photo of a young man wearing thick horn-rimmed glasses.) With this tool, organization could get full loyalty: if a man developed hostility he could not escape by leaving an organization. His card would be revoked and that would be that. Lest readers get too excited, I made the end patently ridiculous: with the card, I said, society would be protected from people who questioned things and rocked the boat. For good measure there was a footnote indicating that the whole thing was a hoax.

To our surprise, a considerable number of people took it seriously. Some thought it was appalling. (*Punch* devoted an article to it, as one more evidence of Yankee boorishness.) Many readers wrote indignant letters, and several newspapers editorialized with great heat. All this we didn't mind; we were sorry they were mad at us but we were glad they were mad at the card.

Unfortunately, however, many who took it literally thought it was a splendid idea and the net effect of the article on them was to embolden them to action. The president of the country's largest statistical firm called in great excitement to find out if anyone had yet started the central processing organization—he said it was the sort of idea you kick yourself for not having thought of first. His firm, he suggested, was just the right outfit on which to build the central unit. When I last heard from him he was on his way to see a testing outfit he might team up with.

The idea of a card I thought so novel, it also developed, was not novel at all. After the article had appeared I came across an account of an index system Westinghouse Electric had had in operation for several years. For each management man they had a "Management Development Personnel Code Card," Westinghouse Form 24908. It is a square card containing basic data on the man, the edges of which are punched so that it can be run through the machines at central files. In fairness to Westinghouse let me point out that it does not delve and there is no personality test information on it. But it does give one ideas.

There is, evidently, not much point at this date in belaboring the moral implications of mass testing. Ethical considerations are paramount, to be sure, but to put the case against testing on these grounds seems to array the critic with the ancient forces of superstition against the embattled followers of science. By default, the basic claims of the testers are left unchallenged. Worse yet, the criticism that portrays testing as a black art only serves to whet the curiosity of organizations all the more.

Rorschach Diagnosis

Kuder Preference Record

Humm-Wadsworth Temperament Scale

Extroversion Rating

Thematic Apperception Test

Bernreuter Personality Inventory

Moss Social Intelligence Test

Moss Social Intelligence Test (wife)

Warner I.S.C. Status Scale (of parents)

Wechsler-Bellevue Intelligence Scale

Political Affiliation

Religion

Salary Gradient

Salary

George B. Follansbee

General Foundry & Casting, Inc.
TrmA7-8 Sls46-9 AsstSupMetalDept50-

118 Crestmere Drive Crestmere Heights, Pa.

5' 10" 168 Hazel Brown None

Oct 1 1922 Jonestown Ohio
BuickSpec2dr'52 Pa 6780 OpLic 204270

175 671 088 B UMich'42 BusAdm .74
ArmyA42-6 1stLt Audio-Visual Cntr

CrpntryIII bwling JrChbrComm Kiwns PTA CommChst Cpt '53
OhioState '43 WAC 2d Lt Audio-Visual Cntr '46
Issue boy 3 girl 2

George B. Follansbee

880671076

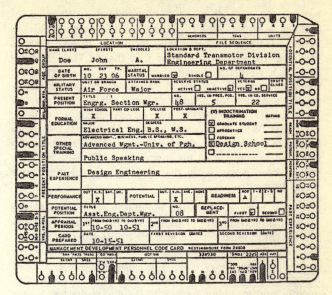

But do the tests do what they purport to do? Let us examine the testers on their own grounds: the scientific method. As a preliminary, let me ask the reader to study the following composite test and its scoring table. To my knowledge, the printing of these guides gives the layman his first opportunity of judging for himself how sensibly prefabricated answers are scored. Until recently, testers have successfully kept such matters within the club; exposure of answers, they have maintained, would be highly unethical—it takes a trained mind to interpret scores, meaningful only to men with Ph.D.s in psychology, individual scores are the property of the organization, the layman would get the wrong idea, etc., etc.

The layman has every right in the world to have a look at the business—in particular, those "right" and "wrong" answers that are not supposed to exist. Whether or not he is unable to distinguish the scientific method from the abuse of it, I leave to the reader.

In detailing scoring methods, I have a practical purpose also. In a small way, I hope to redress the balance of power between the individual and The Organization. When an individual is commanded by an organization to reveal his innermost feelings, he has a duty to himself to give answers that serve his self-interest rather than that of The Organization. In a word, he should cheat. To put it so badly may shock some people—I was scolded severely by several undergraduate groups for giving just such advice. But why be hypocritical? Most people instinctively cheat anyway on such tests. Why, then, do it ineptly? Usually, the dice are loaded in favor of The Organization, and the amateur, unprepared, is apt to slant his answers so badly as to get himself an even worse score than his regular maladjustments would warrant.

A trot is in order. In providing this service, I could not expect the individual to memorize specific questions and answers—there are scores and scores of different tests and far too many hundreds of answers for memorizing to be of any real help. What I have done is to paraphrase the essence of the different types of questions that come up most frequently, and in giving answers in the composite test I have abstracted the basic rules of the game which, once learned, will help the reader master most of the testing situations he may come across.

I suggest to the reader that, before going on to the next chapter, he pause and take the test. If he will then turn to the appendix, he will find a condensed guide on how he should have answered the questions and some tips on test-taking in general. I hope all this may be of some practical benefit, but in asking the reader to pore over these details my main purpose is to give him a chance to evaluate for himself the underlying *principles* of personality testing. To repeat, here is the voice of The Organization, and if one wishes to judge what the future would be like were we to intensify organization trends now so evident, let him ponder well what the questions are really driving at.

COMPOSITE PERSONALITY TEST

SELF-REPORT QUESTIONS

1) Have you enjoyed reading books as much as having company in?

2) Are you sometimes afraid of failure?
3) Do you sometimes feel self-conscious?
4) Does it annoy you to be interrupted in the middle of your work?
5) Do you prefer serious motion pictures about famous historical personalities to musical comedies?

Indicate whether you agree, disagree, or are uncertain:

6) I am going to Hell.
7) I often get pink spots all over.
8) The sex act is repulsive.
9) I like strong-minded women.
10) Strange voices speak to me.
11) My father is a tyrant.

HYPOTHETICAL QUESTION—DOMINANCE TYPE

12) You have been waiting patiently for a salesperson to wait on you. Just when she's finished with another customer, a woman walks up abruptly and demands to be waited upon before you. What would you do?
   a) Do nothing
   b) Push the woman to one side
   c) Give her a piece of your mind
   d) Comment about her behavior to the salesperson

OPINION QUESTIONS: DEGREE OF CONSERVATISM

Indicate whether you agree or disagree with the following questions:

13) Prostitution should be state supervised.
14) Modern art should not be allowed in churches.
15) It is worse for a woman to have extramarital relations than for a man.
16) Foreigners are dirtier than Americans.
17) "The Star-Spangled Banner" is difficult to sing properly.

WORD ASSOCIATION QUESTIONS

Underline the word you think goes best with the word in capitals:

18) UMBRELLA (rain, prepared, cumbersome, appeasement)

19) RED (hot, color, stain, blood)
20) GRASS (green, mow, lawn, court)
21) NIGHT (dark, sleep, moon, morbid)
22) NAKED (nude, body, art, evil)
23) AUTUMN (fall, leaves, season, sad)

HYPOTHETICAL SITUATIONS—JUDGMENT TYPE

24) What would you do if you saw a woman holding a
baby at the window of a burning house:
   a) Call the fire department
   b) Rush into the house
   c) Fetch a ladder
   d) Try and catch the baby
25) Which do you think is the best answer for the executive to make in the following situation:
   Worker: "Why did Jones get the promotion and I
   didn't?"
   Executive:
      a) "You deserved it but Jones has seniority."
      b) "You've got to work harder."
      c) "Jones's uncle owns the plant."
      d) "Let's figure out how you can improve."

OPINION QUESTIONS: POLICY TYPE

26) A worker's home life is not the concern of the company.
            Agree. . . . .   Disagree. . . . .
27) Good supervisors are born, not made.
            Agree. . . . .   Disagree. . . . .
28) It should be company policy to encourage off-hours
participation by employees in company-sponsored social gatherings, clubs, and teams.
            Agree. . . . .   Disagree. . . . .

OPINION QUESTIONS: VALUE TYPE

29) When you look at a great skyscraper, do you think of:
   a) our tremendous industrial growth
   b) the simplicity and beauty of the structural design
30) Who helped mankind most?
   a) Shakespeare
   b) Sir Isaac Newton

CHAPTER FIFTEEN

The Tests of Conformity

IF personality tests are the voice of The Organization it is not that testers mean them to be. A few are lackeys, but the great majority cherish the professional's neutrality; they try hard to be objective, and "value judgments" they shun. And this is the trouble. Not in failing to make the tests scientific enough is the error; it is, rather, in the central idea that the tests *can* be scientific.

They cannot be, and I am going into quite some detail in this chapter to document the assertion. I do so because the tests are the best illustration of the underlying fallacies of scientism—and the underlying bias. As in all applications of scientism, it is society's values that are enshrined. The tests, essentially, are loyalty tests, or rather, tests of potential loyalty. Neither in the questions nor in the evaluation of them are the tests neutral; they are loaded with values, organization values, and the result is a set of yardsticks that reward the conformist, the pedestrian, the unimaginative—at the expense of the exceptional individual without whom no society, organization or otherwise, can flourish.

What I am examining is not the use of tests as guides in clinical work with disturbed people, or their use in counseling when the individual himself seeks the counseling. Neither is it the problems of professional conduct raised by the work of some practitioners in the field, interesting as this bypath is. What I am addressing myself to is the standard use of the tests by organizations as a gauge of the "normal" individual, and the major assumptions upon which the whole mathematical edifice rests.

The first assumption is the idea that if we can measure minor variations in most human beings, we can to a large degree predict what they will do in the future. If the principle of this were true, tests of aptitude—such as vocabulary, or finger dexterity tests—should have long since proved the point. Unlike personality tests, they measure what is relatively measurable, and they have been used so long and on so many people that a vast amount of before-and-after documentation is available.

Aptitude tests have proved useful in distinguishing capabilities. Once past establishing whether a person probably can or cannot meet minimum requirements, however, their predictive success is not impressive. The Army Air Force mass testing experience furnishes perhaps the largest body of evidence available. During the war the Air Force tested hundreds of thousands of men with the standardized battery of tests known as the "Stanines." Now, by going back and comparing the initial prediction with how the men actually performed, we gain a rather clear idea of their usefulness. Here are the conclusions psychiatrist Lawrence Kubie has drawn from the comparison:

The tests of aptitudes were remarkably accurate as far as they went; they selected accurately a small group at one extreme, most of whom would succeed in training, and another small group at the opposite pole, most of whom would fail. (There were exceptions to the results even at both extremes.)

As was to be expected, however, the vast majority of the men tested fell into the central zone of the normal curve of distribution, while only a relatively small percentage of the tested population was placed at the two extremes. With rare exceptions, the individuals who fell into the extremes knew their own aptitudes and ineptitudes before going through any tests. From their experiences at play, in sport, in school, and on various jobs, they knew already that they were specially adept or specially maladroit with respect to certain types of activity. Indeed the representatives of the two extreme ends of the scale were usually able to describe their strong and weak points almost as precisely as these could be measured.

The next important lesson of the entire experiment with the "Stanines" was that for the majority, who fall in the great middle zone of the normal curve of distribution, their minor variations in aptitudes do not determine either success or failure, happiness or unhappiness in a career. For most of us (that is, for the Average Man), a subtle balance of conscious and unconscious forces determines how effectively we use our native aptitudes, whether intellectual, emotional, sensory, neuromuscular, or any combination of these aptitudes. For most of us it is not the minor quantitative differences in the machine itself, but the influence of these conscious and unconscious emotional forces on our use of the human machine which determines our effectiveness. For me this was the ultimate lesson from the experience of the Air Force with the "Stanines."

The personality tester can reply that this merely proves his point—i.e., if a combination of aptitude tests cannot predict the future because of subtle emotional forces, why, then, all we have to do is add some tests that will measure these forces. Once again, the fatal step from science to scientism. In aptitude testing the responses are of a character that can be rated objectively—such as the correctness of the answer to 2 plus 2 or the number of triangles in a bisected rectangle. The conclusions drawn from these aptitude and intelligence scores are, furthermore, limited to the relatively modest prediction of a man's capability of doing *the same sort of thing he is asked to do on the tests.* If the tests indicate that a man has only 5,000 words in his vocabulary, it is a reasonable assumption that he won't do particularly well in a job requiring 50,000 words. If he is all thumbs when he puts wiggly blocks together, he won't be very good at a job requiring enough manual dexterity to put things like wiggly blocks together.

To jump from aptitude testing to personality testing, however, is to jump from the measurable to the immeasurable. What the personality testers are trying to do is to convert abstract traits into a concrete measure that can be placed on a linear scale, and it is on the assumption that this is a correct application of the scientific method that all else follows. But merely defining a trait is immensely difficult, let alone determining whether it can be measured as the opposite of another. Is "emotionalism," for example, the precise statistical opposite of "steadiness"? People are daily being fitted onto linear scales for such qualities, and if their dimensions don't fit they are punished, like those on Procrustes' bed, for their deviance.

But what is "personality"? The surface facets of a man—the way he smiles, the way he talks? Obviously not, the psychologists admit. We must go much deeper. But how much deeper? Few testers would dream of claiming that one can isolate personality from the whole man, yet logic tells us that to be able statistically to predict behavior we would have to do just this. The mathematics is impeccable—and thus entrapping. Because "percentiles" and "coefficients" and "standard deviations" are of themselves neutral, the sheer methodology of using them can convince people that they are translating uncertainty into certainty, the subjective into the objective, and eliminating utterly the bugbear of value judgments. But the mathematics does not eliminate values; it only obscures them.

Let's take the interpretation of test scores. Testers argue that the human element has largely been eliminated from this process; except with "projective" tests the scoring is standardized—if you choose answer (d.) you get so many points, and what the tester may think has nothing to do with it. But you don't take just one test; you usually take several different tests, and the crux of the process comes when the tester attempts to built a composite picture out of all these different sub-scores. The more different scores there are to put together, the more a job of interpretation, not less, the tester has.

With even the most disciplined mind, it is impossible to erase the influence of one's own environment and outlook. Testers likewise, and when any have some stray neuroses themselves, their interpretations can be downright dangerous. Several years ago, a midwest executive sent a job applicant he had investigated and thought very well of to a psychological consultant for testing. The report that came back was surprisingly ominous: according to the analyst, the man was abnormally anti-authority and would have "insufficient feelings of loyalty to the organization." The executive hired the man anyway—he didn't care whether the man loved the company or not; he just wanted a job done. The man worked out fine. A year later, when a similarly ominous report came in on a similarly able man, the executive became curious. He decided to go over and chat with the analyst. "The poor guy was pathetically jealous," the executive recalls. "He was eating his heart out because men his own age that I was sending over had gone way past him. I asked him about the first man he had warned me against. Obviously unstable, he told me; the man had two kids, yet he had bought a convertible. Also, he was building an 'ultramodern' house."

In the case of projective tests, interpretation is even more critical. Originally, they were meant to be used only as part of an exhaustive clinical diagnosis, and the few men who are expert in them have warned against their application to selection. As they point out, the tests can sometimes be more a projection of the man who is doing the evaluation than of the man who is being evaluated.

What do symbols symbolize? David Riesman tells of a Thematic Apperception test taken by a graduate student in history. In these tests you are shown a picture—of a man going out a doorway, for example—and asked to tell a story about it. The history student, not too surprisingly, told a story about a famous historical figure who had had a difficult choice to make. Ah-ha! said the man who interpreted the tests, maladjustment. The student had talked about people who were *dead*. This was the first thought that a historical figure had called up in the mind of the tester.

No matter what tests are used, the interview experience itself is surcharged with values. The dehumanized literature of the field gives little hint of the highly personal overtones that mark the meeting of interviewer and interviewee. Consider the situation in which a man who has reached middle age sees himself weighed in the balance by a man whom he has never seen before. Even were both impossibly "normal" the relationship would be difficult, for all the amenities of civilized discourse cannot suppress in either the consciousness that there is a conflict of interests between the two. There is no interviewee who does not have something within himself that he fears to reveal, and there are few interviewers who do not wish to find it. For professional reasons alone the interviewer wishes to probe for the bared nerve.

And sometimes for personal reasons too. I remember vividly a conversation a colleague and I had with a well-known consultant. Quite voluntarily, he bared his own nerve. In the course of explaining his technique of interviewing he referred to the OSS testing program in World War II and how candidates were submitted to a grueling series of experiences to test their reaction under shock. He spoke warmly of the "final" interview: in this the candidate was taken into a room filled with men dressed as superior officers. They told him that he had done fine and now had only one more test to pass. This was a test of binocular vision in which he was to peer into a box and by turning handles bring two objects together. Unknown to him, one of the onlookers would manipulate a knob which made it impossible to accomplish the task. While the poor devil of a candidate fumbled away, the officers would begin making disparaging remarks. On the very threshold of acceptance, he was told that he had failed. The onlookers then observed his reaction.

The consultant explained that for obvious reasons this sort of thing could not be done in an industrial situation. But the principle could be used. He explained his interview technique. "I sit down with a man with a record of the tests and his vital data in front of me. I am very friendly with him. It is a tense situation, and by increasing the stress I can get him to reveal much more of himself. For example, I will be running down the list and I will read aloud 'married: seventeen years.' Then I will read 'children: none.' I will let my eyebrows go up just a little and then pause thoughtfully. He is probably very sensitive on this point and in a few minutes he will begin to blurt out something about his wife or himself being sterile, and how maybe they have seen doctors about it. Just at this point I may ask him how his sexual relations with his wife are now. After several more minutes of stress I build him up again. Toward the end of the interview I usually smile and say, 'Well, why don't we stop while we're ahead.' That makes him relax and makes him think everything is going to work out all right. Then I shoot a really tough one at him. He is caught off guard."

I am not trying to suggest that testers are abnormal, though there would be, I am tempted to add, a certain poetic injustice in such a suggestion. When they are confronted with recalcitrance or criticism, many testers, as is so characteristic of followers of scientism, do not address themselves to the ideas in dispute but speculate, instead, on the hidden maladjustments that drove one to take a position contrary to theirs. They use sympathy like a weapon.

But turnabout would not be fair play. Most testers are fair and as normal as the next fellow, and as far as underlying hostilities of their own are concerned, they would be abnormal if they didn't have some. They would also be abnormal if they suppressed them completely. The interviewer is sorely tempted to play God—and if the difference in age or salary or background or temperament between himself and the person he is evaluating is wide, the temptation to play somebody else is strong too. This can be resisted by the man with great insight into himself as well as others, the man with wisdom, forbearance, humility. To all such men in the testing field my remarks do not apply.

We have been talking of how testers interpret answers; now let's turn to the questions themselves. Are they free of values? In designing the questions, testers are inevitably influenced by the customs and values of their particular world. Questions designed to find a man's degree of sociability are an example. Do you read books? The reading of a book in some groups is an unsocial act, and the person who confesses he has at times preferred books to companions might have to be quite introverted to do such a thing. But the question is relative. Applied to someone brought up in an environment where reading books is normal—indeed, an excellent subject for much social conversation—the hidden "value judgment" built into the test can give a totally unobjective result. People are not always social in the same terms. A person who would earn himself an unsocial score by saying he would prefer reading to bowling with the gang is not necessarily unsocial and he might even be a strong extrovert. It could be that he just doesn't like bowling.

If the layman gags at the phrasing of a question, testers reply, sometimes with a superior chuckle, this is merely a matter of "face validity." They concede that it is better if the questions seem to make sense, but they claim that the questions are not so important as the way large numbers of people have answered them over a period of time. To put it in another way, if a hundred contented supervisors overwhelmingly answer a particular question in a certain way, this means something, and thus no matter whether the question is nonsensical or not, it has produced a meaningful correlation coefficient.

Meaning what? This is not the place to go into a lengthy dissertation on statistics, but two points should be made about the impressive test charts and tables that so often paralyze common sense. A large proportion of the mathematics is purely internal—that is, test results are compared with other test results rather than with external evidence. Now, this internal mathematics is valuable in determining a test's "reliability"—that is, whether it is consistent in its measurements. If a group of people take Form B of a test, for example, and a mathematical correlation shows that their percentile scores rank just about as they did when they took Form A of the same test, we have an indication of the test's reliability in measuring something.

But *what* is that something? A test's reliability tells us little about its validity. A test may give eminently consistent results, but the results are worthless unless it can be determined that the test is actually measuring the trait it is supposed to measure. Do the tests measure sociability or introversion or neurotic tendencies? Or do they merely measure the number of times an accumulation of questions about putting out fires or reading certain books will be answered certain ways?

To show a test is valid, scores must be related to subsequent behavior of the people tested. Examine the "validation" evidence for many tests, however, and you will find they consist chiefly of showing how closely the average scores for the particular test come to the average scores of somebody else's test. That there should be a correlation between test scores is hardly surprising. Test authors are forever borrowing questions from one another (some questions have been reincarnated in as many as ten or twelve different tests) and what the correlations largely prove is how incestuous tests can be.

But how much have scores been related to individual behavior? Among themselves psychologists raise the same question, and for muted savagery there is nothing to match the critiques they make of one another's tests.[1] The Bernreuter Personality Inventory is a particular case in point. This is by far the most widely used test in business (1953 sales by Stanford University Press, one of several distributors: 1,000,000 copies). Yet a reading of the professional journals shows many reports on it to have been adverse. Some psychologists checked Bernreuter scores against other, more objective, evidence of what the people tested were like and found no significant relationships, and sometimes reverse correlations. "It must be concluded," writes Cecil Patterson in the *Journal of Social Psychology*

[1] For the flavor of this internecine kind of battle read between the lines of the following succession of papers: Peck, R. F. and Worthington, R. E., "New Technique for Personnel Assessment," *Journal of Personnel Administration and Industrial Relations,* January 1954; Clark, J. G. and Owens, W. A., "A Validation Study of the Worthington Personal History Blank," *Journal of Applied Psychology,* 1954, Vol. 38, 85-88; Peck, R. F. and Stephenson, Wm., "A Correction of the Clark-Owens Validation Study of the Worthington Personal History Technique," *Journal of Applied Psychology,* Vol. 38, No. 5, 1954; Owens, W. A., "A Reply to Drs. Peck-Stephenson," *Journal of Applied Psychology,* Vol. 38, No. 5, 1954. This sort of thing can go on for years. The layman who wishes to delve into the field might with profit browse through *The Fourth Mental Measurements Yearbook,* edited by Oscar K. Buros (Highland Park, N. J.: Gryphen Press, 1953). This is a hefty collection of critiques, pro and con, made by psychologists of all the principal aptitude and personality tests. Another, and more readable, book is *Essentials of Psychological Testing,* by Lee J. Cronbach (New York: Harper & Brothers, 1949).

(24, 3-50), "that the results of studies using the Bernreuter Personality Inventory are almost unanimously negative as far as the finding of significant relationships with other variables is concerned. . . . It is no doubt largely due to the nature of the questionnaire approach, which appears to be a fruitless technique for the study of personality."

As top psychologists point out, a really rigorous validation would demand that a firm hire all comers for a period of time, test them, seal away the tests so the scores would not prejudice superiors, and then, several years later, unseal the scores and match them against the actual performance of the individuals involved.[2] This has rarely been so much as attempted. Dr. Robert L. Thorndike of Columbia Teachers College, certainly no fortress of anti-science, points out that most follow-up studies of personality tests known to the field are "contaminated." To make a genuine validation, Thorndike says, it is necessary "to apply the procedure and make the evaluation . . . to keep the results out of the hands of the operating people who can control each man's career and the appraisal of it . . . to get appraisals of job success that are entirely independent of the [original] appraisal, and then to bring together the two *independent* sets of data."

Comparisons have been made between groups that have been tested—for example, a group considered productive may be found to have had an average score on a particular test higher than that of another group less productive. The average of a group, however, tells us very little about the

[2] In the field of projective tests, validation is skimpier yet: psychiatrist Dr. Sol W. Ginsburg, Vanderbilt Clinic, College of Physicians & Surgeons, Columbia University, says, "Rorschach never dreamed his test would be used in the way that it has been used. His most distinguished pupils have also warned against misapplying the test. It has no place in industry for selection purposes. It would be possible to test personalities of future teachers or future executives, but it would be very expensive. You would have to find competent persons to administer the test and such competent persons do not exist in any large numbers. Moreover, it would take more than a generation before one could judge whether the tests one was using were valid." (*What Makes an Executive,* Eli Ginzberg, editor. New York: Columbia University Press, 1955.)

individuals involved. Invariably, some of the people in the "best" group will have lower test scores than some of those in the "poor" ones.

Testers evade this abyss by relying on a whole battery of tests rather than on just one or two. But no matter how many variables you add you cannot make a constant of them. If a man has a high "contentment index" and at the same time a very high "irritability index," does the one good cancel out the other bad? Frequently the tester finds himself right back where he started from. If he is a perceptive man he may pay little heed to the scores and make a very accurate prognosis; if the prognosis later turns out to be correct, however, this will be adduced as one more bit of evidence of the amazing accuracy of the tests.

As an example of how values get entwined in testing, let's watch as a "Worthington Personal History" is constructed. This particular technique is a "projective" one; it is so projective, as a matter of fact, that the tester doesn't even have to bother seeing the man at all. The client company has the applicant fill out what seems to be an innocuous vital-statistics blank and then mails it to Worthington Associates at Chicago. There an analyst studies it for such clues as whether the man used check marks or underlinings, how he designated his relatives, what part of his name he gives by initials, what by the full word. He is then ready to reconstruct the man.

Let the reader match his diagnostic skill against the tester's. In a hypothetical example given in the *Personnel Psychology* journal, we are told that the applicant, one Jonathan Jasper Jones, Jr., writes down that he is twenty-six, that the date of his marriage was November 1951, that he has only one dependent, his wife, that her given name is Bernadine Butterfield, her age twenty-eight, and that she works as a nurse-receptionist in a doctor's office.

Enigma? Carefully, the analyst writes that these clues indicate that Jones "may not take his general obligations very seriously, may have a tendency to self-importance, wishful thinking, may be inclined to be passive-dependent —i.e., reliant on others for direction and guidance—in his general work relationships, may be inclined to take pleasure in unearned status or reflected glory."

How in the world did the analyst deduce all this? Let us peek into the laboratory. The name was the first clue. It told the analyst that Jones was narcissistic. Whenever a man writes his name out in full, the tester notes in his chart that he is "narcissistic." Two initials, last name: "hypomanic." First initial, middle and last name: "narcissistic, histrionic." Any erasure or retracing: "anxious, tense." Characteristically, the applicant gets the short end of every assumption. Even if he adopts the customary first name, middle initial, last name, he is put down as "mildly compulsive."

Deeper and deeper the analyst goes:

Spouse's age: twenty-eight
Fact: married a girl two years older than himself.
Empirical observation: the majority of men marry women younger than themselves.
Primary deduction: may have been influenced in marrying her by unconsciously considering her as a mother-surrogate.
Tentative inference: may like to have an older woman, or people, take care of him.
Provisional extension: may be inclined to be passive-dependent—i.e., reliant on others for direction and guidance —in his general work relationships.

And so on.

Analysts, of course, have just as much right to read between the lines as the next man. What makes their posture interesting is the claim that theirs is the scientific method. There are all the inevitable tables ("the biserial correlation for tenure on Worthington cutoff is 0.34") in which the accuracy of the internal mathematics is confused with the accuracy of the premises. There is the usual spurious humility: the authors caution that no single deduction is necessarily correct; it is only when all the deductions are fitted into a "formal, quantitative scoring procedure based on an organized system of psychodynamic factors" that they become correct. Add up enough wrongs, in short, and you get a right.

The analysis of J. J. Jones is a rather extreme example

but it leads us to a defect characteristic of all tests. Against what specifications is the man being measured? Assuming for the moment that we are able to diagram Jonathan Jones exactly, how are we to know the kind of work the diagram indicates he is suited for? There is not much point in testing people to find out if they will make good salesmen or executives unless we know what it is that makes the good ones good.

There are, of course, some fairly simple common denominators such as energy and intelligence, but beyond these we get into very muddy waters indeed. Is the executive, as is so often assumed, one who was more attached to his father than his mother? And what, for example, of the liking for other people that is supposed to be a key executive trait? Many successful executives are very gregarious, but a great many equally successful ones are not, and some are very cold fish. Conversely, are writers, research people, and the like necessarily introverts? One writer I know rather well was advised by a testing laboratory to go into clerical work and steer clear of writing. While he scored just slightly "introverted," the laboratory still felt that his score indicated enough enjoyment of the company of other people to prove him unsuited for writing. Another laboratory tells people whether they are good at communication by determining their "ability to write freely without blocking or searching for the right word or phrase." You are given a topic and so many minutes in which to write on it. No matter how much gibberish it may be, the more words you write on this glibness test the more "creative" you are rated to be.

Testers often admit their knowledge of personality requirements is still too sketchy, but they feel this can be cleared up by more testing. And thus we come to the "profile." Testers have been busy collating in chart form the personality scores of people in different occupations to reveal how they differ with other adult groups on particular personality traits. These comparisons are generally expressed as a "percentile" rating—if the total of thirty salesclerks' scores on sociability averages somewhere around the 80th percentile, for example, this indicates that the average salesclerk is more sociable than 79 out of 100 adults. With such data a man being considered for a particular kind of job can be matched against the master profile of the group. The closer he fits the better for him.

Profiles are also worked up for work in individual companies. At Sears, Roebuck there are charts that diagram the optimum balance of qualities required. Here is the one an executive values:

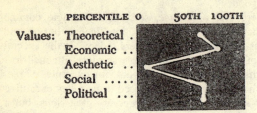

A man does not have to match this profile exactly, but it won't help him at all if his line zigs where the chart zags. Take a man who scores considerably higher than the 10th percentile on aesthetic values, for example; such people, Sears notes, "accept artistic beauty and taste as a fundamental standard of life. This is *not* a factor which makes for executive success. . . . Generally, cultural considerations are not important to Sears executives, and there is evidence that such interests are detrimental to success."

Sears has every right to de-emphasize certain qualities and emphasize others; and in hewing to this type, it should be noted, Sears has built up one of the most alert management groups in the country. But the process should not be confused with science. When tests are used as selection devices, they are not a neutral tool; *they become a large factor in the very equation they purport to measure.* For one thing, the tests tend to screen out—or repel—those who would upset the correlation. If a man can't get into the company in the first place because he isn't the company type, he can't very well get to be an executive in it and be tested in a study to find out what kind of profile subsequent executives should match. Long before personality tests were invented, of course, plenty of companies had proved that if you hire only people of a certain type, then all your successful men will be people of that type. But no one confused this with the immutable laws of science.

Bias doesn't have to be personal. Now it's institutionalized. For the profile is self-confirming; when it doesn't screen out those who fail to match it, it will mask the amount of deviance in the people who do pass. Few test takers can believe the flagrantly silly statement in the preamble to many tests that there are "no right or wrong answers." There wouldn't be much point in the company's giving the test if some answers weren't regarded as better than others. Telling the truth about yourself is difficult in any event. When someone is likely to reward you if you give answers favorable to yourself the problem of whether to tell the truth becomes more than insuperable; it becomes irrelevant. In this respect, let us give the tests their due; they may tell little about personality, but they do tell something about intelligence. "Do you daydream frequently?" In many companies a man either so honest or so stupid as to answer "yes" would be well advised to look elsewhere for employment.

Even when the man who should have looked elsewhere slips through, the profile will be self-confirming. For the profile molds as well as chooses; it is, as Sears puts it, a statement of "the kind of behavior we have found to be desirable." If he is going to get ahead, let alone survive, the man is going to have to adjust. Several years of give and take, and the organization will have smoothed him out, and thus when the psychologists do their "validating," or rechecking, later he will score near enough to the median to show them how right they were all along. At Sears psychologists retested employees about two and a half years after their first test. Of the thirteen personality factors they were investigating, nine showed a definite change. "All the factors," concluded Sears' V. C. Benz, "indicate a 'better' or more adequate psychological adjustment. . . . The individuals are better people."

Up to a point the company "type" has some virtue; any first-rate organization must have an *esprit de corps*, and this requires a certain degree of homogeneity. But the pitfalls are many, for while a self-confirming profile makes for a comfortable organization, it eventually can make for a static one. Even the largest corporations must respond to changes in the environment; a settled company may have its very existence threatened by technological advances unless it makes a bold shift to a new type of market. What, then, of the pruning and molding that adapted it so beautifully to its original environment? The dinosaur was a formidable animal.

The profile can be self-confirming for the individual too. For tests intensify a mutual deception we practice on one another. Who is "normal"? All of us to some degree have a built-in urge to adjust to what we conceive as the norm, and in our search we can come to feel that in the vast ocean of normality that surrounds us only we are different. We are the victims of one another's façades.

And now, with the norm formally enshrined in figures, we are more vulnerable than ever to this tyrant. "Science" seems its ally, and thus, faulty or not, the diagnosis can provoke a sense of guilt or inadequacy; for we can forget that the norm is often the result of the instinctive striving of previous test takers to answer as they think everyone else would answer.

If the organization man escapes the danger of self-tyranny he faces another. At first superiors may scoff at the diagnosis, but if they have been putting reliance on testing they have a stake themselves in the correctness. Suspicion, unfortunately, demands proof, and sometimes it so counterbalances judgment that unconsciously a management will punish the man so that faith in the tests may be confirmed. One large midwestern company was about to promote a man when it decided to have him take a test. The report that the consultant firm mailed back to the company was freighted with warnings about the man's stability. The company was puzzled. The man had consistently done a fine job. Still. . . . The more the company mused, the more worried it became; at last it decided to tell the man the promotion he had expected so long was going to someone else. Six months later, the company reports, the man had a nervous breakdown. As in all such stories, the company says what this proves is how accurate the test was.

Are the people who don't score well necessarily the misfits? Almost by definition the dynamic person is an exception—and where aptitude tests reward, personality tests often punish him. Look at a cross section of profiles and you will see three denominators shining through: extroversion, disinterest in the arts, and a cheerful acceptance of the status quo. Test scoring keys reveal the same bias. As I note in the Appendix, if you want to get a high score you will do well to observe these two rules:

(1) When asked for word associations or comments about the world, give the most conventional, run-of-the-mill, pedestrian answer possible.

(2) When in doubt about the most beneficial answer to any question, repeat to yourself:

> *I loved my father and my mother, but my*
> *father a little bit more.*
> *I like things pretty much the way*
> *they are.*
> *I never worry much about anything.*
> *I don't care for books or music much.*
> *I love my wife and children.*
> *I don't let them get in the way of*
> *company work.*

If you were this kind of person you wouldn't get very far, but, unfortunately, you won't get very far unless you can seem to be this kind. Check the norms and you will find that the advice is not flippant.[3] Norms are based on group scores, and as often as not the group turns out to have been 1,000 college freshmen, 400 high-school students, or some similarly less-than-outstanding aggregation. There

---

[3] Several who have followed this advice, I am glad to report, have profited well. One engineer who was asked by his company to take a battery of tests studied my trot and took the tests in the frame of mind recommended above. To his surprise, he shortly received quite a promotion. The company had found unsuspected depths of normalcy in him; as one executive later confided to him, the tests had eliminated certain doubts some had had about his personality. He has, incidentally, done very well in the new job.

are norms for selected groups like executives, chemists, and the like, and there will in time be more and more. But these can be illusory too. Usually, the norms are based on the responses of people who are being tested by The Organization; in such a situation self-preservation demands a certain circumspection in answering, and the norms are more a playback of what the people taking the tests think The Organization wants to hear rather than the reality of their own selves. Daydream? Of course not.

The sheer mechanics of the tests punish the exceptional man. A test with prefabricated answers is precisely the kind of test that people with superior intelligence find hardest to answer. Writing of the using of "objective." forced-choice college examinations, Jacques Barzun says in his *Teacher in America,* "I have kept track for some ten years of the effects of such tests on the upper half of each class. The best men go down one grade and the next best go up. It is not hard to see why. The second-rate do well in school and in life because of their ability to grasp what is accepted and conventional. . . . But first-rate men are rarer and equally indispensable. . . . To them, a ready-made question is an obstacle. It paralyzes thought by cutting off all connections but one. Or else it sets them to thinking and doubting whether *in that form* any of the possible answers really fits. Their minds have finer adjustments, more imagination, which the test deliberately penalizes as encumbrances."

If the reader has taken the test in the previous chapter he has probably come to the same conclusion about personality-test questions. How big was that fire in the house with the mother and child? What about the worker who wanted a promotion? Was he any good? Maybe the office did want the boss's nephew to get the job. These are not quibbles; they are the kind of questions that occur to the intelligent mind, and the ability to see shadings, to posit alternatives, is virtually indispensable to judgment, practical or otherwise.

How well do group averages fit the outstanding man? For a practical check my colleagues and I decided to do some testing of our own. What would happen, we wondered, if the presidents of some of our large corporations had to take the same tests their juniors do? We obtained a supply of test blanks and scoring keys for the principal tests and managed to persuade a dozen of the most well-known corporation leaders to take the tests and let us do the scoring. For good measure, we gave the same battery of tests to sixteen of the country's most brilliant scientists, and a condensed version to thirty-eight middle-management men who had been picked by their respective companies as outstanding for their age group.

When the tests were scored one thing became clear. If the tests were literally applied across the board today, tomorrow half of the most dynamic individuals in our big corporations would be out pounding the streets for a job. Here are the high lights of the test results.

(1) Not one corporation president had a profile that fell completely within the usual "acceptable" range, and two failed to meet the minimum profile for foremen. On the "How Supervise" questions, presidents on the average got only half the answers right, thus putting them well down in the lower percentiles. They did particularly badly on the questions concerning company employee-relations policies. Only three presidents answered more than half of these questions correctly.

(2) The scientists' Personal Audit profiles were more even than the presidents'—if anything, they scored as too contented, firm, and consistent. They did, however, show up as extremely misanthropic, over half falling under the 20th percentile for sociability.

(3) The middle-management executives scored well on stability and sociability, but on practical judgment only three reached the mean indicated for executive work.

(4) The range of scores was so great as to make a median figure relatively meaningless. On the Thurstone "S" score for sociability, for example, only eight of the forty-three management men fell between the 40th and the 60th percentiles, the remainder being grouped at either extreme.

(5) The scores were highly contradictory. Many of the same people who got high "steadiness" scores on the Per-

sonal Audit scored very badly for "stability" on the Thurstone test. Similarly, many who scored high on "contentment" had very low "tranquillity" scores.

One explanation for the variance between the men and the norms would be that the men in our sample were answering frankly—no job being at stake—and thus their scores could not be properly compared with the standard norms given. But if this is the case, then we would have to conclude that the norms themselves embody slanted answers. Another explanation of the men's poor showing would be that they scored low because they were in fact neurotic or maladjusted, as the tests said. But this would only leave us with a further anomaly. If people with an outstanding record of achievement show up as less well adjusted than the run of the mill, then how important a yardstick is adjustment? Our sample, of course, was small. So is the supply of outstandingly talented people.[4]

Not only do such people disturb the statistical equilibrium, they are the kind of people those of moderate ability frequently distrust. They always did, of course, but now they have a way of rationalizing the distrust; sometimes it seems almost as though they were joined together in a great League of the Mediocre against those who would confound them. The specifications for research people are a case in point. In picking those to be advanced to leadership, some management experts seem to go out of their way to pick the mediocre almost for their mediocrity, as if brilliance in a field disqualifies one for leadership. "When we're looking for a guy to be made a research director," says one consultant, "we try to find a guy who's just a fair chemist but whose test indicates potential leadership qualities. We'd sooner push him up than a guy who is a top chemist but

[4] Management consultant Robert N. McMurry: "Large organizations in particular have a very specific attraction to those with an unusual need for security and so come to have a disproportionate share, a supersaturation, of the passive, dependent, and submissive. This condition would not be such a threat to the morale and organizational integrity of an enterprise if it were recognized for what it is and its implications understood. But this is rarely the case." (*Harvard Business Review*, January-February 1954.)

only an average leader." Sometimes, the consultant adds, they can salvage an introvert. "When we spot a guy with a score like that, we single him out for counseling. Once in a while we're able to make the man over."

A record of achievement is no defense. What a person has actually done over a long period of time would seem to be the single most valuable indication of how he will perform in the future. But a record is not measurable; unlike a forced-choice answer, it cannot be reduced into statistical form, and thus the more anxious an organization is for certainty, the less attention does it pay to past performance. The fault here is management's, it should be noted, more than the psychologists', for management often asks them to deliver much more definite recommendations than they are willing to certify. Even the management consultants, whose chief competence is supposed to be personnel evaluation, frequently farm out the decisions about their own hiring to testing firms.

The study of a man's past performance, the gauging of him in the personal interview are uncertain guides. But they are still the key, and the need is not to displace them but to become more skilled with them. The question of who will be best in a critical situation cannot be determined scientifically before the event. No matter how much information we may amass, we must rely on judgment, on intuition, on the particulars of the situation—and the more demanding the situation the less certain can we be of prediction. It is an immensely difficult task, perhaps the most difficult one that any management faces. But the question cannot be fed into a computer, nor can it be turned over by proxy for someone else to decide, and any management that so evades its most vital function needs some analysis of its own.

Finally, let us suppose that the tests could in fact reveal the innermost self. Would they even then be justified? The moral basis of testing has been tabled in this discussion, but it is the paramount issue. Were the tests truly scientific, their effectiveness would make the ultimate questions more pressing, not less. Is the individual's innermost self any business of the organization's? He has some rights too. Our society has taught him to submit to many things; thousands of civilians who went into the military meekly stood naked in long lines waiting for their numbered turn in the mass physical examinations. Many civilians who have been asked to work on government projects have submitted to being fingerprinted and to the certainty that government agents would soon be puzzling their friends and neighbors with questions about their backgrounds. But in these cases a man can console himself that there is a reason; that if he is to enjoy the benefits of collective effort he must also pay some price.

But there is a line. How much more must a man testify against himself? The Bill of Rights should not stop at organization's edge. In return for the salary that The Organization gives the individual, it can ask for superlative work from him, but it should not ask for his psyche as well. If it does, he must withhold. Sensibly—the bureaucratic way is too much with most of us that he can flatly refuse to take tests without hurt to himself. But he can cheat. He must. Let him respect himself.

PART FIVE

The Organization Scientist

CHAPTER SIXTEEN

The Fight against Genius

SUPPOSE for the moment that you were given this mental exercise: without knowing anything about how scientists work today, you were to imagine what would happen if the Social Ethic were applied to science as it has been in the rest of organization life. The chances are that you would imagine, among other things, that: (1) scientists would now concentrate on the practical application of previously discovered ideas rather than the discovery of new ones; (2) they would rarely work by themselves but rather as units of scientific cells; (3) organization loyalty, getting along with people, etc. would be considered just as important as thinking; (4) well-rounded team players would be more valuable than brilliant men, and a very brilliant man would probably be disruptive. Lastly and most important, these things would be so because people believe this is the way it should be.

Well? Of the $4 billion currently being spent on research and development by government, industry, and the universities, only about $150 million—or less than 4 per cent—is for creative research. The overwhelming majority of people engaged in research, furthermore, must now work as supervised team players, and only a tiny fraction are in a position to do independent work. Of the 600,000 people engaged in scientific work, it has been estimated that probably no more than 5,000 are free to pick their own problems.

And this is because people think it should be so. In the current orgy of self-congratulation over American technical progress, it is the increasing collectivization of research that is saluted. Occasionally the individual greats of the past are saluted, but it is with a subtle twist that manages to make them seem team researchers before their time. In the popular ideology, science means applying ideas; knowing *how*, not asking why.

We have indeed been very good at applying basic ideas. It is our natural bent to be good at exploitation. It is also our natural bent to recognize too late the necessity for replenishing that which we exploit. We have never had a strong tradition of basic science in this country and now, even less than before, we do not seem to care about creating new ideas—the ideas which thirty or forty years from now would nourish the technological advances we so confidently expect.

So far only a few people have had the nerve to come out flatly against the independent researcher, but the whole tenor of organization thinking is unmistakably in that direction. Among Americans there is today a widespread conviction that science has evolved to a point where the lone man engaged in fundamental inquiry is anachronistic, if not fundamental inquiry itself. Look, we are told, how the atom bomb was brought into being by the teamwork of huge corporations of scientists and technicians. Occasionally somebody mentions in passing that what an eccentric old man with a head of white hair did back in his study forty years ago had something to do with it. But people who concede this point are likely to say that this merely proves that basic ideas aren't the problem any more. It's nice to have ideas and all that, sure, but it's American know-how that does something with them, and anyway there are plenty of ideas lying fallow. We don't really need any more ivory-tower theorizing; what we need is more funds, more laboratory facilities, more organization.

The case for more fundamental inquiry has been argued so eloquently by scientists that there is little the layman can contribute in this respect. My purpose in these next three chapters, however, is not to add an amen, though this is in order, but to demonstrate the relationship between the scientist and the management trends I have been discussing in other contexts. The parallels between the organization man and the scientist should not be drawn too closely; their functions are not alike and between the managerial outlook and the scientific there is a basic conflict in goals that is not to be smothered by optimism.

I do not say this in qualification of my argument. It is my argument. For the fact is that the parallels are being drawn too closely, and in a profoundly mistaken analogy The Organization is trying to mold the scientist to its own image; indeed, it sees the accomplishment of this metamorphosis as the main task in the management of research. It may succeed.

Let us look first at the corporation's laboratories. On the surface the corporation would seem to be on the verge of becoming one of the most enlightened of patrons. $1.6 billion of America's total research budget is now concentrated in the great laboratories that corporations have been building up, and proportionately as well as in absolute dollars this is a greater investment in research than industry has ever made before. As industry points out, one result is going to be a speeding up of the production of tangibly better things for more people. But the price may be steep. If corporations continue to mold scientists the way they are now doing, it is entirely possible that in the long run this huge apparatus may actually slow down the rate of basic discovery it feeds on.

Let us ask a brutal question. How good are the corporations' scientists? In the past industry has had many brilliant ones—Langmuir, Steinmetz, Carothers, and many others. But does it have them now? My colleague Francis Bello did a study of young scientists which yielded some very surprising figures. To get a representative group of young scientists, he set out to get nominations of the men under forty in both industry and universities who were thought to be among the most promising. He went first to the foundations and such government agencies as the Office of Naval Research and the Atomic Energy Commission, for it is their business to know who the top men are.

When the many duplications in the names nominated were eliminated, Bello found he had the names of 225 young scientists. He had expected that the nominations would probably split between industry and the universities about half and half. To his amazement, however, he found that only four of the 225 names were of men in industry.

Fearing that the sample was too biased, Bello went directly to the directors of leading corporation laboratories and asked them for nominations. He also asked the top academic scientists to think of scientists in industry and name any they thought top rank.

After all this effort, only thirty-five were forthcoming. Outside of some of their own subordinates, corporation research directors were hard put to it to think of anybody else in their field in industry worth naming—and so were the university people. Most industrial scientists, Bello had to conclude, don't know one another, nor are they known by anybody else.

Two laboratories stood out. In all, there were only seven in which at least two men were nominated as outstanding and in which one man had at least two votes. Of these, General Electric and Bell Laboratories had almost as many men nominated as the other five put together. (The other five: Merck, I.B.M., Lederle, Eastman Kodak, and Shell Development Corporation.)

The chemical industry—the industry that has spent more money on research than any other—fared particularly badly. No scientist in Du Pont was named more than once, and except for American Cyanamid, no one in the other leading chemical firms was named at all. As for discovery, Bello found that chemists could think of only one new chemical reaction discovered by an American chemical company during the last fifteen years.

It is to be expected that industry should spend far less of its time on fundamental research than the universities, and for the same reason it is to be expected that the most outstanding men would tend to stay in the universities. But when all this is said and done, the fact remains that industry has a disproportionately small share of top men.

Why? The failure to recognize the virtue of purposelessness is the starting point of industry's problem. To the managers and engineers who set the dominant tone in industry, purposelessness is anathema, and all their impulses incline them to highly planned, systematized development in which the problem is clearly defined. This has its values. If researchers want to make a practical application of previous discovery—if a group at GM's Technical Center want a better oil for a high-compression engine, for example—they do best by addressing themselves to the stipulated task. In pure research, however, half the trick is in finding out *that there is a problem*—that there is something to explain. The culture dish remained sterile when it shouldn't have. The two chemicals reacted differently this time than before. Something has happened and you don't know why it happened—or if you did, what earthly use it would be?

By its very nature, discovery has an accidental quality. Methodical as one can be in following up a question, the all-important question itself is likely to be a sort of chance distraction of the work at hand. At this moment you neither know what practical use the question could lead to nor should you worry the point. There will be time enough later for that; and in retrospect, it will be easy to show how well planned and systematized the discovery was all along.

Rationalize curiosity too early, however, and you kill it. In the case of the scientist it is not merely that he finds it difficult to foresee what it will prove at the cash register; the sheer act of having to address himself to this or, as management would put it, the $64 question, dampens his original curiosity—and the expectation that the company will ask him to do it is just as dampening as the actual demand. The result is a net loss, not postponement, for if the scientist is inhibited from seizing the idle question at the time, it is not easily recaptured later. Like the nice gestures we so often think of and so often forget to do, many a question that would have led to great discoveries has died as quickly as it was born; the man was too busy to pause for it.

If ever there were proof of the virtues of free research, General Electric and Bell Labs provide it. Consider three facts about them: (1) of all corporation research groups these two have been the two outstandingly profitable ones; (2) of all corporation research groups these two have consistently attracted the most brilliant men. Why? The third fact explains the other two. *Of all corporation research groups these two are precisely the two that believe in "idle curiosity."* In them the usual chronology is often reversed; instead of demanding of the scientists that they apply themselves to a practical problem, they let the scientists follow the basic problems they want to follow. If the scientists come up with something they then look around to see what practical problem the finding might apply to. The patience is rewarded. The work of GE's Irving Langmuir in heated solids, for example, eventually led to a new kind of incandescent lamp; similarly, the recent, and highly abstract, work of Bell Labs' Claude Shannon in communication theory is already proving to be a mine of highly practical applications.

The few notable successes elsewhere follow the same pattern. The succession of synthetic fibers that have made so much money for the Du Pont Company sprang from the curiosity of one man—Wallace Hume Carothers. Carothers did not start out to make nylon. When Du Pont ran across him he was working on molecular structure at Harvard. While the result was eminently practical for Du Pont, for Carothers it was essentially a by-product of the experimental work he had started at Harvard rather than an end in itself. The company's interest was the final product, but it got it only because Carothers had the freedom to pursue what would today seem to many mere scientific boondoggling.

These successes are disheartening. There is nothing at all new in the research philosophy that led to them; both GE and Bell Labs established their basic procedures several generations ago, and their pre-eminence has been commercially apparent for as long. Yet with these models before them, U.S. industry has not only failed to draw any lessons, it has been moving further and further in the opposite direction.

By their own statements of policy the majority of corporations make it plain that they wish to keep their researchers' eyes focused closely on the cash register. Unlike GE or Bell Labs, they discourage their scientists, sometimes forbid them, from publishing the results of their work in the learned journals or communicating them in any way to scientists outside the company preserve. More inhibiting, most corporations do not let their scientists devote more than a fraction of their time following up problems of their own choosing, and this fraction is treated more as a sort of indulgence than an activity worth while in its own right. "It is our policy," one research director says, "to permit our men to have *as much as* 5 to 10 per cent of their time to work on anything they feel would be of interest." (Italics are mine.)

Even this pitiably small fraction is begrudged. Lest scientists interpret "free" work too freely, company directives imply strongly that it would be very fine if what the scientist is curious about during this recess coincides with what the organization is curious about. In "Research: The Long View," Standard Oil of New Jersey explains its policy thus:

The researchers, as a matter of long-range policy, are encouraged, when circumstances permit, to give something like 10 per cent of their time to "free research"—that is, work not currently part of a formal project. [The company] finds, however, that when its research people are kept well informed about the broad areas in which the company's needs and interests lie, a man's independent as well as his closely directed work both tend to have the same objectives. (The Lamp, *June 1954.*)

To some management people the desire to do "free" work is a downright defect—a symptom of maladjustment that demands cure, not coddling. When a man wants to follow his own hunch, they believe, this is a warning that he is not "company-oriented." The solution? Indoctrination. In "Personnel Practices in Industrial Laboratories" (*Personnel,* May 1953) Lowell Steele puts the issue squarely. "Unless the firm wants to subsidize idle curiosity on the part of its scientists," he says, "it must aid them in becoming 'company-conscious.'" Company loyalty, in other words, is not only more important than idle curiosity; it helps *prevent* idle curiosity.

The administrators are perfectly correct. If they get scientists to be good company men like other normal people, they won't be bothered much by scientists' following their curiosity. The policy will keep out that kind of scientist. For what is the dominant characteristic of the outstanding scientist? Every study has shown that it is a fierce independence.

In her study of eminent scientists, psychologist Anne Roe found that what decided them on their career almost invariably was a college project in which they were given free rein to find things out for themselves, without direction, and once the joys of freedom were tasted, they never lost the appetite. The most important single factor in the making of a scientist, she concludes, is "the need and ability to develop personal independence to a high degree. The independence factor is emphasized by many other findings: the subjects' preference for teachers who let them alone, their attitudes toward religion . . . their satisfaction in a career in which, for the most part, they follow their own interests without direction or interference." (*Scientific American*, Nov. 1952.)

In the outstanding scientist, in short, we have almost the direct antithesis of the company-oriented man. If the company wants a first-rate man it must recognize that his allegiance must always be to his work. For him, organization can be only a vehicle. What he asks of it is not big money —significantly, Bell Labs and GE have not had to pay higher salaries than other research organizations to attract talent. Nor is it companionship, or belongingness. What he asks is the freedom to do what he wants to do.

For its part, The Organization can ask only so much in return. The Organization and he have come together because its long-range interests happen to run parallel with what he wants to do. It is in this, his work, that The Organization's equity in him lies. Only one *quid pro quo* can it properly ask for the money that it gives him. It can ask that he work magnificently. It cannot ask that he love The Organization as well.

And what difference would it make if he did? The management man is confusing his own role with that of the scientist. To the management man such things as The Organization and human relations are at the heart of his job, and in unconscious analogy he assumes that the same thing applies to the scientist, if perhaps in lesser degree. These things are irrelevant to the scientist—he works *in* an organization rather than for it. But this the administrator cannot conceive; he cannot understand that a man can dislike the company—perhaps even leave in disgust after several years—and still have made a net contribution to the company cash register infinitely greater than all of his better-adjusted colleagues put together.

Thus, searching for their own image, management men look for the "well-rounded" scientists. They don't expect them to be quite as "well rounded" as junior-executive trainees; they generally note that scientists are "different." They do it, however, in a patronizing way that implies that the difference is nothing that a good indoctrination program won't fix up. Customarily, whenever the word *brilliant* is used, it either precedes the word *but* (cf. "We are all for brilliance, but . . .") or is coupled with such words as *erratic, eccentric, introvert, screwball,* etc. To quote Mr. Steele again, "While industry does not ignore the brilliant but erratic genius, in general it perfers its men to have 'normal' personalities. As one research executive explained, 'These fellows will be having contact with other people in the organization and it helps if they make a good impression. They participate in the task of "selling" research.' "

By insisting on this definition of well-roundedness, management makes two serious errors. For one thing, it seems to assume that the pool of brilliant scientists is so large that it can afford to consider only those in the pool who are well-rounded. There is, of course, no such over-supply; even if there were, furthermore, no such pat division could be made. For brilliance and the kind of well-roundedness management asks are a contradiction in terms. Some brilliant scientists are gregarious, to be sure, and some are not—but gregariousness is incidental to the harmony management is so intent upon. A brilliant scientist can enjoy playing on the company bowling team and still do brilliant and satisfying work. But there is no causal relationship. If the company makes him drop what he wants to do for something he doesn't, he may still enjoy playing on the company softball team, may even lead it to victory in the interurban championships. But at the same time he is doing it he may be pondering how exactly to word his resignation. The extracurricular will not have sublimated his frustration; and for all his natural amiability, in the place where it counts—the laboratory—his behavior will very quickly show it. Quite truly, he has become maladjusted.

He couldn't do otherwise. Management has tried to adjust the scientist to The Organization rather than The Organization to the scientist. It can do this with the mediocre and still have a harmonious group. It cannot do it with the brilliant; only freedom will make them harmonious. Most corporations sense this, but, unfortunately, the moral they draw from it is something else again. A well-known corporation recently passed up the opportunity to hire one of the most brilliant chemists in the country. They wanted his brilliance, but they were afraid that he might "disrupt our organization." Commenting on this, a fellow scientist said, "He certainly would disrupt the organization. He is a man who would want to follow his own inclinations. In a laboratory which understood fundamental research, he wouldn't disrupt the organization because they would want him to follow his own inclinations. But not in this one."

Even when companies recognize that they are making a choice between brilliance and mediocrity, it is remarkable how excruciating they find the choice. Several years ago my colleagues and I listened to the management of an electronics company hold a post-mortem on a difficult decision they had just made. The company had been infiltrated by genius. Into their laboratory three years before had come a very young, brilliant man. He did magnificent work and the company looked for even greater things in the future. But, though he was a likable fellow, he was imaginative and he had begun to chafe at the supervision of the research director. The director, the management said, was a rather run-of-the-mill sort, though he had worked loyally and congenially for the company. Who would have to be sacrificed? Reluctantly, the company made its decision. The brilliant man would have to go. The management was unhappy about the decision but they argued that harmonious group thinking (this was the actual word they used) was the company's prime aim, and if they had promoted the brilliant man it would have upset the whole chain of company interpersonal relationships. What else, they asked plaintively, could they have done?

Listening to some of industry's pronouncements, one would gather that it is doing everything possible to ward off the kind of brilliant people who would force such a choice. Here, in this excerpt from a Socony-Vacuum Oil Company booklet on broad company policy, is a typical warning:

No Room for Virtuosos

Except in certain research assignments, few specialists in a large company ever work alone. There is little room for virtuoso performances. Business is so complex, even in its non-technical aspects, that no one man can master all of it; to do his job, therefore, he must be able to work with other people.

The thought is put even more forcibly in a documentary film made for the Monsanto Chemical Company. The film, which was made to inspire young men to go into chemistry, starts off in the old vein. You see young boys dreaming of adventure in faraway places as they stand by the station in a small town and watch the trains roll by. Eventually the film takes us to Monsanto's laboratories. We see three young men in white coats talking to one another. The voice on the sound track rings out: "No geniuses here; just a bunch of average Americans working together."

This was no mere slip of the script writer's pencil. I had a chance later to ask a Monsanto executive why the company felt impelled to claim to the world that its brainwork was carried on by just average Americans. The executive explained that Monsanto had thought about the point and wanted to deter young men from the idea that industrial chemistry was for genius types.

At the very moment when genius types couldn't agree more, the timing hardly seems felicitous. It could be argued, of course, that since the most brilliant stay in the universities anyway, management's barriers against genius would be at worst unnecessary. But it is not this clear-cut; whether or not they have geniuses, companies like Monsanto do not have their research work carried on by just average Americans, and if they did the stockholders would do well to complain. As Bell Labs and General Electric prove, there are many brilliant men who will, given the right circumstances, find industrial research highly absorbing. For company self-interest, let alone society's, a management policy that repels the few is a highly questionable one.

Society would not be the loser if the only effect on management policy were to make the most brilliant stay in the university. This screening effect, however, is only one consequence of management's policy. What concerns all of us, just as much as industry, is the fact that management also has a very powerful molding effect on the people it does get. They may not all be geniuses, but many are highly capable men, and in the right climate they could make great contributions.

That management is not only repelling talent but smothering it as well is told by management's own complaints. Privately, many of the same companies which stress team play criticize their young Ph.D.s for not being interested enough in creative work—or, to put it in another way, are a bunch of just good average Americans working together. "Practically all who are now Ph.D.s want to be told what to do," one research leader has complained. "They seem to be scared to death to think up problems of their own." Another research leader said that when his firm decided to let its chemists spend up to 25 per cent of their time on "free" work, to the company's surprise hardly any of the men took up the offer.

But it shouldn't be surprising. A company cannot bring in young men and spend several years trying to make them into one kind of person, and then expect them, on signal, to be another kind. Cram courses in "brainstorming" and applied creativity won't change them. If the company indoctrinates them in the bureaucratic skills and asks them to keep their minds on the practical, it cannot suddenly stage a sort of creative play period and then, on signal, expect them to be like somebody else.

In any person a native ability cannot remain very long dormant without atrophying, but this is particularly true in the case of the scientist. Compared to people in other fields, scientists characteristically reach their peak very early in their careers. If the climate is stultifying the young scientist will rarely be vouchsafed a chance later to make up for the sterility of his early years. "It is the effect on the few first-rate men you find in industrial labs that is noticeable," says Burleigh Gardner, of Social Research, Inc. "The most able men generally rise to the top. But how high up the top is depends so much on the environment you put them in. In the average kind of corporation laboratory we have studied, the force of the majority opinion makes them divert their energies to a critical degree. I doubt if any of them could ever break through the group pressures to get up to the blue sky, where the great discoveries are made."

In a perverse way there is one small advantage to society in the big corporation's research policy. If corporation policy inhibits the scientist, it inhibits the flow of really good ideas that will aggrandize the corporation, and this lack may eventually prove a deterrent to overcentralization.

Those who see the growing concentration of technology in Big Business as irrevocable argue that advances are no longer possible except with the huge laboratories and equipment which only the big corporations can afford. But this is not true. For some scientific ends elaborate facilities—cyclotrons for physicists, ships for oceanographers—are necessary means. But this is only part of the picture; historically, almost every great advance has been made by one man with a minimum of equipment—sometimes just paper and pencil—and though this is more true of fundamental research, it is true of applied research as well. Go down the list of commercial inventions over the last thirty years: *with very few exceptions the advances did not come from a cor-*

poration laboratory. Kodachrome, for example, was perfected in Eastman's huge laboratories but was invented by two musicians in a bathroom. The jet engine is an even clearer case in point. As Launcelot Law Whyte points out, none of the five earliest turbo-jet developments of Germany, Britain, and the United States was initiated within an established aircraft firm. "It is usually the relatively isolated outsider," Whyte says, "who produces the greatest novelties. It is a platitude, but it is often neglected."

Because it is small, the small firm has one potential advantage over the big one. It can't afford big research teams to administrate or interlocking committees to work up programs, and it doesn't have a crystallized company "family" to adjust to. Because it hasn't caught up yet with modern management, to put it another way, it provides an absence of the controls that make the scientist restive. Few small corporations have seized the opportunity, and at this writing there is no sign they ever will. But the opportunity is there.

CHAPTER SEVENTEEN

The Bureaucratization of the Scientist

LET's turn now from the corporation to academia, for here we can more clearly see the root of the problem. If the academic scientist is seduced, it cannot be explained away as Babbitt versus the intellectual, the pressures of commercialism, or the managers' misunderstanding of science. Nor can it be blamed on want of talent; there may not be enough quantity, but every man-power survey has shown that so far as quality is concerned, science has been attracting the top slice of our youth.

Yet every one of the trends to be found in corporation research can be found in academic research, and with consequences far greater. There is the same bent to applied rather than fundamental research, the same bent to large team projects, the same bent to highly systematized planning, to committees and programs. Like his brother in management, the scientist is becoming an organization man.

To say that the incubus lies in organization itself would be partially correct, but it would also be somewhat futile. Must the metamorphosis of the scientist be inevitable? The shift from the entrepreneurial to the administrative has been to a large degree a necessary response to the needs of our times, and science cannot remain isolated from it. But it is not the fact of bureaucratization itself that is the central problem. The central problem is the *acceptance* of it. In no field, except the arts, does the elevation of administrative values hold more dangers, yet in this respect science is not even fighting a holding action. To the contrary, the people in the foundations and the universities are reinforcing these values, and by reinforcing them, further molding the scientists to the organization image. Not purposely, no, but this makes it only the worse.

Fundamental versus applied research? It is a truism among American scientists that we have lacked a strong tradition in fundamental research, that we have been borrowing our ideas from Europe, that we can no longer count on the flow of scientific immigrants from abroad, that we urgently need, in short, to create a climate in this country that will encourage basic discovery. And every year, much as in the businessman's plea for the humanities, ideal and practice grow further apart. Of the roughly four billion dollars now being spent on scientific research in this country, approximately 95 per cent is for applied research.

The government has become the major patron, for almost half the research money available in the U.S. is in the form of contracts given out by government agencies, principally the Atomic Energy Commission and the Office of Naval Research. Some very enlightened men have directed these agencies, and considering the pressures under which they must work—secrecy requirements, the need to justify research in terms of national defense—most scientists believe they have fought a very good fight. But they have been able to go only so far; under the watchful eye of Congress, they have spent roughly 93 per cent of the total $5.6 billion distributed in 1953, 1954, and 1955 on applied rather than fundamental research. There has been slight improvement; in 1955 the proportion devoted to fundamental research went up to 7.3 per cent (from 6.6 per cent in 1954).

It can be argued that the proportion is not crucial, because the government sums are now so huge that there is more, in absolute dollars, available for fundamental work. But the proportion *is* crucial. The government monies have not been simply an addition to regular academic research; they have altered the whole structure of it. The universities once conceived themselves as sanctuaries for fundamental work, but the magnetic attraction of government funds has been irresistible.

As the universities have accepted more research contracts, they have relinquished control over the direction of research. The government sets the tune; committees responsible to it specify the problems, pass on the work, and appoint the personnel. The universities provide the setting and the essential housekeeping services. University scientists still do most of the research, but increasingly the allegiance of many is to the "research center," a quasi-academic institution which draws its heat and light from the university, its directions from elsewhere.

The wartime demands of patriotism that justified such diversions to the universities are now gone, but the growth has kept feeding on itself, amoebalike. The more such centers there are in a university, the more likely the university is to get additional contracts, and as a result there has been a concentration of research energy more pronounced than in the corporations. Of the 225 colleges and universities receiving research contracts five have received about as much money as the other 220 put together.

Government research directors themselves have been somewhat disturbed by the acquiescence of the universities. A man well qualified to speak on the matter, E. N. Piore, former Director of the Office of Naval Research, has publicly argued that the universities should look far more zealously to their own interests and bargain well over the conditions on which they will accept money from government, and industry too, for that matter. "The universities," he puts it simply, "have got to stiffen their backbones."

Individual versus collective work? The marked shift to group work is closely related to the emphasis on the applied, for such research puts a premium on highly directed, cooperative effort. It is also related to the wartime "project" approach, and, hopefully, some observers believe that the impulse may therefore soon be on the wane. But there is, unfortunately, more to it than that. The war undoubtedly was a factor, but it only accentuated a trend to collective research long in the making.

The learned journals furnish a yardstick. Look at the issues of thirty or forty years ago and it is difficult to find a paper worked up by more than one man—or, at least, signed by more than one. This is true no longer, and a check of the way group authorship has increased demonstrates that it has not been a sudden, wartime phenomenon but a generational shift.

As a rough index, I have checked all of the papers published in six social-science journals for three periods: The years 1920-22, 1936-38, and 1953-55. With the exception of the *American Economic Review,* in all of the journals there was a notable increase in the number of papers written by two people, and there was an even sharper increase in the number written by teams of three, four, five, or more. No one, of course, can specify any "right" proportion, which in any event would vary from discipline to discipline —applied psychologists, for example, must of necessity do more group work than political scientists. The basic trend, however, transcends disciplinary lines; a considerable increase has been common to all, and though the rate of increase jumped after the mid-thirties, the change in fashion had already started in each of the disciplines.

The chart on the facing page indicates the increase the journals show in papers done by two or more authors. (Chart is based on regular papers; I have excluded short notes, book reviews, and annual proceedings.)

In the physical sciences, the increases have been even sharper. Dr. George P. Bush of American University checked the technical articles appearing in *Science* for the years 1921, 1936, and 1951 to find what trend there had been away from individual authorship. In 1921, he found, 85 per cent of the papers were written by one man, all by himself, and none of the others was written by more than two men. By 1936 only 41 per cent were by one man; 46 per cent were by two men, and there were now beginning to be more multi-man papers: 9 per cent by three; 3 per cent by four men; 1 per cent by five. By 1951 the proportion of papers done by one man was down to 36 per cent, 38 per cent were by two and a good 26 per cent were by three or more men.

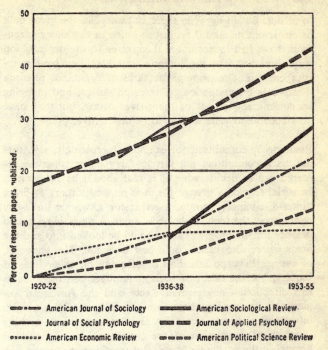

Percent of research papers published.

1920-22   1936-38   1953-55

- - - American Journal of Sociology   ▬▬ American Sociological Review
——— Journal of Social Psychology   ▬ ▬ Journal of Applied Psychology
········ American Economic Review   ═ ═ ═ American Political Science Review

Some argue that these curves don't show an increase in group work so much as an increase in frankness about it; where senior men used to hog the whole show, this argument goes, they are now more disposed to give due credit to associates who work with them. Whether this is true—or whether, as others would argue, it is now a case of the senior man riding his subordinates' backs—the increases still reflect a significant shift in the climate. Group work is fashionable, and if people are franker, it is because the climate almost compels them to be.

It is not that there has been an increase in the kind of people by nature suited to group work. The change has been in the *environment* of research, and its molding effect is felt by all. In degree, of course, there are great differences. The outstanding genius would not prostrate himself before the group; the mediocre would do it whether anyone asked him to or not. But in between these extremes lies the great bulk of our scientists, and they, just as much as the junior executives, have had to acclimate themselves to the organization way. And just like the junior executives, they have overcompensated. The principal features of organized research —emphasis on methodology, research design, and planning by committee—are not of themselves wrong, but they have now become so venerated as to be destructive.

Planning by committee, for example. Increasingly, scientists are using committees not just to carry on or supervise research but to decide what it is that should be researched. In social science, for example, it is now customary to bring "inter-disciplinary" groups together for a two- or three-day conference, the fruit of which is a paper indicating a rough priority for the problems that should be looked into and the areas where discoveries could best be made. The scientists, of course, have no intention of blocking off other lines of inquiry, but the effect of such committees can often be in this direction. Congressman Reece and the American Legion notwithstanding, these committees do not form a tight, interlocking directorate; they are, by and large, nothing more than a reflection of the concentrations of influence normal in the academic world. But for that very reason, the ambitious younger man—and scientists are just as ambitious as anybody else—takes his cues from these guides, and those who prefer to look into questions unasked by others need a good bit of intellectual fortitude to do so.

In stating the problems to be attacked, fund-givers overlook the fact that the first-rate man has a prior intellectual commitment. Occasionally this intellectual commitment will mesh accidentally with the project, but more often the project will divert him from his real interest. Recently, twenty top men in a particular field were brought together to hear the chairman of a great fund describe its plans for the future. One of the scientists recalls the feeling of unease that spread among them. "I knew most of them and I knew that about eight of them were on the verge of some really important work. But the chairman gave no indication that he was at all interested in what they had done before. He talked about starting fresh; all his plans were for new projects, new questions. He meant very well, but we couldn't help but feel that the work he was going to finance would be in the long run a net subtraction."

In stating the problems, the committees are usurping the basic role of the scientist. How do they know that theirs is the problem to be attacked? In applied as well as basic science, many advances have succeeded because they bypassed the problems the majority thought were most pressing. When Frank Whittle first presented his idea for a jet engine, he was met with a massive indifference from the scientific bureaucracy; they were interested in new problems, but the kind of new problems they were interested in were better pistons, improved propellers, and the like. For the very reason that his idea was brilliant, it failed to mesh with the ideas of the fund-givers of the time, and it got support only because a few men, like Launcelot Law Whyte, decided to back the man. "There is a clue here of wide significance," says Whyte. "The most fertile new ideas are those which transcend established, specialized methods and treat some new problem as a single task. . . . Co-operative groups, from great industrial concerns to small research teams, inevitably tend to rely on what is already acceptable as common ground, and that means established, specialized techniques."

Here is one activity where committee *expertise* is an obstacle. In a committee which must "produce" something, the members must feel a strong impulse toward consensus. But if that something is to be a map of the unknown country, there can hardly be consensus on anything except the most obvious. Something really bold and imaginative is by its nature divisive, and the bigger the committee, the more people are likely to be offended.

At this vital moment, the moral responsibility one feels to his colleagues becomes a downright hindrance. A committee member might be inclined to support an idea, but he is also not inclined to put up the fight for it that will be needed. He is constrained by good will. He feels an obligation to his fellow committeemen, who are, after all, only trying to do a good job, like himself. So he compromises, not from mere timidity but from a real desire to show respect for the opinion of others. Even if he has trouble mustering up the respect in some cases, his good will may make him feign it. He has immediate social as well as professional considerations to think of, and throughout any meeting there runs a tacit dialogue that often has very little to do with the ideas being discussed. Who won the last argument? Is this wrangling going to shove us into a night meeting? We voted down Professor So-and-So the last two times; aren't we being a little hard on him? When the minutes get written up, this groping for consensus is left out, but the thin, gray residue is not.

There are a few other activities where committees are even less desirable, but the use of them has become so reflex that the thought of using individuals is hardly even considered. If you want a candid appraisal of a group's performance, a committee is about the most ineffective vehicle, much less a committee composed of the members of the club. Presumably, the virtues of participation offset the inhibitions, and the self-study group has now become a fixture. In a recent test of this principle, the Ford Foundation gave $50,000 apiece to each of five universities for a self-study of their work in the behavioral sciences. For a year, committees and subcommittees and visiting committees met and correlated, and at length five massive documents were produced. The result was thoroughly conventional: in most cases, the really tough issues were noted rather than explored, and the strong implication was that few things were wrong that more financial support couldn't cure. The only trenchant analysis that $250,000 produced was a supplementary report. It was written by one man.

Companion to the team project and planning by committee is the blight of "research design." Instead of being joined together in a flexible arrangement which allows the scientist to follow his own side roads, project members are bound up in a highly detailed, prefabricated master plan of research. In highly applied or urgent research, like making a radar, this discipline is valuable in keeping people focused on the matter in hand, and in any research some coherence and direction is necessary. Too much, however, and the scientist is kept focused on the outward and, in many respects, secondary matters.

To the academic administrator, these are not secondary. The administrators are necessary men, sometimes wise ones, but there is nonetheless an antithesis between the virtues dear to the administrator's heart and the conditions of discovery. Order, clearly outlined direction, precise reporting, tidiness—all these things that are so important in housekeeping and organization are the very things which can make one bridle at the aimless, messy, out-of-program, trivial curiosity that is so wonderfully practical.

As a scientist, the administrator or committeeman knows well the value of unfettered inquiry. But he is now something of a supervisor as well, and one of the most difficult things for a supervisor to do is not to supervise. In fund-giving the opportunities for close supervision are narrow; the only place where the committeeman can have any leeway to pull his oar is in the area of research design. A scientist who has sat on many grant committees, Johns Hopkins's Curt Richter, put the problem to his colleagues this way:

We pick out the one tangible part of the application—the experimental design—how the man plans to work out his project. We are asking more and more questions. Aware of this, applicants elaborate their designs in more and more detail. A vicious cycle has set in. In making application for a grant before World War II, a few lines or at most a paragraph or two sufficed for the experimental design; now it may extend over six to eight single-spaced typewritten pages. And even then committee members may come back to ask for more details. Under these circumstances, passing the buck has come to be practiced very widely. Projects are passed from committee to committee—to my knowledge, in one instance six committees—largely because at no place along the line did anyone believe that he had adequate information to come to a firm decision.

In part, research design is due to a positive quality in the scientist turned administrator. He wants to be constructive. Many feel uncomfortable playing the passive role of middleman of funds; to fully discharge their responsibility, they feel they themselves should play an active role. They should initiate a new line of inquiry, list the problems that should be investigated, and instead of waiting for people to come to them, go out, find people and bring them together on a specific project.

This kind of pre-supervision has several unfortunate results. First, it further depreciates the role of the individual. Revealingly, when such designs are discussed, the talk dwells less on people than on categories of people; the central idea is not to bring together several brilliant men so much as to bring *an* anthropologist, *an* economist, *a* psychologist—as if all that separates us from discovery is the setting of a goal and the right table of organization to carry it out.

Such planning, furthermore, compounds the younger men's already great interest in the externals of research rather than the content of it. In social science, particularly, methodology is being made the route to prestige, and those most likely to get ahead are becoming once or twice removed from the people they are supposed to be studying. It is considered somehow wrong now for first-rate social scientists to have to go out and talk to people themselves. More and more, this is being done by legions of emissaries in order that the social scientist may not be diverted from analyzing what people are like. When younger men talk about "sophisticated" design, this is the sort of thing they are apt to mean.

A lot of them know better, but because of current pressures to rationalize discovery in terms of research design, the true nature of science is thus further obscured from those who will one day follow them. As one young scientist, Walter Roberts, puts it: "There is a tremendous difference between science as it is done in the laboratory and science as it is reported. True science is helter-skelter, depending on one's hunches, angers, and inspirations, and the research itself is done in a very personal fashion. Thirty or forty years ago, it was written up this way. In reporting a great discovery a scientist would say, 'I was working on such-and-such a reaction when I dropped some sulphuric acid by mistake. When I examined it I found, to my surprise, a strange thing going on. . . .' But today nobody would write it up in this way."

Gerald Holton of Harvard uses the example of John Dalton's atomic theory in the 1800s: "It is now well known that this work led Dalton to the epochal concepts of the chemical atom, atomic weight, the law of multiple proportions . . . but it is worthy of note that *each and every one of his steps as just given was factually wrong or logically inconsistent.*" Today? "It is part of the game," continues Holton, "to cover up the transition from the private to the public state, to make the results in retrospect appear neatly derived from clear fundamentals. . . . Months of tortuous, wasteful effort may be hidden behind a few elegant paragraphs, with the sequence of presented development running directly opposite to the actual chronology, to the confusion of students and historians alike."[1]

Thus the organization mystique has grown in science. So far, it has not been an active effort; the decline of the individual researcher has been a by-product, and no identifiable school of thought has promoted it. But a status quo cannot long endure without an ideology to sustain it. In any field, we all want to reassure ourselves that things are the way they are because that's the way they should be, and science is no exception. Of late there are unmistakable signs that a number of people have been groping for a rationale that would openly justify the decline of the individual.

In a recent collection of efforts along this line, *Teamwork in Research*,[2] we see several people of good will taking a crack at this impossible business. The underlying premises

[1] "On the Duality and Growth of Physical Science," *American Scientist*, January 1953.

[2] Edited by George P. Bush and Lowell H. Hattery (Washington, D.C.: American University Press, 1953).

are much the same as we have heard them expressed in the corporation: the group is superior to the individual, the individual contributes by suppressing himself, and so on. Present, among other ideas, is the "self-ignition" theory. This theory does not question that the group is more creative than the individual, but only how *big* the team should be. (With fewer than four members, self-ignition does not take place, while more than ten prevents it.)

There is, however, one illuminating strain in most such efforts. They dwell often on the frustrations of the scientist, but they reveal nothing so much as the frustration of the administrator. In a particularly poignant passage, Howard Tolley, consultant to the Ford Foundation, speaks of the "Individualist" and the "Research Team." After a few nice words to the effect that the individualist can be of value to the team, he gets to the point. "Even when the research team has been constituted for some time," he warns, "individualism may crop out to mar the joint effort. One or another member of the team may get tired and become frustrated. He manifests this in various ways. He fails to show up. He does not come over to see you or talk to you. He withdraws within himself. He sits and looks out the window."

What administrator wouldn't be frustrated? Here is this man who won't come over to talk to you. He doesn't want to be counseled. He sits there staring out the window—off in a little world that you can never enter. Challenge indeed for all the interpersonal skills a man can muster, for if the administrator cannot enter the man's private world, he must somehow get him out of it. The team leader should do this, Tolley suggests, by "talking to this individualist, asking him to lunch, feeling out by counseling that which is at the root of the trouble." Then, as time goes on, there should be fewer repetitions of such behavior. The goal, Tolley says, is "to gradually bend or mold the individualist so that, while retaining a degree of his individualism, he nevertheless more and more inclines toward group approach, group-thinking, team-thinking."

This extraordinary plea is shocking because it is put so

openly. But elsewhere the fight against talent goes on. Others are not so audacious—they make the plea with more nicety of phrasing—but the essential message is the same. They'll make these people happy whether they want to be or not.

In the case against the individual, there is one more ideological point. It can properly be called the final one. *Is there,* some now ask, *anything really left to discover?* When I first heard young trainees state, soberly, that all the basic advances had already been made and that it was now the technicians' turn, I dismissed their proposition as ludicrous. But they have not been alone. Lately some respectable scientists have been saying what amounted to the same thing, though in more sophisticated terms. They don't say there is nothing left to discover; they say that we have now reached the point where *we know what there is left to discover.* Periodically, contributors to scientific journals have attempted to define just where these potential discoveries lie.[3]

An observer of scientific thought sums up this presumably optimistic view thus: "There undoubtedly remain many new ways to combine old discoveries. But this is invention as contrasted with science in the sense of discovering the 'laws' of nature. It is these laws which I think can be compared to charting the geography of the earth. I find it hard to conceive that the laws are anything like endless in number, or are subject to endless refinement. This is not to say that we are anywhere near discovering all the laws, either. *But at least we can, with some confidence, list the things we don't know.* A recent issue of *Scientific American,* for instance, listed these among the major questions in science: What is matter? What holds the nucleus of the atom together? Where do cosmic rays come from? Why are galaxies

---

[3] Physicist George Gamow, writing in *Physics Today* (Vol. 2, No. 1, January 1949): "It seems to me that our science definitely shows signs of convergence, although this statement can also be easily classified as wishful thinking. We see, nevertheless, from our analysis, that in the field of microphenomena there is only one big region remaining to be explored: the theory of elementary length in its relation to the problem of elementary particles."

spiral? Is this a universe of chance or of law? How is a protein made (i.e., what is life)? What is memory?—and a few others." But that's about the long and short of it, many believe.

Furthermore, the argument goes, discovery is inevitable anyway. "The way different people have come to the same discovery independently," one optimist holds, "refutes the 'great-man' concept the layman cherishes. It's mostly luck *who* makes the big discovery. It may be irreverent to suggest, but if there had been no Einstein there would, in all likelihood, still be a relativity theory."

Carried to its ultimate conclusions, this technological interpretation of the history of science is profoundly anti-individualistic. For if it is true either that fundamental discovery is inevitable or that we have exhausted all but a few opportunities for it, there exists less and less reason for encouraging the kind of conditions which lead to that kind of discovery. The trainees would be right after all; the priority should be given to the team work of combining and recombining what we already have.

Speaking to his friend, Lucien Price, Alfred North Whitehead recalled how, in the 1880s in Cambridge, nearly everything was supposed to be known about physics that could be known, and, like others, he thought it was an almost closed subject. "By the middle of the 1890s," he said, "there were a few tremors, a slight shiver as of all not being quite secure, but no one sensed what was coming. By 1900 Newtonian physics were demolished. Done for! Still speaking personally, it had a profound effect on me: I have been fooled once, and I'll be damned if I'll be fooled again."[4]

For his part, the layman can say that he finds it logically inconceivable that we can confidently measure the questions that separate us from total truth; that we can say we know what is unknown. He can say also that we have heard all this before; that epoch after epoch, technicians have assured him of the imminent completion of human knowledge, and

[4] *Dialogues of Whitehead,* Lucien Price (Boston: Atlantic-Little Brown, 1954).

that they have always been wrong. And thank heavens they have been! The implications otherwise would be too awful to accept—for then, with knowledge finite, with all the mystery and the challenge gone, what a crashing, futile bore our world would be!

CHAPTER EIGHTEEN

The Foundations and Projectism

THE bureaucratization can be reversed. For the man who wants to escape the mesh of organization, to ask his own questions, and to ask them for the sheer hell of it, the foundations are the last best hope. Alone of our big institutions, they do not have to yield to the pressures of immediacy or the importunings of the balance sheet. They have the money to invigorate individual research and they have the franchise. The job they have assigned themselves is not to support the status quo but to do what others cannot do or are too blind to do.

And how have the foundations responded to this challenge? They are not countering the bureaucratization of research; they are intensifying it.

Their support of the social sciences is the best yardstick of their performance. They have many other interests: Rockefeller, for example, has a long tradition of support—very enlightened support, too—in the biological sciences. But social-science research is the chief area common to all three, and they have become the critical source of support for it. The money they give is only a small part of the total spent on social science, but most other money has strings on it. Of the $38 million given by the government, all but $2 million goes to applied, large-scale team projects. Business milks basic research, for it eventually uses the techniques developed by academic researchers, but it has shown no disposition to support it at all, and the universities, with few exceptions, have little money left over after salaries and housekeeping expenses are paid. As their "restricted" funds for contract research have gone up, their "free" funds have gone down. If the social scientist wishes to take a leave of absence from the team—in short, if he wishes to exercise his own curiosity and not somebody else's—it is to the foundations that he must turn.

Here is the way they apportion their funds. Of the roughly $11,500,000 a year average (based on 1953-54) they have been giving to social science, only $2.8 million goes to individual projects or fellowships. $8.7 million—or 76 per cent of the total—goes to big team projects and institutions.

One of the anomalies in this situation is that you can't get an argument from foundation people on the subject of the individual. In principle, they are for him, and few are so emphatic, and quite sincerely so, that it's the man and not the program that counts, every time.

But.

They too are organization men. There are difficulties, they explain. The Ford Foundation argues that it just has to give its money in large-scale grants, and while it could give a bit more to individuals and still get rid of its money, it's not likely to get very enthusiastic about such a course. Not only financially, but philosophically, it would be a diversion; the "problem-solving," action approach is the foundation's basic strategy, and this puts something of a premium on the virtues of well-directed, administered, co-ordinated projects. The foundation's officials are quite frank about it. "We'll plead guilty," Rowan Gaither, Jr., president of the foundation, said to me of the disparity. "We do try and take care of the individual, but it's hard in a foundation of this size. It's very hard to support individuals without a staff of about one thousand, so we prefer to rely upon other institutions to provide this service for us."

Giving to individuals, to put it another way, costs too much. Carnegie and Rockefeller have devoted proportionately more to individual research, but their officers make much the same point. It often takes just as much work to make a $5,000 grant to an individual, they argue, as it does $500,000 to a university. The $500,000 grant, they further argue, may be the best way to support individual research; rather than "retail" grants for a certain kind of research, it is more efficient to give a lump sum to an outstanding group to pass on down the line. It was on such grounds of efficiency that Carnegie dropped its program of individual grants-in-aid after the war. The question is not *if* individuals should be supported, Carnegie insists, but *who* should do the selecting.

A poor case. If the big foundations can't afford the staff work, who can? Not the small foundations. With the very notable exception of the Guggenheim Foundation, they don't give much to individuals either.[1] As they can point out, it takes as much work to give $5,000 to an individual as it does $500,000 to a university. Perhaps the big foundations . . .

The big foundations say it costs too much. But need it? Instead of cutting down the number of individual grants, a better solution might be to cut down on the amount of staff work involved. It's been done, and quite successfully. Henry Allen Moe, the wise old bird who directs the Guggenheim Foundation, manages to give $1,000,000 to some 200 to 250 individuals each year. He uses advisers liberally (and gets their advice free), but his basic apparatus consists of no more than himself, two assistants, nine clerks, and a passion for excellence.

What if more individual support did require a heavier staff load? That's what foundations are supposed to be about —to do what others can't. Internal administrative considerations are important, but not as ends in themselves. Administratively, the foundations have a good case only if the other groups they rely on are in fact supporting the individual.

[1] In addition to the Big Three there are seventy foundations which state themselves interested in support of social science. In a questionnaire they were asked (1) how much they gave and (2) how much of this went to individual research. Of the forty-seven who replied, twenty-one actually did give to social-science research (total in 1954: $2,500,000). Only eleven, however, gave any money at all to individuals. Total given in 1954: $480,000.

But are they? Where the foundations specifically earmark funds for individual research, as in fellowship funds given to the Social Science Research Council, the intervening agencies do pass it on for independent work. (And all such grants, no matter how large, I have included in the individual-grants totals.) Where grants are not so earmarked, however, the money has a way of accumulating direction as it gets passed down the line. Eventually, of course, individuals have to do the work, but the work is apt to be what a committee or a department or a center thinks should be done, and while this may be worth while it is not the kind of independent, nondirected work under discussion.

To argue for more individual grants is not to argue against other kinds of support. As the foundations point out, some of the large institutional grants can have the effect of supporting individual work. The foundations have contributed heavily to the creation of "communities of scholars" —the Rockefeller Foundation, for example, founded the National Bureau of Economic Research; Carnegie, the Russian Research Center at Harvard; Ford, the Center for Advanced Study in the Behavioral Sciences. In such communities of scholars the work done is what the scholars wish to be done, and the foundations have been careful not to interpose any control.

But the fact remains that the sums available for the support of an individual doing what he—and he alone—wishes to do is only a fraction. It is such a small fraction, furthermore, that an effective increase in individual support would not jeopardize the support of other kinds of projects. Quite probably, a shift of 15 per cent in the giving pattern would be enough to have a marked effect on the academic world.

One reason no great funds would be needed for a sharp change in the climate is that the chance of a grant can be as important to the researcher as the money. Even a moderate upward shift would stimulate not only the particular people who get them but everyone in the field. In 1952, for example, the Ford Foundation gave $5,500 to fifty-four scholars to use as they saw fit. Quite aside from their effect on the individuals, they lifted the morale, and hopes, of social scientists everywhere, and people who didn't get them praised the idea as warmly as those who did. (The foundation has recently put through another such program, this time with a hundred grants at $4,250 apiece.)

Such grants encourage the scholar to think that he too might be able to follow up that long-shelved idea. Some may not, but the mere knowledge that a grant might be had can deeply influence a man's work—and this applies to the co-operative as well as the lonely, for they too have their private dreams. Let a man feel that he can have the support for the unexpected and he will welcome the unexpected all the more when it comes—not reject it because he sees no time to pursue it and then later sigh over opportunities passed by.

This brings us to the most crucial argument of all. The foundations argue that there are very few people willing and able to do independent work and that all those worthy of support are already taken care of. Assuming for the moment that this is correct, is not a question begged? There is a cause-and-effect relationship in the foundations' position. There are now 162 million people in this country, and proportionately there are just as many people with inherent talent, and in absolute numbers, more. If this talent is growing up in a climate which does not encourage the speculative, independent side of their nature, can the foundations who help shape that climate plead neutrality?

The foundations' own practices are creating the very lack they decry. Almost as important as the actual pattern of foundation giving is the academic's *idea* of how the foundations want to give. Quite plainly, the majority of social scientists believe that the best way for them to get foundation money is: (1) through a large project, and (2) one tailored to foundation interests. Foundations can complain that this is an unjustified stereotype. Stereotype or not, however, it has a way of conjuring up its own reality.

The immediate point at issue is not that the lone genius is being starved. This is by no means an unimportant consideration, but the question of whether or not there are mute, inglorious Miltons is a matter too complex to be explored here. I am talking of the over-all climate, which is to say, the impact of foundation giving on the man in the middle—the nine out of ten who are neither lone genius nor confirmed team "operator." Which side of his work is a man to emphasize? Which of the many problems that can interest him will he choose? What he thinks the foundation wants will have more influence than he cares to think.

Through the grapevine the social scientist hears how so-and-so landed a big grant with one approach and how some-one else didn't with a contrary approach. He also hears that the way he writes up his prospectus is all-important. "I'm gun shy," says one social scientist. "I've seen some of my colleagues sweat long hours writing and rewriting prospectuses. One man I know has been working away at a prospectus for a year now. Every time he rewrites it, he gets further away from his original idea. I don't think he himself realizes how much he has gotten into plain merchandising."

You can get money for any kind of project, goes a standard refrain, except the small one close to your heart. For this reason some don't try at all. "Right now I have an idea that's worth a middling-sized project," says one sociologist. "But I am not going to apply. I want to spend my time on the broad exploratory part, but if I got into it, I would get involved in administration. I would have to spend a year organizing a design that would please the foundation people —people who don't know anywhere near as much about the subject as I do. Then, when we got into the fact-finding part, I wouldn't have time to think." Not entirely facetiously, another sociologist argues that there should be special grant expediters. "We need academic five percenters," he suggests. "Men who would do the organizing work on projects for five per cent of the gross if they landed the grant."

The more usual inclination is not to put off an idea but to bloat it into a big project, and if it is to an image that the academic bends himself, he is nonetheless suborned. He may start out with an idea that requires little more than some time off from the university, travel money, and the help of a few graduate students. But he hesitates to ask for a modest grant; repeatedly, he has heard at the faculty club that foundations don't like that kind of grant. He begins, instead, to think of ways to clothe his basic idea as part of a larger group effort. He will suggest advisory committees, corps of people to collect data, corps to correlate data. Step by step the project grows in grandiosity, and step by step he will get further away from the original idea that impelled him— indeed, in such cases it is a puzzle why he continues to go after the money at all. No imperative of personal gain, or logic, remains. He goes after the foundation's money, as Mallory said of Mt. Everest, because it is there.

But if he gets the money he will be worse off than if he didn't. He has saddled himself with an administrative job— and it will be an administrative job far tougher than that faced by the businessman. For the scientist is particularly vulnerable to the conflicts of group work. The businessman is a professional at this sort of thing; the scientist is not. He too has problems of rank and status: who is going to publish first on the project and where, who is going to be the next chairman of the department, what will this do to his professional reputation? In grappling with these, how- ever, the scientist is not armed with the detachment of the executive; more than the latter, he judges a man for his beliefs and he cannot keep policy differences long separate from personal feelings.

The scientist turned administrator will also find that the project has an insidious way of becoming an end in itself. One social scientist I know helped set up a large area study several years ago in the optimistic belief that this was the best way he could pursue his own inquiry. He is now a much wiser man. "We started by gathering statistics," he says. "Now that I look back on it I am not quite sure why, except that it seemed the best way to get started. But the more statistics we gathered the more statistics we thought of gathering. Pretty soon we had every graduate student in the area out here. Next we had to have more office space, and more clerical help. By the time we'd spent our initial grant, I'd done practically nothing I'd planned to do. But the thing was rolling and there was no stopping it." The experience is not too atypical. Many a project gets to a point where its main reason for being is to produce more research to justify a grant for more research, and if the researcher confesses failure it is apt to be as a disingenuous preface to asking for help to reach the summit now in sight.

If people knew how badly the overblown project frequently turns out, there wouldn't be so many of them. No matter how bad the project, however, there are all sorts of secondary justifications to be made; understandably, researchers don't want to tell the foundations they have been wasting their money, and if nothing comes out of the project there is always the excuse the younger people got some good training. Foundation officials are by no means naïve, but while they may be aware that nothing very important came of an overblown project, they are not so likely to be aware of the far more negative effect of the project. What else could the people have been doing? The wastage of some of the most productive years of many first-rate people is the true blight and it affects the big names in the field quite as well as the newcomer.

It is often assumed in the academic world that the best-known people can write their own ticket if and when they want to. This is not true. For one thing, such men are constantly being approached to head up big projects or become part of one, and it is understandable they cannot resist forever. One well-known sociologist recalls how he got entrapped. "One day a bunch of us were talking to a visiting foundation official about our work. We mentioned one side project we had thought of from time to time. The official was enthusiastic. 'How much would it cost?' he asked. We said, offhand, $150,000. What do you know but two weeks later he sent us a telegram wanting to know if we would go ahead with it. We accepted, dammit, and we have been cursing ourselves ever since. I am not saying that the work wasn't of benefit; we did a fine job. But most of us felt we were marking time for several years."

Even when they want to do some small, independent research of their own, top men often have more trouble getting money for it than colleagues would suspect. Several men who are regarded as great "operators"—men who can raise hundreds of thousands of dollars for surveys on any conceivable subject—privately aver that the one thing they have never been able to do is get money for what they personally would like to do most of all.

Money, money everywhere, they complain, but not a cent to think.

They are apt to be the ones most influential with foundations, but this can be a mixed blessing for them. They, too, are entrapped. "There is a strange clique of advisers which invariably develops around the foundations," says one of the most influential men in U.S. social-science research today. "For instance, take the head of one foundation. I have his ear. If some people convince me their project is good, I can get it through for them much better than they could themselves. But with another foundation I don't even know who to *phone*. So this is how it is: to one clique you belong, to another you have no access at all, and to a third you have secondary access because you have a friend. I suppose it can't be avoided; they have to have advisers. But, if you had a chance to see how we operate without even talking about it! Belonging to one of these cliques is time consuming and nonremunerative. You have to go to the dumbest meetings; it's like the medieval bishopric. . . . It's important to what clique you belong for its own sake. But it doesn't mean you get to do your own personal project. It would be terribly bad taste to ask for special consideration for your own work."

If the men in the mainstream have trouble getting support for individual work, what of the maverick who doesn't fit in? Occasionally, foundation people do wonder about him —when he was head of Carnegie, Frederick Keppel suggested that some kindly benefactor might set up a foundation to look into the matter. Nobody has yet, and foundations don't appear to believe that the problem even needs looking into any more. Where, they ask, is the unsupported "lone wolf," or, as some put it, the *"so-called* lone wolf"? They don't know of any.

We cannot find what we do not seek. To see how justified was the complacency of the foundations I got a list of nominations from several top sociologists of men not working on currently fashionable problems but who were thought first-rate. I wrote the thirteen and asked them their experience with the foundations. Of the thirteen, I found, seven had applied to one of the Big Three for a grant. All but one had been turned down. The other six had not applied at all. With one exception, they felt they would not get sympathetic consideration.

Again, expectations are critical. On any one case there can be honest differences as to whether a grant would be in order, but surely it is significant that some people's image of the foundations is so adverse they won't even apply. It will not do for the foundations to dismiss them as malcontents and their charges as stereotypes. The image is self-confirming, and at the very least the foundations have a serious communication problem on their hands. Their primary public is academia, and if its members are constrained because they believe foundations are hostile to anything that doesn't fit in with currently fashionable trends, the foundations should do something about it. Giving more to individuals, and publicizing the fact, would help. But first must come an awareness that the image does exist and does mold.

That in part it is unjustified is beside the point. It is true, as I have indicated elsewhere, that the frequent charge of an "interlocking directorate" misses the mark. It is obvious that there must be circles of influential advisers and that most of these men should be already great in influence and power in the academic world. What seems at fault is not this fact but the foundations' disinclination to keep reminding themselves of this fact. They must have a main line of direction, yes, but they must for the same reason prod themselves constantly that they will not be inhospitable to people who wish to follow more lonely trails.

The foundations say that individual grants can only be part of their work. They are right. They say that individual grants are not the work that requires great boldness. Again, they are right. But this only compounds their default. If they cannot counter prevailing orthodoxy in an area that requires little audacity or money, where can they? The most serious charge is not that they are failing to give enough to stimulate individual work. It is that they do not concede that such a problem really exists at all.

In these three chapters I have slighted the role of the administrator, the necessity for scientists working together, and the value of applied research. I have done so because these have already been so well praised that further emphasis would be supererogatory. And this is my central point. The foundations, the universities, and the government have not actively conspired to change the climate, but merely by riding with the trends, they have created a growth that can stifle the very progress they seek.

And it is going to keep on feeding on itself. J. A. Gengerelli, head of the Psychology Department at U.C.L.A., has put it well: "We have a social force," he says, "that selectively encourages and rewards the scientific hack. There is a great hustle and bustle, a rushing back and forth to scientific conferences, a great plethora of $50,000 grants for $100 ideas. I am suggesting that scientific, technical, and financial facilities are such in this country as to encourage a great number of mediocrities to go into science, and to seduce even those with creative talent and imagination to a mistaken view of the nature of the scientific enterprise."

Of the two dangers, it is the molding effect that is paramount. When a large group of scientists met several years ago to discuss future basic science, on one point there was unanimous agreement: the contemporary social organization of science has been producing highly competent scientists, but scientists who are trained to work efficiently only in groups and who are not acclimated to individual inquiry. And none have been wholly immune to this force. To talk of the problem in terms of the lone genius or the screwball is to confuse the issue. We cannot have two sets of standards, one for a gregarious majority, another for an introverted minority. What we must concern ourselves with are the conditions that are common to all scientists, for the kind of environment which stimulates the creative side of the average scientist is the same environment in which genius flourishes.

Once we could afford to postpone the creation of such an environment, but we can no longer. In becoming too much the technicians, too little the innovators, we have banked complacently on European thought complementing our application. But we now have little grounds for smugness. European scientists still do more armchair work than American scientists, but this, as the patriot can point out, is partly because the European hasn't the money or facilities to do much else, and as American leadership and money become more influential he may be quite eager to leave the armchair. But this would be cold comfort. The European tradition of fundamental work has not been broken, but it is being severely strained. Why, *The Economist* asked recently, should its country's scientists concentrate on producing ideas that America will exploit? It did not counsel a cut in fundamental science, but it did argue that for Europe's own self-interest, it should put proportionately more effort into technology and application. Let Americans think up their own ideas.

America, as Eric Hodgins has put it, is being offered intellectual leadership in the most compelling way. It is the kind of challenge, candor should force us to admit, that goes against the grain of the American temperament. We are by nature too impatient, too pragmatic, too co-operative for the cause of aimless discovery ever to be a popular one. And that is precisely why leadership is so imperative.

PART SIX

The Organization Man in Fiction

CHAPTER NINETEEN

Love That System

IF you wanted to put in fiction form the split between the Protestant Ethic and the Social Ethic of organization life, you might, if you wanted to be extreme about it, come up with a plot situation something like this.

A middle-management executive is in a spot of trouble. He finds that the small branch plant he's helping to run is very likely to blow up. There is a way to save it: if he presses a certain button the explosion will be averted. Unfortunately, however, just as he's about to press a button his boss heaves into view. The boss is a scoundrel and a fool, and at this moment he's so scared he is almost incoherent. Don't press the button, he says.

The middle-management man is no rebel and he knows that the boss, stupid as he is, represents The Organization. Still, he would like to save everyone's life. Thus his dilemma: if he presses the button he will not be acting like a good organization man and the plant will be saved. If he doesn't press it he will be a good organization man and they will all be blown to smithereens.

A damn silly dilemma, you might say. Almost exactly this basic problem, however, is the core of the biggest-selling novel of the postwar period, Herman Wouk's *The Caine Mutiny,* and rarely has a novel so touched a contemporary nerve. Much of its success, of course, was due to the fact it is a rattling good tale, and even if the author had ended it differently it would still probably have been a success. But it is the moral overtones that have made it compelling. Here, raised to the nth degree, is the problem of the individual versus authority, and the problem is put so that no reader can duck it. There is no "Lady or the Tiger" ending. We must, with the author, make a choice, and a choice that is presented as an ultimately moral one.

The boldness of it makes *The Caine Mutiny* something of a landmark in the shift of American values. Popular fiction in general, as I will take up in the next chapter, has been going in the same direction for a long time, and *The Caine Mutiny* is merely evolutionary in this respect. But it is franker; unlike most popular fare, it does not sugar-coat the precept to adjustment by trapping it up with the words of individualism. It is explicit. Author Wouk puts his protagonist in a dilemma and, through rigorous plotting, eliminates any easy middle course. The protagonist must do what he thinks is right or do what the system thinks is right.

The man caught in the dilemma is one the reader can identify himself with. He is Lieutenant Maryk, the executive officer of the mine sweeper *Caine*. Maryk is no scoffer, but a stolid, hard-working man who just wants to do his job well. He likes the system and all his inclinations lead him to seek a career in the Regular Navy.

Ordinarily he would lead an uneventful, productive life. The ship of which he is executive officer, however, is commanded by a psychopath named Queeg. At first Maryk stubbornly resists the warnings about Queeg voiced by Lieutenant Keefer, an ex-writer. But slowly the truth dawns on him, and in a series of preliminary incidents the author leaves no doubt in Maryk's—or the reader's—mind that Queeg is in fact a bully, a neurotic, a coward, and what is to be most important of all, an incompetent.

In many similar instances subordinates have found ways to protect themselves without overtly questioning the system —they can make requests for mass transfer and thereby discipline the superior, control him by mass blackmail, and the like. Wouk, however, proceeds to build a climax in which such reconciliations are impossible. He places the *Caine* in the midst of a typhoon.

Terrified, Queeg turns the ship south, so that it no longer heads into the wind. Maryk pleads with him to keep it headed into the wind as their only chance for survival. Queeg, now virtually jabbering with fear, refuses to turn the ship around into the wind. The ship is on the verge of foundering.

What shall Maryk do? If he does nothing he is certain that they are all lost. If he takes advantage of Article 184 in Navy Regulations and relieves Queeg temporarily of command for medical reasons, he is in for great trouble later.

Maryk makes his decision. With as much dignity as possible he relieves Queeg of command and turns the ship into the wind. The ship still yaws and plunges, but it stays afloat. As if to punctuate Maryk's feat, the *Caine* passes the up-turned bottom of a destroyer that hadn't made it.

Eventually there is a court-martial for Maryk and his fellow officers. The defense lawyer, Barney Greenwald, makes what appears to be highly justified points about Queeg and, through skillful cross-examination, reveals him to the court as a neurotic coward. The court acquits Maryk. Queeg's career is finished.

Then the author pulls the switch. At a party afterward, lawyer Greenwald tells Maryk and the junior officers that *they,* not Queeg, were the true villains of the piece. Greenwald argues that Queeg was a regular officer, and that without regular officers there would be no going system for reserves to join later. In what must be the most irrelevant climax in contemporary fiction, Greenwald says that he is a Jew and that his grandmother was boiled down for soap in Germany and that thanks be to the Queegs who kept the ships going. He throws a glass of champagne at Keefer.

"I see that we were in the wrong," one of the junior officers writes later, with Wouk's blessing. "The idea is, once you get an incompetent ass of a skipper—and it's a chance of war—there's nothing to do but serve him as though he were the wisest and the best, cover his mistakes, keep the ship going, and bear up."

Here, certainly, is an astounding denial of individual responsibility. The system is presented as having such a mystique that apparent evil becomes a kind of good. What would have happened if Maryk *hadn't* relieved Queeg? We are asked to accept the implied moral that it would have been better to let the ship and several hundred men perish rather than question authority—which does seem a hell of a way to keep a ship going. True, Wouk doesn't extend his premises to this blunt a point, and after it's all over suggests that somehow things would have worked out all right even if Maryk hadn't turned the ship around. But the lesson is plain. It is not for the individual to question the system.

An extraordinary point of view, but did Americans gag on it? In the critical reception of the book most people got the point—and most of them agreed with it.[1] Partly this was a contemporary reaction to the spate of war books which in lazy anger personified the evil of war in officers and discipline. But the larger moral was not overlooked. *The Caine Mutiny* rationalized the impulse to belong and to accept what is as what should be. If we can be shown there is virtue in following a Queeg, how much more reason to welcome the less onerous sanctions of ordinary authority! The "smart" people who question things, who upset people —they are the wrong ones. It was Keefer, with his clever mind, his needling of authority, who led the ordinary people like Maryk astray. Barney Greenwald was too smart for

---

[1] Save for a few articles in the smaller magazines, critical reaction has been overwhelmingly favorable, and, to judge by my sample of reviews, only a handful of critics caviled at the moral. Theater and movie critics, possibly because the three-year time lapse between the book and the screen and stage versions gave them time for a double take, entertained more doubts than book critics. (John Mason Brown in *The Saturday Review:* ". . . he suddenly asks us to forgive the Queeg he has proved beyond doubt unfit for command." Martin Dworkin in *The Progressive:* "Wouk wants us to think less and obey more. . . . There are voices stating this view more clearly than Wouk . . . he, at least, is still confused.") As in the case of the book reviewers, however, the majority applauded, including even such usually perceptive critics as Brooks Atkinson and Walter Kerr. (Kerr: ". . . we are exhilarated by a ringing, rousing, thoroughly intelligible statement in [Queeg's] defense.")

his own good too, and to redeem himself he had to throw a glass of champagne in Keefer's dirty intellectual face.

It could be argued that the public's acquiescence was only apparent and if people had bothered to think about the moral they would have protested it. To get some idea of what would happen if people had to think about its implications, I tried a modest experiment. In co-operation with the authorities of a small preparatory school, I initiated an essay contest for the students. The subject would be *The Caine Mutiny*. Prize winners would be chosen for the literary excellence of their essays and not for their point of view, but it was the moral issue of *The Caine Mutiny* that was their subject. Here are the ground rules we announced:

The essay, which should be between 500 and 1,000 words in length, should consider the following problems:

I. *What is the central moral issue of* The Caine Mutiny?

II. *How does the author, Herman Wouk, speaking through characters in the book, regard the resolution of the moral issue?*

III. *How do the resolution of the moral issue and the author's judgment of that resolution accord with life as you know it?*

At length the essays were finished, and when we sat down to read them we were pleased to find how well they had grasped the essential issue. In a sense, it was a highly nondirective test; not surprisingly, they had gone to some effort previously to cadge some hints from the teachers, and it was obvious they tried hard to cadge hints from Wouk. How they felt about the mutineers depended considerably on how they thought he felt; and, understandably, they were somewhat confused as to what side they were meant to disapprove. On the whole, however, they did grasp the essential issue at stake. Each interpreted its relevance to his life somewhat differently, but most of them saw the problem as that of individual independence versus the system.

With one exception they favored the system. Collusion may have fortified them in this, but their phrasing, and their puzzlement over Wouk's position, left little doubt that their feeling was genuine. Several disagreed with Wouk, but the grounds on which they disagreed with him were that he was too easy on the mutineers. Here is a sampling of final paragraphs:

In everything we do there are certain rules and regulations we have to abide by, and, like Willie Keith, the only way we will learn is through experience. We have to abide by the rules of our particular society to gain any end whatsoever.

I cannot agree with the author in that I believe that one should obey orders no matter what the circumstances.

It seems that life in general is like a baseball game; everywhere there are rules and laws set up by many people for the ultimate benefit of all. Yet there are people who think as the young rookie that their actions should be directed by what they feel is right, not by what everyone else has determined. True, there may be partly extenuating circumstances; but unless the reason is more than subjective, the one who breaks society's laws will be punished by fine, jail, or even death.

This is another example of why a subordinate should not have the power to question authority.

Morally, however, the very act that Maryk committed is against the law.

The underlying causes of the Caine *mutiny have their parallel in everyday life. . . . The teacher who allows personal dislike to enter into his grading; the politician who blames his mistakes on others; both of these are examples of fraudulency. . . . Greenwald, Maryk's lawyer, confused Queeg and twisted his words so that Queeg was made to look stupid.*

Men have always been subjected to the whims of those in command; and so it will be in the future. This plan must exist or anarchy will be the result.

The student who dissented was not rebellious; like the others, he pointed out the necessity for codes and rules and regulations if society is to have any collective purpose. Unlike them, however, he put these points before, rather than after, the "but." "Is a man justified," he asks, "in doing what he truly thinks is right under any circumstances?" After pointing out the dangers of individual conscience, he comes to his conclusion: "A man must realize that a wrong decision, however sincere, will leave him open to criticism and to probable punishment. Nevertheless, and after weighing all the facts, it is his moral duty to act as he thinks best."

It is his moral duty to act as he thinks best. Has this become an anachronistic concept? Fifteen students against, to one for, constitute, let me concede, very few straws in the wind. Nor do they mark any sudden shift in values. Had the question about Queeg been asked in, say, 1939, my guess is that a higher proportion of students would have voted for Maryk than would today; but even then it is probable that a majority would have voted against him.

It is a long-term shift of emphasis that has been taking place. So far we have been talking of only one book and one decade, and, while this gives some sort of fix, it does not illuminate what our popular morality has changed *from*. To this end I would now like to take a look at popular fiction in general—as it used to be, and where it seems to be going.

CHAPTER TWENTY

Society As Hero

I HAVE been talking of one book and one decade. Now I would like to broaden the angle of view, for *The Caine Mutiny* is only one more step in a development that has been going on for a long time. Let me at once concede that much of what seems contemporary in popular fiction is fairly timeless. Black has always been black and white has always been white, with few shades of gray in between; coincidence outrageous and the endings happy, or at least symbolic of a better world ahead. The very fact that fiction does tell people what they want to hear, however, does make it a fairly serviceable barometer. Whether fiction leads people or merely reflects them, it is an index of changes in popular belief that might be imperceptible at closer range.

If we pick up popular fiction around the 1870s, we find the Protestant Ethic in full flower. It was plain that the hero's victories over his competitors and his accumulation of money were synonymous with godliness. The hero was shown in struggle with the environment, and though good fortune was an indispensable assist, it was less an accident than a reward directed his way by a just providence. This didn't always go without saying, but it could. As late as the turn of the century the ethic remained so unquestioned that the moralizing could be left out entirely. Heroes were openly, exultantly materialistic, and if they married the boss's daughter or pushed anyone around on the way up, this was as it should be.

For a farewell look at this hero we have "Ottenhausen's Coup" by John Walker Harrington in *McClure's* magazine, March 1898 (several years before *McClure's* muckraking phase). Young Carl Ottenhausen is sent by his company to take charge of an iron furnace, where, it so happens, the boss's blue-eyed daughter is giving a house party at near-by Eagle's Nest, the boss's palatial summer house. After a brief brush with the daughter, Ottenhausen hears there is a crisis down at the furnace at the bottom of the hill. Some anarchist has gotten the men to revolt. Ottenhausen rushes down to the furnace, pulls out two guns, and advances on the workers. The surly devils cower before him. "The men of Laird's Furnace had met their match."

As Ottenhausen stands triumphant before the workers, the house party group comes down in evening clothes to see what's going on. The president is among them. The last paragraph of the story:

In the top of a tall building, in Columbus, there is a door bearing a porcelain label which reads, General Manager; behind that door sits Carl Ottenhausen, who now directs the destinies of the Mingo Coal and Iron Company. He owns a handsome house in the West End which puts Eagle's Nest to shame. There presides over that household a blue-eyed woman whose very look is merriment.

As time went on the materialism became more muted. Only a few years after "Ottenhausen's Coup," *McClure's* articles were roundly denouncing people like Ottenhausen for their avarice. Fiction was much slower to respond to the changing temper, but once Veblen and Steffens and others had set to work, fiction heroes could not savor riches with the old innocence. By the twenties, money-conscious as they may have been, heroes who married the boss's daughter married a girl who *turned out* to be the boss's daughter. Not so many years later there wasn't much point even in that; and now, with the social changes of the last two decades, stories are just as apt to have the hero who married someone who turns out *not* to be the boss's daughter. In a recent *Saturday Evening Post* story, for example, the hero falls in love with a rich heiress who owns a near-by boat. Actually, she's a secretary who is taking care of her boss's boat. A happy ending comes when the hero finds this out.

But this does not mean that our fiction has become fundamentally any less materialistic. It hasn't; it's just more hypocritical about it. Today's heroes don't lust for big riches, but they are positively greedy for the good life. This yen, furthermore, is customarily interpreted as a renunciation of materialism rather than as the embrace of it that it actually is. The usual hero of the postwar rash of "New York" novels, for example, is overweeningly spiritual on this score. After making his spurious choice between good and evil, the hero heads for the country, where, presumably, he is now to find real meaning in life. Just what this meaning will be is hard to see; in the new egalitarianism of the market place, his precipitous flight from the bitch goddess success will enable him to live a lot more comfortably than the ulcerated colleagues left behind, and in more than one sense, it's the latter who are the less materialistic. Our hero has left the battlefield where his real fight must be fought; by puttering at a country newspaper and patronizing himself into a native, he evades any conflict, and in the process manages to live reasonably high off the hog. There's no Cadillac, but the Hillman Minx does pretty well, the chickens are stacked high in the deep freeze, and no doubt there is a hi-fi set in the stable which he and his wife have converted. All this may be very sensible, but it's mighty comfortable for a hair shirt.

Of late, sanctimonious materialism has been taking a somewhat different tack. Writers have been affected by the era of good feeling too, and heroes are now apt to stick around the market place. But they still have it both ways. Ponder the message of *The Man in the Gray Flannel Suit*. In this story of a man "heroically reconverting" to civilian life, hero Tom Rath is offered a big-money job by his boss. Tom turns it down; indeed, as we heard earlier, he virtually scolds the boss for so much as offering it to him. He'd have to work too hard and he wants to be with his family. Sacrifice? Blessed indeed are the acquiescent. The boss says he will give Tom a good job which won't ask so much, and grandmother's estate Tom inherited, it also transpires, can be chopped up into a development that will make lots of the money that Tom and Betsy so patiently covet. ("One of the rare books of recent vintage," an ad quotes a grateful reader, "leaving one with a feeling of pride to be a member of the human race.")

In *Patterns,* another, equally curious business tale, the hero doesn't mind work so much but he is similarly sanctimonious. He is appalled by the ruthless tactics of an industrial buccaneer. When the buccaneer offers him a top spot the hero says he wants no part of it. He is a moral man and he gives the boss a tongue-lashing. Having thereby saved his soul, he takes the job (at twice the salary). In a masterpiece of the have-your-cake-and-eat-it finale, he tells the boss he'll punch his face if he doesn't act right.

Not in the materialism of heroes but in their attitude toward society is where the change has taken place. In older fiction there was some element of conflict between the individual and his environment; no matter how much assisted by coincidence, the hero had to *do* something—or at least seem to do something—before he got his reward. Rarely now. Society is so benevolent that there is no conflict left in it for anyone to be rebellious about. The hero only *thinks* there is.

Stories must have at least the appearance of a conflict if they are to be stories, but contemporary writers get around this by taking a chunk of environment and then in some fashion disguising its true goodness from the hero. Since this means that the hero's troubles stem from a false image of life, the climax is easily resolved. The author simply tears the veil away. It was really okay all along only the hero didn't know it. Relieved, the hero learns the wisdom of accepting what probably would have happened anyway.

We have the small-town girl planning to marry good, safe old Joe, or already married to him. Just about the time she's getting bored with Joe and the small-town life, an actor or celebrity of some kind comes to town from the city for a short stay. He gives her a mild rush, and she dreams of a glamorous life with him. Then some minor crisis comes up. Who rises to it? Surprisingly, safe old Joe. We leave her as she gazes at Joe, with his briar pipe and his lovable idiosyncrasies and his calm, quiet strength. She would be stuck with him in any event, but now she is swept by a deep inner peace to boot.

It is a churlish critic who would gainsay people the solace of fairy tales. But good fairy tales frankly tell the reader that he is about to enter the land of make-believe and to relax as we go back once upon a time. Current slick fiction stories do not do this; the tales are not presented as make-believe; by the use of detail, by the flagrant plainness of their characters, they proclaim themselves realistic slices of life. They are much like the "situation" magazine covers and the pictures of American family life featured in ads like the "Beer belongs—enjoy it" series. The verisimilitude is superb—from the frayed cord on the bridge lamp to the askew hair of the young mother, the detail is almost photographically faithful to middle-class reality. But it is all sheer romance nonetheless; whether the scene is taking the first picture of the baby, a neighborly contretemps over shoveling snow, or a family reunion of one kind or another, the little humorous squabbles merely serve to high-light how lovable and conflict-less is the status quo beneath.

Let me detour a moment to nonfiction, for it shows the same change of emphasis. Take, for example, that American staple, the self-improvement book. A half-century ago the usual self-improvement book bore down heavily on the theme of individual effort to surmount obstacles. It was a sort of everyman's Protestant Ethic; you too, went the message, can become rich and powerful. This buoyant doctrine reached its apotheosis in the "New Thought" movement, which, by conceiving the individual mind as an emanation of God, confidently asserted that "anything is yours if you only want it hard enough." Typical book titles tell the story: *The Conquest of Poverty, Your Forces and How to*

Use Them, Mastery of Fate, Pushing to the Front, or Success under Difficulty, The Victorious Attitude.[1]

This theme has by no means disappeared. Best-selling books for salesmen preach the same message, and with a gusto that seems downright anachronistic. Frank Bettger's *How I Raised Myself from Failure to Success in Selling,* for example, could, save for a few topical references, have been written in 1910. There is nothing that our old friend Henry Clews would not have subscribed to—and, like him, Bettger winds up with the maxims of Benjamin Franklin. (If I may add a somewhat extraneous comment, the comparative anachronism of this viewpoint helps explain why selling has fallen into such low esteem. The beliefs of the salesmanship ideal remain unchanged—in a world where everything else has changed.)

But the general run of current self-improvement books shows a rather sharp divergence from the old tradition. On the surface they do not seem to, and their titles promise the old fare. Essentially, however, what they tell you to do is to adjust to the situation rather than change it. They are full of ambiguities, to be sure, and many still borrow heavily from the mental-power concept of the New Thought movement. But for all this the picture they present is one of an essentially benevolent society, and the peace of mind or the positive thinking extolled is a kind of resignation to it.

"What should a person do," a puzzled man asks Norman

[1] I am indebted to Reinhard Bendix's analysis of the New Thought movement. In his excellent study, *Work and Authority in Industry* (N.Y. 1956), Bendix points out the dilemma the Protestant Ethic had forced upon the middle class. In the older version there was a sharp division between the haves and have-nots, with very little comfortable middle ground in between. Only a few could be successful; the rest would have to accept their station as an indication of lack of necessary personal qualities. As N. C. Fowler wrote in 1902 in *The Boy, How to Help Him Succeed:* "Many a man is entirely incapable of assuming responsibility. . . . He lacks the courage of willingness to assume responsibility and the ability of handling others. He was born for a salaried man, and a salaried man he had better remain." This, as Bendix points out, was much too harsh a doctrine and the New Thought movement, which denied such exclusiveness to success, furnished a badly needed modification.

Vincent Peale, "who is unhappy and bored in his job after twenty years but who earns a nice salary and hasn't the nerve to leave? He'll never go any higher in salary and position but will always have a job." Peale, one of the few who can preach the Social Ethic and the Protestant Ethic at one and the same time, answers thus: "The trouble here seems to be the tragedy of treadmill thoughts. This individual has gone stale, dull and dead in his thinking. He needs an intellectual rebirth. That job of his is filled with possibilities he never sees, with opportunities he hasn't realized. Tell him to wake up mentally and strive for some understanding of what he can accomplish in his present position." ("Norman Vincent Peale Answers Your Questions," *Look*, March 6, 1955.)

Life, as it is, is beautiful enough, and one could easily gather from current reading that God is so merged with society that the two are just about indistinguishable. In an advertisement for the movie, *A Man Called Peter*, there is a picture of a man walking up a hill through some dry-ice mist. In his white shirt and four-in-hand tie, he looks uncommonly like a thoughtful young executive, but we find that he is a minister: *"He was a first-name kind of guy. . . . He was everybody's kind of guy. . . .* He unpomped the pompous, played baseball with kids, turned a two-hour leave into a honeymoon for a sailor and his girl, and gave voice to all the longings in a man's soul. . . . *He was a lovin' kind of guy. . . .* Every woman secretly had her eyes on him, but he had eyes for only one—Catherine—who learned from him what a wonderful thing it was to be a woman—and wrote this story that topped the nation's best-seller list for 128 weeks. . . . *He was God's kind of guy."*

This profanity, for that is what it is, is bold, even for the popular press, but it is characteristic. God likes regular people—people who play baseball, like movie nuns. He smiles on society, and his message is a relaxing one. He does not scold you; he does not demand of you. He is a gregarious God and he can be found in the smiling, happy people of the society about you. As the advertisements put it, religion can be fun.

Oddly, the only time popular culture gives us a momentary glimpse of the beast in the jungle is when it reverses the usual process and masquerades reality as a fairy tale. Through the thin convention of animals, the animated cartoons show man in conflict with unabashed sadism, and with vicarious enjoyment people roar as human beings gotten up as cats and pigs torture and kill one another. In some television programs, the tradition of the two-reel comedies is perpetuated; here the environment is capricious and sardonic and the protagonist is not merely beset but defeated by the unglamorous impedimenta of everyday life—leeching friends, in-laws, icy sidewalks, stupid waiters, mean superiors. Perhaps it is for the same reason that people still seek out the old W. C. Fields pictures; through the sanction of laughter they can surreptitiously enjoy his detestation for little children, motherhood, and mankind.

Since 1900, to recapitulate, the vision of life presented in popular fare has been one in which conflict has slowly been giving way to adjustment. But there is more to this change than mere degree, and I would now like to take up a further development.

For many years most writers of popular fiction have portrayed society amenably enough, but once they were guileless in this respect, and now they have lost their innocence. Instead of merely showing people not masters of their destiny—and leaving the moral latent—there now seems a disposition to go out of the way to show that people cannot be. Society is no longer merely an agreeable setting in which they place their subjects; it is becoming almost the central subject itself.

Fiction heroes and heroines, as we have seen, have been remarkably passive for some time. It is not enough, however, to show that they are not masters of their own destiny; there now seems to be a growing disposition on the part of writers to go out of their way to show that they *cannot* be. To what degree one can be is of course a matter for deep debate, and many of the best novels of the last decade have been concerned with the impotence of man against society. But where these books deplore, slick fiction seems to rejoice. The new society, it says—often quite forcefully—is such that the hero does not have to wrestle with external forces. He may mistakenly believe this for a while, but eventually he is shown how unnecessary it is.

Society itself becomes the *deus ex machina*. In such cases one of the characters is a sort of accredited spokesman for the system in which the protagonists operate. The system, with an assist from its spokesman, resolves the hero's apparent dilemma, and lest the point be lost on the hero, the spokesman usually has a few sententious words at the end.

In a *Saturday Evening Post* story we see how the system solves the problem of a baffled couple. An Army captain and his wife have gotten in trouble by adopting a Japanese child while they are serving in a regiment stationed in Japan. A mean major and his wife spend most of their time making life miserable for the couple and the child. The captain feels he cannot buck the system by strife with the major; the only way out that he can see is to give up the struggle entirely, resign his commission, and take his wife and the child back to the United States.

Then the wife of the colonel comes to tea. She is especially gracious to the little Japanese girl and thus tacitly announces to all that the little girl is now part of the system. The villainous major is not punished. He and his wife remain just as mean underneath, but they are members of the system too, and thus, we gather, will now be nice to the little girl. The story ends with the captain and his wife happily ascending the stairs to their bedroom.

In a sort of ultimate example of the system spokesman, another *Saturday Evening Post* story rings in the President himself. ("Unexpected Hero," by Paul Horgan, March 26, 1955.) A lawyer is trying to convince a widow to marry him, but her little boy stands in the way; the boy idolizes too much the memory of his war-hero father. One day the lawyer takes him to look at the sights in Washington. The boy is unimpressed. At length, the two stop by the White House where the lawyer runs across an old acquaintance. Suddenly, a presence comes into the room. He puts his arm on the little boy's shoulders, and from above, to judge by the full-page illustration, a luminous light encircles him.

After a long, and what would seem to a taxpayer needlessly garrulous, conversation, the President recognizes the lawyer from the war days in Europe. Wasn't he at the Rhine crossing near Wesel in March 1945? The President recalls the details of the then major's fine work and how he had put him in for the Legion of Merit. The little boy now admires the lawyer and the two go back home, happy.

Sometimes society is personified by an animal or by an inanimate object. In his study of *Saturday Evening Post* fiction, Robert Brustein was struck by the religious overtones writers invoked. "The theme is adoption. A powerful person experiences a difficulty which is resolved through the generous impulse of someone weaker; by his own considerable power or through mysterious intimacy with 'higher-ups,' the stronger then rewards the weaker, and the weaker is subsequently adopted. It is the weaker character —the adoptee—who is the central hero with whom the reader is meant to identify, and his face is featureless so that the reader can substitute his own." ("The New Faith of the *Saturday Evening Post,*" Robert Brustein, *Commentary,* October 1953.)

Popular culture is not monolithic in this counseling of resignation, nor is the audience in accepting it. It too is rife with ambiguity, and just as the executive confuses himself by paying homage to mutually incompatible precepts, so the audience still responds to themes directly contrary to the usual fare. *High Noon,* one of the most successful movies in years, was a clear throwback to the Protestant Ethic. In this morality play the sheriff, who is the hero, starts out as a team player; when he is confronted by evil he diligently seeks the co-operation of the townspeople for a group effort to combat the killers who are coming to town. But the group fails him and the hero is left alone—and afraid. But he conquers his fear and he conquers the killers. The townspeople come out of hiding and congratulate him, but, contemptuous, he spurns them and rides off with his wife, unforgiving. When I saw the movie the audience applauded when the hero told off the townspeople. Conceivably, the same people cheered just as much when Barney Greenwald told off Keefer for questioning the system, but the point is that they can still do both.[2]

In any treatment of man's isolation and his need to belong, diagnosis does not have to lead to precept. In *From Here to Eternity* Prewitt cannot exist outside the cocoon of the Regular Army, but the author presents this as a fact of life and a rather harsh one at that. In many recent books, however, there is an unmistakable note of approval; J. P. Marquand's protagonists, for example, are etched with great detachment yet they are impelled to peace through acceptance, and though there is no exaltation over their acquiescence, neither is there a sense of tragedy. When Sid Skelton, the successful commentator in *Melville Goodwin USA*, goes to a cocktail party for Army brass, the reader braces himself for some sharp comment on Army life. He gets none; Skelton, prototype of the Connecticut suburbanite made miserable by success, envies too much the Army people's sense of belonging and their rootedness in a firm system. He is the man on the outside looking in.

For all the ambiguities and cross currents the dominant strain in popular culture does seem to be adjustment to the system. To what degree this is conscious direction on the part of authors is, of course, impossible to determine. On any one story critics could long split hairs as to whether the author was resolving for or against the system, and perhaps the author might be in some doubt himself. Nonetheless,

---

[2] *High Noon* seems to be susceptible to some much more involved interpretations. In "The Olympian Cowboy" (*The American Scholar*, Summer 1955, Vol. 24, No. 3) a Swedish critic named Harry Schein manages to interpret it as a piece of American propaganda. He writes: "I see *High Noon* as having an urgent political message. The little community seems to be crippled with fear before the approaching villains; seems to be timid, neutral, and halfhearted, like the United Nations before the Soviet Union, China, and North Korea; moral courage is apparent only in the very American sheriff. . . . *High Noon*, artistically, is the most convincing and, likewise, certainly the most honest explanation of American foreign policy."

there does seem to be a sense of direction, and whether it is conscious or not, popular writers are showing an increasing affinity for it.

One way to chart the direction would be to provide a cross section of slick fiction writers with a new plot situation, let each of them make what he will of it, and then do a follow-up study of the results to see how they played back the material. By accident, I found myself involved in what was in effect, if not in design, an almost controlled experiment along these lines, and I would like to present the results in evidence for my thesis.

The plot situation came out of a study my colleagues and I did of the tensions in the life of corporation wives and their families. One article, essentially reportorial, described the growing domination of the family by the corporation and the active "wife programs" some large corporations were instituting to make the domination more absolute. The other article went into the wives' attitudes toward all this. I thought this the more important, for the interviews indicated that most wives *agreed* with the corporation; they too felt that the good wife is the wife who adjusts graciously to the system, curbs open intellectualism or the desire to be alone. There were exceptions, and they were significant ones, but the majority view was so depressingly strong, particularly among the younger wives, that we felt compelled to add a special editorial "In Praise of Ornery Wives." In some small way, we hoped, the articles would be a counter-irritant.

We were soon inundated with letters. Many readers were furious at the conformity described, and so furious they blamed us for it. This wasn't so bad, but the praise was something else again. Soon articles began to appear in trade journals and the women's pages of newspapers on "the wife problem." Congratulations to *Fortune,* they said, for breaking the ice and showing how wrong was the old hands-off policy. The rules of the game we had paraphrased tongue-in-cheek were reprinted verbatim as psychologically sound guides for peace of mind in corporate life; worse yet, the examples of company wife programs we had described were stimulating other companies into devising even more stringently controlled programs.[3]

At length the fiction began to appear, and by the end of the year there was hardly a women's magazine that hadn't printed a story along the lines of "I Was a Company Wife," "Management Bride." On first glance, the stories would appear to be heartening omens of protest. The pictures in the opening layout were of women deeply troubled and apparently in some kind of bondage. As one caption asked, How is a wife to fight when an intangible force comes between her and her husband? But this was only the come-on. No praise of ornery wives; by the end of the story both the heroine and the reader learn that the good wife, as corporations said all along, is highly gregarious and highly adaptable.

In one story, to cite a typical example of the genre, an inexperienced company wife is trying to figure out how to make the next promotion go to her husband instead of the husband of a somewhat older friend down the street. Since the boss and his wife will be making the decision when they come to town for a week's stay, the heroine decides to throw a fancy dinner with caviar and all the trimmings. Her friend, she correctly estimates, will probably serve a much plainer dinner.

The day arrives. The boss and his gracious wife—boss's wives are usually gracious in today's fiction—come to dinner. Too late, our heroine realizes that she has made herself seem pretentious, and, sure enough, the other couple get the job. As with the colonel's wife, however, the system the boss's wife personifies is a warm one, and so she stops by for a friendly chat. Delicately she tells the heroine that it

[3] *Sales Management,* January 15, 1952, describes how U.S. Machine Corporation saw the problem: "All too often, so often in fact that it becomes almost a common situation, a sort of 'love triangle' develops in the lives of salesmen. The three sides of the triangle are salesman, wife, company. The wife sees the company robbing her of her husband's time and companionship, becoming a rival, she feels, for his affection. At first she is slightly resentful. In time she may become openly jealous. This, unless brought under control, can end up in irreparable damage to the salesman's worth to his employer."

would have been better if she had served a plainer meal, but not to worry, her chance will come again.

I found one ostensible exception. It was a story called "Fireworks for Michelle," a complete-in-one-issue novel in the *Ladies' Home Journal*, May 1953. Michelle and her husband are enslaved to a particularly noxious company. The personnel people use all of the many different devices noted in our study and a couple we hadn't heard of yet. The boss tells Michelle's touseled-haired husband, Garry, how Michelle should dress, who her friends should be, and what decoration scheme she should use. Garry doesn't altogether like this, but he's a good corporation man and passes the word along to Michelle. Michelle, apparently made of stronger stuff than her husband, decides that she has had it. She and Garry invite the top executives and their wives for dinner. At dessert they turn and insult their guests.

"Well, ladies and gentlemen," Garry said, "I'm through racing after your mechanical rabbit. I'm not going to climb any further up your blasted ladder. This is where I get off."
She got up somehow on wobbly knees and went to meet him between the tables. His strong arm held her close against his chest.
"To love and to cherish," he said softly.
"To love and to cherish," she repeated.

A soul-searing decision? Not a bit of it; just in time for this bravura scene, it seems, old Grandpa Fitch died and left them a prospering farm.

Phony as this revolt was, most protagonists are not allowed so much as the appearance of one, and if the husbands have a common denominator it is acceptance. The movie *Woman's World* is a particularly good example. The gist is the idea of a company president selecting between men on the basis of their wives. No moral was intended— the writers didn't use the ending of the original magazine story (which antedated our study) and evidently had some trouble settling on the winner. As to the ethics of the whole business, however, they admirably reflect the current climate; they hardly bother to raise an eyebrow over the appalling tactics of the boss (cast as Clifton Webb); they playfully accuse him of being a bit of a torturer, but they make his tactics seem reasonable enough. He needs a general manager, *ergo* he must bring three men and their wives to New York for several days of scrutiny to see which couple should get the job.

Why any of this sorry crew should be considered at all is difficult to understand. One contending couple, Katie and Bill, consists of a juvenile and an equally juvenile wife who is interested chiefly in staying home and being dowdy. Another contender, Sid, is an ambitious fool who has forgotten how to be a husband to his wife; at length he and his wife revisit one of those quaint Italian restaurants with a comic-dialect proprietor (Tomaso, by name), and the emotional hang-over of this experience helps the wife reform him out of his ambition.

This leaves only one man fit for the job. He is Jerry Talbot, a hard-working husband with a sexy, ambitious wife. In terms of the values of the world depicted in the film, she's the only worth-while person in the bunch. Unlike the others, busily sabotaging their husbands, she's actually trying to do something for her husband, albeit a little too pushily. She has the same zest for manipulation as the top man, and her ambition will provide her husband just the same economic motivation companies are so keen on. By the curious morality of popular fiction, however, she is too materialistic. Openly, she savors the idea of high life in New York. The movie does too—that's what its "production values" are all about—but, like the biblical movies, it must in the end smite that which it has exploited. She has to go. Some ten minutes before the dinner at which the boss has promised to award the prize, the husband viciously tells her to get packing. He won't even let her eat supper with the others. He gets the job. The boss explains that by ditching a person inimical to the team the man has shown his true mettle. To quote from the shooting script:

> GIFFORD: *Talbot, I think you have that . . .*
> *"X plus" . . . that makes a big man big.*
> (pause)
> *But there was something that made me*
> *doubt that you could ever function*

successfully as a general manager—
a handicap—and frankly it caused me to
decide against you.

I was convinced you were not aware of
this handicap and I wanted to call it
to your attention. I found an oppor-
tunity that gave me a chance to do so.
I can only guess at the details, but
this much I know: that suddenly you
did become aware of it and had the
courage to get rid of it—and just
as suddenly I'd found my new general
manager! Congratulations!

Jerry looks up at Gifford, dazed, and it is a moment be-
fore he can grasp the hand that is offered him. Liz turns
quickly to Sid and when she sees the unutterable relief in
his eyes her own are suddenly filled with tears. Sid reaches
for her hand.

And now his arms are around Liz and she presses against
him with a warmth he hasn't felt in years. And next to them
Katie and Bill are hugging each other ecstatically.

Hardly a morality tale. Nor are most such stories, singly.
Taken together, however, they constitute a sort of ever continuing serial, and innocent of thought as any one story
may be, cumulatively they have a message. And for all the
fluff, what a dismal one it is! *Accept.*

To compare it with the theme George Orwell tackled in
1984 might seem to be freighting popular fiction with more
portent than it deserves; Orwell was writing of totalitarian-
ism, specifically Communism, and because he makes the
leaders of society so villainous, the terrible world he
sketched would seem far remote, a hell to our heaven. Yet
in the final paragraph there is a scene which is hauntingly
similar to the endings of our current fiction. As the erstwhile rebel Winston sits idly at a café, he gazes up at a
picture of Big Brother. He begins to babble incoherently.
Tears of gratitude well up in his eyes. At last, as the officers
of the *Caine* had learned to love Queeg, he had won the
victory over himself. He had learned to love Big Brother.

PART SEVEN

The New Suburbia: Organization Man at Home

CHAPTER TWENTY-ONE

The Transients

I NOW turn to organization man at home—and, I hope, some clues as to where he is going. In these next chapters I am going to examine him in the communities that have become his dormitories—the great package suburbs that have sprung up outside our cities since the war. They are fascinating institutions in their own right, and here and there I will detour into aspects of them that are tangential to my main theme. What I wish to concentrate on, however, is the way in which they reflect the values of the organization man— and of the next generation to come.

They are communities made in his image. There are other kinds of people there too, and for many a resident the curving superblocks of suburbia are the end of a long road from the city wards to middle-class respectability. But it is the young organization man who is dominant. More than others, it is he who organizes the committees, runs the schools, selects the ministers, fights the developers, makes the speeches, and sets the styles.

Organization people live in many other kinds of places, of course, and some of them are in jobs that don't require them to move away from home at all. But in the new suburbia they are concentrated, and in so pure a state that here they may provide the best indication of the organization life of tomorrow. In suburbia, they can express themselves more clearly than in The Organization itself. They are not subordinates or juniors; they are the elders of the new suburbia, and there they are relatively free of the pressures of older traditions and older people that affect them elsewhere. In such propinquity, they bring out in each other—and at times caricature—tendencies that are latent in organization life, and one sees in bold relief what might be almost invisible in more conventional environments. To an older eye, perhaps, what is to be seen through the picture windows is abnormal, but what may be abnormal today is very likely to be normal tomorrow.

What suburbia best illuminates, I believe, is the nature of organization man's "rootlessness"—and the need to revise our customary assumptions about rootlessness. In speaking of the transients in our society it is interesting how instinctively we describe them by what they *don't* fit—of the homes they'll never go back to again, of the worlds they never made. Related to the usual niches of society, they are anomalies; moving as they are, they cut across the convenient abstractions that have ordered our thoughts, and thus we find it easy to see them as symptoms of malaise, psychological casualties of that world they never made.

Before looking at the transients' suburbia, then, we must first look at the changes in mobility and class structure that brought them there. In suburbia, as we will see in the next chapter, organization man is trying, quite consciously, to develop a new kind of roots to replace what he left behind, and to understand the nature of his quest we need to know what it is he did leave behind, why he left it behind, and how he looks back upon it.

On the matter of how much upward mobility there really is in this country, thinking has fluctuated a great deal—more, perhaps, than the mobility itself. Forty years ago the notion that the U.S. had a fairly fluid society would not have been particularly controversial; observers did point out that the Alger story was more an article of faith than a reality, but for the most part they felt our social structure was dynamic—almost frighteningly so. During the thirties and forties, however, a highly influential series of community studies began convincing people that this was no longer true.

Quite the contrary, it now appeared that the American system was finally shaking down into a fixed order of things in which achievement was more and more closed to the lower classes.

Anthropologist Lloyd Warner and others held that the basic pattern was revealed by the rigidities of the traditional community—the venerable, tree-shaded town in which the Hill, local business ties, and interlocking family relationships firmly fix the individual's position, and from which he can move upward (from the Elks, say, to the Rotary) only by sanction of the next upper group. Short-circuiting of this route, furthermore, was now believed to be more difficult than ever. The old route up through the shop was closing; the worker was unionized, the manager professionalized, and as these lines firmed, the boy from shantytown was going to have less chance than ever of crossing over the tracks. As I noted in the chapter on belongingness, this diagnosis was not without a note of advocacy; students of this school believed there should be some mobility, but they felt that for the most part the individual should not cherish illusions that he was going to go up but instead adjust to the realities of a fairly static environment.

These studies did a service in drawing attention to class and status factors Americans like to pretend don't exist. In focusing on the things that stand still, however, the studies slighted the importance of the things that don't, and in almost all of them there was one rather important omission. What about the man who doesn't fit in because he's not there to fit in? What about the man who *leaves* home?

The man who leaves home is not the exception in American society but the key to it. Almost by definition, the organization man is a man who left home and, as it was said of the man who went from the Midwest to Harvard, kept on going. There have always been people who left home, and the number of them is not decreasing but increasing—and so greatly that those who stay put in the home town are often as affected by the emigration as those who leave.

When a man moves from one place to another he is not necessarily moving socially. If we look at the figures for geographic mobility, however, we find that there is a rough connection between the two kinds of movement. Consider the relationship between the physical movement and age, education, and occupation. Men in the twenty-five-to-thirty-four age group are only 7.5 per cent of the total population, but they account for 12.4 per cent of the migration. The second characteristic is education: the more of it, the more mobility. If a man goes to college now, the chances are almost even that he won't end up in his home state. Recent census figures and *Time*'s study, *They Went to College*, indicate that the educational level is higher among migrants than nonmigrants, and the higher the educational level, the more intensive the migration. Only 27.3 per cent of high-school grads aged twenty-five to thirty-four, for example, were interstate migrants, versus 45.5 per cent of those who had had at least one year of college. Of those who worked their way through in a college outside their home state, 69 per cent don't come back. And for all college men, incidentally, the higher the grades, the more likely they are to move. Next, income. As the correlation with education would suggest, the more the mobility, the more one is likely to be in the higher income brackets. Census figures do not break down migration by income groups, but the experience of direct-mail people indicates that address changes are most frequent in the $5,000 and over bracket. There are also indications that address changes are becoming more frequent in this group. In 1953, 14.8 per cent of *Fortune*'s subscribers changed addresses during the year. In 1954, 16.6 per cent, and in 1955, 17.4 per cent.

Records of long-distance movers show the same concentration of organization people. The greatest single group of their clients—between 40 and 50 per cent—is composed of corporation people being transferred from one post to another (with the corporation directly paying the bill). If to this group are added government, Army and Navy people, and corporation people leaving one company for another, roughly three quarters of all moves are accounted for by members of large organizations.

These people confound the usual concepts of class. Some

can be described as upper class, some middle class, but it is the horizontal grouping in which they come together that is more significant. It does not declass them; however muffled, the differences in family background between organization people will never be erased. But they will be superseded. When organization people speak of the boat they are all in together, it is the horizontal grouping they are describing. They assimilate one another, and the fact that they all left home can be more important in bonding them than the kind of home they left is in separating them.

The export movement that brings them together has become thoroughly basic to our society. It is no longer a case of the special boy who had to get out of town to cross the tracks to find an outlet for his energies; now as many as three quarters of the town's young college men may be in the same position. Where are they to go after college? Back home? Lawyers and doctors can, and the majority do; they are in the happy position of being able to go home, to keep professionally alert, and to make a good bit of money at the same time. But for the others, opportunity seems to be elsewhere—not just for the delivery boy who became an Air Force lieutenant, but for the young man on the Hill who's gone off to join Du Pont.

It is understandable that American literature has been so long fascinated with the small town revisited, or lost.[1] Those who have gone away think often of what they left behind and they are curiously ambiguous in their feeling of estrangement. In the case of the organization transients, they feel they sacrificed much and they often wonder if the gain has been worth it. Most of them came from reasonably prosperous homes, and when they look back they remember the support of the kinfolk and friends about, the reassuring solidity of grandfather's mansard-roof house, and the feeling that they were part of the group that counted. The family name, as they so often say in retrospect, *meant* something. No longer: local prestige, they well know, is not for

---

[1] Recently, *Point of No Return*, by J. P. Marquand; *A Pride of Lions*, by John Brooks; *The View from Pompey's Head*, Hamilton Basso. Forerunners would include Thomas Wolfe's *You Can't Go Home Again*, Willa Cather's *A Lost Lady*.

export, and what is one town's upper-upper would be an-other's middle class.

In leaving this behind, however, the transients also draw solace. They have entered the heavyweight competition, and if they do not enter the arena exactly barehanded, they feel down deep that they have proved themselves just a little bit better than those who didn't. One of the great tacit bonds the transients share is a feeling, justifiable or not, that by moving they acquire an intellectual breadth that will forever widen the gap between them and their home towns.

"Dave and I have often thought about going back to East Wells," a successful young executive's wife explains. "It's a beautiful old New England town and we both had such happy times there. But all the people who had anything on the ball seem to have left. There are a few who took over their fathers' businesses, but the rest—I hate to sound so snob-bish, but, dammit, I *do* feel superior to them." And they can never really go back. Once the cord is broken, a return carries overtones of failure. "I'm fed up with New York," says one executive, "but if I went back to Taylorston I know damned well they'd think my tail was between my legs."

Even if the chance of transfer sends them back they will be strangers. They might still be able to pick up the local prestige they may have inherited, but if they do, it will be at the risk of weakening their new, and now more important, organization ties. One junior executive explained it to me this way: "Because of this last transfer I'm back here, al-most by accident, where I was born. It ought to be a setup; frankly, my family is as old guard around here as they come. Well, it's a lot of crap, sure, but I must say I get a good bit of pleasure knowing I can join the City Club and my boss can't. But it's damned privately I think about it. If I am going to go ahead in this organization, the people I've got to get along with are the office crowd, and don't think I wouldn't get the business if they started reading about me in the social columns." Says another, "It's odd. Here I've got a social position a lot of people would give a fortune to get, but the minute I joined the corporation I had to turn my back on it. We're sort of declassed, and as

far as Amy and I are concerned, it is as if we weren't born
here at all."

But perhaps the most important reason the transients can't
go home is that they won't find it there if they do. It is not
just the physical changes—the new sub-developments on the
old golf course, the shopping-center strip just outside town,
the new factory. As the young transients have left town,
their opposite numbers from other towns have come in,
and in many American communities there has been wholesale displacement from positions of power of the names
that once "meant" something. Even in towns relatively untouched by urbanization the exodus of youth has left a
vacuum the community itself cannot replenish. The venerable Newburyport of "Yankee City" fame is an example.
With a population of about 15,000 at this moment, Newburyport has not shared at all the population growth that
has affected almost every "normal" American community;
physically, it is the Newburyport of the 1800s with the addition of relatively few modern buildings.

But there is considerable mobility. High-school records
show that roughly 25 per cent of the graduating class do not
return to Newburyport but instead go off to join the organization world, and in many cases this geographic movement
represents social movement as well. Meanwhile, the old
upper-upper families of the beautiful houses on High Street
have been giving way here and there; one by one the old
houses are being sold as old ladies with them pass on.
(Several have been bought by executives brought into town
by local companies.) Newburyporters are sad at some aspects of the slow disintegration of the eighteenth-century
idyl, but they are not entirely hostile to the twentieth century. The Newburyport paper is a running stream of items
about efforts of citizens to bring in new industry, and after
a strenuous local debate they got enough land condemned
to make a sort of industrial park. The great suburban trend
has not hit them yet, but the new highway up from Boston
is broad and flat.

For many towns the tensions have been strong. The new

people may be a symbol of growth and prosperity, but much as resort natives view the "summer people" the old residents see them as something of a threat. These people and the corporation that is bringing them not only upset the historically low wage structure of the town, they have upset the whole local order of things. Whether his blood is blue or not, the general manager of the corporation's branch plant wields key power, and the townspeople know it. It is little wonder that corporations think long and hard about the tact of the proconsuls—and their wives—that they send to the far reaches of the empire.

Thus the pleasant young couple driving slowly along in their ranch wagon looking at the old houses can be to a somewhat dispossessed gentry a portent they fear. A member of one of the prominent families in one old town asked me, a comparative stranger, what were the people like that lived in the new houses on the hill across from her farm. "My husband and I are sick about it. We sold the twenty acres over there because we needed the money, but now look what's happened. Those ugly little boxes they're putting up! They cost like sin but there's not one in good taste. These people have no style at all. I wonder where Tom [president of a near-by steel company] finds them all. They are all bright, I suppose. Those wives with their silly babble and their middle-western twangs! They have already just about taken over the golf club, and now Charlie wants me to entertain some of them. I simply won't. I'll be pleasant to them, but they have their way and I have mine."

The newcomers can often sense the distaste. The transients may tell you about a wonderfully exceptional town they hit, but they are more likely to tell you of towns that proffered a cold shoulder. Sometimes they speak of outright antagonism on the part of the locals. If the community is one that has been expanding rapidly, the apprehensions over the newcomers can get translated very quickly into such matters as zoning and club restrictions, and the little developments that encircle some towns form what is in effect a ring of animosities.[2]

[2] A study by New York University's Dr. Marie Jahoda indicates that in its initial stages of development, the people in

The same process of replacement has been going on, somewhat more painlessly, in the great metropolitan centers. Because of the greater number of opportunities it offers, one might assume that the city would much more easily use its home-grown talent to staff its institutions. Even here, however, the natives have been outnumbered by the newcomers. Philadelphia, for example, has long been considered quite inbred, yet a study by sociologist Digby Baltzell reveals that as early as 1940, 64 per cent of the Philadelphia business and professional leaders listed in *Who's Who* were born outside the Philadelphia area; in time, he documents, the influx of new blood in the positions of power is reflected in the Social Register.

The same process is going on everywhere. As the seats of economic power have shifted from the local, home-grown institutions to national organizations, membership in the elite of many a city or town is being determined less by hereditary ties, more by current functional rank. Not only are the national institutions sending in more people, the local institutions themselves are also being opened to outsiders more than before. The urban elite, in short, has become an ex-officio elite.

To document the facts of current mobility is not to furnish proof that it will continue, and I have met many who believe that in its present order of magnitude it is a temporary phenomenon. I think they underestimate the force of momentum in this respect. It is true enough that the postwar physical expansion of industry has been a great factor, and we cannot count on this as a constant. The more intangible aspects of mobility, however, can be just as important. Turnover has a way of begetting turnover, for as people become acclimated to current necessity there is a natural tendency to make it into a desirability.

Let me turn for a moment to corporation transfer policy, for it helps illuminate the self-perpetuating nature of the mobility. When the recruit joins up he does not do so be-

Fairless Hills, Pennsylvania, believed that most of the other people in lower Bucks County disliked them. They were quite right.

cause he *wants* to move a lot, and it is often in spite of it. But moving, he knows, has become part of the bargain, and unsettling as transfer might be, even more unsettling are the implications of not being asked to transfer. "We never plan to transfer," as one company president explains a bit dryly, "and we never make a man move. Of course, he kills his career if he doesn't. But we never *make* him do it." The fact is well understood; it is with a smile that the recruit moves—and keeps on moving—year after year, until, perhaps, that distant day when he is summoned back to Rome.

It is not just more moves per man. Even companies reporting no increase in the number of times each individual moves report an increase in the sheer number of men being moved. GE has compared a cross section of its forty-five-year-old executives with one of its thirty-five-year-olds. In the ten years after they were twenty-five, 42 per cent of the older group had moved at least once; during the same age period, 58 per cent of the younger had moved.

Corporations never planned it quite that way. Decentralization and expansion, rather than deliberate personnel policy, have determined the pattern. Companies have systematized it, to be sure. Moves are settling into more of a rhythm, and almost invariably they are sweetened by special departments that handle all the housekeeping fuss of the trip. By and large, however, the question of the man's personal development—however emphasized when the boss breaks the news to him—has been secondary to the day-to-day necessity of filling vacancies out in the empire.[3]

[3] There are still a number of environments, it should be noted, in which executives don't fit in—and some in which they fit in all too well. A good many companies have belatedly realized they have lost some of their best men by carelessly assigning them to San Francisco or Los Angeles for a spell. Even salary boosts often fail to achieve repatriation; once tasted, the California way of life dulls such appetites—a fact that has sometimes been reflected in a salary differential between the West Coast and the East. When Shell Chemical moved its head office to New York from San Francisco some of its management group resigned rather than go along, and several who did go along eventually decided to go back. Another company recently located a lab on the Coast, it admits, mainly to hang onto talent it might otherwise lose.

That is, up until now. Periodic transfer, some companies are coming to believe, is a positive good in itself; and even where no immediate functional reason exists, it might often be important to move the man anyway. What better way, they ask, to produce the well-rounded executive? Instead of leaving transfer to be determined haphazardly by different departments, some companies, like GE, have made such decisions part of a systematic managerial program. By thus making a man's "permanent" assignment (i.e., one lasting at least three years) part of a deliberate rotation policy, the man is given "more choices in life to make," and the company, as a result, is given a pool of seasoned talent. Other companies agree. By deliberately exposing a man to a succession of environments, they best obtain that necessity of the large organization—the man who can fit in anywhere. "The training," as an I.B.M. executive succinctly puts it, "makes our men interchangeable."

And is not this the whole drift of our society? We are not interchangeable in the sense of being people without differences, but in the externals of existence we are united by a culture increasingly national. And this is part of the momentum of mobility. The more people move about, the more similar the American environments become, and the more similar they become, the easier it is to move about.

More and more, the young couples who move do so only physically. With each transfer the *décor,* the architecture, the faces, and the names may change; the people, the conversation, and the values do not—and sometimes the *décor* and the architecture don't either. If there are no company people to help the newcomers break the ice, there are al-

---

On the other hand, there are some kinds of environments many people can't be tempted into trying at all. This has been particularly evident in the postwar moves of entire headquarters to the hinterlands. Making a small town a way station on the executive route is one thing; making it Mecca, another. An organization's creative and professional people usually will move permanently to a small town only if it is in striking distance of a large city and the professional contacts it affords. Similarly, almost any executive is likely to balk—for a while at least—if the town is so small that the influx of the company threatens a resurgence of the paternalistic company town.

most bound to be some fellow transients near by, and the chances are good that some of them will be couples that the most recent arrivals have run into somewhere else in this great new freemasonry of transients. It is, they like to observe, a small world. "I just jump to read the new-arrivals list in the local paper," says a typical transient. "We've already run up against a couple from our Cambridge days at the Business School, and we're sure that some from Park Fairfax or Fresh Meadows will be along soon too." But even if they know no one it will not make too much difference. Whatever their respective organizations, they will share the same problems, the same kind of memories and aspirations. To use a favorite phrase, they talk the same language.

This communality among organization people would seem to support one of the more unpleasant prophecies that have been advanced in the U.S. Will not this freemasonry of talent freeze into an elite more and more closed to outsiders? From Veblen's "soviet of engineers" to Burnham's "managerial revolution," the idea that a professional ruling class was jelling—or should jell—has been a strong undercurrent in American thought. Today, on the face of it there would seem more reason than ever for such an elite to coalesce.

I do not think this is the direction of our main problem. As the new generation of management has been maturing, whole groups, not merely individuals, have moved into the middle class. The fact, for example, that a declining number of businessmen comes from farm homes is not due to oligarchy so much as to the decrease in the proportion of farmers to the rest of the U.S. population. So with laborers. It is true that few top executives come up from a working-class background, but we tend to exaggerate the number who ever did. If we go back to 1870, we find that very few of the business leaders of that time had been laborers or even laborers' sons. As a study by Gregory and Neu[4] demon-

---

[4] In *Men in Business,* edited by William Miller; a publication of the Research Center in Entrepreneurial History, Harvard University, 1952.

strated, the business leaders of that day were overwhelmingly of middle- or upper-class background, and more, not fewer, of them were sons of heads of companies than today.

As the middle class has expanded, the hereditary advantages of the upper strata have declined drastically. The spread of American education, the growing accessibility to culture, have so ironed out regional and social differences that a vastly greater number of Americans can now compete on even terms in what might be called a national society. The rate of expansion within high-prestige occupations tells part of the story. As Nelson Foote has pointed out, the occupations which have shown the greatest relative gain compared to 1910 are those, like teaching and engineering, in which education is far more important than family and community ties. Similarly, within business, those more dependent on family connections—the proprietors, for example—have decreased while the white-collar people have increased.[5]

For further evidence of this upward movement we are indebted to none other than Lloyd Warner. He has collaborated in a study of big-business leaders, and with a willingness to revise former conclusions that compels awe as well as respect, he concludes that it is people who move who are the key. Hereditary advantages can be important, he and co-author James C. Abegglen note, but what seems to be the more essential denominator of top executives is a recurrent cycle of "arrival and departure"—an ability to leave one set of friends and circumstances and affiliate with another, and to repeat this whenever necessary, and repeat it again. "All evidence," Warner and Abegglen say, "indicates that in American society opportunity continues to be realized, and increasingly so. Rather than closing in on men of low birth, holding them to the positions into which they were born, our social system continues to make it possible for men from all levels to move into elite positions in commerce and industry."[6]

[5] Nelson N. Foote and Paul K. Hatt, "Social Mobility and Economic Advancement," *The American Economic Review,* May 1953.

[6] W. Lloyd Warner and James C. Abegglen, *Big Business*

Aside from the fact that the managerial group is open to all comers, there is another fact which disqualifies its members as a ruling class. They have no collective sense of direction. They have none because their organizations have none. Owing to essential differences in functions and goals, and not unimportantly, the American inability to put things together into a doctrine until after it's all over, our many different hierarchies are not so comparable as might appear. Like the union man who becomes an industrial-relations executive, the ex-government lawyer turned a corporation counsel, the erstwhile blue blood who becomes a sales trainee, many organization men have a conflict in loyalties they must resolve. The men who move are not vouchsafed a common, all-purpose religion.

Their allegiance is more to The Organization itself than to any particular one, for it is in the development of their professional techniques, not in ideology, that they find continuity—and this, perhaps, is one more reason why managerial people have not coalesced into a ruling class. "They have not taken over the governing functions," Max Lerner has pointed out, "nor is there any sign that they want to or can. They have concentrated on the fact of their skills rather than on the uses to which their skills are put. The question of the *cui bono* the technician regards as beyond his technical competence."

The evidence, in short, is that whatever the faults of American society at this time, lack of dynamism is not one of

Leaders in America (New York: Harper & Brothers, 1955). This study, based on 8,562 businessmen, gives an even stronger picture of mobility than did Herrymon Maurer's provocative study, which concentrated on the 900 top executives (*Fortune*, Nov. 1952). Using categories comparable to those used in earlier studies, Warner and Abegglen found that since 1900 there had been an *increase* of 8 per cent in the proportion of executives whose fathers were laborers, a decrease of 10 per cent in those whose fathers were owners of businesses. A study by Mabel Newcomer, *The Big Business Executive* (New York, 1955) documents the same trend; in her sample, 7.5 per cent of the executives of 1950 were sons of workers—versus 4.2 per cent for the executives of 1900.

them. The routes to advancement are not closing down, our classes are not freezing; quite the opposite, there have never been so many people moving in so many different ways. How much to the good, or bad, this change will be is a question we must defer. There is no virtue in change per se; whether or not it is to be for the good depends on what the change is *to*, and that, as the young suburbanites' way of life would indicate, is at once unsettling and encouraging.

A focus on the dynamic can breed a shallow optimism, and one can revel so much in the variety in American life as to believe that no matter how bad a particular trend may be there is always a counter-trend around to offset it, and so why worry? (Or why generalize, some might add.) Yet I do believe the emphasis on change to be the most valid point of view and one, furthermore, that bespeaks a considerable faith in the capacities of the individual. Observers who would like to see less change argue that change breeds anxieties, tensions, and frustrations. This is true, and certainly the suburban transients pay a great price for the uprooting that has put them there. But how ideal for them would be the alternative? Before we explore their troubles let us remember that only a fixed order of things, or total allegiance to one encompassingly benevolent organization, would give them freedom from this kind of worries.

CHAPTER TWENTY-TWO

The New Roots

To FIND where the mobility of organization life is leading, the new package suburbs may be the best place of all to look. For they are not merely great conglomerations of mass housing. They are a new social institution, and while the variations in them are many, wherever one goes—the courts of Park Forest, the patios of Park Merced in San Francisco, Philadelphia's Drexelbrook, the new Levittown, Pennsylvania—there is an unmistakable similarity in the way of life.

It is a communal way of life, and the residents are well aware of it. They are of many minds how to describe it. Sometimes they lean to analogies like the frontier, or the early colonial settlements. Other times they are a little more wry; "sorority house with kids," a projection of dormitory life into adulthood, or, slightly better, a lay version of Army post life. But no matter how sharp the coinages—"a womb with a view," "a Russia, only with money"—it is a way of life they find suited to their wants, their needs, and their times. They are not unwitting pawns; educated to be more aware of social trends than their forebears, they discuss their situations with considerable sophistication; at times, the way they casually toss out words like "permissive" and "kid-centered," it almost seems as if everyone was his own resident sociologist.

In part, these communities are a product of the great expansion of the middle class, for the new suburbs have become a mecca for thousands of young people moving up and out of city wards. It is not these people, however, who are dominant. In his wanderings, the organization man has found in the new suburbs an ideal way station. He is the one who is most quick to move out, but as soon as he does another replaces him, and then another. It is he who sets the tone, and if he is as uncertain as any in keeping up with the Joneses, it is because he *is* the Joneses.

Park Forest, the community I studied most intensively, has its unique features, but its most salient characteristic is that it is virtually a controlled sample of organization people. As elsewhere, there are other kinds of people too, and for many a newcomer from the city such communities are an education in middle-class values. What might be called the modal man, however, is a twenty-five-to-thirty-five-year-old white-collar organization man with a wife, a salary between $6,000 and $7,000, one child, and another on the way.

If one wishes to study the next generation of organization men, a pretty good form chart is the record of how the younger ones handle their problems when they are away from their elders. Because they are jammed into such propinquity with one another in their new suburbia, everything they do carries a certain degree of exaggeration: the schools are a little more modern than elsewhere, the politics a little more intense, and most certainly the social life is a lot more social. Abnormal? Or the portent of a new normality? The values of Park Forest, one gets the feeling, are harbingers of the way it's going to be.[1]

This kind of suburbia is a natural phenomenon. They bear

[1] These chapters are based on research I did for a *Fortune* study in 1953, and on subsequent research in 1955 and 1956. Originally, I had started to study Drexelbrook, Pennsylvania, but in late 1952, after visiting several other suburbs, I decided to use them for reference and comparison and concentrate on Park Forest, for it was the largest one that was a political as well as a social unit. Work commenced in December 1952 and continued over a six-month period until June 1953. During this period additional research was done at Drexelbrook, Levittown, Pennsylvania, and several developments in California. In 1955 I

a resemblance to such utopian ventures as the Oneida community or the Fourier settlements, but where earlier utopias were an expression of revolt and idealism, the new suburbs are a response to social and economic realities. Park Forest, for example, was set up, quite simply, to make money, lots and lots of it. Looking at the real-estate situation right after the war, a group of Chicago businessmen saw that there was a huge population of young veterans, but little available housing suitable for young people with (1) children, (2) expectations of transfer, (3) a taste for good living, (4) not too much money. Why not, the group figured, build an entire new community from scratch for these people? The group, incorporated as American Community Builders, bought up 2,400 acres in the cornland thirty miles south of Chicago and brought in a remarkable man, former Federal Public Housing Commissioner Philip Klutznick, as president.

The plan was to build clusters of rental garden apartments (rent for two-bedroom duplex: $92) around a central shopping center, and then, as time went on, build ranch-type houses for sale ($11,995) on the periphery of the area. The housing would be merchandised at bargain rates. The real money would come from the waterworks and the company's cut (ranging up to 10 per cent) of every dollar spent in the shopping center. In effect, the developers were building a city to provide a sort of captive market—a constantly replenished, nonsatiable reservoir of 30,000 people, many of whom would ever be poised at that stage when families just begin to lay up possessions.

returned to Park Forest, after a deep breath, to check up on what had happened in the intervening time, and in January and February 1956 did further research at Levittown, Pa.

I would like to acknowledge the help of Mrs. Selma Wolff, the principal researcher on the study; of Edward Engberg (who, as an ex-Park Forester, was well equipped to do research in Levittown, Pennsylvania; of the Mesdames Priscilla Shames and Jean Martin, two of the shrewdest of Park Forest's many shrewd social observers. Thanks also to Philip Klutznick and his organization, American Community Builders, Inc., the developers of Park Forest, who gave us their full co-operation. A word of thanks too to the people of Park Forest, Levittown, and Drexelbrook who gave so much of their time, thought, and coffee.

When the doors were thrown open in 1948 the rental courts were islands in a sea of mud, but the young people came streaming out of Chicago. The first wave of colonists was heavy with academic and professional people—the place, it appeared, had an extraordinary affinity for Ph.D.s. Since Chicago is one of the great business-training grounds of the U.S., however, another kind of affinity proved even stronger: poised at the nexus of America's junior-executive migration, Park Forest quickly became a haven for the organization man. Out came trainees for the big corporations, research chemists with the AEC, captains and majors with the Fifth Army, airline pilots, FBI men—in total, a cross section of almost every kind of organization man in America.[2]

Why the attraction? Since I am going to emphasize some of the nonmaterial factors let me at once put first things first. The people who went to Park Forest went there because it was the best housing for the money. Some psychiatrically-minded observers have hazarded the thought that they really went there to seek a father image and such, and that Park Forest is not a normal sampling because it tends to select such people. I do not agree. Undoubtedly, it does have some selective appeal, but it should be noted that people in the

---

[2] The cross section has remained constant. Old settlers at Park Forest like to tell you that they are being replaced by an "element" less worthy, but though the population has been greater each year (about 25,000 in mid-1956), there has been little change in basic characteristics. Median educational level for *all* adults remains about 2.5 years of college—the highest of any Illinois community. As far as occupation is concerned, a check of move-ins to the rental area in 1955 shows no change, save a few less university people. Here is a random sampling of newcomers in 1955: research chemist, Sinclair Oil Co.; salesman, Swift & Co.; major, Fifth Army; investigator, FBI; purchasing agent, Ford Motor Co.; industrial psychologist, Swift & Co.; space salesman, *Business Week* magazine; underwriter, Prudential Life; salesman, Du Pont Co.; buyer, Carson, Pirie, Scott store; trainee, Burroughs Adding Machine Co.; lieutenant colonel, Fifth Army; research engineer, Continental Can Co.; engineer, Western Electric; sales trainee, Atlas Box Co.; engineer, General Electric; pilot, American Airlines; public-relations assistant, Acme Steel Co.; teacher, Rich High School; labor-relations assistant, Ford Motor Co.; writer, Time, Inc.; accountant, Gulf Oil Co.; copywriter, Chicago advertising agency.

income and age group of Park Forest have very little luxury of choice in housing. Even though they might dislike the idea of so much propinquity—many Park Foresters, indeed, say that they almost decided not to go there because of the propinquity—other considerations weigh far more in the balance. The space for the money, the amenities not elsewhere available, and, most important, the fact that it was so well set up for children have been in most cases the dominant factors.

Park Foresters, in short, went there for quite rational, and eminently sensible, reasons. Once there, however, they created something over and above the original bargain. Together, they developed a social atmosphere of striking vigor, and while it might have been as one to ten with the more material attractions, it was to be a significant extra. The developers were quick to recognize it. At first they had advertised Park Forest as housing. Now they began advertising happiness. They retained an advertising agency, Weiss and Geller, famed as the most motivation-minded of all agencies, and after a bout of depth interviews and psychiatric panel discussions, the ads began belting away at the overtones of Park Forest more than the homes themselves.

Here's the way they went:

> You *Belong*
>   in PARK FOREST!
> The moment you come to our town you know:
> You're welcome
> You're part of a big group
> You can live in a friendly small town
>   instead of a lonely big city.
> You can have friends who want you—
>   and you can enjoy being with them.
> Come out. Find out about the spirit of Park Forest.
> (*Ad for Park Forest Homes, Inc., November 8, 1952*)

Here is a magnificent one:

> a cup of coffee—symbol of
> PARK FOREST!
> Coffeepots bubble all day long
> in Park Forest. This sign of

friendliness tells you how much
neighbors enjoy each other's company—
feel glad that they can share their daily
joys—yes, and troubles, too.

Come out to Park Forest where small-
town friendships grow—and you still live
so close to a big city. (*November 19, 1952*)[3]

The ads are quite right. Let's take, for example, a couple
we shall call Dot and Charlie Adams. Charlie, a corporation trainee, is uprooted from the Newark office, arrives at
Apartment 8, Court M-12. It's a hell of a day—the kids are

[3] One can only stand in admiration of these ads—and hard
selling they were. I have always wondered, however, why the
developers and the advertising people neglected another, and quite
important, appeal. In exploiting the loneliness of contemporary
life they hit a nerve, but they left untouched the more material
service of Park Forest as a temporary home for people who know
they'll be transferred. Many transients would be better off
if they bought a home, and some discover this after a year or so
at Park Forest. But often it is when it is too late and the knowledge that buying a home—even for a stay of only two years—
as a riskless and economical proposition has not been openly
advertised, and as a consequence many transients in the Chicago
area never think of this possibility. In time this new concept of
home-buying will probably become accepted practice, but it is
still an appeal that offends many sensibilities. Those who want
to stay put bridle at it. Even the developers themselves hate
to say it out loud. They have become Park Forest citizens too,
and hard-headed as they are on most things, they are a bit touchy
on the matter of Park Forest's turnover. It is quite a normal
phenomenon, but they sometimes spend their own good money
in ads that imply that nobody's leaving Park Forest any more.
The developers have a proper concern, of course, in that it
takes some explaining before most nontransient home seekers
will recognize that turnover is normal and not a rejection of
the community. I still think, however, an opportunity is being
overlooked, and since I have great respect for the resource-
fulness of the developers I have no doubt that in time they'll
be advertising openly how good a way station for transients
they have. In a decade or so, indeed, what may worry them is that
people aren't *enough* aware of the turnover. Park Forest is not so
a home of aging people, of has-beens, they may feel impelled to
argue; our junior-executive people get promoted and transferred
as fast as people anywhere.

crying, Dot is half sick with exhaustion, and the movers won't be finished till late.

But soon, because M-12 is a "happy" court, the neighbors will come over to introduce themselves. In an almost inordinate display of decency, some will help them unpack, and around suppertime two of the girls will come over with a hot casserole and another with a percolator full of hot coffee. Within a few days the children will have found playmates, Dot will be *Kaffeeklatsching* and sunbathing with the girls like an old-timer, and Charlie, who finds that Ed Robey in Apartment 5 went through officers' training school with him, will be enrolled in the Court Poker Club. The Adamses are, in a word, *in*—and someday soon, when another new couple, dazed and hungry, moves in, the Adamses will make their thanks by helping them to be likewise.

In the court, they find, their relationships with others transcend mere neighborliness. Except for the monastic orders and the family itself, there is probably no other social institution in the U.S. in which there is such a communal sharing of property. Except for the $200 or $300 put aside for the next baby, few of the transients have as yet been able to accumulate much capital or earthly possessions, and so they share to make the best of it. One lawn mower (with each man doing his allotted stint) may do for the whole court. For the wives there may be a baby-sitting "bank" (i.e., when one wife baby-sits for another she is credited with the time, and when she wishes to draw on it one of the wives who has a debit to repay will sit for her). To hoard possessions is frowned upon; books, silverware, and tea services are constantly rotated, and the children feel free to use one another's bikes and toys without asking. "We laughed at first at how the Marxist society had finally arrived," one executive says, "but I think the real analogy is to the pioneers."

But the court social life, important as it is in rooting the transient, is only part of the acclimation. Before long Charlie Adams may feel the urge to shoot out a few extra roots here and there and, having normal joining instincts, may think a mild involvement in some community-wide organization just the thing. When the matter is bruited to him he may be tentative—nothing strenuous, understand, awfully busy with company work; just want to help out a little. Instantaneously, or no longer than it takes one person to telephone another, the news is abroad. Charlie will never be quite the same again.

He has plunged into a hotbed of Participation. With sixty-six adult organizations and a population turnover that makes each one of them insatiable for new members, Park Forest probably swallows up more civic energy per hundred people than any other community in the country. For the wife who gets fully involved, the blackboard in the kitchen is indispensable, for scheduling oneself to keep from being expected at two different meetings at the same time is not always easy. Every minute from 7:00 A.M. to 10:00 P.M. some organization is meeting somewhere. Looking through the picture windows of one of the community buildings one typical night I saw: on the top floor, the church choir rehearsing; the Explorer Scouts (waiting for a quorum to plan next week's hike); world politics discussion group (to discuss what causes war; a second discussion group was to meet on a different evening to take up American foreign policy). Bottom floor: school board meeting (to talk over interior decoration of the new school); an organizing committee to organize a new organization (the Protestant Men's Club); Husanwif Club (to watch slides on safety rules for children).

As elsewhere, of course, the apathetic greatly outnumber the active—but not by so much as elsewhere, and the active are so active that they generally feel compelled to laugh at themselves for their folly. "Actually, neither Fred nor I are joiners, like some of these silly characters around here," one wife explains, "but it's gotten so now I practically have to make an appointment to see him Saturdays. During the week we alternate; when I have my meetings, he baby-sits for me, and when he has his political meetings, I baby-sit for him." Says another: "What a rat race! Even staying at home I do a lot more than you think. I act as Dick's secretary and handle all the phone calls when he's away, and then there's my League [of Women Voters] work and the PTA and the Great Books Course. Some of my friends think I'm nuts. They ask me, what do you do it for? Sometimes I wonder myself."

They hate it and they love it. Sometimes it seems as if they are drawn to the participation just for participation's sake—the ease with which signatures for petitions—any petition—are obtained, for example, is nothing short of startling. Nor are meetings necessarily directed to any substantive purpose. Sometimes they appear to be chiefly a medium by which anxious, uncertain people can vent aggressions they must elsewhere repress. Without the disciplining effect of a dominant older group and of custom, they are enticed into precocity, and this, unfortunately, stimulates many to a form of free expression in which name-calling and rancor seems to be an end in itself.

But there is real purpose to all this. If they do act like precocious brats at times, they do, eventually, get a great deal accomplished, and the fact that the community has solved so many problems so well outweighs the bloody noses and ferocities along the way. But the most important compensation is of another nature. The civic activities are in no sense make-work, but while they have grown out of quite practical community needs, they have also grown out of personal needs, and these are needs that far transcend Park Forest.

I speak of the problem of "rootlessness." It is a term that needs re-examination. Are the transients a rootless people? If by roots we mean the complex of geographical and family ties that has historically knitted Americans to local society, these young transients are almost entirely rootless. They are very much aware of the fact; surprisingly often they will bring up the home town, and though they have no intention whatsoever of going back, they dwell on what they left behind. Interestingly, the minor note that recurs most frequently is trees. "You know, the birds don't sing here yet," one transient explained to me, waving disgustedly at the little sapling outside the picture window. "The trees are so small. When I was a child in Jeffersonville I remember so well the great big trees outside the house. There were squirrels and birds around all the time. I think that's what I miss most of all."

Always, they will be moving on. For most of its renters Park Forest is a sort of way station, a phase in life, and beyond a certain point continued residence can carry overtones of failure. Very few "flunk out" of Park Forest because they are not making the grade; far more leave precisely because they *have* made the grade. However glowingly they speak of the no-keeping-up-with-the-Joneses and the other attractions of Park Forest, transients say frankly that they expect eventually to graduate to someplace like Winnetka, the Main Line, or Westchester County. Anyway, they explain, the decision is out of their hands; someday soon the boss may call John in for a little chat and they will be moving on.

They speak of their impermanence in terms of their children more often than of themselves, but the overtones are unmistakable. "The kids look forward to moving, and yet they dread it," as one young parent put it. "They hear that if they move to a house they can have a little dog or cat. They like that. But their friends—they hate to leave their friends. My little daughter got worried over this and I had to reassure her we are going to stick around for a while. . . . It's this temporary attitude we all have."

But unsettling as this mobility has been, it has provoked its own compensations. The transients are rootless, in the old sense of the term, but is the old sense the only possible one? The analogy we usually think of involves a large, venerable tree. But another analogy may now be as appropriate. I cite from a catalogue for a forest nursery:

Stock is transplanted in our nurseries from one to four or more times. Each time, the longer, more easily damaged roots are reduced so that more small feeder roots develop near the stem. The more feeder roots, the more quickly the tree is established on your land. Also, the resulting compact mass of small feeder roots makes the tree easier to plant. Each year in the spring and summer, we transplant hundreds of thousands of seedlings to build more feeder roots. Results prove extra cost is repaid many times over. (From 1954 catalogue of Musser Forests' Catalogue.)

The more small ones, in short, the easier the transplanting. The transients do hunger for deeper roots, but because they have sought so hard they have found something of what they have been looking for. They are beginning to find it in one another. Through a sort of national, floating co-operative, they are developing a *new* kind of roots. The roots are, to be sure, shallow—but like those of the redwood tree, even shallow roots, if there are enough of them, can give a great deal of support.

In much of the current writing about the need for belong-ingness, it is implied that participation is a kind of unity and that differences in what people are participating about are only differences in degree. Park Forest proves that it is not this simple; that there is a profound antithesis between different kinds of participation. But Park Forest indicates this, let me now point out, not because it is a failure, but because it is a success. Precisely because it comes so much closer to providing so full a spectrum of participation than other communities, the dilemmas of participation are more apparent there.

In the huge new life-insurance housing developments there is often a good bit of social activity—the "patio" at Park Merced, for example, functions very much like Park Forest's courts in this respect. There is little real civic or political activity, however. The developments are not po-litical entities but parts of established communities, and the old residents do not solicit the help of the newcomers, nor are the newcomers particularly interested in giving it. Within the development itself, furthermore, issues remain latent. With what can be called semi-benevolent paternal-ism, the developers have attended to almost all of the com-munity's physical problems, including even the cutting of grass (done at Park Merced by a corps of uniformed at-tendants). The developers provide room for hobby shops and the like, but they are not at all anxious to stimulate too active a sense of community. As one landlord confided to me, some originally innocuous group might easily become the nucleus of a tenants' organization and there would be no telling what would happen then.

Going up the scale of participation, there are quite a few new communities in which the developers do encourage social activities. Drexelbrook is an outstanding prototype. Here the paternalism is fully benevolent; builder Dan Kelly, a genial promoter who loves parties himself, runs his development on a bread-and-circuses principle. Unifying the 1,223 garden apartment units is the Drexelbrook Swimming and Tennis Club—a handsome affair with veranda terrace, swimming pools, and clubrooms which is made available at bargain rates. There is a full-time recreation director and in summer a corps of young girls to shepherd the children so mothers can take off for some shopping or the theater. Parties abound: "hunt balls" on Washington's Birthday, celebrity parties, "splash" parties (all you can eat for a dollar).

When residents want to start a social activity on their own, Kelly is usually glad to lend a hand. Several years ago, for example, a group of wives were sitting around wondering what they could get up. Somebody suggested maybe a garden club. They called up Kelly and he told them to count on him. As soon as they got things going he provided free busses for the club's first trip to the Philadelphia flower show and stimulated them in every way he could. The garden club now absorbs more of the wives' excess energies than any other activity. Another tradition partially subsidized by Kelly is the annual Christmas decoration contest. During December each court vies with the others to win the prize for the best Christmas displays, and they do such a striking job that over 100,000 people drive out each year to see the sight.

But it remains a development, more than a community. Understandably, no group has turned into a protest group against the developer; there have been mutterings about paternalism, but they have never coalesced into any active movement. As for the politics of the township of which Drexelbrook is a part, there occasionally is some ferment about matters which touch the immediate interests of the residents, like school-bus arrangements, but other than this, residents don't take much interest. Besides, they don't have the time.

Statistically, the people at Park Forest are much the same

as those of the Park Merceds or the Drexelbrooks. What makes their community so much more expressive than the demi-utopias lies in two factors: (1) it is a town in its own right, a real town with real problems;[4] (2) it has had a socially conscious developer.

From the beginning Klutznick decided that the affairs of the town would be turned over to the citizenry. This would put the tenants in the curious position of being able to tax the landlord, but Klutznick, a practical visionary, reasoned that this would be best for all—and for commercial reasons as well as idealistic ones. The more people get involved in running the place, he figured, the more they take root and thus the more stable would be the community—and the investment.

What happened was a severe wrench for Klutznick. Like many extremely dynamic men, he is not patient with what he feels is misguided opposition, and in no time he had plenty of it. Park Foresters fell to organizing their community, and what unified them more than anything else was the developer. Instinctively, they were against what he was for, and while they talked darkly of feudal barony and serfs, they certainly didn't act like serfs. No matter what the issue —the developer's rule against dogs, school appropriations— they reacted with the vigor of all those who feel they must do battle against tyranny. When Klutznick, in a moment of anger, expelled an activist tenant they organized a mass march on Klutznick's office complete with sound truck and placards. Even when Klutznick came bearing gifts they were contentious. "Father Klutznick, father of the village, eh!" I heard one tenant exclaim after a particularly handsome gift of land to the community was made by Klutznick. "He won't get away with it!"

[4] The experience of Levittown, Pennsylvania, demonstrates the importance of political unification. It straddles four townships, and quite possibly always will. There was a chance early for Levittown being incorporated as a town in its own right, but the civic leadership was inept and the move failed. Since then there has been less community-wide spirit, and many who otherwise would have been active have withdrawn from participation. There is plenty of local activity in the "sections," but it does not stir banked passions.

But the autonomy was good for all concerned. For the tenants the result was a rich diet of issues on which to cut their teeth, and for the developers a disciplining force that helped them resist the temptation to cut corners. Klutznick, who can reflect that it will be a hell of a day when Americans come to love the landlord, became more philosophical about it all. Heavy as the cross may have appeared, he is a formidable debater, and few things were so stimulating to him as a public tussle with the equally vigorous young lawyer who was the village president.

But the pot had to simmer down. Democracy, Klutznick once remarked, meant the day when he could drive around Park Forest in his Cadillac Sixty Special without anyone's saying, "Look at that lousy bastard Phil Klutznick driving a Cadillac." That day has long since arrived. Patently, Park Forest works superbly, and even those for whom tilting with the landlord is reflex hold that while Klutznick has an immensely shrewd eye for the dollar, he has proved himself a wise and fundamentally idealistic partner. The new era of good feeling has by no means dulled the citizenry's reflexes, but lately some have confessed that they did wish there were more iniquities to get excited about. Writing in a vein unthinkable before, a local columnist, Al Engelhard, has asked for a substitute ogre: "Of itself, harmony between tenant and landlord is a salutary thing, testifying to the tenant's intelligence and the landlord's good will. But the price has been high. Apathy has been the child of Peace, Indifference the spawn of Concord. . . . Since he is a man of many parts, I have hope that Phil Klutznick, alert to the disservice he has done us by becoming a sweet and lovable old bug, is even now pondering some issue which will redynamize us. We need a common enemy we can magnify into a monster, whisper about, conspire about, hang in effigy."

Writing of the period 1848-1853 in the California mining camps, Charles Shinn wrote how a great wave of communal sharing and democratic participation stirred people to believe that "the 'social contract' ideas of Rousseau and his followers seemed to have suddenly found a practical expression." Shinn also tells how in very short order this dream soured as the camps became more organized and the lawyers came in. Now, old-timers complained, the camps were just like any other place. Somewhat similarly, the Kibbutzim of Israel have lost something of their former communitarianism as they have grown larger. In *Life in a Kibbutz* (New York: The Reconstruction Press, 1955) Murray Weingarten sketches the impact of hired labor on one Kibbutz. "It seems much easier to maintain a communal setup in a poorly developed, impoverished society where there is little to divide and no opportunity to become an 'executive' than it is when the community begins to expand its wealth and activity."

So at Park Forest. Because the emergency pressures have vanished, the emergency spirit has too, and many pioneers see this as a flight from virtue. Several, indeed, actually moved away they were so disappointed. Many of those who remain are similarly disillusioned to find that without the stimulus of necessity most people can take issues or leave them alone, and you will be assured that it's disgraceful how few turn up for meetings.

The rather high quotient of idealism generated there is immensely valuable; without it there would not be the *esprit*, the agitation that so animate the community. All the idealism does, however, tend to make some residents discontented with anything less than the complete Welfare Community. Thus aroused, they measure the very achievements against perfection—and the result is a sense of paradise lost that bedevils many of them. "We moved here because we decided this would be a brave new world," says one resident, without conscious irony. "But so many compromises have been made. We're disgusted." Now they say it's just like any other place.

It isn't, of course. Apathy is a relative matter, and to newcomers from outside the amount of participation is still a phenomenon. Since the issues are now those of a "maturing" community rather than one a-borning, there has of necessity been some change in the way of meeting them—symptomatically, the able young chemist who is the new village president is known as a noncontroversialist. But the *élan* is still there, and if Park Foresters are a little more good humored about their new furors these days, they can still burn over them. For an idea of the flavor, I append a sampling of recent headlines in the Park Forest *Reporter:*

ACB, TRUSTEES CLASH ON BLDGS
TEMPORARY SCHOOLS WRANGLE CONTINUES
DEVELOPER OBJECTS TO NEW REGULATIONS
TRUSTEES REFUSE APPROVAL OF ACB'S AREA TO UTILITY
 PLANS
LIQUOR LICENSE HASSLE CONTINUES AT SECOND PUBLIC
 HEARING
TRUSTEES PONDER ACB PARK AND SEWER OFFER
CAT ORDINANCE AROUSES FUROR
AREA 11 PLAT OKAYED BY VILLAGE IN SHORT AND PEACE-
 FUL MEETING

I would not maintain that this activity fully compensates for the old kind of roots. The participation, as I have remarked, is often participation for the sake of it, and sometimes one is tempted to apply H. G. Wells's description of the town of Bromstead—"a dull, useless boiling up of human activities, an immense clustering of futilities." But this would miss an important point. In a community where there are real issues—schools to be built, segregation problems—its residents are immersed in the main stream of life, not insulated. If they appear stimulated over and above the call of community necessity, this itself is evidence of how very much they seek ties more meaningful than those of bridge and canasta and bowling.

For no one is this quest more important than the organization man. One of the dangers in the transient life is that these young people, because they must move about so frequently, will more and more identify their total destiny with one particular organization. For society as well as for themselves, the organization transients need to multiply their allegiances—to the church, to community, and the like. These additional allegiances provoke no great ideological conflicts with the office, certainly, but they do turn the executive away from complete preoccupation with one encompassing organization. Places like Park Forest do not solve this problem—The Organization will still come first—but they do ameliorate it.

This becomes evident when you talk to organization transients who have made their pause in more conventional environments. As might be expected, those who are in the cities have the least chance for participation, but the traditional small towns are not much better, and transients who have spent a tour in them speak feelingly of rebuffs and cold shoulders. "We just play around with company people," says a resident of one elm-shaded town. "The regular people here are pleasant enough, I suppose, but they don't want our help in anything that really counts—except when they come around to solicit money for the hospital." Such transients may make common cause with one another; in many a ranch-type block on the new outskirts of old towns the Du Pont engineers and the GE men and other fellow transients turn inwardly to one another and create something of the *Gemütlichkeit* of life at a Drexelbrook or a Park Merced. But it doesn't mean much. The activity is at a superficial level and the residents know it. One may dispute how much deeper is the activity of a Park Forest. The fact remains, however, that its people do feel an importance there they do not elsewhere.

The ability to chew on real problems is functional in another respect too. On a purely utilitarian level it provides young transients a leadership training it would take them years to get otherwise—and one of their few opportunities to acquire a sense of capital. "We are a young group without mature leadership," explains a rising young banker, "so we are forced to take on responsibilities that older people usually assume. For the last two years I have been chairman of the board of the church, a job held by a fifty-five or sixty-year-old man in most communities. This gives me a training valuable in business. The church is a corporation with a $50,000 budget, and we've had to think about a $100,000 capital loan. How else could people our age get a chance to deal with that much capital? We're forced ahead of our time."

Many feel that community work is viewed with high approval by their companies—a fact that Park Forest leaders do not forget to mention in proselyting the laggard. Both of the two contenders for the village presidency in a recent election, they point out, worked in the research department of the same oil company, and it is a reasonable conclusion that the company does not view such activity with displeasure.

Compared to lawyers, academic, and professional people, the young businessman is not markedly a civic joiner. There is evidence that those who are, however, are more likely to be "comers." A few of the civically active may have seized on the activity as compensation for a blocked career, but on the whole the active would appear to be more likely to get ahead than their less active brothers.

Undeniably, places like Park Forest do tend to spoil one. While most of the people who move to package communities move out of a simple economic necessity, after exposure to such an environment some people find a warmth and support in it that makes the prospect of other environments seem unduly cold to them—it is somewhat unsettling, for example, to hear the way some residents of the new suburbs refer to "the outside." Frequently, alumni of package communities go considerably out of their way to seek out a similar community when the next move comes up, even when they are making quite enough for a more fashionable spot.

On balance, however, the training of a Park Forest stimulates them more than it coddles them. The test is what happens to Park Foresters when they leave. Those who haven't left like to tell stories of how "lonely" ex-residents have become in other places, and there is the strong imputation that it very well served them right for leaving. But most are not homesick. Thanks to the "bringing out," transients are all the better fitted for the moves ahead of them. If they are annoyed at the disinterest they find in a traditional town, it is because they want to be active, and know how to, and the disinterest serves more often to challenge than inhibit them. We looked up ex-Park Foresters now living in other kinds of communities and found that most were more active in the community than their contemporaries. "I learned at Park Forest how to take the initiative," goes a typical explanation. "It certainly stood me in good stead. I found out when I got here that most of the people really didn't know one another, and I just naturally started getting them to-gether." The majority of alumni confess they wouldn't want to go through Park Forest again, but they look back with fondness on Park Forest. "It all got pretty hectic at times," one recalls, "but one thing's sure—we were *living*."

I am not trying to argue that more places just like Park Forest are to be the pattern of the future, or should be. I do believe, however, that the kind of rootedness it illustrates will be. Better than most communities, it reveals the tran-sients' need for a conscious, almost professional, attitude to-ward the environment, but transients everywhere feel this need. The shifting, fluid course of their lives demands it, and if our society continues to expand, this increasingly profes-sional approach to human relationships is going to be more and more evident, whatever the nature of the community. Critics may mourn the passing of the days when people didn't have to think about roots, but it is futile nostalgia for the transients and they know it. Give them credit. In becom-ing so self-conscious about adjustment and participation they are erecting some shaky idols, but we should not turn to this side of the coin until we recognize how tremendously difficult a problem they face.

They *have* to be professional. On the one hand, they can-not sink roots too deep. They will be moving on some day, and if they become too involved they risk an emotional shock they do not wish to sustain. On the other hand, how-ever, they cannot forever wait for the eventual home, for they do not know when, if ever, they will find it. They must, in short, make a home of the home away from home, and to accomplish this feat they must act in the present. "The trick," one veteran puts it, "is to pretend to yourself that you're here for keeps and to join. If you don't, you'll keep putting off doing anything year after year, and you'll just make yourself feel more temporary than you actually are."

All of this puts a tremendous premium on "adjustment." "The best-adjusted people are the ones who are constantly adjusting," says the wife of a plant engineer. "My father says we're just a bunch of gypsies. Maybe so, but we always have something ahead of us. People who have houses already—what's left for them? For us, though, there is always something that's coming up next. You couldn't exactly call it adventure, but it is a challenge."

Once adjusted to the mobile life, transients say, they find as much stability in the new kind of roots as in the old, geographical ones. "If you haven't been moving around before, a development like this makes you unsettled," an Army wife explains. "These places are not right for people who want to stay forever. But for people like us, who are already 'unsettled,' it makes you settled, if you know what I mean."

If one loses some old friends, there will always be comparable ones to replace them. Furthermore, because the old friends are being exposed to the same kind of environment, you can pick up with them where you left off when you meet again. "Even if you're separated by time and space, you know their thinking will be the same," says a transient. "It's the underlying values that count, and they'll stay the same."

CHAPTER TWENTY-THREE

Classlessness in Suburbia

As far as social values are concerned, suburbia is the ultimate expression of the interchangeability so sought by organization. It is classless, or, at least, its people want it to
be. As in The Organization, so in its dormitories there has
been a great broadening of the middle, and a sort of "de-
classification" of people from the older criteria of family
background. But there is also another parallel. As in The
Organization, the more that distinctions are broken down,
the more exquisite they become. The suburbanites' impulse
to the Social Ethic is understandable; to live without social
class you must be socially skillful—consciously and continuously.

Like the office with no division between carpet and lino-
leum, suburbia demands perception. How in the world, you
wonder when you see Park Forest, can anyone tell rank—
or, for that matter, pull it? To the stranger's eye the usual
criteria of status are almost entirely absent. There are a few
exceptions; in the rental area there are some duplex units
situated on roads rather than grouped court fashion, and
these, renting for $117 (versus $92 to $104 for most court
units) make something of a local Gold Coast. Similarly,
though most homes are in the $13,000 bracket, there are a
few areas with houses around $10,000, several in the $17,-
000 to $20,000 class, and a small area with "custom" houses
ranging anywhere from $17,000 to developer Klutznick's

$50,000 home. These differences, as I will touch on later, are not without significance. For the great bulk of residents, however, the houses are uniform enough in cost as to make them comparatively unimportant as a prestige factor, and physically they are so uniform that if it weren't for paint and trim, newcomers would have trouble finding their unit in the labyrinth.

Cars aren't much help, either. Of the thousands that lie in the parking bays, few are more expensive than the Buick Special, and rakish touches are not too frequent. Only in near-by industrial towns do people show exuberance in the captainship of the American car; foxtails and triumphant pennants, like Cyrano's plume, fly defiantly on cars there, and occasionally from the radiator a devil thumbs his nose at the passing mob. Not at Park Forest; whatever else it has, it has no panache.

Suburban residents like to maintain that their suburbia not only looks classless but is classless. That is, they are apt to add on second thought, there are no extremes, and if the place isn't exactly without class, it is at least a one-class society—identified as the middle or upper middle, according to the inclination of the residents. "We are all," they say, "in the same boat."

They are not. People may come out of the new suburbs middle class; a great many who enter, however, are not. Middle-class, college-educated organization people give the communities their dominant tone, but there are other residents for whom arrival in the Park Forests and Levittowns is, psychologically at least, a crossing of the tracks. This expansion of the lower limits of the middle class is happening in towns and cities as well, but it is so pronounced in the new suburbs that it almost seems as if they were made for that function.

They have become the second great melting pot. The organization man furnishes the model, and even in suburbs where he is a minority he is influential out of all proportion to his numbers. As the newcomers to the middle class enter suburbia, they must discard old values, and their sensitivity to those of the organization man is almost statistically demonstrable. Figures rather clearly show that people from big, urban Democratic wards tend to become Republican and, if anything, more conservative than those whose outlook they are unconsciously adopting. Pondering the 1952 Park Forest vote, the *Chicago Tribune*, with vengeful pleasure, attributed the large Republican majority to the beneficial influence of fresh country air on erstwhile Democrats. Whatever the cause, it is true that something does seem to happen to Democrats when they get to suburbia. Despite the constant influx of Democrats, the size of the Republican vote remains fairly constant from suburb to suburb. (The vote for Eisenhower in 1952: 66 per cent in Levittown, Long Island; 69.4 per cent in Park Forest.)

Suburbanites make a great to-do about being independent—the 1952 plurality, they maintain, was due to their crusading spirit. Maybe so, but even without this extra stimulus they vote Republican just the same. In the 1950 senatorial election, Everett Dirksen—a Republican never accused of any great appeal for "independents"—polled 68.5 per cent of the Park Forest vote, only .9 per cent less than Eisenhower two years later. After a study of all the different election returns, local Democrats have concluded that the best they can hope for is a 14 per cent spread—30 per cent of the vote at worst; 44 per cent at best.

The social factor is only one of many in the making of converts to Republicanism, but it is a powerful one. "I'll be frank about canvassing," one Democratic precinct leader told me. "We've got to concentrate on people with foreign names and Jewish names." He took out a voter list and showed me the check marks he had made. "I'll try to concentrate on these people. On form, the Jews are more likely to be the intellectual type and the people with foreign names strong Democrats. But we've got to get to them quick."

The conversion process can take place rather rapidly. A Democratic allegiance is part of an environment which the newcomers wish to leave behind, and in attuning themselves to the values of the group they now wish to join, they soon find that "acceptance," to use a favorite word of suburbia, is more difficult if one persists in obdurately sticking to what others regard as a lower-class habit. They should graduate, and though the gang may adopt a live-and-let-live attitude most of the time toward such idiosyncrasy, when election time comes near and morality complicates the issue, the pressure becomes intense. In desperation, local Democratic organizations have turned to fighting fire with fire. To counteract the social process, they have been giving a series of parties for newcomers; at these events they dress up the house with the most respectable Democrats available, command them to put on their best bib and tucker, serve tea, and in every way possible try to fortify potential waverers with the knowledge that they can have kindred souls just as chic and well educated as anybody else.

Acclimation to suburbia also stimulates switches in religious affiliations, and the couple from, say, a small Ozark town is likely to discard their former fundamentalist allegiance to become Methodists or Presbyterians. So with personal tastes: wives are particularly quick to pick up the cues from the college-educated girls on the street, and their clothes, be they slacks or cardigans and pearls, begin to show it. Home furnishings are another symbol of emancipation. Merchants are often surprised at how quickly their former customers in city stores discard old preferences when they arrive in suburbia. "They won't touch 'Polish Renaissance' any more," the manager of a chain store in Levittown, Pennsylvania told me. "When I was over in the Trenton store I had to stock the most hideous stuff you ever saw. I couldn't sell them a nice Lawson sofa; they'd go for borax and the purplest purples and pinkest pinks. When they get over here they want something plainer—exactly the same people who only a year or so ago would have wanted some overstuffed thing."

Suburbanites are perfectly aware of this educating process, and though they may want to be egalitarian, they are not unconsciously so. They miss few of the clues to family background provided by slips in speech or peculiarities of taste, and in almost every block there is someone—to use a favored euphemism—who the others say "has not had all the advantages some people have had." As the use of the word "advantages" implies, such a person is not snubbed; quite the opposite—the others will go out of their way to make him feel at home and, through a sort of osmosis, to educate him in the values of the group. There are, of course, failures; some newcomers are so shy, so sensitive about their background that they rebuff advances, and occasionally they see no reason to acclimate themselves at all. (One court was thoroughly confounded by the arrival of a housewife who was an ex-burlesque stripper and, worse yet, volubly proud of the fact. She never learned, and the collision between her breezy outlook and the family mores of the court was near catastrophic. "They're just jealous because I'm theatrical folk," she told an observer, as she prepared to depart with her husband in a cloud of smoke. "All these wives think I want their husbands. What a laugh. I don't even want my own. The bitches." The court has never been quite the same since.)

For newcomers, the teaching of sociability is perhaps the greatest achievement of suburban education. The newcomers need it. They are more lonely than the others, for they are strangers to this world, yet they markedly lack the social skills by which to overcome their loneliness. This is particularly apparent in a new block that does not have the leavening influence of one or two organization couples. Often it is months before the people even strike up a conversation with the neighbors about them. They don't know how, and they want so desperately to know that they will respond to any activity, no matter what the ostensible purpose, that furnishes a catalyst. This is one of the reasons for the popularity of the "home commercial parties" in such neighborhoods. In one small subdivision outside Hartford, Connecticut, it was not until ten months after everyone had moved in that they got to know one another, and a Stanley Home Party was the cause; the first party broke the ice, and in a surge of gratitude all the wives pleaded to be hostesses in turn. It was the best way they knew of to get friendship started.

To understand how suburbia fills this kind of void, an understanding of the nature of turnover within them is necessary. It is not a subject suburbanites like to talk about. When I first went to Park Forest, I found the residents rather touchy about the fact that the turnover in the rental apartments was running at roughly 35 per cent annually, and in the homes area at about 20 per cent. Only temporary, many assured me. One man even went so far as to work up an ingenious mathematical formula to demonstrate the imminent decline of turnover. Of every 100 persons moving in, he argued, a given number will stay permanently; the more these people move in, accordingly, the fewer apartments and houses there will be on the market for the transient type—*ergo,* in time there should be practically no turnover at all.

Meanwhile, the turnover continues. In the rental courts a third of the tenants still move out every year. In 1954, out of 3,000 rental apartments there were 1,059 move-outs; in 1955, 1,100. As Park Foresters are quick to point out, some of these move-outs didn't leave the community but moved to the homes area, and this movement has lent a measure of stability to the community. Nonetheless, over-all turnover remains high. A comparison of the 1954 phone directory with the 1955 directory indicates that in one year's time 18 per cent of Park Foresters had moved on to other communities (948 families out of a total listing of 5,363). A closer check on one court shows that since 1953 all of the original thirty-nine couples had left save eight; of the couples who left, a third had moved to other parts of Park Forest, while the rest moved away.

It is a perfectly normal phenomenon. Some of the people who leave Park Forest do so because they want something "better," but most leave because they *have* to. In 1953, 44 per cent of the move-outs were corporation couples being transferred away from the Chicago area; 12½ per cent were Army and Navy couples assigned to new stations. Since then there has been little shift in this pattern and little shift in the kind of people who are moving in to fill up the vacancies. Periodic checks on the occupational breakdown of the rental people show that from year to year the proportion of engineers, junior executives, and such remains roughly the same.[1]

[1] As of April 1954, a check made by Thomas McDade of ACB of 700 rental families showed the following breakdown:

This constant replenishing assures that, as the community ages, there will always be a cadre of young, middle-class organization people on the way up. People who stay are not necessarily less successful; Park Forest has a strong adhesive power for those who have become involved in its activities, and many people who ordinarily would have moved away to the North Shore or its equivalent have stayed on. But the transients are still the key. Whether they actually move or not, it is the people successful enough to have the option who set the dominant style of life in suburbia.

While it cannot be called a "class" division, there is an important difference in attitude between these transients and the others, and to explore it is to recognize the great amount of insecurity many of the latter have over their middle-class status. A resident's attitude toward the community is an index. The usual organization man tends to affect an attitude of fond detachment—swell place, lots of kicks, but, after all, the sort of place you graduate from. For others, however, such an attitude is impossible. It is most impossible of all for the man who has expected to go ahead in the organization world but finds that he will not. He dislikes thinking about turnover, not so much that he sees it as a slur on the community, but as a slur on himself. For him, the ever-present moving van is a standing rebuke—a reminder of an organization world to which he does not truly belong.

Then there are the people for whom suburbia is a social achievement. They are not envious, like the unsuccessful organization man, of those who leave; much as enlisted men feel toward a comrade who has won a bid to officer's training, they can speak quite equably, sometimes proudly, of ex-neighbors who have gone on to better things. But it is the permanence of the community, not its impermanence, that they wish to see. They cannot joke about it with detachment, and they can be extraordinarily sensitive about references that no one else would think invidious. When I

business administration, 28.2 per cent; professional, 25.2 per cent; sales, 22.1 per cent. Of the remaining 24.5 per cent: supervisors, production workers, and independents, 6.3 per cent; publicity, 4.2 per cent; retail workers, 5.7 per cent; transportation workers, 6.1 per cent; miscellaneous, 2.2 per cent.

first started interviewing, one of the women's magazines had just come out with a picture story on life in the homes area. It was a pleasant story, full of praise, but the housewives were very annoyed. "Those pictures they published are absolutely disgraceful," one exclaimed to me. "Why did they have to take so many of back yards? The way they angled them makes it look like a development!"

Let us pause briefly to retrace their steps back from suburbia. It is important to remember that the move is not a sudden one from the lower to the middle class but rather the most critical of several moves. To a degree the people affected have been moving simultaneously with others—which is to say, the mobility hasn't been a case of the individual outracing the people he was brought up with, but a concurrent movement. Yet it is not so uniform a movement that some have not gone past others, and the awareness of this competition has produced some very powerful tensions.

This was brought home to me when I made a study of several new Philadelphia row-house neighborhoods of the kind that are the stepping stones to suburbia. There were many similarities to suburbia—the median income was only slightly beneath the Park Forest and the Levittowns; the population was predominantly a young one, and they give it the look of the new market wherever you see it: the great forest of television aerials, the hard-top convertibles, the housewives in blue jeans and plaid slacks *Kaffeeklatsching* on the lawns, the hundreds of husbands stopping off at the giant supermarket to pick up the extra groceries on the way back home from work.

But there were differences, and if I had to single out the one that impressed me most, it would be, simply, the amount of plain, ordinary disagreeableness. Compared to the suburban communities, the tensions seemed much closer to the surface, the jealousies more intense. Nobody seemed to have settled down to take a long breath; the notion of survival of the fittest was omnipresent, and few blocks seemed to have the graces, the rules of the game that suburbia has acquired to muffle the conflict. These neighborhoods happen to be in Philadelphia, and there are factors peculiar to them. Yet I was persuaded by the talks I had there that this somewhat intangible atmosphere was a reality which all sensed and which had its roots in causes fairly universal.

As a check of former addresses indicated, these people are members of the great outward movement from the inner city wards—as they have been moving geographically toward the suburbs, they have been moving socially as well. But it is a *transition,* and there is the rub, for though they have left one world—the close-knit society of the *padrone,* for example—they have not quite joined another, and the influx of Negroes into the houses they left behind is a specter they do not for a moment forget. Except for the older people, for whom such neighborhoods can be ideal, suburbia is the dream, and the neighbor who puts the "For Sale" sign up as he prepares to move to suburbia does so with a feeling that he has made it.

It is not stretching the sense of the word too much to say that he has not *made it* so much, but that he is *passing.* Still fundamentally urban and lower middle class in his reflexes, he has a long acculturation ahead of him, and if he is not entirely sure how it is going to end up, neither can we be. His social enfranchisement is a great tribute to the vigor of our democracy, but we would do well to recognize the pitfalls of this dynamic.

Psychologically at least, the newcomers to suburbia are living on the brink of a precipice. It is true that they are better buttressed than were their parents against a depression, but that much more have their expectations been raised. Broad as the middle class may be, there is a line, and a rather firm one, beneath which middle-class life is impossible. The line, suburbia would indicate, is somewhere between $4,800 and $5,200. It is not, furthermore, a static figure. It is constantly moving up as the couple ages, for while it may be all right to enter suburbia strapped for money, as time goes on it is abnormal for one's income not to rise, and this will be painfully evident to the family which cannot follow other contemporaries as they expand the little luxuries of their life.

When they studied Middletown of the depression years, the Lynds were struck by the way in which the blurring of class lines denied people a sense of "sheltered arrival." "Democracy under private capitalism," they wrote, "has shaved off the edges of these plateaus, and the whole population moves, according to the ethos of our culture, endlessly and breathlessly up one long, unbroken sandy slope of acquisition. . . . from every point on the unbroken incline one can look ahead and see others with more than one has oneself."

But private socialism offers no resting place either. The upward struggle is easier now, or seems easier, and though the couple who move into suburbia may do so with a feeling of "we made it," their satisfaction is quite temporary. The longer they stay the more they recognize subtle gradations that at first were not apparent. There is no plateau in front of them, only the rungs of a ladder.

In this climb the young management man who sets suburbia's styles can be a dangerous pace-setter. At a given time, his income and the income of the newly arrived white-collar man may be identical.[2] The potential rate of increase, however, is quite different. With much more safety can the organization man extend himself, for unless he does something extremely stupid in the company, his income will automatically increase by 30 per cent at the very least in the next three or four years. His white-collar neighbor is not in the same position, even though his salary be identical. This kind of disparity, however, is muffled by surface similarities, and many who will never enter management are stimulated

[2] How illusory the "average" income of a community can be is apparent if you plot the rate of increase of its members' incomes. In 1953 we obtained financial data on every tenth rental family in Park Forest which included the husband's salary on entering the community and the periodic raises he may have obtained in succeeding years. At the end of their second year, most of the husbands were fairly near the median income of $5,800, but their rates of ascent varied considerably. Salesmen, for example, went up only about $150 a year, while chemists went up in $500 to $600 leaps, and lawyers raced past everybody. People in the latter categories could afford to mortgage themselves very heavily and they did. The others could not afford to, but they did too.

to live as if they would. It is particularly hard for wives to grasp the fact, and husbands who are in a fairly static job are under constant pressure from them to keep up.

In those sections of the new suburbia where the houses are slightly less expensive than the norm, people are closest to the thin edge, and the social importance of small differences becomes assertive. The case of the Eastgate area is illustrative. Several years ago, the Park Forest developers decided to add a group of houses in the $10,000 class. The difference between these houses, in either price or attractiveness, and the $12,000 to $13,500 houses is not great, but there has been enough to strain Park Foresters' pretensions of classlessness. (Asked to describe the kind of people living in Eastgate, Park Foresters grope with difficulty. No one can bring himself to say "working-class people"; the phrases are more likely to be "people who work with their hands more than their heads," "artisans," or, at worst, "blue collar.") The homes are nice—some think the design better than the more expensive ones—and they are well kept up. But both the Eastgaters and the others in the community sense that Eastgate is not quite a part of Park Forest. Many Eastgaters have moved to another sector at the first opportunity, and it will probably always remain a bit of alien soil in the one-class society.[8]

[3] The segregating effect even small differences can provoke has been well illustrated in the new towns of England. F. J. Osborn, in *Green Belt Cities* (London, 1946), tells how homes had been sited in the new towns of Letchworth and Welwyn Garden City so there would be much mixing of classes. At first they did seem fairly classless; their residents were caught up in the same wave of pioneer spirit that characterized Park Forest's early days. As in Park Forest, however, the unifying pressures slackened, and latent differences began to show up. "There is less segregation of the classes than in other towns," writes Osborn. "It has been found, however, that whatever the town planner may desire, people have a marked tendency to segregate themselves by class or income. . . . The better-off tenants (whether they are clerical workers or the more highly paid factory workers) spontaneously move to streets in which, even if the houses are no larger, the social atmosphere is regarded as superior." (Quoted from Harold Orlans, *Utopia, Ltd.*, New Haven, 1953, p. 89.)

While the vulnerability of the newcomers may never be put to a large-scale test, the effect of several localized recessions is suggestive. Economically, the impact has not been serious; most of the plant layoffs have been temporary, and in the midst of a generally rising economy the families affected have been able to weather the squall through renegotiated loans. Psychologically, however, the effect has been considerable. The possibility of going much under $4,800 does not threaten merely to rob a family of some luxuries; it threatens to take them away from a style of life. Suburbia does not condone shabby gentility. The amenities that a severe cutback in expenditures would put in jeopardy are not marginal; to the family on the edge of the middle class they are social necessities.

Those who have counseled with people in such situations say that in almost every case the prime fear is the fear of "going back." Often it is an unreasoning fear—houses in suburbia, after all, are often the cheapest houses available—but it can be a tremendous one nonetheless to those who suffer it. They can feel so isolated. Back in the depression, millions were in a predicament not of their own making, yet social workers tell us that despite the generalness of the depression people had strong feelings of individual guilt. Today the feelings of guilt could be much more intense. Psychologically, they have more to lose than any other group in our society, and a turndown that would be moderate by the standards of two decades ago would place them in a perilous position. They are not going back, and if their fears were exploited, their discontent could become ugly indeed. If our economy has an Achilles' heel, this might be it.

But if return seems a specter, let us remember, it is because there is advance, and on balance it is the dynamic of this forward movement rather than the danger of it that seems most impressive. There must be a thin edge, for we cannot expect to celebrate the gains of a rising standard without bearing this price. The fruits of social revolution are always more desirable in anticipation than fact, and the pink lamp shade in the picture window can be a sore disappointment to those who dreamed that the emancipation of the worker would take a more spiritual turn.[4] It is a sight, however, that we can well endure. The phase in which people stand poised on the brink of the middle class is not a pretty one, but it is a phase. In somewhat the same way that Americanization affected succeeding waves of immigrants, acclimatization to the middle class will lessen the feeling of social vulnerability that can turn these newcomers ugly.

The melting-pot analogy is still apropos. For all the differences in background, no fixed class structure has congealed in places like Park Forest. Occupation and family background have provided a certain kind of status—but for individuals, and the individuals have not jelled into groups on this basis. Similarly, while many people get together according to common interests—interest in world politics, for example, or in gardening—these are only part-time associations and they are so fluid that they carry few overtones of social status. The same is true of religion: vigorous as church activity is, religious allegiances have far less of the clan effect than they have in traditional communities. Not so incidentally, many mixed-marriage couples have come to Park Forest, for here, they have correctly sensed, is a refuge from the conflicting loyalties that would beset them elsewhere.

The nearest thing to an upper class are the remaining

---

[4] This kind of disappointment has been very strong in England. For years liberal intellectuals fought to extend middle-class security to the workers, and now that they are succeeding they are discomfited. Writing in *The Spectator* (January 20, 1956), Charles Curran talks of life in the vast municipal housing estates where so many workers now live. He speaks of how they read the tabloids exclusively because the tabloids "offer a simple, cheerful, manageable universe, a warm, cozy place of sex, excitement, triviality and fantasy . . . the daydream heaven of wealth, luxuries, and sexual attraction to which the football-pool coupon will one day provide a ticket of admission. An interior life of this kind and on this scale is something that has not previously existed in England. It contrasts sharply with the expectations that buoyed up the social reformers—that once the manual worker was free from the clutches of poverty and insecurity, he would begin to participate in our social heritage. Nothing of the kind has happened."

pioneer settlers who are still active in the village government. Interestingly, this group has a heavy representation of Democrats of the egghead kind, for though the Democratic leaders can't get much support during national elections, as private citizens and "independents," they virtually run the place. To some intellectuals this has been something of a cruel blow; for those who like to feel themselves embattled against the forces of Philistinism, it has been almost embarrassing to be so powerful, and a few, almost eager to see the hopelessness of it all, have left lest they compromise their idealism. Most are quite happy, however, and though they speak harshly of the anti-intellectualism of suburbia, they are—aside from the developer's people they so regularly combat—the nearest thing to fat cats Park Forest has. Because of the fact of their having been there quite some time, most of them are now in the income bracket which can support one of the more expensive houses (the block in which they are concentrated is called "Government Row").

But though the civic leaders have prestige, they are not, in any customary sense, an upper class. An elite, perhaps, but not a social one. Their cohesion is functional; they are not, like the upper class of Newburyport, members of a primary group which envelops most of one's allegiances and kinship ties. True, they tend to come from a middle-class background, but this is a corollary, not a cause, of their situation. Like the national elite of which they are fractions, their prestige is a sort of ex-officio prestige, awarded for performance and function and revocable for lack of it. And they do not want for people eager to do the revoking. By reflex, the new suburbanites are stringently anti-cabal, and indignant letter writers to the newspapers habitually refer to "self-appointed" leaders, "so-called" saviors, and similar threats to the open utopia.

When the current "Aquacenter" pool was a-building, there was resistance to the idea and, significantly, the principal basis was the fear of people that this might be a first step toward stratification. Instead of there being a municipal pool, as many had hoped, a private organization was set up to undertake the business. "The town pool that was originally planned was right," says one resident, "but then we would have had to admit Chicago Heights people and some of our 'democratic' people wouldn't like that at all." Modest as the family expenses are ($100 bond plus usage fees), many believe that it is just high enough to keep many of the marginal-income people in Park Forest away from the pool and the result will be the formation of a "country-club set."

The classlessness also stops very sharply at the color line. Several years ago there was an acrid controversy over the possible admission of Negroes. It threatened to be deeply divisive—for a small group, admission of Negroes would be fulfillment of personal social ideals; for another, many of whom had just left Chicago wards which had been "taken over," it was the return of a threat left behind. But the people who were perhaps most sorely vexed were the moderates. Most of them were against admission too, but though no Negroes ever did move in, the damage was done. The issue had been brought up, and the sheer fact that one had to talk about it made it impossible to maintain unblemished the ideal of egalitarianism so cherished.

But the force of the ideal should not be deprecated. Let me make perverse use of the concept of those who believe we are highly stratified: if one holds that class divisions exist because people think there are class divisions, to be consistent one would have to concede that they do not exist when people think they do not exist. The new suburbanites do indeed obscure some harsh realities when they talk of their democratic ideals, yet their unwillingness to concede class divisions is itself a very powerful factor in keeping the divisions from crystallizing. I am not trying to argue that paradise is imminent; the breakdown of the old divisions of class has left people vulnerable to other kinds of webs, and these too have their tyrannies. But they are not tyrannies fixed upon the individual, like class; they are self-imposed, and the individual has at least the choice of declining them.

CHAPTER TWENTY-FOUR

Inconspicuous Consumption

IN defining the good life, the suburbanites have to get down to cases, and when they do these social pressures can become highly visible. On the one hand, suburbanites have a strong impulse toward egalitarianism; on the other, however, they have an equally strong impulse to upgrade themselves. Somewhere in the middle lies the good life, but like that elusive plateau they seek in The Organization, it vanishes as quickly as one finds it.

In an environment that seems so homogeneous, one might think there were few distinctions one would have to worry about. To the practiced eye, however, there is much more diversity in the scene than the bystander sees, for the more accustomed one becomes to the homogeneity, the more sensitized is he to the small differences. At Levittown, Pennsylvania, residents are very much aware of who has what "modification" of the basic ranch-house design, and one house on which the owner mounted a small gargoyle became so famous a sight that many residents used to drive out of their way to show it to visitors. People have a sharp eye for interior amenities also, and the acquisition of an automatic dryer, or an unusually elaborate television set, or any other divergence from the norm is always cause for notice. Those who lack such amenities, conversely, are also noted. In one suburb, to cite a rather extreme example, a wife was so ashamed of the emptiness of her living room that she smeared the picture window with Bon Ami; not until a dinette set arrived did she wash it off.

Necessity has been buttressed with ideology. It's inconspicuous consumption now, and suburbanites are quite articulate about it. One of the most frequent observations they will volunteer is that "there's no keeping up with the Joneses here," and they protest it with unwonted frequency. The precept does more than condone their lack of money to do anything else; it praises the behavior as ultimately ethical. It is a social compact they are voicing. Openly stated, the reasoning would go something like this: Most of us are at a pretty critical stage in our careers; it is just about now that we will realize that some of us are really going to go ahead and some of us aren't. If you find you're going ahead, it's rubbing it in unfairly to make it obvious to the others who aren't. You have broken the truce.

The job, then, is not to keep up with the Joneses. It's to keep *down* with them.[1] Even those sophisticated enough to talk, albeit a trifle nervously, about "other-directed" consumption of their group see a valid reason for it. When they see a neighbor vaunting worldly goods, they can see this is an offense—not to them individually, mind you, but to the community. When people comment unfavorably about conspicuous display, they usually stress that they themselves see nothing wrong with it, *but that other people might;* and the purchase, therefore, was ill advised.

The group has always conditioned purchases, of course, and the women who gathered over the clothesline thirty years ago could form as influential a group as any *Kaffeeklatsch* session of today. But there is an important difference. It is the matter of choice. In previous times the

[1] Ad in *The New York Times,* January 10, 1954: "Gimbel's takes note of a new trend in American living. The 'Booming Middle Class' is taking over—and no longer are we living up to the Joneses (Chauncey Montague Jones et familia)—we're living down to the Joneses (Charlie Jones and the wife and kids). It's bye-bye, upstairs chambermaid—ta, ta, liveried chauffeur—good riddance to the lorgnette, limousine, and solid-gold lavatory. The new Good Life is casual, de-frilled, comfortable, fun—and isn't it marvelous. Gimbel's is all for the bright, young, can't-be-fooled Charlie Joneses."

group had less effect on what a person bought because there wasn't as much of a choice to make. Today, with more people with the money to buy more things, consumers have a bewildering multiplicity of choices to make. In making them, furthermore, they have less and less tradition to lean on.

And the very similarities of suburbia are pitfalls. When everyone lives in an identical house, the most important item of their estate is washed out as a factor, and the marginal purchases become the key ones. How to choose, then? Would an automatic dishwasher be right at this stage of the game—or would it seem like putting on the dog? On this knotty problem of whether an item is a luxury or a necessity, aggregate national statistics are no guide. Some purchases, such as a car, can be accurately described as a necessity; others, such as a swimming pool, a luxury. But in between these two categories is a great shadow area in which national averages can be illusory. Even in a single neighborhood, what in one block would be an item eminently acceptable might in another be regarded as flagrant showing-off.

It is the group that determines when a luxury becomes a necessity. This takes place when there comes together a sort of critical mass. In the early stages, when only a few of the housewives in a block have, say, an automatic dryer, the word-of-mouth praise of its indispensability is restricted. But then, as time goes on and the adjacent housewives follow suit, in a mounting ratio others are exposed to more and more talk about its benefits. Soon the nonpossession of the item becomes an almost unsocial act—an unspoken aspersion of the others' judgment or taste. At this point only the most resolute individualists can hold out, for just as the group punishes its members for buying prematurely, so it punishes them for not buying.

Item by item, the process is constantly repeated, and the norm never stays still. As soon as a certain range of items becomes standard in the neighborhood group, its members grow restive for a new necessity. What it will be is only partly determined by national trends; even when neighborhoods are identical in age and income levels, they can vary a lot in the luxuries that are being turned into necessities. Home freezers, for example; like air conditioners, they are not distributed uniformly, and in some blocks there may be a 60 per cent "saturation" while in the very next one no more than one or two. Similarly, in some blocks hi-fi sets are considered an affectation; in others, only a stone's throw away, they are almost mandatory.

In this process, merchandisers have been comparatively passive. In the check I made of air-conditioner ownership in Philadelphia, I found only two cases where the original suggestion to buy had been made by a salesman; in almost all cases the initiative in the purchase had been taken by the consumer himself. To a surprising degree, retailers—and most manufacturers, for that matter—fail to appreciate the power of these word-of-mouth networks. Few use "outside" salesmen to speed up the process, and those who do tend to have the salesmen scatter their calls over a wide area rather than work on natural neighborhood groupings.[2]

[2] The combination of dealer passivity and the growing influence of the group network has a lot to do with the pricing troubles now worrying manufacturers and retailers. Many manufacturers talk about the cut-price problem as if it were due largely to the machinations of discount houses and will be solved by "stabilizing" the market and "protecting the ethical retailer." It is not quite so simple. What has been happening is that the consumer has been taking over part of the selling burden historically allotted to the retailer. Just as the consumer has shared in the markup on groceries by sharing in the physical burden of distribution, so now with the "big ticket" items; he has worked for part of the markup by sharing the selling burden, and he wants his cut. Because discount houses give it to him, they are often cited as the villains of the piece. But they are not the cause, only the manifestation, and though they are filling the vacuum, it was produced for them. Manufacturers still give retailers a markup big enough to justify the missionary work retailers once did. With few exceptions, however, retailers no longer do this kind of work; they *service* demand, but they have discarded their former techniques, such as the use of outside sales forces, to create the demand. The burden of introducing new products, as a result, now falls upon a combination of advertising and the word of mouth of the consumer group. The real selling job, in short, is done before the customer comes into the store. Guided by the group, the customer already has determined almost everything about the purchase—including the fact that he will make

For which fact, I make haste to add, the susceptible can be thankful. With mingled admiration and horror, I heard a door-to-door selling expert explain how a smart merchandiser could exploit the group contagion. First, he said, he'd make a special effort, even if it involved a slight loss, to place air conditioners in the key homes in a neighborhood. Then, after the rest had succumbed, he'd leave them alone for a while. Just about the time they would be feeling guilty that there wasn't a conditioner in the children's room, he would return to trigger the next round of purchases. "All you do now," he said, "is pull the trap. Here's the way I would do it. I'd go in to 'check' the first conditioner, and while I was about it I'd mention to the couple that my wife and I had just bought a second conditioner for the little ones. I'd pause and let that hang in the air for a while. Then, very quietly, I'd say, 'You know, Mr. and Mrs. Jones, now my wife and I *really* sleep nights.'"

The good-life standard is being revised upward so rapidly that planners of suburban shopping centers have had a hard time keeping up with it. If one has to err, this experience suggests, it is safer to overestimate than underestimate—even to aim at the center is to be unsynchronized with the suburban rhythm. At what they fancy are slights to their taste level suburban housewives are quick to take injury. When it was announced at Park Forest that the new department store would be a branch of a people's department store, there was a good bit of who-do-they-think-we-are-anyway muttering on the part of housewives. They wanted Marshall Field. Eventually, Marshall Field did install a store there. To some shoppers it looks almost forbiddingly stylish, but not to most; sales have been good, and on some lines—higher-priced men's suits, expensive dresses, and moderately expensive home furnishings—beyond expectations. (Hosiery, lingerie, and cosmetics sales were surprisingly poor.)

it—except the price and a few minor options. So he shops for price; he is earning the price cut, and whether manufacturers like it or not, he is going to get it. For years merchandising people have loved to say that the consumer is their boss. Now some of them would like to eat their words. He really is.

The pattern has been similar at Levittown, Pennsylvania. For several years the principal stores were chain stores featuring an economy-priced line. Newcomers to the community were well satisfied; those who had been there long enough to pass through the necessity phase, however, were not. Convenient, some said, but, frankly, a little tacky. When the Allied Stores Corporation decided to put in a department store, it correctly saw that the matter of its "character" was all important. In its preliminary survey in early 1954, it found a strong demand for higher-priced brand lines and better "taste." In furniture, for example, 25 per cent of Levittowners had mixed-style furniture—i.e., otherwise indescribable—but only about 2 per cent said they would buy this kind again; 67 per cent wanted modern. When Allied put in the store, Pomeroy's, it found that the people bought just the way they said they would—upward.

The word "rhythm" is justified, for, increasingly, this upgrading trend seems to be following a regular, cyclical pattern. In early 1954, Levittown, Pennsylvania, had been settled for only two years, yet despite this small time span it was found that small differences in the age of a neighborhood made for considerable differences in average income. In the area settled between a year and one half and two years, Allied Stores found, 24 per cent of the families had incomes over $7,000; in areas settled a year to a year and a half, 19 per cent; areas settled a half to one year, 13 per cent; areas settled up to six months, 7 per cent.

These differences in average income may seem small, but they are translated into palpable differences in what has come to be called "life style." Even the degree of wives' slenderness; as incomes rise, waistlines go down. In their Levittown survey, Allied Stores found that in the area settled long enough for income to have risen to between $5,000 and $7,000, 59 per cent of the women wore the small "misses" sizes; by contrast, in the newer, $3,000 to $4,000 area the sizes were larger—only 42 per cent wore the small sizes and 7 per cent wore the large 38-44 sizes (versus only 3 per cent of the wives of the $5,000 to $7,000 area).

In this upward course there is physical movement as well.

Because small differences are magnified in suburbia, people can upgrade themselves in one location just so long; after they reach a certain income level, there is a strong pressure on them to move, for they cannot otherwise live up to their incomes without flouting the sensibilities of the others. This is true everywhere, of course, but in suburbia so many people regularly find themselves in this position that periodic house changing is becoming an increasingly accepted phenomenon. Not only do people move out and on, but, in a sort of musical-chairs cycle, there is a growing amount of movement *within* the communities.

Developers did not plan it this way. When Park Forest was first put up, the developers thought of sticking pretty much to the basic $13,000 house; but they were nothing if not pragmatists. More or less as an experiment, they put in several blocks of houses at $17,000. When these were snapped up almost immediately, the developers started putting in more blocks, and before long they were putting up some $19,000 houses.

Half in jest, but only half, they are now talking about the possibility of the "life cycle" community. It would work like this: At age twenty-six, a junior-executive trainee, his wife, and baby join the cycle by moving into a two-bedroom court apartment. This is ideal for quite a while, but at the end of three years his income is up to $6,800, they are getting fed up with the court, and the third baby is on the way. As another junior-executive couple takes over their apartment, they move into a three-bedroom, $13,000 house in the homes-for-sale area.

For five years this is fine too, but as the husband's salary has gone up, so has that of his successful friends, and one by one they have been moving into the $18,000 area. At age thirty-five, the husband sells the ranch house and moves into a $19,000 split level. Fifteen years later, when the children have married and moved away, they sell the house and move back into a two-bedroom apartment in one of the old courts. The kids playing in the court make good proxies for their missing grandchildren, and the gang is delighted to have them around to baby-sit for them. The cycle draws to a close.

Too many people are transferred—or begin making too much money—to stay within the cycle, but the basic idea is not so farfetched as it sounds. It is now plain that the best customers for the $13,000 houses are people who moved into Park Forest as renters; the best customers for the $19,000 houses have been either ex-renters or people who had $13,000 homes. Meanwhile, the declining demand for two-bedroom houses by young couples has been offset by a potential market originally not considered. With some signs of success, the developers are beginning to merchandise these to older people without children. (A SECOND HONEYMOON! the ads promise.)

Somewhat the same kind of movement has been taking place in Levittown. Of 17,600 dwellings, roughly 3,000 change hands annually, and a good part of this turnover is caused by residents trading in old houses as their rising income enables them to move to somewhat more expensive ones in the same community. After about five years a man with one of the early Cape Cod Levittown houses (original price: $8,000) finds that he can get up to $10,000 for it, and he transfers his equity to the purchase of a later, ranch-type model. This will cost him as high as $18,000, depending on the location and the improvements that the owner has added.[3]

The optimism that powers this upgrading movement is tremendous. In any period, of course, it is characteristic that couples are most consumption-minded—and sanguine—during the time they are raising their children and accumulating their basic possessions, and as they grow older, their aspirations tend to level out. But there is a real generational difference as well. Even people in their late thirties feel a

[3] The disposition to segregate by age and income is also demonstrated by the Florida trailer-camp settlements. These have become permanent institutions, and the nature of the turnover and the social life of the old people within them is in many ways quite similar to that of the younger people's suburbia. For a good description, see G. C. Hoyt's "The Life of the Retired in a Trailer Camp" and L. C. Michelon's "The New Leisure Class," both in the *American Journal of Sociology*, January 1954.

fundamental difference between their outlook and that of the younger neighbors, and they speak with awe of the liberal spending habits about them. "When we were that age we wouldn't have dreamed of getting so much in debt," goes a typical observation. "Even now, when we have more than they do, we put off getting things like dishwashers." The memory of the depression is still so vivid that they cannot be sure the cornucopia will remain open; and their outlook was shaped in that distant period when Social Security, hospital insurance plans, and other such cushions were not a part of life.

For the younger couples, however, there has been an almost unbroken momentum; they came to adolescence at a time of rising hope, and throughout their early adult years they have known nothing but constantly increasing prosperity, personal as well as general. Suburbia has further confirmed them in their optimism. Here they are surrounded by others like themselves—too young to have failed. Disillusionment and diminishing raises are yet to come, and there are few about them whose example would temper their aspirations. No crazy drunkards, no embittered spinsters— there is rarely even death in the new suburbia—and though there are some whose hopes are already blighted, it is without the cruel finality that one can see elsewhere.

Depression? They don't even think about it. If they are pressed into giving an opinion on the matter, their explanations would suggest that America has at last found something very close to the secret of perpetual motion. And the gears, they believe, can no longer be reversed. "They can't dispossess everybody," goes a frequent observation, and equally frequent is the even more optimistic thought that the government not only wants to keep prosperity from slipping even slightly, but that it knows exactly how to do it. "The depression would be a political issue," explains a twenty-six-year-old junior executive. "The government would certainly see to it that a depression would not take place." In the unlikely event one did take place, some add, it wouldn't hurt them personally. Whatever their occupation, almost all organization people feel their particular job is depression-proof. ("People always need electricity"; "The food business couldn't go down much," etc.) Furthermore, it would all be relative. "If my salary goes down," as one puts it, "prices would be going down too, so in the end I would be just about as well off as I was before."

But all this is highly academic. Not only do the younger people accept the beneficent society as normal; they accept *improvement,* considerable and constant, as normal too. In a continually expanding economy, they reason, future prosperity will retroactively pay for today, and there is, accordingly, no good sense to self-denial. They have a point. The great expectations have a certain self-enforcing quality, and in an instinctive kind of way suburbanites sense this—at times, after hearing one after the other refer to that same boat they're all in, one gets the feeling that they have ganged together in a great collective blackmail operation.

Suburbanites have a wonderful capacity for interpreting demands for more of the good life as the expression of idealism. Back in 1953, to cite one instance, Park Foresters demanded that a special $60,000 multi-purpose room be added to a new school then a-building. Klutznick said no; eventually the town was going to have to take over the financial burden and it was questionable whether they would have the tax base to pay for the regular classrooms, let alone the extra facilities. I asked the young head of the school board about this. With great heat, he declared that it was a matter of principle. "Our children deserve the best," he said, and since a multi-purpose room was part of modern education, that should be that. I asked him about Klutznick's argument. He shook his head sadly; he didn't know where the money would come from either. "But," he repeated, "our children deserve the best." To ask why, of course, would be unpardonable in suburbia.

They save little. The average bank savings deposit throughout the country—$1,342—sounds reassuring, but the average is illusory. Examine the individual accounts that make up this average, and it becomes evident that older people contribute to the aggregate out of all proportion to their numbers. Significantly, in both Park Forest and Levittown,

Pennsylvania, where there are few older people to swell the figures, the banks report the average deposit is $300.

Most young couples carry life insurance, but the actual cash value of their policies is very little. A considerable number make modest accumulations of E Bonds through pay-roll savings plans, and here and there the venturesome few buy stocks. But that's about it. A check of budgets of a cross section of younger-marrieds in the $5,000-to-$7,500 bracket indicates that the median equity in savings deposits, bonds, and stocks is about $700 to $800. The median amount of loan money outstanding: $1,000.

The exceptions to the rule are revealing. Among younger people, bankers reports, there is one kind of couple that in matters of money remains conspicuously faithful to the Protestant Ethic of eighteenth-century America. They are the first-generation children of foreign-born parents.

For the middle-class majority, however, saving is no longer a virtue in itself. What the average young couple does save is not put aside in the old rainy-day sense; it is, rather, accumulated for some anticipated expense—e.g., the next baby or a down payment on the next house. So much, they explain, is being saved *for* them. It's not government Social Security they talk about so much; middle-class people became uncomfortable dwelling on the benefits of welfare statism; and, anyway, they point out, the retirement payments won't amount to so very much. What they refer to freely are the compulsory savings bestowed by the organization they work for. Thanks to annuity plans, profit-sharing funds, and the like, they argue, the future is already in good part prepaid. To save heavily on one's own initiative would be redundant. It would also, according to another rationalization, be bad economics. "Why should I save today's dollars to spend tomorrow," asks one young husband, "when they will be worth less than they are now?"

For short-term emergencies the young suburbanites expect to take shelter under personal loans. They use loans for planned purchases too, but the primary reason they take out personal loans is for debt consolidation and for emergency medical expenditures. Significantly, medical loans are rarely taken out to cover obstetricians' bills; these, being a highly anticipated expense, are generally taken care of by savings.

Even when suburbanites have not taken out a loan, the knowledge that loans are so readily available today has a pronounced effect on their budget habits. They have a highly inflated idea of the amount they can borrow. When the young couples are asked how much they could raise in an emergency, the median response is usually $2,000 to $3,000. As a check with bank officers indicated, many of them would be lucky to raise $500. Going by the usual rule of thumb, on a personal, unsecured loan the husband could borrow up to roughly 20 per cent of his annual income. This would mean that couples in the $5,000-to-$7,500 bracket would be able to raise little more than $1,500— provided they had no other debt outstanding. Which would be most unusual.

Not that the suburbanites are irresponsible. Indeed, what is striking about the young couples' march along the abyss is the earnestness and precision with which they go about it. They are extremely budget-conscious. They can rattle off most of their monthly payments down to the last penny; even their "impulse buying" is deliberately planned. They are conscientious in meeting obligations, and rarely do they fall delinquent in their accounts.

They are exponents of what could be called "budgetism." This does not mean that they actually keep formal budgets. Quite the contrary; the beauty of budgetism is that one doesn't have to keep a budget at all. It's done automatically. In the new middle-class rhythm of life obligations are homogenized, for the overriding aim is to have oneself pre-committed to regular, unvarying monthly payments on all the major items. Come the first of the month and there is practically nothing left to decide. And so it will be the next month, and the month after—a smooth, almost hypnotic rhythm so compelling that suburbanites will go to great lengths to gear any expenditure to it.

Two decades ago, one could divide Americans into three sizable groups: those at the lower end of the income scale who thought of money obligations in terms of the week, those who thought in terms of the month, and those who thought in terms of the year. There are still many people at both ends of the scale, but with the widening of the middle class, the month has become the standard module in Americans' budgetary thinking. Salary checks, withholding deductions, mortgage payments—the major items in middle-class finances are firmly geared to a thirty-day cycle, and any dissonant peaks and valleys are anathema. Just as young couples are now paying winter oil bills in equal monthly fractions through the year, so they seek to spread out all the other heavy seasonal obligations they can anticipate: Christmas presents, real-estate taxes, birthdays, spring cleaning, outfitting the children for school. If vendors will not oblige by accepting equal monthly installments, the purchasers will smooth out the load themselves by floating loans.

It is, suburbanites cheerfully explain, a matter of psychology. They don't trust themselves. Occasionally bankers ask them why they don't build up a constantly replenished savings fund to finance purchases rather than rely on loans. The answer is standard: "We're sure we'll pay back the bank," the young couple explains, "but we couldn't be sure we'd pay ourselves back." In self-entrapment is security. They try to budget so tightly that there are no unappropriated funds, for they know these would burn a hole in their pockets. Not merely out of greed for goods, then, do they commit themselves. It is protection they want, too; and though it would be extreme to say that they go into debt to be secure, carefully charted debt does give them a certain peace of mind—and in suburbia this is more coveted than luxury itself.

They have little sense of capital. The benevolent economy has insulated the organization man from having to manipulate large personal sums; indeed, it has relieved him from even having to *think* about it. Tax withholding, that great agent of social revolution, has almost removed from his consideration one of the largest single items in his finances, and package mortgages have done the same for real-estate taxes. So with all the other major items. No longer does he have to think about setting aside large sums; the government and the corporation have assumed the prerogative. It is not merely that you don't have to worry about big sums, a young couple can explain; you don't even have the choice.

With budgetism, in short, one is passive, and this passivity helps explain why saving is losing its moral imperative. In the Protestant Ethic morality was identified with savings because of the idea that man, rather than society, was ultimately responsible for his destiny, and that, considering the way things were stacked, he'd better well attend to it. As our society has grown more beneficent, external forces, like the corporation personnel department, have assumed much of the protective job, and it is this defensive alliance, not a slackening of moral fiber, that has robbed saving of its moral imperative.

They are acquisitive, yes, but, like the heroes of popular fiction, for the good life, and in the good life it is stability—or at least the illusion of it—that is all important. Money itself is secondary. These sober people have become prey to a state of mind in which the form of payment is almost as important as money itself or, for that matter, the purpose of payment. Up to a point, the regular monthly payment is functionally useful, but young suburbanites have gone far beyond this point; like Pavlov's dog, they have become so conditioned to outward form that they will respond even when it poorly serves their actual needs. In their budgetism they do not seem to care about money at all. Goods, yes, but about money itself they are apathetic.

They don't care very much what they pay for their money. As to interest rates, young suburbanites are inconsistent. They know what they are getting on their savings but they show colossal indifference toward the interest charged on loan money. This is the more remarkable since they borrow so much more than they save, and the interest on loans is usually so much higher that the yield on savings is by contrast almost irrelevant. Yet they don't care. They much prefer banks to finance companies, for the trip up the flight of stairs to the finance company is a trip away from middle-class respectability, and they do know vaguely that the bank will charge them less than finance companies. But how much less they have no idea. They don't even ask. All they really want to know, loan officers say, is the size of the monthly payment.

Even when the suburbanites do imagine they know the interest, they delude themselves. Most young people would be amazed to discover that almost invariably they pay the bank a minimum of 10 or 12 per cent. If they have any notion at all, they believe they are paying about 6 per cent. Very few ever pause to realize that the 6 per cent is on the *face* amount and, though they are constantly paying off the principal, they continue to pay as if they retained the face amount, and thus, in effect, pay double the interest they think they do.

They are relatively uninterested in total cost. The monthly charge is the only figure that they feel is relevant, and unless the item is a brand-name appliance they often are quite hazy about the real price. Occasionally a couple will ask the salesman to tell them what the whole thing will come to, itemized, but when he says how glad he is that they raised the question and goes on to other matters most couples seem almost relieved. The truth is, they don't *want* to know.

Their powers of suspicion are rather dormant. A pathetic spectacle is the show of zeal the husband will affect when reading a sales contract; it wouldn't make the slightest difference what outrageous provisions were inserted, he would still read on, comprehending nothing. Among young people there seems to be a strong faith that the protective legislation of the last twenty years, such as the small-loan acts, has somehow reversed the law of *caveat emptor*. One would think, for example, that they had lived long enough to be implacably suspicious of any automobile dealer, but they are not. They are so trusting that they almost never multiply to find out how much of a "pack" the dealer is taking them for. When they raise the money somewhere else so they can pay him cash, they throw away the advantage; on the mistaken assumption that the dealer prefers a cash transaction, they will prematurely announce their intention to pay cash and thereby forewarn him to pad the list price by enough to compensate for the finance charges he won't get.

The symbols of reputability easily disarm them. If an automobile dealer or furniture merchant can say that he will arrange the financing through a local bank, they relax their guard completely. The coupon book will have the reassuring good name of the bank on it, and the suburbanites take it for granted that, as the dealer offhandedly promises, they will be paying "bank rates." Occasionally a purchaser will bother to add up the coupons and come storming into the bank. There must be some mistake, he will say; the interest comes to 12 per cent on the face amount alone. At this point the banker must delicately explain that everything is quite in order but that the dealer, rather than the bank, sets the interest rates. If pressed, the banker must add that the difference between 6 per cent and what the dealer has charged is returned to him as a kickback for throwing the business the bank's way.

For a future capitalist, the organization man displays a remarkable inability to manipulate capital. His handling of "debt consolidation" is a case in point. The growing popularity of loans for this purpose conjures up a picture of chastened citizens tightening their belts and cannily reducing total interest charges. The picture is quite misleading. It is true enough, of course, that in taking out one large loan from the bank a person can cut down the interest he has been paying on a variety of purchases from 25 to 30 per cent to a low of 12 or 18 per cent. But this is not the reason most purchasers take out the loan. In actual practice their consolidating is a sort of check-kiting operation by which they can square themselves away for yet another round of commitments. When these are halfway digested, they will be back again. And again.

They pay dearly for the convenience. Consider, for example, a possible alternative. A mythical couple we will call the Frugals decide to defer all but necessary purchases for enough months to accumulate an extra $500. They will then have a revolving fund of their own which they can use for cash purchases, and instead of paying out a fixed amount each month in installment loans, they will use these sums to replenish the $500.

Now let's take a normal couple. The Joneses, with precisely the same income, don't put off purchases but instead commit themselves to a combination of installment loans and revolving-credit plans. At the end of ten years the Joneses would have paid out somewhere around $800 in interest. The Frugals, by contrast, would have earned interest—roughly $150. Not counting the extra benefits they would have reaped by being able to buy for cash, they would be, in toto, almost a thousand dollars better off.

The Frugals, to repeat, are somewhat mythical. Most suburbanites fail to accumulate capital to produce capital, and they fail to manipulate what capital they do have. It rarely occurs to them, for example, to use their savings as collateral in taking out a loan. Were they to do this they could frequently get an actual rate as low as 4¼ to 4½ per cent instead of the usual 10 to 12 per cent—and their savings would still earn them the regular rate of interest.

Were budgetism carried to its ultimate conclusion, the result would be a plan something like this: A store would assign a couple a credit limit of, say, $150. After buying up to this limit the borrower would pay off in equally scaled monthly payments, with the interest charge on the unpaid balance 1 to 1½ per cent a month, depending on the cupidity of the store. There would always be an unpaid balance. Once a couple started using revolving credit they would never stop, for if they continued to buy as fast as they paid off, they would then enjoy absolutely rhythmic regular payments, month in and month out. True, they would be paying between 12 and 18 per cent annually on a perpetually unpaid balance, but they wouldn't have to think about this.

In department store revolving credit plans the young couples have found just such a service. And they are enthusiastic. Even the most hardened credit men are flabbergasted; so many people have been staying "bought up" that on some lines the stores are making more profit on the interest charges than on the goods themselves. Department store people don't quite have a guilty conscience on the subject, but when they start talking about high administrative overhead, the service to the customer, etc., only the humorless can keep a straight face. "It's fantastic," a department store executive exclaimed to me, closing the door. "Eighteen per cent a year! Imagine it. We didn't expect they'd all stay bought up, but if you want to know whether we like the plan, just ask us if we like money."

The growth of revolving credit has been an interesting reversal of the usual trickle-down effect. Originally, these plans were designed for the needs of a lower economic group, but they blended so well with the prevailing budget psychology that they have been growing steadily more popular with middle-class stores and middle-class people. To the surprise of stores, even customers well enough off to rate charge accounts now frequently prefer revolving credit.

Here is the ultimate in regularity. For one thing, revolving credit evens out purchases so that there are no seasonal peaks, such as occur when the children must be outfitted for school, or Christmas presents bought. It is, better yet, a disciplining factor for the wife. The old coupon-book plans that preceded revolving credit had many of the same features, but the coupon book was "hot money," and, more often than not, the wife spent every bit of it on the trip between the credit department and the store's exit. The regular monthly limit provided by revolving credit has a different psychological effect, and the wife, to the delight of her husband, can confidently pre-plan her impulse buying to the penny.

So far, budgetism has operated largely to put people more in debt, but there is nothing inherent in the process that requires it to do that. Budgetism, essentially, is a person's desire to regularize his finances by having them removed from his own control and disciplined by external forces. This urge could apply to savings as well as debt. To a degree, budgetism has subsumed thrift, most noticeably in pay-roll deduction plans; but on balance, most of the external services offered the consumer are for ease in spending rather than accumulation.

Bankers, for the most part, have not yet recognized how

inclusive is the urge for the organized life. They have heavily exploited the obsession for monthly regularity in their loan business, but they have not done the same for savings. Except for the Christmas Clubs, which bankers rather dislike, few banks have merchandised compulsory, fixed plans by which people can trap themselves into accumulation. Either people save or they don't save, bankers argue, and special plans would have very little effect.

If this were true, however, the Christmas Clubs would be highly unpopular. As many bankers privately remark, the Christmas Clubs are in some ways rather silly; the term is too short for the bank to net any profit from the funds, and the customer, who has to come in once a week, gets nothing extra in interest for his trouble. And Christmas, it has turned out, doesn't have much to do with the plans; when they withdraw their money in December, the depositors apply it to real estate and federal taxes more often than presents, and roughly a third of the depositors transfer the sums to regular savings accounts or convert them into bonds.

Illogical? What people have really been begging for in the Christmas Clubs is an external discipline, and the one feature that banks most dislike—the short time period—is what many depositors also dislike. They want entrapment—constant entrapment—and those banks which have abstracted the moral think the urge can be requited quite easily. Instead of merchandising the idea of saving, they would merchandise the apparatus of it. The external stimulus, they reason, already exists. Thanks to the young couples' familiarity with loans, they have a conditioned response to coupon books, and to exploit this, the banks simply set up loans in reverse (one such plan is called Sav-a-Loan). Instead of having payments optional, they supply coupon books with specified payments and specified dates. It is only a change in form, but where such plans have been pushed they have been successful.

Whatever expression it may take, the rhythm of budgetism is going to become more compelling. Organization man's suburbia provides only a foretaste. Our whole population is moving toward the more regularized life, and as the guaranteed annual wage becomes a reality, the conditions for middle-class budgetism will become yet more universal. And then, finally, there are the children of suburbia—a generation of organization people for whom the Depression is not a father's tale but a grandfather's. Nobody, as suburbanites sometimes remark, is going back.

CHAPTER TWENTY-FIVE

The Web of Friendship

IN such characteristics as budgetism the organization man is so similar from suburb to suburb that it is easy to fall into the trap of seeing a "mass society." On the surface the new suburbia does look like a vast sea of homogeneity, but actually it is a congregation of small neighborly cells—and they make the national trends as much as they reflect them. The groups are temporary, in a sense, for the cast of characters is always shifting. Their patterns of behavior, however, have an extraordinary permanence, and these patterns have an influence on the individual quite as powerful as the traditional group, and in many respects more so.

Propinquity has always conditioned friendship and love and hate, and there is just more downright propinquity in suburbia than in most places. Yet in the power of the group that we see in suburbia we can see something of a shift in values as well. Just as important as the physical reasons is a responsiveness to the environment on the part of its members, and not only in degree but in character it seems to be growing.

In suburbia friendship has become almost predictable. Despite the fact that a person can pick and choose from a vast number of people to make friends with, such things as the placement of a stoop or the direction of a street often have more to do with determining who is friends with whom. When you look at the regularities of group behavior, it is very easy to overlook the influence of individual characteristics, but in suburbia, try as you may to bear this in mind, the repetition of certain patterns makes the group's influence abundantly obvious. Given a few physical clues about the area, you can come close to determining what could be called its flow of "social traffic," and once you have determined this, you may come up with an unsettlingly accurate diagnosis of who is in the gang and who isn't.

Now this may be conformity, but it is not *unwitting* conformity. The people know all about it. When I first started interviewing on this particular aspect of suburbia, I was at first hesitant; it is not very flattering to imply to somebody that they do what they do because of the environment rather than their own free will. I soon found out, however, that they not only knew quite well what I was interested in but were quite ready to talk about it. Give a suburban housewife a map of the area, and she is likely to show herself a very shrewd social analyst. After a few remarks about what a bunch of cows we all are, she will cheerfully explain how funny it is she doesn't pal around with the Clarks any more because she is using the new supermarket now and doesn't stop by Eleanor Clark's for coffee like she used to.

I believe this awareness is the significant phenomenon. In this chapter I am going to chart the basic mechanics of the gang's social life and what physical factors determine it, but it is the awareness of the suburbanites themselves of this that I want to underline. They know full well why they do as they do, and they think about it often. Behind this neighborliness they feel a sort of moral imperative, and yet they see the conflicts also. Although these conflicts may seem trivial to others, they come very close to the central dilemma of organization man.

For comprehending these conflicts, Park Forest is an excellent looking glass. Within it are the principal design features found separately in other suburbs; in its homes area the 60 x 125 plots are laid out in the curved superblocks typical of most new developments, and the garden duplexes of its rental area are perhaps the most intense development of court living to be found anywhere. Park Forest, in short, is like other suburbs, only more so.

Some might think it a synthetic atmosphere, and even Park Foresters, in a characteristically modern burst of civic pride, sometimes refer to their community as a "social laboratory." Yet I think there is justification for calling it a natural environment. While the architects happened on a design of great social utility, they were not trying to be social engineers—they just wanted a good basic design that would please people and make money for the developers— and some of the features they built into the units turned out to be functional in ways other than they expected.

But functional they have been. Perhaps not since the medieval town have there been neighborhood units so well adapted to the predilections and social needs of its people. In many ways, indeed, the courts are, physically, remarkably similar to the workers' housing of the fifteenth century. Like the Fugger houses still standing in Augsburg, the courts are essentially groups of houses two rooms deep, bound together by interior lines of communication, and the parking bay unifies the whole very much as did the water fountain of the Fugger houses.

Park Forest is revealing in another respect. There are enough physical differences within it to show what the constants are. When the architects designed the 105 courts and the homes area, they tried hard to introduce some variety, and because of differences in the number of apartments, the length of streets, and the way buildings are staggered around the parking bays, no two courts or superblocks are alike. Neither are they alike socially; some neighborhood units have been a conspicuous social success from the beginning, while others have not. There are more reasons than physical layout for this, of course, yet as you relate the differences in design of areas to the differences in the way people have behaved in them over a period of time, certain cause-and-effect relationships become apparent.

Let us start with the differences. In "spirit" they are considerable, and the lottery that takes place in the rental office when a couple is assigned to Court B 14 or Court K 3 is a turning point that is likely to affect them long after they have left Park Forest. Each court produces a different pattern of behavior, and whether newcomers become civic leaders or bridge fans or churchgoers will be determined to a large extent by the gang to which chance has now joined them.

Court residents talk about these differences a great deal. In some areas, they will tell you, feuding and cussedness are chronic. "I can't put my finger on it," says one resident, "but as long as I've been here this court has had an inferiority complex. We never seem to get together and have the weenie roasts and anniversary parties that they have in B 18 across the way." In other courts they will talk of their *esprit de corps*. "You would be lucky to get assigned here," says one housewife. "At the beginning we were maybe too neighborly—your friends knew more about your private life than you did yourself! It's not quite that active now. But it's still real friendly—even our dogs and cats are friendly with one another! The street behind us is nowhere near as friendly. They knock on doors over there." Community leaders explain that they have to become professionally expert at diagnosing the temper of different areas. In a fund-raising campaign they know in advance which areas will probably produce the most money per foot pound of energy expended on them, and which the least.

When I first heard residents explain how their court or block had a special spirit, I was inclined to take it all with a grain of salt. But I soon found there was objective proof that they were right. I began a routine plotting of the rate of turnover in each area, the location of parties, and such, and as I did so the maps revealed geographical concentrations that could not be attributed to chance. The location of civic leaders, for example. In the nucleus of courts that were settled first one would expect to find a somewhat higher proportion of leaders than elsewhere, but except for this I thought the distribution of leaders would be fairly random. Where potential civic leaders live, after all, had been determined more or less by chance, and three years of turnover had already shifted the personnel in every court.

But when I plotted the location of the leaders of the

church civic organizations, certain courts displayed a heavy concentration while others showed none at all. The pattern, furthermore, was a persistent one. I got a list of the leaders for the same organizations as of two years previous and plotted their location. The same basic pattern emerged. Some of the similarity was due to the fact that several leaders were still hanging on, but there had been enough turnover to show that the clustering was closely related to the influence of the court.[1]

Other indexes show the same kind of contagion. A map of the roster of the active members of the United Protestant Church indicates that some areas habitually send a good quota of people to church while other areas send few. Voting records show heavy voter turnouts in some areas, apathy in others, and this pattern tends to be constant—the area that had the poorest showing in the early days is still the poorest (six people voting out of thirty-eight eligibles). Sometimes there is a correlation between the number of complaints to the police about parking-space encroachments, litter left on the lawns, and similar evidences of bad feeling. Much in the way one college dorm remains notorious as a "hell's entry," some courts keep on producing an above-average number of complaints, and these courts will prove to be the ones with relatively poor records of churchgoing and voting. Another key index is the number of parties and such communal activities as joint playpens. Some courts have many parties, and though the moving van is constantly bringing in new people, the partying and the group activities keep up undiminished. On closer investigation, these areas with high partying records usually prove to be the ones with the layout best adapted to providing the

---

[1] In only slightly lesser degree the same kind of patterns are visible in other suburbs. As one check, I plotted on a map the members of the Garden Club at Drexelbrook. Again, the map indicated the power of the group. The 120 members were not scattered in the 84 buildings at Drexelbrook, but tended to concentrate in clusters—of the 84 buildings, 33 had no members at all, 20 had one member apiece, and 31 had two, three, or four members. To put it another way, of the 120 members, only 20 were sole members of the group in their building, while 78 were in buildings containing three or four members.

close-knit neighborly group that many planners and observers now feel needs to be re-created on a large scale.

Let me now get ahead of my story a bit with a caveat. These indexes I have been speaking of do not necessarily measure different aspects of the same quality. I had mistakenly thought that if I put all these indexes together I would have a rough over-all measure of group cohesion. But I found that areas that had an excellent score on one kind of participation, for example, often had a markedly poor one on another. This pattern was common enough, furthermore, to indicate that there must be some basic reasons why the groups couldn't have their participation both ways.

I believe there is a lesson to be learned from these disparities. Most of those who speak of man's need to belong tend to treat belongingness as a sort of unity—a satisfying whole in which the different activities a man enters into with other people complement one another. But do they? The suburban experience is illuminating. The comparison of physical layout and neighborliness will show that it is possible deliberately to plan a layout which will produce a close-knit social group, but it also will show that there is much more of a price to be paid for this kind of neighborliness than is generally imagined.

Before going into the conflict between types of neighborliness, let's look first at how these traditions came about. It is much the same question as why one city has a "soul" while another, with just as many economic advantages, does not. In most communities the causes lie far back in the past; in the new suburbia, however, the high turnover has compressed in a few years the equivalent of several generations. Almost as if we were watching stop-action photography, we can see how traditions form and mature and why one place "takes" and another doesn't.

Of all the factors, the character of the original settlers seems the most important. In the early phase the impact of the strong personality, good or otherwise, is magnified. The relationships of people within a small area are necessarily rather intense; the roads separating one court from another will become avenues but they are more like moats at this stage, and the court's inhabitants must function as a unit to conquer such now legendary problems as the mud of Park Forest, or the "rocks and rats" of Drexelbrook.

But though the level of communal sharing and brotherhood is high in all courts in this period, even then important differences develop. Two or three natural leaders concentrated in one court may so stimulate the other people that civic work becomes something of a tradition in the court; or, if the dominant people are of a highly gregarious temper, the court may develop more inwardly, along the one-big-family line. Conversely, one or two troublemakers may fragment a court into a series of cliques, and the lines of dissension often live long after they have gone.

In time, the intensity of activity weakens. As the volunteer policemen are replaced by a regular force, as the mud turns to grass, the old *esprit de corps* subsides into relative normalcy. First settlers will tell you that the place is in a dead calm. "We used to become so *enraged*," one nostalgically recalls. "Now it is just like any other place."

Not really. What seems like dead calm to the now somewhat jaded pioneers will not seem so to anybody from the outside world, and for all the settling down the court continues to be a hothouse of participation. Occasionally, there are sharp breaks in the continuity of tradition; in one court, for example, several forceful women ran for the same post in a community organization, and the effect of their rivalry on the court spirit was disastrous. Most courts, however, tend to keep their essential characters. The newcomers are assimilated, one by one, and by the time the old leaders are ready to depart, they have usually trained someone to whom they can pass on the baton.

The rules of the game that are transmitted are more tacit than open, yet in every court there are enough rules to provide an almost formal ritual. "We live as we please," the old resident will tell the newcoming couple, who then proceed to learn about the tot yard, about the baby-sitting service, about the history of the court and The Incident, how the round-robin bridge group alternates, and how, frankly, they are lucky they didn't get assigned to the next court—broth-er, what a weird crew they are!

There are more subtle aspects to the court character, and through sheer absorption the couple will pick these up too. Their language, for example. With surprising frequency, residents of a particular area will use certain vogue words and phrases, and the newcomers' vocabularies will soon reflect this. (In one group of duplexes at Drexelbrook, the girls use the word "fabulous" incessantly; in a Park Forest court once dominated by a psychology instructor and his wife, both "interaction" and "permissive" frequently punctuate the most humdrum conversations.) Leisure-time hobbies are similarly infectious. "Charlie used to make fun of us for spending so much time planting and mowing and weeding," one superblock resident says of a neighbor. "Well, only the other day he came to ask me—oh so casually —about what kind of grass seed is best for the soil around here. You should see him now. He's got sprays and everything."

We have been looking at the differences between courts and blocks as they affect behavior; now let us move in for a close-up of the differences within areas. Here the tremendous importance of physical design becomes apparent. The social patterns show rather clearly that a couple's behavior is influenced not only by which court they join but what particular part of the court they are assigned to.

This was first brought home to me when I was talking to a housewife in one large court. She had been explaining to me how different people went with each other and how they decided who was to be included in parties and who was not. When I seemed somewhat surprised at the symmetry of these groupings, she asked me if I had heard about The Line. They wouldn't know what to do without it, she said, with some amusement. The court was so big, she went on, that things had to be organized, and so they had settled on an imaginary line across one axis of the court. This made the larger division; certain secondary physical characteristics, such as the placement of a wing, took care of the subgroupings.

Was layout that important? Intrigued, my associates and I decided to make this court the object of considerable study. For a month we went into every other factor that could account for the friendship patterns. We looked into the religion of each one of the forty-four couples, their family background, where they were born, how much education they had, their taste in books, in television, whether or not they drank, what games they liked to play, the husband's salary, and so on. With all this in hand we correlated this way and that way, but when we were finished we found we were right back where we had started from. Just as the resident had said, it was the layout that was the major factor.

The social notes of the Park Forest newspapers offer further corroboration. On this matter I speak with no modesty; I have read every single one of the social notes in the *Park Forest Reporter* for a three-and-one-half-year period and, believe me, that's a lot of social notes. The *Reporter* is an excellent paper and the social doings are reported in sometimes overpowering detail. If you plot the location of the members of each gathering reported in the social notes, you will see certain recurring patterns appear. Wherever areas have common design characteristics—such as a cul-de-sac road—the friendship groupings also tend to be similar.

On pages 374-75 is a fair sampling of parties held in the homes area of Park Forest between December 1952 and July 1953. It you look closely you will note certain patterns—and these patterns, it should be added, would be even clearer if all the parties could be put on the map. You will note, for one thing, that the guests at any one party came from a fairly circumscribed geographic area. Gatherings that drew their cast from a wide area, like the meeting of the Gourmet Society, were the exception. Note also that the groups usually formed along and across streets; rarely did the groupings include people on the other side of the back yard. And these patterns persist. On pages 376-77 is a sampling of parties in the same area three years later (Jan.–June 1956). New people have moved in, others have moved out, yet the basic patterns are unchanged.

Social notes, needless to say, are a highly incomplete

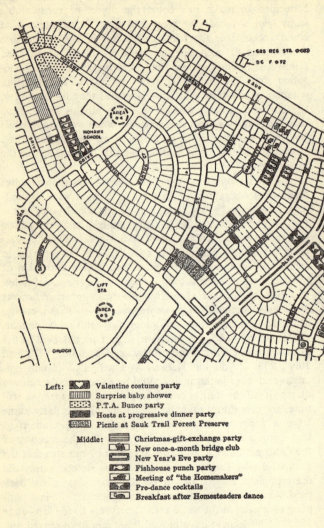

Left:
- Valentine costume party
- Surprise baby shower
- P.T.A. Bunco party
- Hosts at progressive dinner party
- Picnic at Sauk Trail Forest Preserve

Middle:
- Christmas-gift-exchange party
- New once-a-month bridge club
- New Year's Eve party
- Fishhouse punch party
- Meeting of "the Homemakers"
- Pre-dance cocktails
- Breakfast after Homesteaders dance

Period covered above is January–July 1953.

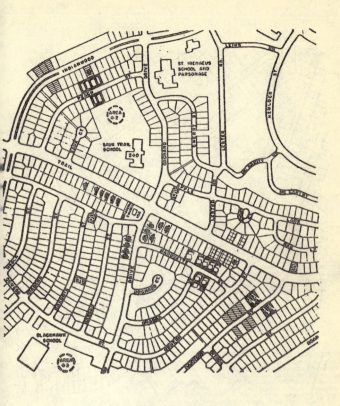

Right:
- Saturday-night party
- New Year's Eve party
- First meeting of new bridge group
- Eggnog before Poinsettia Ball
- Come-as-you-are birthday party
- Saturday-night bridge group
- Gourmet Society

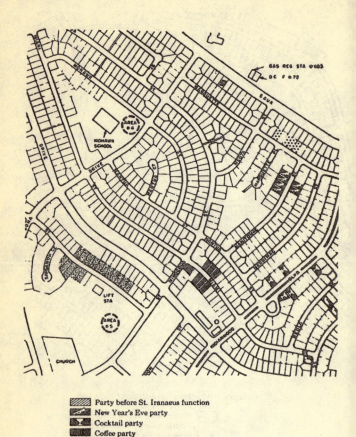

Period covered: January–June 1956. (As with the previous map, the party groupings above show the most typical patterns, but are only a fraction of the parties that actually took place in the area.)

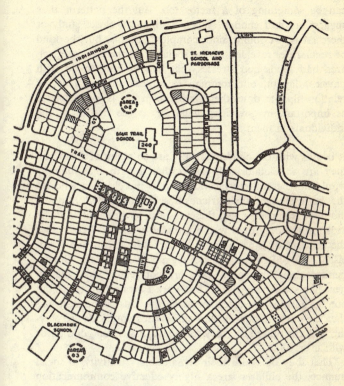

Bridge party
Goodbye party
Canasta party
Nassau Bridge Club
Fourth birthday party
Bridge Club

guide—some areas are over-reported, others are under-reported, and the personal inclinations of the social reporter can be something of a factor too. But the patterns they suggest are real enough. When we made a closer study of these areas, we found more complex patterns, but the kind of regularities revealed by the social notes were there. Each area had feuds and stresses that had nothing to do with physical layout, but common to almost all was a set of relationships—at times they almost seem like laws—that were as important in governing behavior as the desires of the individuals in them.

It begins with the children. There are so many of them and they are so dictatorial in effect that a term like *filiarchy* would not be entirely facetious.[2] It is the children who set the basic design; their friendships are translated into the mother's friendships, and these, in turn, to the family's. "The kids are the only ones who are really organized here," says the resident of a patio court at Park Merced in San Francisco. "We older people sort of tag along after them." Suburbanites elsewhere agree. "We are not really 'kid-centered' here like some people say," one Park Forester protests, "but our friendships are often made on the kids' standards, and they are purer standards than ours. When your kids are playing with the other kids, they force you to keep on good terms with everybody."

That they do. With their remarkable sensitivity to social nuance, the children are a highly effective communication net, and parents sometimes use them to transmit what custom dictates elders cannot say face to face. "One newcomer gave us quite a problem in our court," says a resident in an eastern development. "He was a Ph.D., and he started to

[2] Characteristic of all the new suburbs is a highly skewed age distribution in which children between 0 to 10 and parents between 25 to 35 make up the overwhelming bulk of the population. At Levittown, Pennsylvania, for example, a 1953 census revealed that 40 per cent of the people were between 0 and 10, 33 per cent between 25 and 35. Only 1.4 per cent were teenagers between 15 and 20, only 3.7 per cent were 45 or older. (Source: Philadelphia Council of Churches survey.)

pull rank on some of the rest of us. I told my kid he could tell his kid that the other fathers around here had plenty on the ball. I guess all we fathers did the same thing; pretty soon the news trickled upward to this guy. He isn't a bad sort; he got the hint—and there was no open break of any kind."

Play areas: Since children have a way of playing where they feel like playing, there congregating areas have not turned out to be exactly where elders planned them to be. In the homes area the back yards would seem ideal, and communal play areas have been built in some of them. But the children will have none of it; they can't use their toy vehicles there and so they play on the lawn and pavements out front. In the court areas the children have amenably played in and around the interior parking bay out of traffic's way. The courts' enclosed "tot yards," however, haven't turned out to be as functional as was expected; in some courts the older children have used them as a barricade to keep the younger children *out*.

Find where the flow of wheeled juvenile traffic is and you will find the outlines of the wives' *Kaffeeklatsch* routes. Sight and sound are important; when wives go visiting they gravitate toward the houses within sight of their children and within hearing of the telephone, and these lines of sight crystallize into the court "checkerboard movement."

In the courts, as a consequence, the back door is the functional door and the front door might just as well be walled in. As a matter of fact, this has been done in some buildings; when they learned how the residents centered their activities around the inner parking bay, the architects decided to incorporate the fact into a new apartment building recently added. There is no front door at all; the space is given over to a picture wall, and all traffic has to funnel through the back area. By all accounts, the design is a conspicuous success.

Placement of driveways and stoops: If you are passing by a row of houses equally spaced and want a clue as to how the different couples pair off, look at the driveways. At every second house there are usually two adjacent driveways; where they join makes a natural sitting, baby-watching, and gossip center, and friendship is more apt to flower there than across the unbroken stretch of lawn on the other sides of the houses. For the same basic reasons the couples who share adjoining back stoops in the courts are drawn together, even though equidistant neighbors on the other side may have much more in common with them.

Lawns: The front lawn is the thing on which homeowners expend most time, and the sharing of tools, energies, and advice that the lawns provoke tends to make the family friendships go along and across the street rather than over the back yards. The persistence of this pattern furnishes another demonstration of the remarkable longevity of social

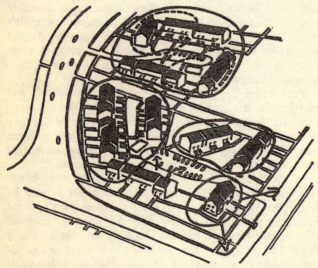

What makes a court clique: In the rental courts formed around parking bays social life is oriented inward. In the large court at the bottom, for example, wings whose back doors face each other form natural social units. Buildings sited somewhat ambiguously tend to split the allegiance of their inhabitants, or else, like the lonely apartment unit at lower right, isolate them. Smaller courts like the one at the top are usually more cohesive; and though there may be subgroupings, court people often get together as a unit.

patterns. Two years ago I was assured by many that lack of over-the-back-fence fraternization was strictly temporary. It has not proved to be so. As the areas have matured, some of the reasons for the concentration of activity in the front area have disappeared; but despite this fact and despite the turnover, over-the-back-fence socializing is still the exception. Many residents joke about not having the slightest idea who lives in back of them, and those who know one or two rear neighbors generally met them through a community-wide activity, like politics, or the church.

Centrality: The location of your home in relation to the others not only determines your closest friends; it also vir-

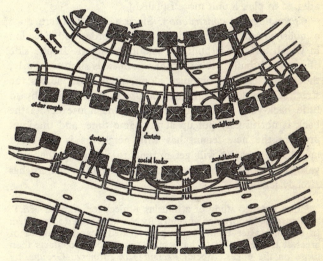

How homeowners get together: (1) Individuals tend to become most friendly with neighbors whose driveways adjoin theirs. (2) Deviates or feuding neighbors tend to become boundaries of the gang. (3) People in the most central positions make the greatest number of social contacts. (4) Street width and traffic determine whether or not people make friends across the street. (5) People make friends with those in back of them only where some physical feature creates traffic—such as the short-cut pavement one woman on the lower street uses on her way to the supermarket.

tually determines how popular you will be. The more central one's location, the more social contacts one has. In the streets containing rental apartments there is a constant turnover; yet no matter who moves in or out, the center of activity remains in mid-block, with the people at the ends generally included only in the larger gatherings.[3]

Some Park Forest veterans joke that a guide should be furnished newcomers so that if they had a choice of sites they would be enabled to tell which would best suit their personality. Introverts who wished to come out of their shell a bit could pick a house in the middle of a block; while introverts who wished to stay just as they are would be well advised to pick a unit more isolated.[4]

Chronology of construction: Since a social pattern once established tends to perpetuate itself, the order and direction in which an area is built are enduring factors. If one side of a street is built first rather than both sides simultaneously, the group tends to organize along rather than across the street. The order of construction also helps explain why so little back-yard socializing develops. The house across the back is not usually put up at the same time, and the joint problem the new tenant has with neighbors is the front lawn. Later on he will get around to fixing up the back yard, but by that time the front-lawn neighbor pattern has already jelled.

[3] In a detailed study of a housing project for married M.I.T. students, the importance of centrality has been well documented. In building after building, couples located near the routes of greatest traffic tended to have many more social contacts than those on the edges. (*Social Pressures in Informal Groups,* by Leon Festinger, Stanley Schacter, and Kurt Back. New York: Harper & Brothers, 1950.)

[4] It's not such an outlandish idea. William L. Wheaton, Professor of Planning at the University of Pennsylvania, came to somewhat the same idea as the result of studies his students had made of five communities. The social patterns he found were substantially the same as those in Park Forest, and he noted well the hothouse effect of the tightly knit unit. Streets or courts, he advised planners, should be so laid out as "to allow any one family the choice of two groups or benevolent despotisms in which to live."

The chronology also has a lot to do with the size of the group. If a person moves into a new block the social group to which he will belong is apt to be a large one. The reasons are visible. Mud, paving, the planting of trees, the sharing of tools—problems common to all—and in each new block you will see the pioneer phase all over again. Go down the street to where the lawns are green and the lucite awnings long since up, and there the group will probably be smaller. Once the pressure of common pioneering problems is lifted, the first great wave of friendliness subsides, and the potential fissures present from the beginning start to deepen.

This process is almost visible too. To find how one block had matured we put on a series of identical maps each gathering that had taken place over a year; riff through these maps quickly, and in the few seconds that represent a year's parties you can see in crude animation the fissures begin to widen as the original group splits up into more manageable components.

Limitations on size: One reason it's so important to be centrally placed is that an active group can contain only so many members. There is usually an inner core of about four to six regulars. Partly because of the size of the living rooms (about twenty by fifteen), the full group rarely swells beyond twelve couples, and only in the big functions such as a block picnic are the people on the edges included.

Barriers: But the rules of the game about who is to be included are not simple. Suppose you want to give a party? Do you mix friends out of the area with the neighbors? How many neighbors should you invite? Where, as social leaders chronically complain, do you draw the line? Physical barriers can provide the limiting point. Streets, for example, are functional for more than traffic; if it is a large street with heavy traffic, mothers will forbid their children to cross it, and by common consent the street becomes a boundary for the adult group.

Because of the need for a social line, the effect of even the smallest barrier is multiplied. In courts where the parking bays have two exits, fences have been placed across the middle to block through traffic; only a few feet high, they are as socially impervious as a giant brick wall. Similarly, the grouping of apartment buildings into wings of a court provides a natural unit whose limits everyone understands. All in all, it seems, the tightest-knit groups are those in which no home is isolated from the others—or so sited as to introduce a conflict in the social allegiance of its residents.

Ambiguity is the one thing the group cannot abide. If there is no line, the group will invent one. They may settle on an imaginary line along the long axis of the court, or, in the homes area, one particular house as the watershed. There is common sense behind it. If it's about time you threw a party for your neighbors, the line solves many of your problems for you. Friends of yours who live on the other side understand why they were not invited, and there is no hard feeling.

In this need, incidentally, the deviant can be of great benefit. The family that doesn't mix with the others or is disliked by them frequently furnishes a line of social demarcation that the layout and geography do not supply. So functional is the barrier family in this respect that even if they move out, their successors are likely to inherit the function. The new people may be quite normal enough themselves, but unless they are unusually extroverted the line is apt to remain in the same place.

What lessons can we deduce from these relationships? All other things being equal—and it is amazing how much all other things are equal in suburbia—it would appear that certain kinds of physical layouts can virtually produce the "happy" group. To some the moral would seem simplicity itself. Planners can argue that if they can find what it is that creates cohesiveness it would follow that by deliberately building these features into the new housing they could at once eliminate the loneliness of modern life.[5]

[5] The English experience has been instructive. In his acerb account of the development of the new town of Stevenage (*Utopia, Ltd.* New Haven: Yale University Press, 1953), Harold Orlans found planners impaled by the dilemmas of happiness. Some planners, and there were many schools of thought among them, had a considerable faith in certain geometric arrangements

Not all planners go along with this line of thought, but some are enthusiastic. At several meetings of planners I have talked to about suburbia, I have noticed that the most persistent discussion is on this point. Planners involved with urban redevelopment are particularly interested. Concerned as they are with the way housing projects break up old family and neighborhood ties, they see in the tight-knit group of suburbia a development of great promise.

I hope they pause. I would not want to malign planners for becoming interested in sociology—it is a common complaint in the field, indeed, that most planners aren't interested enough. But a little sociology can be a dangerous weapon, for it seems so objective that it is easy to forget the questions of value involved. Certainly, the more we know about the social effects of planning the more effectively we can plan. But on such developments as the integrated group it is necessary to ask not only how it can be planned but *if*.

How good is "happiness"? The socially cohesive block has its advantages, but there is a stiff price to be paid for them. In the next chapter I am going to sketch the impact of this cohesiveness on the suburbanites. It is a highly mixed picture and must be entirely a matter of personal opinion as to whether the cohesion is more good than bad. It is very

---

as the means to more happiness. The planners differed on the size of the ideal neighborhood, but they all agreed on the idea of breaking up the larger neighborhood unit into a series of smaller ones which, it was hoped, would at once produce neighborliness and stimulate community-wide activity at the same time. Orlans, strongly anti-utopian, is skeptical. "Can it have been scientifically established that the 'neighborhood unit' will increase human happiness or neighborliness when some planners [arguing for a different type unit] . . . believe the opposite?" Orlans notes that while most of the planners believed that a series of neighborhood units would integrate the community, others believed that they would break up, rather than unite, the towns. "Fortunately, many planning decisions are unlikely to affect the happiness of new-town residents one way or the other," Orlans laconically observes, "for the residents will probably be less concerned about them than are planners, and, being ordinary people and not abstractions, will be able to adjust satisfactorily to a variety of physical and social environments."

evident, nonetheless, that this cohesion brings the suburban-ite up against a serious conflict of values. It is important not only in its own right, it is important as a symbol of the conflict that pervades all of organization life.

CHAPTER TWENTY-SIX

The Outgoing Life

THE effect this web of friendship has on the individual is a problem suburbanites think about a great deal. Like them, I am going to deal with the good aspects first, the adverse second. But the two are really inseparable, and it is this duality I wish to underscore. The Social Ethic denies it, and there is the problem. Finding a middle way in the conflicts of interest between the group and oneself has always been difficult, but it has become particularly difficult as people have come to believe there should be, ideally, no conflicts—and the happier the group, the more, not the less, intense is the problem. In the chapters on the corporation I argued that it was the very beneficence of the environment that made resistance to it so difficult. So in suburbia. As many people have sensed, it is all very well to say one should belong. But how much? Where is the line between co-operation and surrender?

On the credit side the suburbanites have much to say about the group. One of the first points they make is how it has altered their personality—or how they and the rest of the group altered someone else's. For the good. "I've changed tremendously," says one typical transient. "My husband was always the friend-maker in the family—everybody always loves Joe; he's so likable. But here I began to make some friends on my own; I was so tickled when I realized it. One night when the gang came to our house I suddenly realized *I* made these friends."

The cumulative effect can be summed up in a word. One is made *outgoing*. If the person is too shy to make the first move, others will take the initiative. In almost every court, patio, or superblock there is usually someone who enjoys doing the job, and the stiffer the challenge, the more the enjoyment. "When Mr. and Mrs. Berry came, they wouldn't give you the time of day," one leader recalls. "But I knew they were real shy and unhappy beneath it all. I said to myself, 'I'm going to conquer them if it kills me.' I have, too. She was one of the organizers for the Mothers' March and he's gotten tremendously interested in the school. They're part of the gang now—you wouldn't know they were the same people."

Those who have been "brought out" bear witness to the transformation. They speak enthusiastically of it, and if their experiences had to be summed up in a phrase, it would boil down to one heartfelt note of joy: *they weren't introverts after all*. "One of the reasons I took technical training in college," explains one ex-introvert, "was that I thought I wasn't the mixing type and wouldn't be much good with people. Well, here I am, leading meetings and what not, and, frankly, not doing too bum a job. It's changed a lot of ideas I had about myself."

In theory, one could keep entirely to oneself, and some people attempt to do so. It is not, however, an easy alternative. The court, like the double bed, enforces intimacy, and self-imposed isolation becomes psychologically untenable. People so ingoing that they have been proof against "bringing out" usually seem to be rather troubled people, and though the causes of their unhappiness may antedate their entry into the court, some leave at the first opportunity. The court checks off another failure. "At the very end the Smithers were beginning to come out of their shell," one outgoing resident recalls. "But it was too late; they'd already given up their lease. The night they left, you could tell by their faces, the way they tried to get friendly, they wished they weren't leaving. It was so pathetic."

On the matter of privacy, suburbanites have mixed feelings. Fact one, of course, is that there isn't much privacy. In most small towns there is at least enough living room to soften the shock of intimate contact, and, besides, there is usually some redoubt to which the individual can withdraw. In Park Forest not even the apartment is a redoubt; people don't bother to knock and they come and go furiously. The lack of privacy, furthermore, is retroactive. "They ask you all sorts of questions about what you *were* doing," one resident puts it. "Who was it that stopped in last night? Who were those people from Chicago last week? You're never alone, even when you think you are."

Less is sacred. "It's wonderful," says one young wife. "You find yourself discussing all your personal problems with your neighbors—things that back in South Dakota we would have kept to ourselves." As time goes on, this capacity for self-revelation grows; and on the most intimate details of family life, court people become amazingly frank with one another. No one, they point out, ever need face a problem alone.

In the battle against loneliness even the architecture becomes functional. Just as doors inside houses—which are sometimes said to have marked the birth of the middle class —are disappearing, so are the barriers against neighbors. The picture in the picture window, for example, is what is going on *inside*—or, what is going on inside other people's picture windows.

The walls in these new apartments are also dual purpose. Their thinness is occasionally a disadvantage; one court scandal, as a matter of fact, was provoked by a woman who chronically inverted a tumbler against the wall to eavesdrop. But there is more good than bad, many transients say, to the thinness. "I never feel lonely, even when Jim's away," goes a typical comment. "You know friends are near by, because at night you hear the neighbors through the walls."

Even the most outgoing, of course, confess that the pace of court life occasionally wears them down, and once in a while they reach such a point of rebellion they don't answer the phone. Such a purely negative response, however, is not enough. To gain privacy, one has to *do* something. One court resident, for example, moves his chair to the front rather than the court side of his apartment to show he doesn't want to be disturbed. Often a whole court or a wing of it will develop such a signal; a group in one Drexelbrook court has decided that whenever one of them feels he or she has finally had it, she should draw the venetian blinds all the way down to the bottom of the picture window. This lowered position is an unusual one, and the rest spot it as a plea to be left alone—for a little while, anyway.

But there is an important corollary of such efforts at privacy—*people feel a little guilty about making them.* Except very occasionally, to shut oneself off from others like this is regarded as either a childish prank or, more likely, an indication of some inner neurosis. The individual, not the group, has erred. So, at any rate, many errants seem to feel, and they are often penitent about what elsewhere would be regarded as one's own business, and rather normal business at that. "I've promised myself to make it up to them," one court resident recently told a confidant. "I was feeling bad that day and just plain didn't make the effort to ask them in for coffee. I don't blame them, really, for reacting the way they did. I'll make it up to them somehow."

Privacy has become clandestine. Not in solitary and selfish contemplation but in doing things with other people does one fulfill oneself. Nor is it a matter of overriding importance just what it is that one does with other people; even watching television together—for which purpose, incidentally, several groups have been organized—helps make one more of a real person.

However one may view this responsiveness to the group, it is important to acknowledge its moral basis. That friendship in the new suburbia transcends personal characteristics so much is due in part to the increasing homogeneity of American middle-class values. But it is also due to a very active kind of tolerance, and unless this is recognized one cannot appreciate the true difficulty of the suburbanites' dilemmas.

Very consciously, they try to understand one another's backgrounds and prejudices. As the unresolved segregation problem indicates, the millennium is still some way off, but the fact remains that they make a great effort to meet one another halfway. If misfortune strikes a family, the neighbors are not only remarkably generous but remarkably tactful. If, say, the child of a couple in straits accidentally breaks someone's windshield, the group may not only chip in to pay for the damage but will try to conceal the fact that they have done so. Those in trouble are often irrationally antagonistic, but this the group takes in stride. They may have "a personality problem," and there is nothing so challenging to the others as its diagnosis and therapy.

In the more humdrum aspects of daily life, much of what could pass for lazy conformity is in fact a very energetic, and in many ways unselfish, quest for consensus. Just as the Bunco player may put his mind to mastering bridge, so the shy housewife makes herself have fun at a coffee party; just as the Fundamentalist unbends with a risqué story and a beer now and then, so his neighbors tone down their own stories.

For the intellectual also Park Forest is a melting pot. "When I first came here I was pretty rarefied," a self-styled egghead explained to me. "I remember how shocked I was one afternoon when I told the girls in the court how much I had enjoyed listening to *The Magic Flute* the night before. They didn't know what I was talking about. I began to learn that diaper talk is important to them and I'm not so highbrow about it now. I still listen to *The Magic Flute,* but now I realize that it's not wrong that most people care about other things."

In similar fashion, farm-bred Republicans learn to appreciate that not all urban Democrats are Communists. "The people who lived in the other half of our duplex," recalls one Republican, "were as different as could be from us. They were the kind who worshiped F.D.R.'s name. But we got to like them just the same. We just didn't talk politics. We used to go bowling together and that sort of thing. I didn't make him a Republican, but I think he appreciates my views a lot more than he did before, and I understand him better."

This seeking of common values applies markedly to religion. The neighborhood friendship patterns would be impossible unless religious beliefs had lost much of their segregating effect. And it is more than a passive, live-and-let-live attitude. Several people of other faiths, for example, have joined the National Council of Jewish Women; they like the intellectual content of its discussion programs, and they feel no conflict with their own beliefs.

Even where there is conflict, suburbanites lean over backward to see the other point of view. "When Will and Ada had to dash East last month—they're devout Catholics—I took care of little Johnny for them," recalls one non-Catholic. "It really tickled me. Here I was picking Johnny up at St. Irenaeus School every afternoon and seeing to it that he said his Rosary every night before he went to bed." Park Forest abounds with such stories, and the good will implicit in them is real.[1]

The suburban group also has a strong effect on relations between husband and wife, and in many ways a beneficent one. The group is a foster family. In the transient organization life the young family has to take a good part of its environment with it; no longer is there the close complex of aunts and uncles and grandparents to support the couple, and when they come to their first crisis this absence can have a devastating effect. Thus the function of the suburban

[1] This denominator-seeking is also illustrated in the commercial "parties" held in suburbia (Linda Lee clothes demonstrations, the Beauty Counselor, etc.). Stanley Home products demonstrators, for example, ask the hostess to serve only two refreshments, preferably coffee and doughnuts. If the choice is left to her, she may overdo it and others will fear to be hostesses lest their own offerings suffer in comparison. Similar care marks the games that precede the product demonstration. "The best kind of thing to start with," says one Park Forest housewife who has demonstrated Stanley products, "is something like the waistline game. That's where you lay a piece of rope on the floor and start making an ever-bigger circle; one by one the girls tell you when they think it's as big as their waistline. They always overestimate, because your waistline is oblong and not a circle. They get a big charge out of that. But if you do anything that shows up people's intelligence, it's tricky. With a spelling game or naming states—you'd be surprised how many people can't name ten states—they just get uncomfortable."

group. All the other young couples are in the same boat, and in a sort of unspoken mutual assistance pact they provide for one another a substitute for the big family of former years.

What unites them most are the concerns of parenthood, and this preoccupation with children is a potent factor in keeping marriages on keel. "The kind of social situation you find here discourages divorce," says United Protestant Church minister Dr. Gerson Engelmann. "Few people, as a rule, get divorces until they break with their groups. I think the fact that it is so hard to break with a group here has had a lot to do with keeping some marriages from going on the rocks."

So pervasive are the concerns of parenthood that adjustment to court life is almost impossible for childless couples. Unless the wife obviously loves children—unless she is the kind, for example, who keeps a cooky jar for the neighbors' kids—her daily routine is painfully out of kilter with the others'. Understandably, the recourse of adopting a child is sought very frequently. Complementing the social pressure of the group on the couple is the readiness of social agencies to give a Park Forest couple preference, for they look on the environment as ideal for adjustment. (Social workers' liking for Park Forest has been so strong as to force local authorities to yell uncle; so many problem children have been sent out that in several areas the problem children are having more impact on the normal ones than the normal ones on the problem children.)

Personal morals? The court is the greatest invention since the chastity belt. In company, young suburbanites talk a great deal about sex, but it's all rather clinical, and outside of the marriage no one seems to do much about it. There have been, to be sure, some unpleasant occurrences: in one court there was talk of wife-trading several years ago, and there have been affairs here and there since. The evidence is strong, however, that there is less philandering in the package suburbs than in more traditional communities.

For one thing, it's almost impossible to philander without everyone's knowing about it. One's callers are observed, and if neighbors feel there is anything untoward, suburbia's phenomenal grapevine will speed the news.[2] This is not mere venom; in a web of relationships as delicate as that of the court an affair can harm not only two marriages, it can upset the whole court applecart. Infidelity, to put it another way, is an ethical as well as a moral problem.

More important, the neighborliness of court life fills a void in the life of the young wife that is not always filled elsewhere—and this is particularly important for the wife whose husband travels. "You don't find as many frustrated women in a place like this," says one young wife. "We gals have each other. A young girl who would get to brooding if she was in an apartment all by herself on the outside can talk things over with us. She's just too busy to get neurotic. Kitty, for example. She's married to a real creep—pardon me, but that's what he is—but when she's disturbed she comes over here for coffee and a little chat, and we have a fine old time yakking away. It helps, for people like her."

The participation also mitigates the "retrograde wife" problem that affects many corporation couples. If the husband is moving up rapidly this introduces a wedge between husband and wife, for while he is getting a postgraduate finishing through travel and exposure to successful older men, her tastes are often frozen at their former level by lack of any activity but child rearing. In the new suburbia this is somewhat less likely to happen. "Before we came here," one wife, typical of many another, says, "I was such a stupid little thing. I didn't think about anything except

---

[2] One of the occupational hazards of interviewing is the causing of talk, and I am afraid my presence seriously embarrassed some housewives in several suburbs. In one of the instances I later learned about, a husband arrived home to be greeted by a phone call. "You don't know who I am," a woman's voice announced, "but there's something you ought to know. A man stopped by your house this afternoon and was with your wife *three* hours." This was malicious, but not all such gossip is. Unless he is a deliveryman or doctor or such the man who enters suburbia during the day can make the female group feel that here comes Trouble, and their protective instincts come to the fore—stroll by a bunch of wives *Kaffeeklatsching* on a lawn and you will feel very forcefully their inquiry.

shopping and the babies and things like that. Now that I'm in the League of Women Voters and the school board I feel so much more worth while. When Joe comes home at night I have so many interesting things to talk to him about."

In this mutual seeking of denominators, to recapitulate, the young suburbanites have been re-creating something of the tight-knit group of old. It is an achievement not to be dismissed lightly. They have come together with many more differences in religion, background, and expectations to adjudicate than troubled communities of old. Tensions they suffer for the suppression of their differences, but the consensus that is the result bespeaks a pretty high quotient of kindliness and fundamental decency.

But there is another side to the coin. Contemporary prophets of belongingness point out the warmth and security the tight-knit group produces for the individual, but they generally stop short at diagnosing some of the other things it produces. The suburbanites are more troubled, for they experience the double-barreled effects of belongingness, and in highly practical, immediate ways. It is not the question of conformity, though many speak of it as such. It is, rather, the question of determining *when* one is conforming, when adjustment is selflessness, or surrender. It is a moral dilemma—the one, I believe, central to the organization man, and while the suburban group affords the most concrete illustration, the underlying problem will not be shed when he moves on.

Let's take a second look at that tolerance. There is one trouble with it. In the happy group, people are very intolerant of those who aren't tolerant. This is using the same word in two senses, I admit, but suburbanites are ambiguous about it too. Their tolerance, as they are so proud to point out, goes downward. It does not, however, go *upward* very far. The leveling process is just that—leveling—and those financially above the norm who let the fact be visible are risking trouble. Though neighbors speak kindly of someone who "has not had all the advantages," the phrase "they are more . . . fortunate than the rest of us" is likely to be spoken with a real bite.

Now let me make an important qualification. How much bite depends on how happy the group is. In the block which never quite jelled there is little of the belongingness, the mutual support characteristic elsewhere; for the same reason, however, there is not much pressure on the individual to adjust. There is no working group to adjust to. In the tight-knit group, however, each member feels an equity in others' behavior. With communication so intensive, the slightest misunderstanding can generate a whole series of consequences. If Charley ducks his turn at the lawn mower, if little Johnny sasses Mrs. Erdlick just once more, if Gladys forgets to return the pound of coffee she borrowed, the frictions become a concern of the group and not just of the principals.

The more vigorous the search for common denominators, the stronger the pressure to alikeness. Sometimes this extends even to house design. The architects have tried to vary the façades of each house, and one might assume that in putting up aluminum awnings, making alterations, repainting and the like, residents try hard to enlarge the differences. This is not always so; in some areas residents have apparently agreed to unify the block with a common design and color scheme for garages and such.

In such blocks an otherwise minor variation becomes blatant deviance; if a man were to paint his garage fire-engine red in a block where the rest of the garages are white, he would literally and psychologically make himself a marked man. So with fences; if they are obviously designed to keep the children safe, eyebrows are not raised. But if the height or elaborateness of the fence indicates other motives, there will be feeling.

An unkempt lawn is another symbol of malaise. The state of the lawn is an effect as well as a cause, and in talking to owners of neglected lawns one gets the suspicion that they have subconsciously used the unkemptness as a weapon to tell the others where they can head in. "I suppose I should do more about it," said one resident, waving to a rather weedy expanse outside, "but my wife and I think there are other things more important in life."

Reprisal is inevitable. The sanctions are not obvious—indeed, people are often unconscious of wielding them—but the look in the eye, the absence of a smile, the inflection of a hello, can be exquisite punishment, and they have brought more than one to a nervous breakdown. And the more social the block, the rougher it is on those who don't fit in.

In some areas it is questionable if the *Gemütlichkeit* of the gang compensates for the misery of the deviate. It is frightening to see the cruelty with which an otherwise decent group can punish the deviate, particularly when the deviate is unfortunate enough to be located in the middle of the group, rather than isolated somewhat out of benevolence's way. "Estelle is a case," says one resident of a highly active block. "She was dying to get in with the gang when she moved in. She is a very warmhearted gal and is always trying to help people, but she's, well—sort of elaborate about it. One day she decided to win over everybody by giving an afternoon party for the gals. Poor thing, she did it all wrong. The girls turned up in their bathing suits and slacks, as usual, and here she had little doilies and silver and everything spread around. Ever since then it's been almost like a planned campaign to keep her out of things. Even her two-year-old daughter gets kept out of the kids' parties. It's really pitiful. She sits there in her beach chair out front just dying for someone to come and *Kaffeeklatsch* with her, and right across the street four or five of the girls and their kids will be yakking away. Every time they suddenly all laugh at some joke she thinks they are laughing at her. She came over here yesterday and cried all afternoon. She told me she and her husband are thinking about moving somewhere else so they can make a fresh start." (The woman in question has since moved.)

Perhaps the greatest tyranny, however, applies not to the deviate but to the accepted. The group is a jealous master. It encourages participation, indeed, demands it, but it demands one kind of participation—its own kind—and the better integrated with it a member becomes the less free he is to express himself in other ways.

In the planners' meetings I spoke of earlier, most of those

who wanted to plan for more participation assumed there is a unity to participation—that is, a layout that will stimulate neighborly social participation is the layout that will stimulate civic and cultural participation. They saw no antithesis; their primary goal was to develop "citizenship" rather than social activity, but they saw both kinds of participation as indivisible—parts of a satisfying whole.

When I first went to Park Forest I thought so too. The courts and blocks that were most notable for the amount of friendliness and social activity, I presumed, would be the ones that contributed the greatest number of civic leaders, and as a check I plotted the location of all the leaders in the principal community organizations. To my surprise, the two did not correlate; if anything, there was a reverse relationship. By and large, the people who were active in the over-all community did not tend to come from the courts that were especially "happy."

The cause-and-effect relationship is not too difficult to determine. For some people, of course, it does not make much difference whether the neighborly gang is a happy one or not; they would be leaders in any event. But such people are a minority. The majority are more influenced by the good opinions of the group, and the cohesiveness of it has a considerable bearing on whether they will become active in community-wide problems. Where the group has never jelled enough to stimulate a sense of obligation, the person with any predilection for civic activity feels no constraints. The others would not be annoyed if he went in for outside activity; they don't care enough. If the group is strong, however, the same kind of person is less likely to express such yearnings. It would be divisive. There are only so many enthusiasms a person can sustain, only so many hours in the day, and the amount of leisure one expends outside the group must be deducted from that spent inside.

It is not merely that the group will resent the absenteeism. Again, on the part of the individual himself, there is a moral obligation, or, at least, the feeling that there should be. I recall how a young housewife put it to me. She had been toying with the idea of getting involved in the little theater, for she felt she and her husband were culturally very lacking. But she decided against it. "If we do it'll mean we'll have to spend more of our free evenings away from the gang. I'd hate to be the first to break things up. We've really worked things out well here. The two play areas for the kids —my, how we all pitched in on that! I know we spend too much time just talking and playing bridge and all. Frankly, Chuck and I are the only ones around here who read much more than the *Reader's Digest*. But have we the right to feel superior? I mean, should we break things up just because we're different that way?"

Is this simple conformity? I am not for the moment trying to argue that yielding to the group is something to be admired, but I do think that there is more of a moral problem here than is generally conceded in most discussions of American conformity. Let me go back to the case of the man who is wondering about something he knows would upset the group—like not painting his garage white, like the rest. He may have been one of the first settlers of a block where the people have suppressed potential dislikes in a very successful effort to solve their common problems. Quite probably, a piece of bad luck for one of the group might have further unified them. If one of the wives had come down with polio, the rest might have chipped in not only with their money but with their time to help out the family through the crisis.

In other words, there has been a great deal of real brotherhood, and the man who is now figuring about his garage faces a decision that is not entirely ludicrous. He knows instinctively that his choice will be construed by the others as an outward manifestation of his regard for them, and he does feel a real obligation to help sustain the good feeling.

If he goes along with them he is conforming, yes, but he is conforming not simply out of cowardice but out of a sense of brotherhood too. You may think him mistaken, but grant at least his problem. The group is a tyrant; so also is it a friend, and *it is both at once*. The two qualities cannot easily be separated, for what gives the group its power over the man is the same cohesion that gives it its warmth. This is the duality that confuses choice.

This duality is a very unpleasant fact. Once you acknowledge how close the relationship is between conformity and belongingness—between "good" participation and "bad" participation—you cannot believe in utopia, now or ever. But progress is not served by ignoring it. Many current prescriptions for a better society do ignore it, and thus are delusory. However shrewd their diagnosis of what is wrong, their precepts could intensify the very problems they are intended to solve.

Even so perceptive an observer as Erich Fromm has fallen into this trap. In his plea for *The Sane Society,* Fromm makes a searching diagnosis of man's desperate efforts to escape the burdens of freedom in group conformity. In documentation Fromm cites the conformity of suburbia. Appropriately enough, he singles out Park Forest as an example and dwells at considerable length on the baneful aspects of the group pressures found there. But what is his antidote? In conclusion, he advocates a "democratic communitarianism"—a society in which, through a multitude of small, local groups, people learn to participate more actively with others.

Well? Fromm might as well have cited Park Forest again. One must be consistent. Park Foresters illustrate conformity; they also illustrate very much the same kind of small group activity Fromm advocates. He has damned an effect and praised a cause. More participation may well be in order, but it is not the antidote to conformity; it is inextricably related with it, and while the benefits may well outweigh the disadvantages, we cannot intensify the former and expect to eliminate the latter. There is a true dilemma here. It is not despite the success of their group life that Park Foresters are troubled but partly because of it, for that much more do they feel an obligation to yield to the group. And to this problem there can be no solution.

Is there a middle way? A recognition of this dilemma is the condition of it. It is only part of the battle, but unless the individual understands that this conflict of allegiances is inevitable he is intellectually without defenses. And the more benevolent the group, the more, not the less, he needs these defenses.

For ultimately his tyranny is self-imposed. In earlier chapters on life within The Organization we saw how the increasing benevolence of human relations, the more democratic atmosphere, has in one way made the individual's path more difficult. He is intimidated by normalcy. He too has become more adept at concealing hostilities and ambitions, more skillfully "normal," but he knows *he* is different and he is not sure about the others. In his own peculiarities he can feel isolated, a fraud who is not what he seems.

Wives also. Like their husbands in the office, they are easily misled by the façades of those about them in suburbia, and a frequent consequence is the "superwoman" complex. Only a minority of wives are really successful at handling both a large agenda of social or civic obligations and their home duties, but everyone puts up such a good front that many a wife begins to feel that something is wanting in her that she is not the same. Determined to be as normal as anyone else, or a little more so, they take on a back-breaking load of duties—and a guilt feeling that they're not up to it. "I've seen it so many times," says Arnold Levin, Park Forest's overworked family counselor. "They may feel inadequate because they haven't a college degree, or haven't made the League of Women Voters, or can't be a 'model' mother like someone else in the court. 'I'm not worth *enough*,' they tell me."[3]

---

[3] The impulse to self-punishment sometimes takes a more pathological form. Barbiturate addiction and attempted suicides are not over average at Park Forest related to national statistics, but there is enough to mock the façade of well-adjusted normality. In the spring of 1955 there was a rash of publicity over the number of women found lifting groceries in the supermarket. Actually, the number was not really very high, the main reason for the excitement being the merchants' faith in publicity as a deterrent. The news about who the women were, however, was something of a shocker. The average shoplifter, the police chief told the newspapers, was not a low-income wife; she was the wife of a junior executive making $8,000, she belonged to a bridge club, was active in the PTA, and attended church. Usually she had about $50 a week to spend on food and sundries.

To bring the problem full circle, you often find wives in deep emotional trouble because they can no longer get understanding or help from their husbands on their social problems. The wife's talk about the court or the block is not just idle gossip; this is the world she and the children must live in, and the personal relationships in it are quite analogous to the ones that are the basis of the husband's worries. But husbands have a double standard on this: office politics they see as part of a vitally important process, but the same kind of relationships in the community they dismiss as trivia, the curse of idle female tongues. "I often wonder," says Levin, "does the husband look to the job in self-defense against his wife's lack of interest? Or does she go in for civic activity because he's withdrawn into the job? I don't know which cause comes first, but it's tragic how many couples have lost the ability to meet each other's inadequacies."

Those who seem best able to steer their own course care about the good opinion of the group, but they have this distinction: they are professionals. They know the conflicts of interest between themselves and others are natural; they have been through many environments and they have the intelligence to grasp this recurring feature of group life. To use Everett Hughes's phrase, they know how to routinize crisis.

Unlike the deviate, they pay the little surface obeisances to the group. Thus do they defend themselves. They have to. Usually, those who seek their friendships through civic or cultural interests have palpably different tastes than those who accept propinquity. Members of the League of Women Voters, for example, are apt to be somewhat absent-minded about their clothes and their housekeeping. ("Most of us League gals are thin," says one, after some comments on the Women's Club. "We're so busy, and we don't have time

---

Perplexed, the police chief and the village chaplain had to put it down as part of the "middle-class neurosis." Rarely was there any obvious motive; even the repentant of the wives could not explain. Perhaps, as some psychiatrists might venture, they stole to be caught—as if they were asking to be punished for wearing a false face to the world.

for coffee and doughnuts.") Such people, however, have much less friction with their neighbors than might be imagined. They do not give the group enough familiarity to breed contempt; although they may draw a firm line at intimacy, they are good about baby-sitting, returning borrowed lawn mowers, and the other neighborly graces.

Above all, they do not get too close. The transients' defense against rootlessness, as we have noted, is to get involved in meaningful activity; at the same time, however, like the seasoned shipboard traveler, the wisest transients don't get too involved. Keeping this delicate balance requires a very highly developed social skill, and also a good bit of experience. "It takes time," explains one transient. "I had to go through fraternity life, then the services, and a stretch at Parkmere before I realized you just get into trouble if you get personally involved with neighbors."

More basically, what they have is a rather keen consciousness of self—and the sophistication to realize that while individualistic tastes may raise eyebrows, exercising those tastes won't bring the world crashing down about you. "One day one of the girls busted in," one upper-middlebrow cheerfully recounts. "She saw I was reading. 'What you got there, hon?' she asked me. You might have known it would be Plato that day. She almost fell over from surprise. Now all of them are sure I'm strange." Actually they don't think she's overly odd, for her deviance is accompanied by enough tact, enough observance of the little customs that oil court life, so that equilibrium is maintained.

Just where the happy mean lies, however, still depends greatly on the degree of the group's cohesion. Relatively, the seasoned transient steers his course more intelligently than the others. But he too is not proof against beneficence. "Every once in a while I wonder," says one transient, in an almost furtive moment of contemplation. "I don't want to do anything to offend the people in our block; they're kind and decent, and I'm proud we've been able to get along with one another—with all our differences—so well. But then, once in a while, I think of myself and my husband and what we are not doing, and I get depressed. Is it just enough not to be bad?" Many others are so troubled. They sense that by their immersion in the group they are frustrating other urges, yet they feel that responding to the group is a moral duty—and so they continue, hesitant and unsure, imprisoned in brotherhood.

CHAPTER TWENTY-SEVEN

The Church of Suburbia

THIS brings us to a question. Is the organization transients' emphasis on the social a passing phase in their lives—a convenient accommodation to current reality? In the early stages of their life in suburbia, patently, the sheer fact of living so close together is bound to make them put a heavy premium on fellowship, and to a degree they are preoccupied with other people because they have to be. Yet there is more than expediency to this impulse. There is internal conviction as well, and in evidence I would now like to turn to the church. I will concentrate largely on one church, Park Forest's United Protestant Church, for it is perhaps the most outstanding example of its kind in the country. It is outstanding, however, precisely because it so well expresses the temper of organization man, and the needs that it fulfills are deeply felt by him wherever he may be.

The story begins in 1946. To church the community, Klutznick decided to give free land to the churches. But to how many and which? Obviously there would be a Catholic church and a Jewish synagogue, but the Protestant denominations posed a problem. To help him out, the leading denominations made estimates of how many people each would probably serve. Not too surprisingly, each was generous in its projections, and when Klutznick added up the estimates, it appeared that there would be more Protestant churchgoers than people.

Klutznick tried a different tack. In effect, he would give the land to the people rather than to the churches. He would provide the church sites, he told the denominations, but only if they got together and, by impartial survey, determined what the young people themselves wanted. What was the actual number in each denomination? As time went on, how many would probably switch from one denomination to another? Or were they tired of denominations altogether? If the churches would send out a man to make the study—preferably a veteran—Klutznick said he would abide by the results.

Thus, one day in 1948, Chaplain Hugo Leinberger arrived in Park Forest. It was one of those catalytic moments when the man and the environment come together. Leinberger had no strong denominational bias; he was, furthermore, a veteran. During the war he had served as a Navy chaplain at sea, and this experience, in an analogy he was later to draw on often, was almost a dry run for the chaplaincy of a village.

Leinberger's philosophy, in brief, was that a specific philosophy wasn't something to worry about. "This business of denominational theologies should come later," he explained. "Take schools, for example. When you move into a formative community like this, you don't worry first about what the educational philosophy is. You want to know if there is a good building, teachers with degrees to indicate they are equipped, multi-purpose rooms, and things like that. You worry about the detailed philosophy only later. Because of disagreements on details of theological implications, the Protestant Church gets there 'last with the least' and ultimately makes very little impact on these new communities."

He wanted a *useful* church, and to emphasize theological points, he felt, was to emphasize what is not of first importance and at the price of provoking dissension. "We try not to offend anybody," he explains. "In the Navy I learned it was important to conduct services to emphasize the areas where there was theological agreement and not bring up the theological points anyone could take exception to."

Human relations, he felt, were of key importance. "I think this is the basic need—the need to belong to a group. You find this fellowship in a church better than anywhere else. And it is contagious. In a community like Park Forest, when young people see how many other people are going to church regularly, they feel they ought to. Another need we fulfill is that of counseling. Young people want a place to take their problems and someone to talk to about them. Put all these things together and you get what we're after —a sense of community. We pick out the more useful parts of the doctrine to that end."

When Leinberger began making his rounds, he found that Park Foresters couldn't agree with him more. Their mobility, far from making them cling to a single church affiliation as a sort of constant in their lives, had weakened the denominational barriers. In moving from one community to another, many of the transients had gone where there was either no church of their faith or one that to them seemed mediocre, and as a consequence they had got in the habit of "shopping."

Of all the factors that weighed in their choice, denomination had become relatively unimportant. In a house-to-house survey of their religious preferences, Park Foresters were asked, among other things, what counted most to them in choosing a church. Here, in order, are the factors they listed: (1) the minister, (2) the Sunday school, (3) the location. In fourth and fifth places the denomination and the music.

Here, by percentages, are the denominational backgrounds of suburbanites in Levittown and Park Forest:

	PARK FOREST			LEVITTOWN, PA.	U.S. 1955
	As of May 1950	As of Dec. 1955		As of 1953	
	Renters (no home-owners		Home-		
Denomination	then)	Renters	owners		
Methodist	17.4	13.6	9.1	9.7	12.1
Presbyterian	12.1	11.7	7.3	8.5	3.9
Lutheran	8.5	9.3	11.4	7.6	7.1
Episcopal	7.7	5.0	5.4	7.2	2.7
Baptist	5.9	4.5	3.4	3.6	19.0
Congregational	4.1	3.0	2.4	.4	1.3
Other Protestant	8.7	12.3	10.6	3.7	15.7
Total Protestant	64.4	59.4	49.2	41.2	
Roman Catholic	25.0	23.5	30.7	38.9	33.0
Jewish	8.7	9.4	11.0	14.7	5.2
No denomination	1.5	7.7	8.7	5.7	not reported

SOURCES: *Park Forest figures were gathered by the chaplain in his calls on incoming families. Levittown figures, which have been readjusted to eliminate nonreporting residents, were gathered by the local churches in co-operation with the Philadelphia Council of Churches. The figures for the U.S., most of which are based on* claimed *membership, are from the Census of Religious Bodies of the United States, based on the Yearbooks of American Churches and the* World Almanac *questionnaire.*

Thanks to a question included in the 1950 Park Forest survey, there are some clues as to the latent desire for upgrading denominational ties. Of 3,919 respondents, 593 showed an inclination to switch. Comparing the number who wished to switch to a particular faith with the number who wished to leave it, we find that the Congregational, Episcopal, and Presbyterian faiths, in that order, come off best. Methodists, almost fifty-fifty, are in the middle, while the greatest potential emigration is from the Baptists and the Lutherans. The Catholic and Jewish faiths were both alike in that though more people showed a preference to leave than to join, the ratio of potential switchers to the total affiliation was so small that the two faiths appeared to be the most stable of all.

Why not, then, one United Protestant Church? The young people did not want what is usually called a "community church." This kind of church, they heard, had not worked too well in some of the communities where it had been tried, for it was too often simply a gambit on the part of a denomination to draw people in before the church flew its true sectarian colors. What the young people wanted was a true union of the leading Protestant denominations. And for practical as well as idealistic reasons. "Why spend a lot of money building a lot of little churches," one layman argued, "when one church would do the job better, and do it now? Why give small salaries to five so-so pastors instead of a decent salary to one good one?"

Leinberger agreed; like the residents, he saw the spiritual and the practical as reasonably synonymous. "It was just common sense. Central management is always more efficient and less expensive. Furthermore, I began to realize that it was a good thing for the church itself. Protestantism loses a lot because there is so much choice of churches. Protestants spend a lot of time shopping around, whereas the Catholics immediately become a part of the religious life of the community. Where there is too much choice, people often end up making no choice at all."

The denominations didn't think much of the idea, but their opposition merely stimulated the Park Foresters to new efforts. "The kids said that if that was the story, then they'd go ahead on their own," recalls Leinberger. "It was a real grass-roots thing. When the kids said they wanted it, I fought for it with them." A fight there had to be, but before long, worn down by the sheer pressure of mass meetings, petitions of one kind or another (and some scoldings from the *Christian Century*), the denominations agreed to compromise. The Lutherans and Episcopalians, because of differences of liturgy and polity too great to be encompassed in the United Protestant Church, went ahead and set up their own churches, but under the leadership of five denominations (Methodist, Presbyterian, Baptist, United Presbyterian, Evangelical and Reformed), twenty-two denominations agreed to co-operate in setting up the church. There would be one basic service, but, unlike community churches, this church would encourage its members to retain their original affiliations. Doctrinal differences would not be obliterated—in baptism, for example, the pastor would both immerse and sprinkle, and there would be both pew communion and altar communion.

To finance the church, the Park Foresters had to break some precedents. Without sufficient money from the denominations they had to float bank loans with pledges of collateral—an action that caused much rethinking about church financing elsewhere. When a bond issue was floated, the parishioners dipped into their savings to make it a success; they sacrificed even more of their time, and a good part of the physical plant represents evening and week-end hours given up by many a weary young executive. In all of this they felt not too much sympathy from churchmen outside Park Forest. Few clergymen, they complained, were equipped to understand or meet the needs of Park Forest. "I found a great lack of insight into our kind of problem," said one layman who was engaged in looking for the new minister. "I remember talking to one man we were considering. He kept talking to me about having to wait for the Call of God. Well, sir, I got the feeling that the Call of God was going to have to come over the telephone—and also going to have to say something about a pretty good salary. I tell you it's hard to get across to most clergymen the frontier we are offering."

But the church has been successfully kept to its original vision. In choosing the first pastor, Dr. Gerson Engelmann, Park Foresters were hesitant at first because of his advanced age (he was forty-five), but in his own way he has proved to be ideally suited to the community. Dr. Engelmann, who is an ex-sociologist, has a keen understanding of the pressures that beset transients, and in talking over their problems with them, he has proved to be a wise and friendly counselor. He has been particularly effective in getting people rooted through community work, and in pointing out the advantages of the church in this respect he is refreshingly free from sanctimony. "Gerson realizes how terribly important church work is for young couples like us," says a transient. "If you're going to have any stability in our kind of life, you have to get involved with other people in things that really count. I can't think of a better way than the kind of activity we have in the United Protestant Church."

In the meantime a second United Protestant Church has been set up to take over the growing load. It appears to be cast in the same spirit as the first. Its pastor, Rev. Robert Crocker, has, like Dr. Engelmann, put great emphasis on Christian fellowship, and he too draws heavily on young business talent for its leadership. (The chairman of the church board is a lab technician at Swift's; the chairman of the finance committee is an advertising-agency man; the chairman of the trustees is a salesman for Cities Service; the chairman of admission, a salesman at Swift's; the young counselor, a professor.) The church building has not yet been raised, but all the indications are that the laymen of the second will display the same practicality and energy in tackling the job. Meanwhile, in the newest subdivision of the community a third United Protestant church has been formed with the Rev. Vernon Flynn as minister.

Clearly, the United Protestant Church represents the basic temper of Park Forest. In proportion to the increase in population, the two United Protestant churches and the Jewish congregation have made the greatest increase. Except for the Catholic Church, the sectarian groups have increased the least, and some haven't even kept up.

Characteristically, the village chaplain the community selected, the Rev. Joseph Hughes, is of the same pragmatic stamp as Leinberger (who has since gone off, at the request of a near-by suburb, to revamp the approach of a more traditional church).[1] He has expanded the services offered by the chaplain—among other things, he follows up every police car and, like an M.D. referring a patient to a specialist, he will refer problems he discovers to the appropriate minister. When there was a temporary wave of shoplifting, Hughes worked on each case and, together with the police chief, did such an effective job of case work that not one of the housewives apprehended was ever found to be a repeater. He, too, is strong for the breaking down of denominational barriers. In calling on newcomers to find their religious preferences, he does not proselytize for any one church, but it is a matter of satisfaction to him that the idea of a United Protestant Church interests them very much.

There are, to be sure, misgivings. Is it a church, some ask, or is it a social center? One wife who was trying to explain to me why she didn't go to any church at all explained her feelings by referring to her child. "My little girl made a very shrewd comment," she said. "She had been telling me that she didn't want to go to the United Protestant Church Sunday School any more. I was asking her why. She told me, 'I don't want to learn about how Christian people live. I want to learn about God.' " This remark smells

[1] Partly as a result of the Park Forest experiment, Leinberger was also called in to set up a chaplaincy program for Paducah, Kentucky, and for the taconite communities in Minnesota. Recently he had to decline a request from Chicago Heights to become a community chaplain and help out with the 3,000 new homes expected to be built there soon.

a bit of the parental lamp, but it succinctly expresses the objection of some Park Foresters. Between the two poles, between faith and authority on one hand and the social and the pragmatic on the other, they feel the United Protestant Church has leaned much too far toward the latter. "I told Gerson Engelmann that if the Catholic Church got wise," says one resident, "they'd send out a smart young Jesuit of the Monsignor Sheen type. If they did, I told Gerson, he'd better watch out, for half his flock would stray over the fence."

Certainly there is little likelihood of flight in the other direction. As the Unitarians have found out, there's not much room left. Many had at first thought Park Forest would be ideal proselyting ground for Unitarianism. To a population predominantly indifferent to theology, it offered more freedom from doctrine than any other group. Like the U. P. Church, it stressed participation too and, if anything, with more conscious intellectualism. From the beginning, the local congregation has been very active in the community's more serious cultural and civic activities, and the church's own projects have had a marked secular appeal. (Most successful projects in 1955: a Modern Jazz Concert and a Folk Sing.) Yet the congregation has remained small, now numbering about 120 members. The full-time minister who recently took over is a thoughtful man and he may succeed in enlarging the membership considerably. For the time being, however, Unitarianism has not exerted a strong popular appeal.

It is something of a case of stolen thunder. The Unitarians maintain that the Christian Message is a strait jacket to thought, but of the U. P. Church they say only that the Message is "latent" there. Similarly, while they advertise their church as the one for those who think, they cannot bear down too hard on this distinction either. Even if they did, furthermore, the interests of the U. P. Church would not be hurt; the more strongly the Unitarian position is delineated, that much closer to the middle of the road does the U. P. Church appear. "I get annoyed at the Unitarians' ads," says a U.P. member, "but I'll tell you one good thing about them. It's wonderful, for a change, to have someone imply we're *too* doctrinal."

At the other end of the scale is the Catholic Church. It is convenient to see it as the direct opposite of the United Protestant approach—and the contrast is one Park Foresters often make. The tug between tradition and social utility, however, is not confined to Protestantism. Among young Catholics, too, there is a ferment for a more socially useful church, and suburbanism has greatly accentuated it. At Park Forest, as elsewhere, many parishioners feel that some of the customs traditional in the church were a response to social needs of former times and could without theological conflict be better attuned to those of today. For some, the problem is personified by their priest, Father Coogan. They like him, but they have the feeling that he embodies an authoritarian approach better suited to a city ward than middle-class suburbia.

An interesting development has been the growth of the Catholic Action Movement at Park Forest. In the form of the Christian Family Movement, it is essentially an effort to apply religion to social and personal problems and it has proved to have strong appeal for many Catholics who have not otherwise been heavily involved in community activities. There are now about a hundred couples meeting regularly —a very high number for the population represented—and the leaders feel the number could grow still higher. The assistant priest, Father Didier, has helped them greatly, but they are now at a stage where they need an extra man assigned to them by Father Coogan. They do not feel that Father Coogan is especially enthusiastic.

Some Catholic laymen are most definitely not enthusiastic. Noting uneasily the references to "group dynamics" in Catholic Action literature, they feel that a more pragmatic church would be a contradiction in terms: let the United Protestants try it if they wish, goes the argument, but Catholics cannot look to God and John Dewey at the same time. I append some observations on this score written down by a former member of the parish:

Take the social aspect. Actually, the Roman Catholic Church can offer a better deal in this respect than the United Protestant Church. Look at it in pragmatic terms and you have everything that the social dynamists want: in one package you have an "explicitly stated consensus" (doctrine), a sense of direction (a reason for, or why), hygienic, interpersonal relation (participation in the Mystical Body), nondirection psychotherapy (confession), and an educational system that insures constant adjustment. From any of these pragmatic viewpoints the church has been servicing her transients for many years, no matter where they are or where they happen to alight. This, it seems to me, is what the United Protestants are looking to. But there's one great difference. They don't make the heavy moral and intellectual demands of the Catholic Church.

The church must be socially useful, and I'll admit that it hasn't adjusted to the new problems as well as it should. But to get involved in "social dynamics" in a misguided attempt to meet "the needs of modern man" is to defeat the ancient purpose of the church. It would make an important concession to the view that man is more animal than rational and would deny his capabilities for social growth. It would deny, in fact, his free will, and this, to understate the issue, lies at the root of Christian doctrine.

The church failed once before and the Reformation resulted, and she failed a second time, and Marxism grew and thrived. If she fails this time—by not adjusting or by adjusting too much—she may well be doing herself in.

In the Jewish community also there is a pull between the religious and the social, and a more complicated one than affects Protestants and Catholics. In matters secular Jews have been adopting the values and customs of the middle-class majority; not only does suburbia tend to attract Jews who are less "different"; it speeds up the process in which anyone—Jewish or non-Jewish—becomes even less "different." At the same time, however, there has been a revival among Jews of religious and cultural practices which intensify one's sense of Jewishness.

Yet, in some respects, this emphasis on revival stems from much the same drives that animate the Protestant suburbanites. In the more fixed community of old, people did not need so much to be aware consciously of the bonds which united them, but in suburbia they have had to think about them, to dramatize them, and this is why their emphasis on fellowship can seem so noticeable to those from more cohesive, aged communities. So with the Jews; the revival of interest in many traditional practices, such as the dietary laws, may seem a far cry from the Protestants' emphasis on fellowship, but it too represents the impulse to make explicit a kind of belongingness that once was an almost involuntary, normal part of life. The new Jewish institutions of suburbia particularly emphasize the education of the children, but they have grown also, Herbert Gans has suggested, by serving social needs that Jews living in predominantly Jewish city neighborhoods could satisfy without benefit of formal organization—or did not feel to be desirable until they had begun to become more a part of middle-class American life. As Will Herberg has observed, less and less do they then feel the need to reject the Jewishness of the immigrant generation.

Doctrinally, Jews too are trying to find the middle of the road. Park Forest's Temple Beth Sholom is not interdenominational like the United Protestant Church; it is Reform—a "warm, liberal kind of Reform," as the rabbi has put it—and could not well accommodate Orthodox Jews.[2] Its services, however, include many ritual and ceremonial elements usually associated with those of a Conservative synagogue.

At Park Forest, as in other new suburbs, Jews have set up what amounts to a sub-community of their own, for in addition to the synagogue and the Sunday schools there are men's and women's social and fund-raising organizations which parallel the organizations of the Protestant majority. For most of Park Forest's Jews, furthermore, closest friendships seem to be with other Jews. It would be wrong, however, to attribute this to a drive for "separatism." Despite their heavy involvement in purely Jewish activity, Park For-

[2] The quote is from Herbert Gans's "The Origin and Growth of a Jewish Community in the Suburbs," to appear in a forthcoming reader of sociological studies of the American Jewish Community, edited by Marshall Sklare, to be published by the Free Press.

est's Jews are also outstandingly active in community-wide affairs as well. Jews from middle-class backgrounds and with upper middle-class aspirations feel a strong pull for activities that cut across ethnic lines, and a great many Park Forest Jews are at an educational and income level considerably higher than that of the community average.

Were they to compete in North Shore suburbs, their qualifications for leadership might be more offset by the fact of Jewishness, but at Park Forest such an obstacle is minimized. Jews make up less than ten per cent of the population, but out of all proportion to their numbers they staff positions in the community's civic and cultural organizations (both the current village president and his predecessor are Jews). There is latent antagonism on the part of some Gentiles, but what is noteworthy is how little there really is. When Herbert Gans made his excellent study of the Jewish community in 1949, he did not feel there was any appreciable anti-Semitism, and neither, several years later, did I.[3]

Even the well-educated Jews do tend to associate more with one another in their close friendships, but, as Gans noted, this is not due so much to ethnic considerations as to the fact that these Jews are apt to be culturally higher-browed in their tastes than most of their neighbors. "Jews who seek other people with whom they can share these attitudes and interests tend to find other Jews," Gans said. "This culture—which includes an important proportion of other Park Forest non-Jews—itself is largely devoid of Jewish content, and the Jews who come together in it would seem to do so primarily not because they are Jews but because they share a culture." Indeed, some non-Jews with upper-brow tastes often mix more easily with Jewish friends than with others.

As in the Protestant community, there is some soul-searching among Jews about the new synagogues and com-

---

[3] "Park Forest, Birth of a Jewish Community," April 1951. As is so often the case with first-rate social reportage, the magazine was *Commentary*. The main staple of this remarkable journal consists of articles on Jewish topics, but it has consistently published some of the most searching, and hardheaded, comment on U.S. life in general that can be found anywhere.

munity centers of suburbia, and somewhat the same question is asked of them as of the United Protestant Church. Are they religious institutions—or social ones? Perhaps, as Nathan Glazer suggests, "One could have reason to believe that the Jewish religious institutions have won such wide support lately precisely and merely because they enable Jews, in the guise of a denomination, to survive as a separate group in America."

So far, I have been talking chiefly of Park Forest, but wherever young organization people are to be found the same urge for a more socially useful church manifests itself. The fact that the current "religious revival" has a strong social basis has been widely observed, of course, but it is significant how much more clearly this social emphasis is discerned when you narrow the focus from people in general to the strata of young organization people. They need to have emphasized what others take for granted. For those who stay put in one place, the church has always been socially useful, and the by-products of church affiliation they take as a matter of course. But the transients cannot. Stability, kinship with others—they want these demonstrated, and in the here and now.

In one Protestant church in Levittown, Pennsylvania, the young minister was surprised when his congregation began to complain about the cathedral chairs with which the church was furnished. They were excellent chairs and, for a growing church, more practical than fixed pews. They conceded all this but they still complained. "At last I figured it out," he said. "The chairs *moved*. All the young people here have come from somewhere else—from up state, Philadelphia, or New Jersey, and even though the distance isn't great, they have had to break with their old home ties. They are extremely eager for stability and for any signs of it. So I figured out a compromise. We fixed up kneeling stools so that they would hold the chairs firm. I didn't hear any complaints after that."

They seek friendship, and this yen is now becoming so evident that wherever there is a transient population it has been an irresistible temptation for the churches to make friendship their chief appeal. Symptomatically, even within the more conservative denominations recently there has been a good bit of use of advertising appeals frankly based on the how-to-win-friends theme. Here, for example, in an ad in the New York *Herald Tribune* (May 20, 1955), "spiritual force" is advertised as a means to friendships:

Lots of acquaintances—not many friends. Is this increasingly true for you? Look at your life. You may find that it lacks those spiritual experiences which bring people together in understanding and friendship.
Participation in the activities of the neighborhood church supplies the spiritual force to weld lasting friendships. Meet future friends in church next Sunday.
A cordial welcome awaits you at
YOUR NEIGHBORHOOD EPISCOPAL CHURCH.

This is a rather exceptional ad, but the sensitivity to practicality that it illustrates is growing more general. Even though they might themselves feel that spiritual considerations are basic, a considerable number of churchmen now have been persuaded they should ask people in the door by mentioning only the social and practical benefits one will find inside. A bulletin put out by the Protestant Council of New York City, to cite another somewhat exceptional example, gives this advice to speakers on its radio and television programs:

Subject matter should project love, joy, courage, hope, faith, trust in God, good will. Generally avoid condemnation, criticism, controversy. In a very real sense we are "selling" religion, the good news of the Gospel. Therefore admonitions and training of Christians on cross-bearing, forsaking all else, sacrifices, and service usually cause the average listener to turn the dial. Consoling the bereaved and calling sinners to repentance, by direct indictment of the listeners, is out of place (with designated exceptions). . . . As apostles, can we not extend an invitation, in effect: "Come and enjoy our privileges, meet good friends, see what God can do for you!"

If transients are so disinterested in theological and doctrinal matters, many churchmen ask, why have there not been more united churches of the Park Forest variety? It is true enough that there are few; this seems due not so much to strong denominational spirit on the part of younger people, however, as to strong denominational spirit on the part of the church hierarchies. At Levittown, Pennsylvania, for example, there was for a while a fair chance of making the first church there, the Dutch Reformed, a united church deliberately patterned on the Park Forest model. The minister, the Rev. Bert Bonte, was, like Park Forest's Hugo Leinberger, eager to make the church a vehicle for bringing together people of different faiths in meaningful civic, cultural, and religious activity. For a variety of reasons the effort failed, but the church is, if not in name, in fact something of a united church. Of its 325 members, only a few were raised in the Dutch Reformed Church. The rest are Methodists, Presbyterians, Lutherans, Baptists, Congregationalists, and twelve are ex-Catholics. Like Park Forest's United Protestant Church, it has become the center of community activity. "What fires young people today is the urge to co-operate," says Bonte. "The old fire of denominationalism is gone. The young people are ready for union now, but the vested interests—the bureaucrats of the church—are against it. They would stand to lose their jobs. But the young people are ready, and I think it significant that the ones who are most eager for the ecumenical movement are the best-educated ones." (Roughly 50 per cent of Bonte's congregation is college educated.)

In near-by Fairless Hills, another united church almost came into being. The Philadelphia Council of Churches sent out a chaplain, and when he discerned the popular movement on the part of the residents for a common church, the denominational authorities were persuaded to set up such a church. It was run by the Methodists, but the understanding was that it would serve all the Protestant denominations. So it continued for several years, but in time it became more a Methodist church, and while it numbers many denominations among its members, it cannot be considered a true united church—a fact that other ministers in the neighborhood take pains to emphasize.

Whether they take the form of a united church or not, however, the desires that produced the Park Forest experiment are well illustrated everywhere. Let me go back a moment to the priorities that Park Foresters indicated in 1950. They listed, in order of importance, the minister, the Sunday school, the location, the denomination, the music. Some churchmen have been shocked at this, but subsequent experience has proved that, whatever one may think of the order, it has proven rather accurate.

That the minister is of primary importance has been well borne out by the unusually heavy demand among suburbanites for personal counseling. "So many young people around makes counseling my main worry," says a forty-two-year-old minister in one package suburb. "I simply haven't time for any more, and I am getting an assistant to help me out. But the thing is, you feel you can do so much in a place like this. My last parish was in a run-down city neighborhood. I had a lot of counseling work there, but so much of it was with people who had no hope—people you knew you couldn't do very much for. But here it's different. These young people have all their adjustments to make at once, and you feel you can do so much for them. No case seems hopeless, and you're tormented by the thought that how you help them will be important for years to come."

Because of this demand the age of the ministers has been more of a factor than expected. At first glance, the ideal minister for suburbia would seem to be a man of the same age as the others, and many churches have sent young men on that assumption. The age similarity does not always work out well, however. In a community where most people are the same age, and when that age is one in which they are meeting their first marital conflicts, the couples feel drawn to a man who is somewhat more fatherly than brotherly. Some young ministers have done well, but the failures—there have been very many—have been disproportionately concentrated among the younger men. Elderly ministers have their problems, too, but one of these is the heavy strain put upon them by their popularity as counselors. One elderly minister virtually suffered a breakdown—there were so few others in his age group that he had to bear an unconscionable load, and at length he left, for the burden was too much.

The second factor, Sunday school, is at times even more important than the minister. Customarily, new suburbanites approach the church through their children, and a lively youth-education program can often offset many other factors in a church's popularity. In time, the parents may join, but on the average there is a waiting period of about a year before they will themselves become regular parishioners.

The relationship between location and churchgoing has been similarly demonstrated. At Park Forest, for example, it has been found that traffic flow is a lot more important than sectarian ties in determining churchgoing habits; people tend to go to a church located between them and the center of a community, and a mainroad location is so important that placing a church only one or two blocks away will make for considerably decreased attendance. The same seems to be true elsewhere: if you plot the location of the members of a particular congregation, you will find nearness to the church a much larger factor than some ministers would like to believe. Because of the split between the two branches of the Lutheran Church, to take another example, Park Forest has two Lutheran churches, one for each branch. Despite the doctrinal differences, however, the people divide up between the two more because of geography than theology, and to all intents and purposes the two have become regional churches.

What the transients want most urgently, in short, is a sense of community—and they are coming to care far less than their elders about matters of doctrine that might get in the way. For some people, the result may be far too secular, but before one casts a stone at such as the United Protestant Church, he must first face up to the question its people can posit: *What is the alternative?* The United Protestant Church, they maintain, is at least taking the initiative in meeting the needs of the new transients as it sees them.

Are the denominations doing so? Thanks to increased mobility, they have one of the greatest proselytizing opportunities they have ever had. But they are not seizing it. So say Protestant transients, and the more religiously inclined they are, the more harsh their judgment. Neither the mystery nor the fellowship, neither the sacred nor the secular, they complain, are being pushed forward with any real vigor. Says an executive of one of America's largest apartment-house developments, "In a community like this there isn't a well-heeled older group to get a church going, so it's up to the church authorities to step in and take the initiative. But what's happened here? The churches have missed the boat. We set aside space for the three faiths to have a center. They didn't show much interest; the Episcopalians did put up a Quonset hut, and the Jews put up a temple. But that's all so far."

The writer feels no competence to enter any judgment on the spiritual issues raised by these questions. I do think, however, that this ferment, from whatever standpoint one views it, is a clear indication that the quest among the transients for a socially useful church is a deeply felt one. They do not seek fellowship simply because they cannot avoid the need. They seek it actively, and they feel that it is ultimately a moral quest.

CHAPTER TWENTY-EIGHT

The Organization Children

THE organization man's emphasis on the group, I have been maintaining, is not a temporary phenomenon dictated by external necessity; it is a response to what he feels is a moral imperative, and more and more he is openly articulating it. I have looked at the church in this perspective; now I would like to turn to the schools. Like the churches they had to be built from scratch, and in building them the young parents had to declare themselves. Their children will be transients too, and the pressures of the organization life ahead for them will be, if anything, more intense. What, then, should be emphasized? In helping shape the curriculum, parents are at once giving a guide and revealing themselves.

The Park Foresters threw themselves into the job of creating a school system with tremendous energy. With few precedents to go on and virtually no industrial tax base, they have developed a system which includes a spankingly attractive high school, six cheerful elementary schools, and several more a-building. Educators all over the country have been lavish in their praise. In 1954 the high school was selected as one of the five winners in the "All-America Schools" contest of the National Municipal League, and other awards for the school have been streaming in.

They have both profited and suffered from an unusual turnover problem. The leadership of the school boards, for example, is constantly turning over. The first elementary-school superintendent, Robert Anderson, and the young chemist who headed the school board could never be sure from one month to the next just who would be working with them. While they were there, board members worked devotedly. Just about the time one became saturated in the school problems, it seemed, his company would transfer him, and the break in continuity persists to this day.

Teachers have also been a worry. There is a high turnover of younger teachers in any community, but Park Forest is at an especial disadvantage in this matter. There aren't any bachelors around. (Of some 5,000 males in 1954 only one was unmarried, and he has since left.) Several court units have been set aside for unmarried girl teachers, but this kind of sorority life doesn't jibe with the community, or with the girls, and the rate of departure has been heavy.

More important, the children move too. The impact is as severe on the teachers as on the children themselves, for the teachers are thereby robbed of a good bit of the feeling of achievement they get from watching the children develop. As Anderson put it: "In any school you have to put a six-months' investment in a child before the two of you can start functioning right—you have to test them, get the parents involved, get the kids settled down in a group. We do this all right—but then what happens? They move, and you have to start all over again."

The children, however, have proved to be highly adaptable material, and the teachers who have had experience in traditional communities are quick to note how much more socially responsive the children of transients are than others. "Social maturity comes faster here for children like this," explains one teacher. "The adjustment to the group doesn't seem to involve so many problems for them. I have noticed that they seem to get the feeling that nobody is the boss—there is a feeling of complete co-operation. Partly this comes from early exposure to court play."

Like their parents, in short, the children already have a high degree of social skill, and the environment itself will further intensify this in them. This being the case, it could be argued, there is no necessity for the school to duplicate, and thus they are all the more free to concentrate on the other, more inward, aspects. But neither the parents nor the schools feel this way. From the beginning the curriculum has borne down very heavily on the pragmatic and the social, and the concept of adjustment has been dominant.

The first superintendent left, with a well-earned sigh of relief, to be a professor at the Harvard Graduate School of Education. What curriculum changes have ensued, however, have not been major. Anderson's successor, Superintendent Gerald Smith, has talked of introducing the "Fourth R, Responsibility," but this seems largely another way of describing the established policy. The disciplining vehicle, Smith explains, is the group. The teacher strives not to discipline the child directly but to influence all the children's attitudes so that as a group they recognize correct behavior. If a child falls out of line, he does not have to be subjected to authoritarian strictures of elders; he senses the disapproval of the group and, in that way, the school believes, learns to discipline himself as much as possible.

The child who tends to be withdrawn is given special attention. "Johnny wasn't doing so well at school," one mother told me. "The teacher explained to me that he was doing fine on his lessons but that his social adjustment was not as good as it might be. He would pick just one or two friends to play with, and sometimes he was happy to remain by himself." There are many such instances, and, save for a few odd parents, most are grateful that the schools work so hard to offset tendencies to introversion and other suburban abnormalities.

Park Forest schools are not extreme in this respect, and most Park Foresters are anxious that the curriculum be recognized as middle of the road. But they do agree that there is a noticeably permissive atmosphere. They point out, for example, that the schools follow a method by which the student group is encouraged to take a strong hand in the planning of what they are to be taught. The children are not exactly put in charge, but the teacher makes a point of asking them what it is they would like to know about a particular subject, rather than unilaterally giving them what she thinks they ought to learn. As Superintendent Smith explained it: "If the topic under discussion is India, the children are asked what they would like to know about that country. Queries might range from elephants to the mysteries of bathing in the Ganges. By the time juvenile curiosities are satisfied, the children have a reasonable knowledge of India's terrain, vegetation, animal life, religions, caste systems, and politics."

The schools are similarly flexible in grading. To use fixed standards of performance, the authorities feel, would straitjacket the child. As a consequence, the primaries, as in many other schools, are ungraded, and in later classes formal reports of the A-B-C-D-F or percentage type have been discarded. "It is obviously impossible," curriculum consultant Lucille Thimblin explains, "for a teacher to reduce the many-sided aspects of a pupil's development to an accurate numerical value." Under the old method, she says, a bright pupil who has made little effort might get the highest mark while another child who works hard might fail to get a respectable mark. The school could get around this by simply using the two terms "satisfactory" and "unsatisfactory" and this would be helpful, Mrs. Thimblin points out, in that "this type of report does reduce the competition for scholastic leadership." Unfortunately, however, while it would make for better adjustment, "it is very likely also to reduce some pupils' incentive to do better work." The solution: a check list to supplement parent-teacher conferences. In this the student's academic progress is rated on the basis of his individual capabilities rather than against an arbitrary norm. He is also rated in terms of his social group and whether or not he meets the standards attainable for every member of the group.

There are a few parental misgivings about the elementary schools. As far as discipline is concerned, parents sometimes wonder if perhaps the school isn't a bit too permissive. Occasionally parents talk of sending their children to Park Forest's parochial school so they would "get some discipline"; they rarely get around to trying, but they still sigh aloud over the elementary schools' laxness. Even parents who are satisfied with the children's behavior are sometimes critical, for though not many may think their own children lack discipline, they are very sure that everybody else's children do. Habitual is the complaint of their "freshness." ("The kids here call everybody by their first names. If one of my neighbors' children ever came up and called me Mrs. George, I think I would drop dead from surprise.") As a few Park Foresters take pains to note, however, parents are somewhat unreasonable about this; whatever their faults, harsh parental discipline is not one of them, and they cannot fairly ask the schools to do what they won't.

There is always a controversy of some kind going on over the elementary schools, but it is more on administration and taxes than matters scholastic.[1] On the whole, it seems clear, the parents are very well satisfied with the curriculum. At Park Forest, a PTA committee proudly agreed, learning is a "painless process." "The teacher and the pupils plan together," the committee's report went on, "and everyone has a conscious feeling of belonging—as an individual and as a group participant. . . . Everything they learn is related to something they've experienced in their everyday life or through TV, radio, movies, or on the playground." A few parents are still not altogether adjusted to the absence of primary grades, but this criticism usually comes from people who arrived from a town with a more traditional school, and in time evaporates. Similarly, though

---

[1] A notable fracas was over the schools' use of tests to screen kindergarten applicants. Parents whose children flunked were outraged, and when Superintendent Smith's contract came up for renewal in early 1956 many parents were on hand to protest. The board voted to retain Smith but the proceedings were unusually acrimonious—even for Park Forest. From the Park Forest *Reporter*, February 2: "An unruly crowd of nearly 180 jammed the Sauk Trail multi-purpose room to hear the verdict . . . rules of order were violated left and right as spectators voiced opinions . . . [board member] Glassner's prepared speech was two-pronged and included a tabulated 'score' of Smith's administrative successes and failures . . . even more bitter was his indictment of his fellow board members during which he accused former President Albertz of breach of faith . . . Joseph Egan's immediate criticism was of the 'betrayal' of private conversations held with members of the board and employees of the school district." Participation, as I noted earlier, has not died out at Park Forest.

some feel there is a slighting of fundamentals, all are impressed with the reports from Park Forest alumni that their children are doing very well academically in their new communities because of their Park Forest schooling. If they had to choose, furthermore, most Park Foresters would hate to see the schools discard the emphasis on practical, contemporary problems. "Janet is studying marketing," one parent told me, "and she's only in the sixth grade. She's studying ads and discounts—things I didn't get until college. These kids are certainly getting a broad view of things."

It is in the high school, however, that the new suburbia's philosophy gets its most significant expression. The philosophy is by no means unique to Park Forest. High-school superintendent Eric Baber speaks very much like many superintendents elsewhere, and his writings do not show unorthodoxy but, rather, a deep grasp of contemporary educational literature. What makes Park Forest's high school unique is that, where in traditional communities what has been called the "life adjustment" curriculum has been introduced a bit at a time, at Park Forest it has been the foundation. The new $1,600,000 "learning laboratory" is not only one of the most modern in the country; in spirit as well as brick it is the embodiment of the suburban temper.

Five years ago, when the school was still in the planning stage, Baber told parents that the trouble with U.S. education is that it is concentrated far too much on the intellectual aspect of education. Even teachers' colleges, he observed sadly, still require plane geometry for admission. Except for a small coterie, he asked, of what value to most people are the traditional academic disciplines? "The so-called 'bright student' is often one of the dumbest or least apt when he gets away from his textbooks and memory work," Baber told a teachers' workshop. "This is evidenced by the fact that many $20,000-to-$100,000-a-year jobs in business, sales, sports, radio . . . are held by persons with I.Q.s of less than ninety."

Baber is not actually against intelligence. He believes it should be channeled toward real-life, vocational needs more than to the academic requirements of the colleges. Since

Park Forest, unlike many towns, is predominantly college-educated, most students will be going on to college anyway; thus the "two-school," vocational versus academic problems might not seem particularly pertinent. A large share of the school plant nevertheless was designed with great attention to the vocational, and so was the curriculum.

Of the total of seventy subjects originally offered, only one half were in traditional academic subjects—and the latter, furthermore, were by no means ivory tower. Of seven offerings in English available to juniors and seniors, the one devoted to grammar, rhetoric, and composition was a one-semester "refresher course . . . for students who feel the need for additional preparation." Of more appeal to teen-agers would be the full-year courses in journalism and in speech (for which, in the "communication laboratory," facilities are available for practical things like radio and TV debating).

The seventy formal subject offerings by no means exhausted the life-adjustment curriculum. Baber felt that the schools must assume more responsibility for the *total* growth of the child. Conceivably, this could be left to other agencies—to the family, or the church, or society itself, for example. Nevertheless, through such media as courses in family group living (twelfth-grade elective) and "doing" sessions in actual situations, the school tackled it. "Ours is an age of group action," Baber says.[2]

Partly because so many parents are college-educated, Park

[2] Lest I seem to be applying the word *vocational* unfairly, let me note that Dr. Baber is equable about it. From a letter to the writer from Dr. Baber: "In general, I believe you have given a reasonably accurate description of the high-school situation. The frequent use of the word *vocational* as applied to our educational program is acceptable if broadly defined as useful or functional. . . . We emphasize *general education* and the development of understandings, skills, and critical thinking directly related to current problems of social living. If I were to attempt to define the bases of our educational program I believe it would be in terms of three fundamental concepts: (1) the philosophy of experimentalism, compromised somewhat by the pressures of tradition, (2) an organismic (or Gestalt) psychology, and (3) democratic educational leadership."

Forest would not seem to be ideal soil for the full development of the life-adjustment curriculum. When the curriculum was first being planned several years ago, a questionnaire was sent to parents, and somewhat to Baber's surprise, over half of the parents checked French, Spanish—and Latin, of all things—as desirable electives. Most, furthermore, showed a disinterest in vocational courses of the craft type.

As elsewhere, of course, colleges have also been a stumbling block. Most colleges, Baber regrets, still require specified academic credits for admission, and this has been a brake on further enrichment. Core courses like Unified Studies offer some flexibility: if a student lacks a credit in English, for example, Unified Studies can be translated as English; if he needs history credit, as history. But this only mitigates, and like many another educator, Baber feels that the colleges continue to lag behind secondary education in acceptance of modern trends.

Another cloud has developed. While the school board and the majority of parents have been well satisfied with the school, what is usually referred to as a "vocal minority" has materialized. In 1955 a special curriculum advisory committee was formed. The laymen, each under the impression that he might be a lone dissenter, were surprised to find that they shared the same misgivings. After a survey they drew up quite a caustic report, the gist of which was that while Baber deserved tribute for the formidable job he had done, much too large a share of the school's energies were devoted to what was essentially extracurricular. The ideal of education might be Mark Hopkins on one end of a log and a student on the other, the initial report tartly observed, but it isn't Mark Hopkins and an administrative assistant and a guidance counselor and a psychologist and a curriculum consultant in between.

The final report was somewhat more tempered, but its conclusions were inescapably combative. "We believe in hard work per se, and, therefore, until educators discover some harder work, we believe in such courses as Latin and algebra as 'disciplines.' We do not believe that all knowledge must have an immediate or even, indeed, an eventual 'use.'

. . . There is a tendency to design courses of study so that students will not be able to fail. This is completely unrealistic so far as life is concerned. Real life includes failures as well as success, and failure *can be* a challenge to make greater efforts to succeed."

Because the critics have been responsible ones, their work has had some effect. Baber has taken it all in good humor and while he still feels there are things more important than academic studies and memory learning, the pamphlets the school has been lately turning out could easily mislead the bystander into thinking the school has slipped back into medievalism. ("There are no substitutes for subject-matter information," one pamphlet declares.) The school points to the larger number of students in academic courses than in vocational ones, albeit with repressed enthusiasm; it also speaks of its increasing interest in the gifted student and the desire to accelerate such students by special classes.

Justifiably, Baber also points with pride to his strong academic teaching staff. The challenge of teaching in a new community like Park Forest has attracted an unusually able group, and on statistics alone the school is well over-average in the number of M.S.s and Ph.D.s. In view of the salaries they are paid, indeed, they would seem a good bit better than the taxpayers deserve. Their average salary, $4,500, is less than the income of the lowest-salaried junior executives who enter the community, and where the latter can expect to double their salaries in ten or fifteen years, the teachers will be lucky to inch up a hundred or so a year. As was pointedly observed in the biographical sketches recently printed in the papers of the teachers, a majority perform outside work to make ends meet.[3]

[3] While the taxpayers have displayed parsimony in this matter, the schools themselves are partly to blame. Events indicate that if the school administrators were a little less fascinated with physical facilities, they would have an easier time getting better salaries for the teachers. While the cement was still cooling on the new $1,600,000 school, Baber and his board went to the voters with a request for an additional $1,250,000 bond issue for a five-year package of additional construction. The voters balked. Baber's estimates of the high-school population needs have been consistently high, for he has tended to project the elementary-

Essentially, however, the school has been kept to the original vision, and little of the emphasis on the practical has been sacrificed. "Family Living," for example, has been built into one of the key offerings, and the school is proud that boys as well as girls take it. ("All aspects of family group life are open to study. Units of study include money management, everyday social relationships, care of the sick, nutrition and food management, clothing and housing the family, and preparation for marriage. Home and community resources are used. The accent is on 'shared responsibility' in building a successful, happy home.") The testing program is extensive. In addition to a battery of achievement tests, such as the Iowa tests, and intelligence tests, the school has given students the Kuder Vocational Preference Record, the Bell Adjustment Inventory, and the California Personal Adjustment Test.

Part of the concentration in the academic column of the curriculum is due to the large number of students enrolled in Unified Studies, and for this reason some of the laymen feel that they still have plenty of work cut out for them. They are not yet satisfied as to what the studies unify. Here is part of a description written by the school for a local paper:

How can I improve my study habits? Is going steady a good idea? How can I pick a career? Why does Park Forest call its governing body a board of trustees, when Chicago Heights has a mayor and aldermen? Why does my family expect so much of me?

If you stepped into a Unified Studies classroom at Rich High you might hear students discussing any one of these or other problems of a personal, group, or community nature. You might find John Scott, Village Manager, or Colonel

school figures without taking sufficient account of the peculiar nature of Park Forest's turnover. In balking at the bond issue, unfortunately, the taxpayers rather heedlessly turned down a companion request for an educational levy increase that would up salaries. Eventually, after two unsuccessful tries and some scolding from its friends, the school got the bond issue by scaling it down to $450,000. In so doing, however, it also had to scale down the levy increase for salaries, which, as a result, continue to be lower than the Park Forest average.

Plavsic, Director of Public Safety, discussing the government of Park Forest or the problem of juvenile delinquency.

If laymen cavil, the school can count on the moral support of professional educators elsewhere. The school's way of reporting grades is a case in point. Some parents are disturbed because the reports seem to give as much weight to "co-operating with the group" as they do to academic marks. (Grades on examinations are only one of sixteen sub-grades.) Precisely because of this weighting, however, the Park Forest report system has been cited as one of the most advanced in the country by Dr. Ruth Strang of Teachers College, Columbia.

Dr. Strang is well aware of the difficulties a school's concern with total growth can provoke from some parents. "If the parents' philosophy is one that emphasizes rugged individualism and competition," she says, with scarcely concealed disapproval, "a report that emphasizes development as a co-operative social person may not have much meaning for the parent." But such a report can also help educate parents. Criticism notwithstanding, Dr. Strang argues, the reports should clearly reflect the underlying philosophy of the school—and in this respect, certainly, Park Forest parents have no cause for complaint.[4]

It is possible, if not very probable, that there will be shifts in the future. Significantly, the few critics are from what is regarded as the progressive element in Park Forest, and they are poles apart from the right-wing reactionaries who have muddied the issue in some communities. But they remain very much a minority, and at present writing it must be concluded that the philosophy of the elementary and high schools is a fair reflection of the community. If any debate

[4] As this book was going to press, the school board announced, with what appeared genuine regret, that Baber was going to accept the very excellent post of head of the Waukegan, Illinois, high-school system and oversee its ambitious expansion program. To fill his shoes the board secured Dr. Robert G. Andree, previously head of the Brookline, Massachusetts, high school. It is clear, however, that the majority of the citizens do not expect, or want, any basic changes in school philosophy.

has developed, it is because Baber has been so eminently fair in making his position explicit.

The majority do not see any basic philosophic differences. Differences of degree, yes—they don't want the school to be *too* progressive, *too* practical—but on the basic concept of social utility they have no argument to make. If one wishes to quarrel with the philosophy, he must address himself to the people themselves. The educators may be in the vanguard, but they are going with, not against, the grain of their society.

For what is it that the parents want most emphasized by the school? At Park Forest they were asked just such a question, and when they wrote the answer in their own words, one note was found more often than any other. The primary job of the high school, they wrote, should be to teach students how to be citizens and how to get along with other people.

CHAPTER TWENTY-NINE

Conclusion

HERE, finally, is the apotheosis of the Social Ethic. Some might summarize the suburban temper in different terms—pragmatism, perhaps, or utilitarianism—and their intonation would depend on their own outlook. But the dominant motif is unmistakable. Not just as something expedient, but as something right, the organization transients have put social usefulness at the core of their beliefs. Adaptation has become more than a necessity; in a life in which everything changes, it has become almost a constant.

Since I am using suburbia as a vehicle to bring together many strands, it can be asked if it is fair to generalize from such places to organization man in general. Suburbs like Park Forest are not typical places—even as lodging for organization people—and it is obvious that in degree many of the pressures there are peculiar to such places. No matter how stanch an individualist you might be, if you have to live in such close union with others, the sheer instinct of survival, let alone good sense, is likely, at the time, to make you emphasize the extroverted side of your nature. The suburbanites' group-mindedness, it could be argued, is merely a passing phase, an expedient dictated by necessity and not by any inner impulse.

But I am not talking about overt behavior; I am talking about values, and the suburbanites themselves provide evidence that their values are a great deal more than a function of the physical environment. That they respond to the pressure of the court or the tight-knit block is not so significant. They have to. What is significant is how they feel about these pressures—and how, ideally, they think a person should feel about them.

Their children, for example. In building the school system the suburbanites have had to face the question, and if the passing-phase explanation were correct, we could find the answer in the kind of well-roundedness they ask for. In deciding what the children needed most to learn, or least, parents might reason that since the children were already so well instructed by the environment in social skills the schools should teach them not to overcompensate. For the sake of mental health, if nothing else, it would follow that the schools would emphasize the more neglected, inner aspect of the child to the end that personality development be truly balanced. In this light, the more asocial, intellectual disciplines could be utilized as highly pragmatic tools—not to mention any utility their content might have.

But this, we know, is not the way the great majority of parents feel. They do not wish the great cycle of which they are a part reversed, but intensified. It is an age of group action, they well agree, and skilled as they are in the ways of group living, it is a source of pride to them, rather than concern, that their children may be even more so. As some parents point out, they themselves have had to learn adjustment the hard way, without the benefit of an education anywhere near as contemporary, or socially-conscious, as that the schools are now offering. If they have made their adjustments as successfully as they have, they wonder, how much more successfully may their children when they come of age?

The potential leaders differ, as we have noted, from most of their neighbors. But how much do they differ? They are more the individualist than the rest of their contemporaries, but this is only a relative comparison, for the leaders' values also indicate how very far the balance between the group and the individual has shifted. In a more muted fashion most of the potential leaders hold the same view of man as a social animal, and though they say it much more intelligently—and know that they are saying it—they, too, tend to equate the lone individual with psychic disorder. "We have learned not to be so introverted," one junior executive, and a very thoughtful and successful one too, told me. "Before we came here we used to live pretty much to ourselves. On Sundays, for instance, we used to stay in bed until around maybe two o'clock reading the paper and listening to the symphony on the radio. Now we stop around and visit with people, or they visit with us. I really think we've broadened."

The bare quote does not do him justice; he is not a fool who would rather chatter than listen to music. The point he was trying to make was that for him doing things with and for other people was ultimately more fulfilling. Whether one agrees or not, it is a point that must be understood. To repeat, the basis of the Social Ethic is not conformity but a sense of moral imperative.

Let us now broaden our view to organization man in general and ask what this climate of thought portends. If, as I believe, the people I have been examining in this book are representative of the main stream of organization life, one thing seems clear. If ever there was a generation of technicians, theirs is it. No generation has been so well equipped, psychologically as well as technically, to cope with the intricacies of vast organizations; none has been so well equipped to lead a meaningful community life; and none probably will be so adaptable to the constant shifts in environment that organization life is so increasingly demanding of them. In the better sense of the word, they are becoming the interchangeables of our society and they accept the role with understanding. They are all, as they say, in the same boat.

But where is the boat going? No one seems to have the faintest idea; nor, for that matter, do they see much point in even raising the question. Once people liked to think, at least, that they were in control of their destinies, but few of the younger organization people cherish such notions. Most see themselves as objects more acted upon than acting —and their future, therefore, determined as much by the system as by themselves.

In a word, they *accept,* and if we do not find this comforting at least we should recognize that it would be odd if they did not feel this confidence. For them society has in fact been good—very, very good—for there has been a succession of fairly beneficent environments: college, the paternalistic, if not always pleasant, military life, then, perhaps, graduate work through the G.I. Bill of Rights, a corporation apprenticeship during a period of industrial expansion and high prosperity, and, for some, the camaraderie of communities like Park Forest. The system, they instinctively conclude, is essentially benevolent.

No one should begrudge them the prosperity that has helped make them feel this way. If we have to have problems, after all, the adversities of good times are as worthy as any to have to worry about. Nor should we regard the emphasis on co-operation as a reversal of our national character. When the suburbanites speak of re-establishing the spirit of the frontier communities, there is a truth in their analogy. Our country was born as a series of highly communal enterprises, and though the individualist may have opened the frontier, it was the co-operative who settled it. So throughout our history. Our national genius has always lain in our adaptability, in our distrust of dogma and doctrine, in our regard for the opinion of others, and in this respect the organization people are true products of the American past. "The more equal social conditions become," De Tocqueville, no friend of conformity, presciently observed, "the more men display this reciprocal disposition to oblige each other."

And there is the crux. When De Tocqueville wrote this a century ago it was the double-edged nature of this disposition that haunted him. He understood its virtue; he was an aristocrat and he confessed that he missed the excellence of the few in the good of the many, but he saw clearly that our egalitarianism and our ease of social co-operation were the great fruits of democracy. We could not sustain these virtues without suffering their defects. But could we keep them in balance? De Tocqueville made a prophecy. If America ever destroyed its genius it would be by intensifying the social virtues at the expense of others, by making the individual come to regard himself as a hostage to prevailing opinion, by creating, in sum, a tyranny of the majority.

And this is what the organization man is doing. He is doing it for what he feels are good reasons, but this only makes the tyranny more powerful, not less. At the very time when the pressures of our highly organized society make so stringent a demand on the individual, he is himself compounding the impact. He is not only other-directed, to borrow David Riesman's concept, he is articulating a philosophy which tells him it is right to be that way.

My charge against the Social Ethic, then, is on precisely the grounds of contemporary usefulness it so venerates. It is not, I submit, suited to the needs of "modern man," but is instead reinforcing precisely that which least needs to be emphasized, and at the expense of that which does. Here is my bill of particulars.

It is redundant. In some societies individualism has been carried to such extremes as to endanger the society itself, and there exist today examples of individualism corrupted into a narrow egoism which prevents effective co-operation. This is a danger, there is no question of that. But is it today as pressing a danger as the obverse—a climate which inhibits individual initiative and imagination, and the courage to exercise it against group opinion? Society is itself an education in the extrovert values, and I think it can be rightfully argued that rarely has there been a society which has preached them so hard. No man is an island unto himself, but how John Donne would writhe to hear how often, and for what reasons, the thought is so tiresomely repeated.

It is premature. To preach technique before content, the skills of getting along isolated from why and to what end the getting along is for, does not produce maturity. It produces a sort of permanent prematurity, and this is true not only of the child being taught life adjustment but of the organization man being taught well-roundedness. This is a sterile concept, and those who believe that they have mastered human relations can blind themselves to the true bases of co-operation. People don't co-operate just to co-operate; they co-operate for substantive reasons, to achieve certain goals, and unless these are comprehended the little manipulations for morale, team spirit, and such are fruitless.

And they can be worse than fruitless. Held up as the end-all of organization leadership, the skills of human relations easily tempt the new administrator into the practice of a tyranny more subtle and more pervasive than that which he means to supplant. No one wants to see the old authoritarian return, but at least it could be said of him that what he wanted primarily from you was your sweat. The new man wants your soul.

It is delusory. It is easy to fight obvious tyranny; it is not easy to fight benevolence, and few things are more calculated to rob the individual of his defenses than the idea that his interests and those of society can be wholly compatible. The good society is the one in which they are most compatible, but they never can be completely so, and one who lets The Organization be the judge ultimately sacrifices himself. Like the good society, the good organization encourages individual expression, and many have done so. But there always remains some conflict between the individual and The Organization. Is The Organization to be the arbiter? The Organization will look to its own interests, but it will look to the individual's *only as The Organization interprets them.*

It is static. Organization of itself has no dynamic. The dynamic is in the individual and thus he must not only question how The Organization interprets his interests, he must question how it interprets its own. The bold new plan he feels is necessary, for example. He cannot trust that The Organization will recognize this. Most probably, it will not. It is the nature of a new idea to confound current consensus—even the mildly new idea. It might be patently in order, but, unfortunately, the group has a vested interest in its miseries as well as its pleasures, and irrational as this may be, many a member of organization life can recall instances where the group clung to known disadvantages rather than risk the anarchies of change.

It is self-destructive. The quest for normalcy, as we have seen in suburbia, is one of the great breeders of neuroses, and the Social Ethic only serves to exacerbate them. What is normalcy? We practice a great mutual deception. Everyone knows that they themselves are different—that they are shy in company, perhaps, or dislike many things most people seem to like—but they are not sure that other people are different too. Like the norms of personality testing, they see about them the sum of efforts of people like themselves to seem as normal as others and possibly a little more so. It is hard enough to learn to live with our inadequacies, and we need not make ourselves more miserable by a spurious ideal of middle-class adjustment. Adjustment to what? Nobody really knows—and the tragedy is that they don't realize that the so-confident-seeming other people don't know either.

Now let us ask if these defects are inevitable. Does The Organization *have* to require acquiescence? Many critics of American civilization, European critics in particular, see our spiritual conformities as an unavoidable consequence of an industrial society, and further growth and prosperity of our kind, they believe, will lead to the ultimate dehumanization of man. The external similarities of American life, in short, they hold as inextricably related to the inner similarities.

We should never allow ourselves to be complacent about the external similarities of American life, or use prosperity as an apologia for Babbittry. But it is a retrograde point of view that fails to recognize that these similarities are in great part a consequence of making the benefits of our civilization available to more people. The monotonous regularity of ranch-type houses that can so easily appall us is not the product of an inner desire for uniformity so much as the fact that modular construction is a condition of moderate-cost housing. This kind of housing is no more or less a pressure for inner conformity than the rows of identical brownstones of the 1890s or, for that matter, the identical brick fronts of the 1700s.

Science and technology do not have to be antithetical to individualism. To hold that they must be antithetical, as many European intellectuals do, is a sort of utopianism in reverse. For a century Europeans projected their dreams into America; now they are projecting their fears, and in so doing they are falling into the very trap they accuse us of. Attributing a power to the machine that we have never felt, they speak of it almost as if it were animistic and had a will of its own over and above the control of man. Thus they see our failures as inevitable, and those few who are consistent enough to pursue the logic of their charge imply that there is no hope to be found except through a retreat to the past.[1]

This is a hopelessly pessimistic view. The fault is not in the pressures of industrial society—an agrarian society has pressures as powerful—but in the stance we assume before these pressures. If we reverse our current emphases, we will not reverse progress, for individualism is more necessary, not less, than it ever was.

[1] In *Tomorrow Is Already Here*, to cite one example, Robert Jungk touches on many of the things I have gone into in this book, but his underlying premise seems to be that it is morally wrong for man to try to control his environment the way Americans are doing. In this indictment he fails to distinguish between the kinds of control, and with little qualification he equates aberrations like "soul engineering" with such activities as trying to find better air medicine techniques, scientific agriculture, etc. This is very sloppy thinking. One kind of activity represents man's attempt to control his physical environment; the other is an attempt at social manipulation, and its relation to science lies only in its pretensions.

Where man uses science to control the physical, the result is to enlarge the area of his potential freedom. This point shouldn't need to be labored, but some of our own critics similarly fail to distinguish between control of the physical and control of the social, with the result that they see the I.B.M. machine, fluorescent lighting, and the like as symbols of spiritual decline. This false personalization of the inanimate seems to me a very sentimental viewpoint and one that militates against any comprehension of the real problems. The I.B.M. machine has no ethic of its own; what it does is enable one or two people to do the the amount of computing work that formerly required many more people. If people often use it stupidly, it is their stupidity, not the machine's, and a return to the abacus would not exorcise the failing. People can be treated as drudges just as effectively without modern machines.

This does not mean a "return" to the Protestant Ethic as preached a century ago. It is futile to speak of individualism as if unrestrained self-interest will somehow produce the greater good. It is for this reason, perhaps, that the right wing has remained a comparatively negative force in American thought. Even more than those who preach the Social Ethic slough over the individual's rights against society, the right sloughs over the individual's obligations to society—and the lack of realism is sensed by the middle as well as the left.

The pendulum analogy that suggests itself would be misleading, for it implies a return to some ideal state of balance. What we need is not to return but to reinterpret, to apply to our problems the basic idea of individualism, not ancient particulars. The doctrines of the nineteenth-century businessman and our modern society are disparate, but that they are disparate is little cause for us to assume that individualism must be too. The central ideal—that the individual, rather than society, must be the paramount end—animated Western thought long before the Industrial Revolution, or Calvinism, or Puritanism, and it is as vital and as applicable today as ever.

But what is the *"solution"*? many ask. There is no solution. The conflict between individual and society has always involved dilemma; it always will, and it is intellectual arrogance to think a program would solve it. Certainly the current experience does suggest a few steps we can profitably take, and I would like to suggest several. Common to all, however, must be a fundamental shift of emphasis, and if this is evaded, any change will exist largely on the level of language. The organization man has a tremendous affinity for vogue words by which the status quo can be described as dynamic advance, and "individualism," alas, is such a word. Let us beware, then, the hard-sell, twelve-point program. Many have been touted as in the name of individual expression, but as those suppressed by them will sense, they are usually organization-serving loyalty devices that fool only those who administrate them.

This caveat made, let me suggest several areas where constructive proposals are in order. First, "human relations."

We need by all means to continue to experiment and study. Whatever we call human relations, they are central to the problem of The Organization and the individual, and the more we find out about the effect of the one on the other the better we can find more living room for the individual. But it's not going to be done if many of those who propagate the doctrine cling to self-proving assumptions about the overriding importance of equilibrium, integration, and adjustment. The side of the coin they have been staring at so intently is a perfectly good one, but there is another side and it should not be too heretical at least to have a peek at it. Thousands of studies and case histories have dwelled on fitting the individual to the group, but what about fitting the group to the person? What about *individual* dynamics? The tyranny of the happy work team? The adverse effects of high morale?

One does not have to be in favor of unhappiness to explore such hypotheses, and now, encouragingly, a few whose good will is unquestionable are showing more disposition to do so. The Harvard Business School, which almost grew old with human relations, has been using the word *administrator* less, the word *leader* more, and lately its best research seems directed at the matter of individual initiative more than of group happiness. Rensis Likert, the leader of the "group dynamics" school, has announced that recent studies of organization are leading him and his colleagues to question their earlier conclusions that good morale necessarily produces high productivity. They still believe that the work group should be supervised as a group rather than on a man-to-man basis, but they do warn that the supervisor who concentrates on making the group happy may produce belongingness but not very much else.

Another fruitful approach would be a drastic re-examination of the now orthodox view that the individual should be given less of the complete task, the team more of it. For a century we have been breaking down tasks into the components and sub-components, each to be performed by a different cell member, and this assembly-line mentality has affected almost everything that men do for a living, including the arts. We can grant that to a degree the benefits of compartmentalized work have surpassed the disadvantages. But do we have to grant that progress demands more of same? That the monotony, the sacrifice of individual accomplishment are inevitable? On the assembly line itself, where specialization would seem most necessary, some companies have found that a reversal of emphasis can actually lead to more productivity. Instead of trying to offset the monotony of a task with externals, such as bowling alleys and "economic education," they have enlarged the task itself. By giving the worker more of the total job to do—asking him to wire the whole set, for example, instead of just one relay—they have given him that wonderful thing that is challenge, and he has responded with more effort, more skill, more *self-respect*.

Is there not a moral here for all organization life? If we truly believe the individual is more creative than the group, just in day-to-day routine there is something eminently practical we can do about it. Cut down the amount of time the individual has to spend in conferences and meetings and team play. This would be a somewhat mechanical approach to what is ultimately a philosophical problem, but if organization people would take a hard look at the different types of meetings inertia has accumulated for The Organization, they might find that the ostensibly negative act of cutting out many of them would lead to some very positive benefits over and above the time saved. Thrown more on their own resources, those who have nothing to offer but the skills of compromising other people's efforts might feel bereft, but for the others the climate might be invigorating. Of itself such a surface change in working conditions would not give them more freedom, but it would halt a bad momentum, it would force organization to distinguish between what are legitimate functions of the group and what are not, and even if it yielded only a few more hours, this would be no small blessing. Once enjoyed, room to move around in is sweet indeed, and men partially liberated might be tantalized into demanding more.

In fighting the incubus of team work, we need to look more understandingly at the frustrations of those involved. Let's go back a moment to the situation of the professional employee. Studies have now convinced organization people that engineers and scientists in industry make up its most disaffected group, and that something should be done about it. The diagnosis is valuable. But how does organization interpret it? Organization people have concluded that the trouble is that the professional tends to be career-oriented rather than company-oriented. What The Organization must do, they believe, is to direct its efforts at integrating him by giving him more company status, indoctrinating him more effectively in the "big picture," by making him, in short, a company man.

How futile, how destructive is this solution! Why should the scientist be company-oriented? Is he to be called maladjusted because he does not fit the administrator's Procrustean bed? And of what profit would be his integration? It is not to his self-interest, neither is it to that of The Organization. Leave him his other allegiance. It is his work that must be paramount, and efforts to divert him into contentment are the efforts best calculated to bridle the curiosity that makes him productive.

Is it so practical? There is a magnificent piece of evidence that it is anything but. In the great slough of mediocrity that is most corporation research, what two laboratories are conspicuous exceptions in the rate of discovery? They are General Electric's research department and Bell Labs: exactly the two laboratories most famous for their encouragement of individualism—the most tolerant of individual differences, the most patient with off-tangent ideas, the least given to the immediate, closely supervised team project. By all accounts, the scientists in them get along quite well, but they do not make a business of it, and neither do the people who run the labs. They care not a whit if scientists' eyes fail to grow moist at company anthems; it is enough that the scientists do superbly well what they want to do, for though the consequences of profit for The Organization are secondary to the scientist, eventually there are these consequences, and as long as the interests of the group and the individual touch at this vital point, such questions as belongingness are irrelevant. Hard-boiled? No, tough-minded—and what more moral basis, it can be asked, for people working together, scientists or others?

It is not just for the scientist, not just for the brilliant, that the moral should be drawn, and this brings us to what ultimately is the single greatest vehicle for constructive change—education. The many points against the social adjustment emphases now prevailing are being vigorously sounded, and it is right that they should be, but one point needs to be made much more emphatically. The case for a rigorously fundamental schooling can be made on the utilitarians' own grounds: social usefulness. There are better reasons for the development of the individual, but until this point is made more clearly we seem by default to leave the debate on the either/or grounds of "democratic education" versus a highly trained elite. This is false antithesis. The great bulk of people will face organization pressures as inhibiting for them as for the few, and they need, as much if not more, to have the best that is within them demanded early. Is it "democratic" to hold that the humanities can have no meaning for them? They do not have to be taught to shake hands with other people; society will attend to this lesson. They have to be taught to reach. All of them. Some will be outstanding, some not, but the few will never flourish where the values of the many are against them.

I have been speaking of measures organizations can take. But ultimately any real change will be up to the individual himself, and this is why his education is so central to the problem. For he must look to his discontents with different eye. It has been said that dominance of the group is the wave of the future and that, lament it or not, he might as well accept it. But this is contemporaryism at its worst; things are not as they are because there is some good reason they are. Nor is the reverse true. It may one day prove true, as some prophets argue, that we are in a great and dismal tide of history that cannot be reversed, but if we accept the view we will only prove it.

Whatever kind of future suburbia may foreshadow, it will show that at least we have the choices to make. The organization man is not in the grip of vast social forces about which it is impossible for him to do anything; the options are there, and with wisdom and foresight he can turn the future away from the dehumanized collective that so haunts our thoughts. He may not. But he can.

He must *fight* The Organization. Not stupidly, or selfishly, for the defects of individual self-regard are no more to be venerated than the defects of co-operation. But fight he must, for the demands for his surrender are constant and powerful, and the more he has come to like the life of organization the more difficult does he find it to resist these demands, or even to recognize them. It is wretched, dispiriting advice to hold before him the dream that ideally there need be no conflict between him and society. There always is; there always must be. Ideology cannot wish it away; the peace of mind offered by organization remains a surrender, and no less so for being offered in benevolence. That is the problem.

APPENDIX

How to Cheat on Personality Tests

THE important thing to recognize is that you don't win a good score: you avoid a bad one. What a bad score would be depends upon the particular profile the company in question intends to measure you against, and this varies according to companies and according to the type of work. Your score is usually rendered in terms of your percentile rating—that is, how you answer questions in relation to how other people have answered them. Sometimes it is perfectly all right for you to score in the 80th or 90th percentile; if you are being tested, for example, to see if you would make a good chemist, a score indicating that you are likely to be more reflective than ninety out of a hundred adults might not harm you and might even do you some good.

By and large, however, your safety lies in getting a score somewhere between the 40th and 60th percentiles, which is to say, you should try to answer as if you were like everybody else is supposed to be. This is not always too easy to figure out, of course, and this is one of the reasons why I will go into some detail in the following paragraphs on the principal types of questions. When in doubt, however, there are two general rules you can follow: (1) When asked for word associations or comments about the world, give the most conventional, run-of-the-mill, pedestrian answer possible. (2) To settle on the most beneficial answer to any question, repeat to yourself:

a) I loved my father and my mother, but my father a little bit more.

b) I like things pretty well the way they are.

c) I never worry much about anything.

d) I don't care for books or music much.

e) I love my wife and children.

f) I don't let them get in the way of company work.

Now to specifics. The first five questions in the composite test are examples of the ordinary, garden variety of self-report questions.[1] Generally speaking, they are designed to

---

[1] Leading Tests of this type include:

The Personality Inventory by Robert G. Bernreuter. Published by The Stanford University Press, Stanford, California. Copyright 1935 by The Board of Trustees of Leland Stanford Junior University. All rights reserved.

125 questions; measures several different things at once; scoring keys available for neurotic tendency; self-sufficiency; introversion-extroversion; dominance-submission; self-confidence; sociability.

Thurstone Temperament Schedule by L. L. Thurstone. Copyright 1949 by L. L. Thurstone. Published by Science Research Associates, Chicago, Ill. 140 questions. Measures, at once, seven areas of temperament: to wit, degree to which one is active, vigorous, impulsive, dominant, stable, sociable, reflective. "The primary aim of the Thurstone Temperament Schedule . . . is to evaluate an individual in terms of his relatively permanent temperament traits. One of the values of the schedule is that it helps provide an objective pattern, or profile, of personal traits which you can use to predict probable success or failure in a particular situation."

Minnesota T-S-E Inventory by M. Catherine Evans and T. R. McConnell. Copyright 1942 by Science Research Associates, Chicago, Illinois.

150 questions. Measures three types of introversion-extroversion—thinking, social and emotional.

The Personal Audit by Clifford R. Adams and William M. Lepley, Psycho-Educational Clinic, Pennsylvania State College. Published by Science Research Associates, Chicago, Ill. Copyright 1945 by Clifford R. Adams. All rights reserved.

450 questions. Nine parts, of 50 questions each. Each part measures "a relatively independent component of personality." Extremes of each trait listed thus: seriousness-impulsiveness; firmness-indecision; tranquillity-irritability; frankness-evasion;

reveal your degree of introversion or extroversion, your stability, and such. While it is true that in these "inventory" types of tests there is not a right or wrong answer to any *one* question, cumulatively you can get yourself into a lot of trouble if you are not wary. "Have you enjoyed reading books as much as having company in?" "Do you sometimes feel self-conscious?"—You can easily see what is being asked for here.

Stay in character. The trick is to mediate yourself a score as near the norm as possible without departing too far from your own true self. It won't necessarily hurt you, for example, to say that you have enjoyed reading books as much as having company in. It will hurt you, however, to answer every such question in that vein if you are, in fact, the kind that does enjoy books and a measure of solitude. Strive for the happy mean; on one hand, recognize that a display of too much introversion, a desire for reflection, or sensitivity is to be avoided. On the other hand, don't overcompensate. If you try too hard to deny these qualities in yourself, you'll end so far on the other end of the scale as to be rated excessively insensitive or extroverted. If you are somewhat introverted, then, don't strive to get yourself in the 70th or 80th percentile for extroversion, but merely try to get up into the 40th percentile.

Since you will probably be taking not one, but a battery of tests, you must be consistent. The tester will be comparing your extroversion score on one test with, say, your sociability score on another, and if these don't correlate the way the tables say they should, suspicion will be aroused. Even when you are taking only one test, consistency is important. Many contain built-in L ("lie") scores, and woe betide you if you answer some questions as if you were a life of the party type and others as if you were an excellent follower. Another pitfall to avoid is giving yourself the benefit of the doubt on all questions in which one answer is clearly preferable to another, viz.: "Do you frequently daydream?" In some tests ways have been worked out to penalize you for this. (By the same token, occasionally you are

stability-instability; tolerance-intolerance; steadiness-emotionality; persistence-fluctuation; contentment-worry.

given credit for excessive frankness. But you'd better not count on it.)

Be emphatic to the values of the test maker. Question five asks:

"Do you prefer serious motion pictures about famous historical personalities to musical comedies?" If you answer this question honestly you are quite likely to get a good score for the wrong reasons. If you vote for the musical comedies, you are given a credit for extroversion. It might be, of course, that you are a very thoughtful person who dislikes the kind of pretentious, self-consciously arty "prestige" pictures which Hollywood does badly, and rather enjoy the musical comedies which it does well. The point illustrated here is that, before answering such questions, you must ask yourself which of the alternatives the test maker, not yourself, would regard as the more artistic.

Choose your neurosis. When you come across questions that are like the ones from 6 to 11—"I often get pink spots all over"—be very much on your guard. Such questions were originally a by-product of efforts to screen mentally disturbed people; they measure degrees of neurotic tendency and were meant mainly for use in mental institutions and psychiatric clinics.[2] The Organization has no business at all to throw these questions at you, but its curiosity is powerful and some companies have been adopting these tests as standard. Should you find yourself being asked about spiders, Oedipus complexes, and such, you must, even more than in the previous type of test, remain consistent and as much in character as possible—these tests almost always have lie scores built into them. A few mild neuroses conceded here

---

[2] Outstanding example is the *Minnesota Multiphasic Personality Inventory,* Revised Edition, by Starke R. Hathaway and J. Charnley McKinley. Published by The Psychological Corporation, N.Y. 495 questions. This yields scores on hypochondriasis, depression, hysteria, psychopathic deviation, masculinity and femininity, paranoia, psychoasthenia, schizophrenia, hypomania. It also yields a score on the subject's "test-taking attitude," with a score for his degree of "defensiveness-frankness." If the subject consistently gives himself the benefit of the doubt, or vice versa, the scoring reveals the fact. This is not a test for the amateur to trifle with.

and there won't give you too bad a score, and in conceding neuroses you should know that more often than not you have the best margin for error if you err on the side of being "hypermanic"—that is, too energetic and active.

Don't be too dominant. Question 12, which asks you what you would do if somebody barged in ahead of you in a store, is fairly typical of the kind of questions designed to find out how passive or dominant you may be. As always, the middle course is best. Resist the temptation to show yourself as trying to control each situation. You might think companies would prefer that characteristic to passivity, but they often regard it as a sign that you wouldn't be a permissive kind of leader. To err slightly on the side of acquiescence will rarely give you a bad score.

Incline to conservatism. Questions 13 through 17, which ask you to comment on a variety of propositions, yield a measure of how conservative or radical your views are.[3] To go to either extreme earns you a bad score, but in most situations you should resolve any doubts you have on a particular question by deciding in favor of the accepted.

Similarly with word associations. In questions 18 through 23, each word in capitals is followed by four words, ranging from the conventional to the somewhat unusual. The trouble here is that if you are not a totally conventional person you may be somewhat puzzled as to what the conventional response is. Here is one tip: before examining any one question closely and reading it from left to right, read vertically through the whole list of questions and you may well see a definite pattern. In making up tests, testers are thinking of ease in scoring, and on some test forms the most conventional responses will be found in one column, the next most conventional in the next, and so on. All you have to do then is go down the list and pick, alternately, the most con-

---

[3] An example of this kind of testing is the *Conservatism-Radicalism Opinionaire* by Theodore F. Lentz and Colleagues of The Attitude Research Laboratory. Published by Character Research Association, Washington University, St. Louis, Mo., Dept. of Education. Copyright 1935. 60 statements are given; the subject indicates whether he tends to agree or disagree. His score is obtained by checking the number of times he sides with the conservative statement side *vs.* the radical one.

ventional, and the second most conventional. Instead of a high score for emotionalism, which you might easily get were you to proceed on your own, you earn a stability score that will indicate "normal ways of thinking."

Don't split hairs. When you come to hypothetical situations designed to test your judgment, you have come to the toughest of all questions.[4] In this kind there are correct answers, and the testers make no bones about it. Restricted as the choice is, however, determining which are the correct ones is extremely difficult, and the more intelligent you are the more difficult. One tester, indeed, states that the measurement of practical judgment is "unique and statistically independent of such factors as intelligence, and academic and social background." He has a point. Consider the question about the woman and the baby at the window of the burning house. It is impossible to decide which is the best course of action unless you know how big the fire is, whether she is on the first floor or the second, whether there is a ladder handy, how near by the fire department is, plus a number of other considerations.

On this type of question, let me confess that I can be of very little help to the reader. I have made a very thorough study of these tests, have administered them to many people of unquestioned judgment, and invariably the results have been baffling. But there does seem to be one moral: don't think too much. The searching mind is severely handicapped by such forced choices and may easily miss what is meant to be the obviously right answer. Suppress this quality

---

[4] Two tests of this type are:

Test of Practical Judgment by Alfred J. Cardall, N.B.A., Ed.D. Published by Science Research Associates, Inc., Chicago, Ill. Copyright 1942, 1950 by Science Research Associates, Inc. All rights reserved. 48 Forced-choice questions "designed to measure the element of practical judgment as it operates in everyday business and social situations." How were the "best" answers chosen? "Rigorous statistical analysis was supplemented by consensus of authority. . . ."

Practical Social Judgment by Thomas N. Jenkins, Ph.D. Copyright 1947. All rights reserved. Executive Analysis Corporation, N.Y. 52 questions about hypothetical situations; subject must choose the "best" and the "poorest" of given answers.

in yourself by answering these questions as quickly as you possibly can, with practically no pause for reflection.

The judgment questions from 25 through 28 are much easier to answer.[5] The right answers here are, simply, those which represent sound personnel policy, and this is not hard to figure out. Again, don't quibble. It is true enough that it is virtually impossible to tell the worker why he didn't get promoted unless you know whether he was a good worker, or a poor one, or whether Jones's uncle did in fact own the plant (in which case, candor could be eminently sensible). The mealy-mouthed answer d)—"Let's figure out how you can improve"—is the "right" answer. Similarly with questions about the worker's home life. It isn't the concern of the company, but it is modern personnel dogma that it should be, and therefore "agree" is the right answer. So with the question about whether good supervisors are born or made. To say that a good supervisor is born deprecates the whole apparatus of modern organization training, and that kind of attitude won't get you anywhere.

Know your company. Questions 29 and 30 are characteristic of the kind of test that attempts to measure the relative emphasis you attach to certain values—such as aesthetic, economic, religious, social.[6] The profile of you it produces is matched against the profile that the company thinks is desirable. To be considered as a potential executive, you will probably do best when you emphasize economic motivation the most; aesthetic and religious, the least. In question 29,

[5] An example of this kind of test is *How Supervise?* by Quentin W. File, edited by H. H. Remmers. Published by The Psychological Corporation, N.Y. Copyright 1948, by Purdue Research Foundation, Lafayette, Indiana. 100 questions on management policy and attitudes.

[6] *A Study of Values,* Revised Edition, by Gordon W. Allport, Philip E. Vernan, and Gardner Lindzey. Copyright 1951, by Gordon W. Allport, Philip E. Vernan, and Gardner Lindzey. Copyright 1931 by Gordon W. Allport and Philip E. Vernan. Published by Houghton, Mifflin Co.

45 forced-choice questions. Answers are scored to give a measure of the relative prominence of six motives in a person: theoretical, economic, aesthetic, social, political, and religious. A profile is charted to show how he varies from the norm on each of the six.

accordingly, you should say the skyscraper makes you think of industrial growth. Theoretical motivation is also a good thing; if you were trying out for the research department, for example, you might wish to say that you think Sir Isaac Newton helped mankind more than Shakespeare and thereby increase your rating for theoretical learning. Were you trying out for a public relations job, however, you might wish to vote for Shakespeare, for a somewhat higher aesthetic score would not be amiss in this case.

There are many more kinds of tests and there is no telling what surprises the testers will come up with in the future. But the principles will probably change little, and by obeying a few simple precepts and getting yourself in the right frame of mind, you have the wherewithal to adapt to any new testing situation. In all of us there is a streak of normalcy.

INDEX

ANCHOR BOOKS

AMERICAN STUDIES

ANTHROPOLOGY

PSYCHOLOGY

RELIGION

SOCIOLOGY